29.95

Arabs in America

Arabs in America

Building a New Future

EDITED BY

Michael W. Suleiman

TEMPLE UNIVERSITY PRESS

PHILADELPHIA

Temple University Press, Philadelphia 19122
Copyright © 1999 by Temple University
All rights reserved
Published 1999
Printed in the United States of America

∞ The paper used in this publication meets the requirements of the American
National Standard for Information Sciences—Permanence of Paper for
Printed Library Materials, ANSI Z39.48-1984

Library of Congress Cataloging-in-Publication Data

Arabs in America: building a new future / edited by Michael W. Suleiman.
    p.   cm.
    Includes bibliographical references and index.
    ISBN 1-56639-726-x (alk. paper). — ISBN 1-56639-727-8 (pbk.:
alk. paper).
    1. Arab Americans—Social conditions.   I. Suleiman, Michael W.
E184.A65A72   1999
305.8927073–dc21   99-22775
                                                           CIP

Excerpts from the poems "Breath" (p. 331 herein), "Available Light" (p. 331), and
"Lasts" (p. 332), David Williams, in TRAVELING MERCIES (Farmington, ME: Alice
James Books, 1993), reprinted courtesy of Alice James Books.

Excerpts from the poem "Shrines" (p. 329 herein), Naomi Shihab Nye, from AN-
THOLOGY OF MODERN PALESTINIAN LITERATURE, edited by Salma Jayyusi.
Copyright © 1989 Columbia University Press. Reprinted with permission of the pub-
lisher.

Excerpts from the poems "Different Ways to Pray" (p. 328 herein), "Remembered" (p.
329), "Kindness" (p. 329), "For Lost and Found Brothers" (p. 330), and "The Man Who
Makes Brooms" (p. 328), Naomi Shihab Nye, reprinted by permission of the author,
from WORDS UNDER THE WORDS: SELECTED POEMS, copyright © 1995, and
used by permission of Far Corner Books.

To Penny, with love

Contents

Part VI: Arab-American Identity Negotiations

Preface

Until the past 20 to 30 years, scholars ignored or were ignorant of Arabs in North America. Although the situation has changed somewhat, there is still a dearth of information on the subject, especially because many early studies tended to be general, concerned largely with providing background information. Much of the available literature on Arabs in America has not found its way into the main body of scholarship and has instead been restricted to a limited audience, primarily the educated and active members of the Arab-American community. Such a situation is clearly a disservice to the Arab-American community and to the host countries—the United States and Canada. Recent academic studies have been more widely disseminated and have started to change this unhealthy neglect and marginalization of a vibrant community.

This volume continues this trend. It constitutes a multifaceted look at the Arab community in North America. It provides new information and original studies based on primary sources and using a variety of research approaches. It addresses the main challenges and concerns facing the Arab-American community at the start of the twenty-first century.

A word about the transliteration of Arabic words is in order. In general, I have followed the usage common in general surveys about the subject. When a name appears in more than one essay, the same spelling is used, except when it is part of a quotation.

I want to express my deep gratitude to all the authors in this volume. They have been most patient and responsive to requests for revision. The Association of Arab-American University Graduates (AAUG) deserves much credit for its 1996 conference on Arab Americans, which recognized the need for scholarly writings on the subject and inspired the development of this book. I am also grateful to the two anonymous readers of the manuscript. At Temple University Press, Doris Braendel, the Senior Acquisitions Editor, has been wonderful to work with, always providing quick and efficient responses to my many queries. Finally, although I have had many assistants who helped with typing the various iterations of the chapters in this volume, the contributions of two deserve special mention: Katie Carnahan, the former secretary of the Political Science Department at Kansas State University, and Kelly Wagner, my student assistant for the last three years. I am grateful to both of them, especially to Ms. Wagner, who has been with the project from its inception through the final manuscript production.

Michael W. Suleiman

Introduction:
The Arab Immigrant Experience

In 1977, William E. Leuchtenburg, the prominent American historian, remarked, "From the perspective of the American historian, the most striking aspect of the relationship between Arab and American cultures is that, to Americans, the Arabs are a people who have lived outside of history."[1] Professor Leuchtenburg could have just as accurately made the same observation about Arabs in America.

Ignorance about Arab Americans among North Americans at large means that, before looking at more detailed accounts of the Arab-American experience, we may benefit from a quick overview of Arab immigration to North America and what the Arab-American communities here have been like.

There have been two major waves of Arab immigration to North America. The first lasted from the 1870s to World War II and the second from World War II to the present. Members of the two waves of immigrants had somewhat different characteristics and faced different challenges in the social and political arena. Any examination of the immigrant communities must take into account these differences. As we shall see, the two communities began to come together in the 1960s, especially after the 1967 Arab-Israeli war,[2] and this rapprochement must also be taken into account.

The term "Arab Americans" refers to the immigrants to North America from the Arabic-speaking countries of the Middle East and their descendants. The Arabic-speaking countries today include Algeria, Bahrain, Egypt, Iraq, Jordan, Kuwait, Lebanon, Libya, Mauritania, Morocco, Oman, pre-1948 Palestine and the Palestinians, Qatar, Saudi Arabia, Sudan, Syria, Tunisia, United Arab Emirates, and Yemen. Somalia and Djibouti are also members of The League of Arab States and have some Arabic-speaking populations. Most Arab immigrants of the first wave came from the Greater Syria region, especially present-day Lebanon, and were overwhelmingly Christian; later immigrants came from all parts of the Arab world, but especially from Palestine, Lebanon, Syria, Egypt, Iraq, and Yemen, and had large numbers of Muslims among them. Although most Muslim Arab immigrants have been Sunni (reflecting the population in the region), there is a substantial Shi'a minority. Druze started immigrating in small numbers late in the nineteenth century.

Immigrants from the Arabic-speaking countries have been referred to and have referred to themselves by different names at different times, including Arabs or Arabians, but until World War II the designation Syrian or Syrian-Lebanese was used most often. The changeability of the name may indicate the absence of a definite and enduring identity, an issue that is discussed later. For the purposes of this chapter, the various names are used interchangeably, but the community primarily is referred to as Arab or Arab American.[3]

It is impossible to determine the exact number of Arab immigrants to North America, because U.S. and Canadian immigration officials have at different times used different classification schemes. Until 1899 in the United States, for instance, immigration statistics lumped the Arabs with Greeks, Armenians, and Turks. For this and other reasons, only estimates can be provided.

According to U.S. immigration figures, which generally are considered to be low, about 130,000 Arabs had immigrated to the United States by the late 1930s.[4] Estimates of the size of the Arab-American community by scholars and community leaders vary widely. A conservative estimate is that there were approximately 350,000 persons of Arab background in the United States on the eve of World War II.[5] In the 1990s, the size of the Arab community in the United States has been estimated at less than one million to the most frequently cited figure of two and one-half to three million.[6]

Numerous reasons have been given for the first wave of Arab immigration to America, which began in large numbers in the 1880s, but the reasons usually fall into two categories: push and pull factors, with the push factors accorded greater weight.

Most scholars argue that the most important reasons for emigration were economic necessity and personal advancement.[7] According to this view, although the economy in geographic or Greater Syria (a term encompassing the present-day countries and peoples of Syria, Lebanon, the Palestinians, Israel, Jordan, and possibly Iraq) registered some clear gains in the late nineteenth and early twentieth centuries, this progress was uneven in its impact and did not manifest itself in a sustained manner until "after emigration to the New World began to gather momentum."[8] The economy of Mount Lebanon suffered two major crippling blows in the mid-1800s. The first was the opening of the Suez Canal, which sidetracked world traffic from Syria to Egypt and made the trip to the Far East so easy and fast that Japanese silk became a major competitor for the Lebanese silk industry. The second blow came in the 1890s, when Lebanese vineyards were invaded by phylloxera and practically ruined.[9]

Also contributing to the economic stress in the Syrian hinterland was a rapid increase in population without a commensurate increase in agricultural or industrial productivity. Many families found that the subsistence economy could support only one child, who eventually inherited the farm or household. Other male children had to fend for themselves, and emigration to a New World of great wealth became an irresistible option.[10]

Many Lebanese Christians, who constituted most of the early Arab arrivals in North America, emphasize religious persecution and the lack of political and civil freedom as the main causes of their emigration from lands ruled by an oppressive Ottoman regime.[11] Under Ottoman rule, Christians in the Syrian province were not accorded equal status with their Muslim neighbors. They were subjected to many restrictions on their behavior and often suffered persecution. These oppressive conditions worsened and discriminatory actions occurred more often as the Ottoman rulers became weaker and their empire earned the title of the "Sick Man of Europe." As the power of the sultan declined, the local rulers began to assert greater authority and power, which they at times used to suppress and oppress further their subjects, particularly Christians. In part, this persecution took place in response to the increased power and prestige of "Christian" Europe and the encroachment of its rulers on Ottoman sovereignty. This effect, combined with the Christian population's desire for greater equality, threatened the Muslim public's sense of security. Like the "poor white trash" of the American South at the time of the Civil War and the Civil Rights Movement, the Muslim population in the Syrian province was poor and oppressed—but it still enjoyed a social status that was superior to that of the non-Muslims, particularly the Christians. The threat of losing that "high" status made many Muslims susceptible to suggestions from local Ottoman rulers that their Christian neighbors were the cause of rather than companions in their troubles. The worsened social and economic conditions in Syria in the mid-1800s and the beginning of the disintegration of feudalism, especially among the Druze, produced social turmoil that erupted in sectarian riots in which thousands of Christians perished.[12] Many Christian Lebanese, especially Maronites, cite the 1860 disturbances and massacres as the main factor contributing to the exodus from their homeland.

In addition to the economic, political, and social causes of the early Arab immigration to North America, some incidental factors should be cited. Among these are improved transportation and communication facilities worldwide, development of steam navigation that made the sea voyage safer and shorter, and aggressiveness of agents of the steamship companies in recruiting new immigrant passengers. Although American missionaries often actively discouraged Syrians or Arabs from migrating to the United States, their very presence as model Americans, their educational activities, and their reports about American life ignited a desire, especially among the graduates of American schools and colleges in Syria, to emigrate to America.

After the feasibility and profitability of immigration to the United States and to "America" in general were well established, chain migration became the norm, with immigrants making it possible for the ambitious and the disgruntled in the old homeland to seek newer horizons. Those wanting to escape military service in the Ottoman army and those craving freedom from oppression and the liberty to speak and publish without censorship or reprisal left their homeland quickly and stealthily and sought what they thought would be a temporary refuge in America.

The Early Arab Community in America

Before World War II, most Arabs in America were Christians who came from the Mount Lebanon region of geographic Syria. Especially until the turn of the century, these travelers were mainly poor, uneducated, and illiterate in any language. They were not trained for a particular profession. As unskilled workers, after they learned the rudiments of the English language, they could work in factories and mines. However, such jobs were taxing and monotonous and, most importantly, did not offer opportunities for the fast accumulation of wealth, which was the primary objective of these early Arab arrivals. Farming presented them with the added hardships of isolation, loneliness, and severe weather conditions. Peddling therefore was an attractive alternative. It did not require much training, capital, or knowledge of English. With a few words of English learned on the run, a suitcase (*Kashshi*) full of notions (e.g., needles, thread, lace) provided by a better-established fellow Lebanese or other Arab supplier, probably a relative who helped bring them to the New World, many new arrivals often were on the road hawking their wares only a day or so after they landed in America. Success in peddling required thrift, hard work, very long hours, the stamina to endure harsh travel conditions (mostly walking the countryside on unpaved roads), and not infrequently, the taunting and insults from children or disgruntled customers. These conditions were made tolerable for most early Arab arrivals by their vision of a brighter economic future and the concomitant prestige they and their families would eventually acquire in the old country. When they could afford to do so, they switched to the "luxury" of a horse and buggy and later to a dry-goods store.[13]

Before World War I, Arabs in North America thought of themselves as sojourners, as people who were in, but not part of, American society. Their politics reflected and emulated the politics of their original homeland in substance and style, because they were only *temporarily* away from home. In New York, *Kawkab America* (*Kawkab Amirka*), the first Arabic-language newspaper established in North America, declared in its very first issue its unequivocal support for the Ottoman sultan, whose exemplary virtues it detailed at length.[14] All other newspapers had to define in one way or another their attitude toward and their relationship with the Ottoman authorities. Although *Kawkab America* was pro-Ottoman, at least initially, *Al-Ayam* (*al-Ayyam*) was the most vehement opponent of the Ottoman authorities, a role it later shared with *Al-Musheer* (*al-Mushir*).[15] It excoriated the cruelty and corruption of Ottoman rulers, especially in the Mount Lebanon region. It also called for rebellion against the Turkish tyrants and urged its readers to exercise their freedom in America to call for freedom back home. Other newspapers, including *Al-Hoda* (*al-Huda*) and *Meraat-ul-Gharb* (*Mir'at al-gharb*), fell between these two extremes of total support or clear rejection of Ottoman authority.

The orientation of early Arab Americans toward their homeland meant that their political activities were also focused on issues that were important in their country or village of origin. There was communal solidarity, but the community was a collective of several communities. The sectarian and regional disputes that separated the Arabs back home were also salient in this "temporary" residence. The newspapers they established were in the main socializing agencies conveying the messages of their sectarian leadership. Because the Orthodox already had their *Kawkab America*, *Al-Hoda* was set up to represent and speak for the Maronites. Later, *Al-Bayan* (*al-Bayan*) proclaimed itself the newspaper of the Druze.[16] Within each community there were rivalries and competing newspapers, each claiming to be the best defender or representative of its sect.

World War I was a watershed event for Arabs in North America, cutting them off from their people back home. This separation from the homeland became almost complete with the introduction of very restrictive quota systems in the United States and Canada after World War I, which practically cut off emigration from Arab regions. These developments intensified the community's sense of isolation and separation, simultaneously enhancing its sense of solidarity. One consequence was a strengthening of the assimilationist trend—a trend already reinforced by the American-born children of these Arab immigrants.

The substance and style of the Arab community's politics changed after the war, with a clear realization that they had become part of American society. Intersectarian conflicts became less intense and fewer in number. Calls for unity were heeded more often. For instance, Syrian-Lebanese clubs formed regional federations that joined together to form a national federation.[17] A process of socialization into American politics resulted in greater participation in voting and party membership and in public and political service at local or state levels. "Syrian" Republican and Democratic Clubs were formed in the United States, and the arena for political competition changed as the Arab community became part of the American body politic. There also emerged a clear change in matters of style—generally for the better. By the 1930s and 1940s, conflicts became fewer and somewhat less personal, and the language of discourse became much less offensive.

Whereas first-generation Arabs in America managed as best they could in an alien environment, their children were thoroughly immersed in American society and culture—and their first or only language was English. Consequently, English-language newspapers and journals were established to cater to young Americans of Arab heritage.[18] Eastern churches began to translate some of the liturgy and conduct part of the services in English to prevent the loss of members,[19] although many members left the church nonetheless. Some intellectuals, including some of the most celebrated Arab-American writers and poets, took advantage of the blessings of freedom and democracy in North America to attack the tyranny and corruption of the clergy, especially in the old homeland but also in America. Some also expressed atheistic or agnostic views, and others left their old churches and joined new ones.[20]

As Arabs assimilated in American society, they also worked harder for a better image of themselves and their people in the old homeland. More effort was spent on campaigns to inform Americans about the rich Arab heritage. In the political arena, especially in the United States, there were many, serious efforts to get the government to support foreign policy positions favored by the Arab community, especially in regard to Palestine. During World War I and its aftermath, the main political preoccupation of the Arabic-speaking groups in North America was to achieve the liberation of their homelands from Ottoman rule and to provide economic assistance to their starving relatives, especially in the Mount Lebanon region. To accomplish these objectives, their leaders set up relief committees, raised funds, and sent money and supplies whenever it was possible to do so. They also urged Arab young men in the United States to join the American armed forces to help their new country and to liberate their old homeland.[21] Leaders organized campaigns to have their people buy American Liberty bonds to help with the war effort.[22]

After the war, the Arabs in America were divided over the destiny of the regions liberated from Ottoman rule. In general, there was a strong sentiment among the Maronites to support French control over Syria and Lebanon under the League of Nations' Mandate.[23] Others argued for complete independence, viewing France as a new occupying power.[24] On the question of Palestine, there was general agreement in support of the Palestinian-Arab population and for eventual, if not immediate, independence. There was widespread opposition to Zionism as a movement bent on establishing a Jewish state there.[25] Arabs in America showed their support for the Palestinians through lectures, publications, fund raising, and political lobbying, especially with U.S. government officials.[26]

Until World War I, Arabs in North America may be considered sojourners exhibiting many traits of a middleman minority—a community whose members primarily engage in one particular specialized activity such as migrant farm work or peddling. Substantial numbers of Arabs in America engaged in commerce, most often beginning as peddlers commissioned by their own countrymen. Their objective was to make the greatest amount of money in the shortest possible time to help their families in the old country and eventually to retire in comfort in their village or neighborhood. In the meantime, they spent as little as possible of their income in America, often living in crowded tenements and, while on the road, in barns or shacks to avoid expensive hotel costs. They did not live rounded lives, allowing themselves no luxuries and finding contentment and solace in family life. Because they could pull up stakes anytime, they sought liquidity in their economic enterprises. Long-term investments were avoided. For that reason, in addition to other advantages, they preferred peddling, dry goods stores, restaurants, the professions, and a cottage industry in lace and needlework. In all of these activities, their primary contacts were with other Arab Americans, especially relatives or people from the same town, religious sect, or geographic region.[27] They developed few lasting relationships with "Americans." *Al-Nizala*, the term the Arab-American community used to refer to itself, is a name that clearly describes its status and purpose. It means a temporary settlement, and it was used in contrast to "the Americans" to indicate the alien or stranger status of Arabs in America. At first, Arabs in America formed their own residential colonies, especially in New York and Boston. Even when they did not, they encouraged within-group marriage, frequently praising its virtues and especially pointing out the disadvantages of marrying "American" girls. In other words, they resisted assimilation, even after their intellectuals began to urge acculturation to life in America.[28]

Arabs in America, sharing an attitude common to other middleman or sojourner communities, were charged with being "clannish, alien, and unassimilable."[29] Such attitudes were fairly common among influential American journalists and public officials, who also viewed Arabs as inferior to whites. In the economic field, Arabs were sometimes seen as parasites, because they allegedly did not engage in any productive industry, merely being engaged in trade. They were sometimes attacked as a drain on the American economy, because they sent part of their income back home.[30]

The Process of Americanization

Arab immigrants soon found out that the land of opportunity was also strewn with hardship and an "unwelcome" mat. In response to insults and charges of inferiority, they did occasionally defend themselves.[31] However, to add injury to insult, the U.S. and Canadian authorities began to claim that Arabs had no right to naturalization and citizenship because they allegedly were Asian and did not belong to the white race.[32] This problem of racial identification and citizenship traumatized the Arabic-speaking community. In their attempt to resolve this crisis, the "Syrians" searched for their roots and found them in their *Arab* background, which ensured them Caucasian racial status and therefore eligibility for U.S. citizenship—or so they argued.[33] Beginning in 1909, Arabic-speaking individuals from geographic Syria began to be challenged in their citizenship petitions. It was not until 1914, however, that George Dow was denied a petition to become a U.S. citizen because, as a "Syrian of Asiatic birth," he was not a free white person within the meaning of the 1790 U.S. statute.[34] In 1915, the Dow decision was reversed based on the argument that the pertinent binding legislation was not that of 1790 but the laws of 1873 and 1875, and in accordance with these, Syrians "were so closely related to Europeans that they could be considered 'white persons.'"[35] Despite this precise and authoritative language, "Syrians" in the United States continued to be challenged and to feel insecure about their naturalization status until the period of 1923 to 1924.[36]

Even during World War II, the status of Arabs remained unclear. In 1942, a Muslim Arab from Yemen was denied U.S. citizenship because "Arabs as a class are not white and therefore not eligible for citizenship," especially because of their dark skin and the fact that they are "part of the Mohammedan world," separated from Christian Europe by a wide gulf.[37] On the other hand, in 1944, an "Arabian" Muslim was granted citizenship status under the 1940 Nationality Act, because "as every schoolboy knows, the Arabs have at various times inhabited parts of Europe, lived along the Mediterranean, been contiguous to European nations and been assimilated culturally and otherwise by them."[38]

Apart from the legal battles to ensure they were allowed to reside in their new homelands, especially in the United States, Arabic-speaking persons had to figure out what identity best fit their indeterminate status. They knew who they were and had a very strong sense of personal identity centered first and foremost in the family. There were, however, other lesser but still important identities related to clan, village, or sect. Because these identities were strong, a "national" identity could remain amorphous or at least indeterminate, shifting from one orientation to another with relative ease and without much psychological dislocation. In practical terms, the Arabic-speaking people in North America functioned as a collective of communities whose bonds of solidarity beyond the family were mainly related to sect or country, such as Maronite, Orthodox, Muslim, Druze, and Palestinian affiliations. Before World War II, the primary or most acceptable designation for the group was "Syrian." However, when Lebanon emerged as a country in the 1920s, some Maronites, especially N. Mokarzel, the editor and publisher of *Al-Hoda,* spearheaded a campaign to get the community to change its name to Lebanese, because Lebanon was where most of its members originally came from.[39] The campaign was not a big success, although, many of the clubs did change their name to Syrian-Lebanese.[40]

Another and more important identity crisis occurred when these peripatetic sojourners realized that they had to decide whether to become "settlers" or return to the old homeland. It had become increasingly difficult for them to function as temporary aliens. After World War I, it became clear to large numbers of Arabs in North America that it was not possible to go "home" again and that the United States and Canada were their homes.[41] This change from sojourner to permanent settler necessitated and was accompanied by other changes in the way Arabs in America thought and in the way they behaved. The substantial investments they had made in homes, property, and real estate in the old country lost their original purpose, and much more attention was paid to material improvements and investments in their new countries. In the United States, one manifestation was the migration by substantial numbers of the New York Arab community from the run-down and extremely crowded tenements of Manhattan to the nicer environment of South Ferry in Brooklyn and beyond.[42]

Arabs in America saw that they had to become full-fledged Americans. Assimilation became strongly and widely advocated, and citizenship training and naturalization were greatly encouraged. Although out-marriage was still not favored, some now claimed that success in such situations was possible if the American partner (usually female) was a "good" person who behaved in a conservative or traditional manner.[43] Along the same lines, Arab women were told to retain the modesty code of the old homeland.[44]

Although Arab women in America constituted a major asset to their kinfolk, they also presented the community with many difficulties, primarily related to issues of honor and modesty. This problem was most acute among the Druze, some of whom asked to restrict or totally ban the immigration of Druze women to America. Among Christians, women peddlers were a big concern. The complaints and areas targeted for reform included the act of peddling itself, the personal appearance and dress of the woman peddler, the distance she covered and whether she had to stay away from home overnight, and her demeanor or behavior. These problems were viewed as especially serious because large numbers had decided to stay in America and wanted to become "acceptable" to the host society. The preference was for Arab women to help their kinfolk by crocheting or sewing at home or by minding their family's store. Work in factories was also acceptable, although not favored, especially among the rising middle-class Arab Americans.[45]

The decision to settle in America meant setting a higher priority on children's education for boys and girls. This was viewed as more important than any contribution the children might make to the family's economic welfare. The result was a marked improvement in women's education and an increase in the number of male and female graduates from universities and professional institutions.

Another consequence of the decision to stay in America was that parents and children had to learn to be good Americans, and they flocked to citizenship classes. Parents attended English-language classes and studied the American governmental system in preparation for their new role as American citizens. Americanization was seen as a process of shedding old loyalties, the traditional culture, and the Arabic language. The children therefore grew up barely aware of their Arabic heritage.

Although the assimilationist approach began to gain favor and was encouraged by the leadership, it was not presented in ideological terms. Often, it took the form of a suggestion that Arabs should no longer feel like strangers in their new country and that they should make a positive contribution to American society.[46] Nevertheless, in the heyday of the melting pot approach to assimilation, the Arabs in America strove to remove any differences, except perhaps food and music, that separated them from the general

American population. They also neglected or chose not to teach their children Arabic or to instill into them much pride of heritage.[47] The result was that, by World War II, Arabs in North America were, for all practical purposes, an indistinguishable group from the host society. It took a second wave of immigration and other developments to rekindle interest in their Arab heritage and to revive them as an ethnic community.

Post–World War II Immigration

The second wave of Arab immigration brought to North America a much more diverse population, one that differed greatly from the early pioneering group. Whereas the first-wave immigrants came almost exclusively from the area of Greater Syria and were overwhelmingly Lebanese, the new immigrants came from all parts of the Arab world, including North Africa. Unlike early arrivals, who were predominantly Christian, the new immigrants were Christians and Muslims.

The two groups' reasons for immigration were also somewhat different. In addition to economic need and the attraction of a major industrial society, new immigrants often were driven out of their homes as a result of regional conflicts (e.g., Palestine-Israel, Arab-Israeli, Iraq-Iran, Iraq-Kuwait) or civil wars (e.g., Lebanon, Yemen) or as a consequence of major social and political changes in the homeland that made life difficult, especially for the wealthy or the middle class in Egypt, Iraq, Syria, and other countries. The search for a democratic haven, where it is possible to live in freedom without political or economic harassment and suppression by the government was a strong motivation, even more so than during the earlier period, that affected much larger numbers of individuals. To these political and economic motivations can be added a psychological one. The great improvements in transportation and communication facilitated the process of immigration, and by making the world seem smaller, they made it much easier for people to accept the notion of migration to other parts of the world, especially to the United States and Canada.

Whereas the early Arab immigrants were mainly uneducated and relatively poor, the new arrivals included large numbers of relatively well-off, highly educated professionals: lawyers, professors, teachers, engineers, and doctors. Many of the new immigrants began as students at American universities who decided to stay, often as a result of lack of employment opportunities back home or because of the unstable political conditions in the homeland—conditions that often threatened imprisonment or death for returnees.[48] Besides these comparatively affluent immigrants, especially in the 1990s, relatively large numbers of semi-educated Arabs, primarily engaged in commerce, came to North America as political refugees or as temporary residents to escape the wars and violence of the Middle East region.

An important difference between members of the two immigration waves is the way each group thought of itself in terms of American society and politics. First-wave immigrants were viewed and thought of themselves as mere sojourners staying in the United States on a temporary basis with the primary or sole purpose of making a fortune they could enjoy back home. This orientation remained dominant at least until World War I and probably well into the 1920s. Such a stance meant that they avoided participation in American society beyond taking care of basic needs such as commerce. They were "Syrians" or "Arabians" and sought to establish their own churches, clubs, or newspapers. They sought (and preached to their people) not to "meddle" in the affairs of the host society. They were anxious not to offend their hosts, not to break the law, and not to behave in a manner offensive to Americans, but they also tried not to imitate American social customs (i.e., Americanize), not to mix socially with Americans, and not to intermarry. Although most did not participate in politics much beyond voting, they nevertheless expressed pride in the occasional Arab who was able to make it as a city alderman, political party functionary, or a candidate for local political office.

The change from these conditions came slowly and as a result of changes in the world around them, especially World War I, the Ottomans' oppressive treatment of their subjects in the Syria-Lebanon region, and the success of Zionism in securing Western, especially British and American, support for its objective of establishing a Jewish homeland in Palestine.

Immigrants who arrived after World War II came with a well-defined view of democracy and the role of citizens in it—ideas they had learned in their homeland but that had originally been imported from Europe and America. Their higher level of education and social status gave them greater confidence about participating in American politics almost as soon as they arrived in their new country. Even when they thought about returning to their Arab homeland, they were anxious to live full and productive lives in the United States or Canada for themselves and their children. The Arab-American community today constitutes a combination of the diversities of the early and more recent immigrants. In addition to the sectarian and mainly social clubs that the early immigrants formed, new political organizations were gradually established. In the United States, Syrian Democratic and Syrian Republican clubs were formed in the 1920s and 1930s. These were, as the Arab Democratic and Arab Republican clubs are today, adjuncts to the main two major parties designed to encourage political participation and to integrate Arabs into the American body politic. What was new and significant was the establishment of bona fide Arab-American pressure groups and voluntary associations whose main function has been to protect themselves against harassment from private groups or public agencies and to influence policy in the United States and Canada concerning different parts of the Arab World or Middle East.

As World War I had marked a watershed for the early Arab immigrants, the 1967 Arab-Israeli war did for the entire community. The older and newer Arab-American communities were shocked and traumatized by the 1967 war. In particular, they were dismayed and extremely disappointed to see how greatly one-sided and pro-Israeli the American communications media were in reporting on the Middle East.[49] The war itself also produced soul-searching on the part of many Arab Americans, old and new, and often reinforced or strengthened their Arab identity. This group included many members already active in various Palestinian, Syrian, and Lebanese clubs, which were mainly social in nature.

By 1967, members of the third generation of the early Arab immigrants had started to awaken to their own identity and to see that identity as Arab, not "Syrian." Elements of this third generation combined with politically sophisticated immigrants to work for their ethnic community and the causes of their people in the old homelands. The result was establishment of the Association of Arab-American University Graduates (AAUG) in late 1967, which was the first post-World War II national, credible, non-sectarian organization seeking to represent diverse elements of the Arab-American community and to advance an Arab rather than regional or country orientation.

To the AAUG, however, American hostility to "Arabs" and the concept of Arabism was so extreme and so widespread among policy makers and the general public that influencing the political process or public policy, especially in the United States, seemed futile. The Republican and Democratic parties were almost completely and solidly one sided in their support of Israel and in their hostility to Arab causes, even though the United States had huge economic and military assets in the region and was on the friendliest terms with most leaders and countries of the Arab world. The AAUG sought support from or identified with other individuals and groups. Among these were a few politicians such as Senator William Fulbright and others who were courageous enough to voice criticism of U.S. policy in the Middle East, other minority or disenfranchised groups in American society, and some intellectuals who began to criticize the administration and its policies.

The AAUG's first priority was the need to provide accurate information about the Arab world and Arabs in North America and to distribute this literature to the public at large, wherever access was possible. It sought to educate the Arab countries and people about the true nature of the problems facing the region and to educate Arab intellectuals and political leaders about U.S. and Canadian policies and the American political process. While the AAUG sought mainly to inform and educate, it also performed other tasks, because no other organizations existed to perform them. Among the tasks to which the AAUG devoted some time and effort were political lobbying, attacks against defamation of and discrimination against Arabs and Arab Americans, and activism among Arab Americans to get them to participate in politics.

These ancillary tasks were later championed and performed by newer organizations. The National Association of Arab Americans (NAAA) was formed in 1972 in the United States to act as a political lobby to defend and advance Arab-American interests and causes. In 1980, in response to the continuing slanders and attacks against Arabs and Arab Americans, the American-Arab Anti-Discrimination Committee (ADC) was established and quickly drew widespread support from the varied elements of the Arab community. In 1985, the Arab American Institute (AAI) was formed, primarily to encourage Arab Americans to become active in the American political arena.[50]

Building a New Future

To get a feel for how the Arab community has fared in America, it is useful to review some of the challenges and concerns that Arabs have faced in their new homeland and how they have coped with building a new future. Among the most important issues with which Arabs in America have had to wrestle is the definition of who they are, their sense of identity as a people, especially as they encountered and continue to encounter bias and discrimination in their new homeland.

Although Arabs in the United States and Canada constitute an ethnic group, they were not an ethnic minority in their old homeland. Their new identity has been shaped by many factors but especially by continuing interactions between conditions in the old and new homelands and by the interplay between their perceptions of themselves and how others see them. The early immigrants spoke Arabic and came from a predominantly Arabic culture and heritage, but they did not think of themselves as "Arabs." The main bond of solidarity among them at that time was based on familial, sectarian, and village- or region-oriented factors. The plethora of names by which they were known in the New World reflects their lack of "national" identity and ignorance or confusion on the part of the host society. Another factor in this process was the American, especially U.S., obsession with the idea of race and the various attempts early in this century to classify every immigrant group, no matter how small, by its racial composition.[51] The early Arabic-speaking groups were called Asians, "other Asians," Turks from Asia, Caucasian, white, black, or "colored."

Although immigration officials and the general press looked down on Arabic-speaking peoples, they nevertheless viewed them as part of the "white race," at least for the first thirty years or so of their presence in North America. These authorities then decided those immigrants were not white. With their very identity questioned and maligned, the reaction of the early Arab Americans was to try to refute what they saw as demeaning and untrue charges. They argued that they were very much part of the white race.[52] Stung by accusations of inferiority in terms of scientific and technological accomplishments, Syrian-Arab Americans developed a two-cultures thesis long before C. P. Snow discussed it.[53] Their argument, which became popular in the community, especially among Arab literati, was that, although America was the most advanced country in the world in science, technology, and industrialization, the East was spiritually superior.[54] Coming from the Holy Land, they offered themselves as guides and instructors to Americans in their search for and desire to experience the life and times of Jesus—where he was born, preached, was crucified, and rose from the dead.[55] Arab Americans spoke and wrote about the "spiritual" East in terms that suggested perpetuity: it was always so and would always be so. By accident or not, these writers in essence condemned the East to an absence of material progress and desire to produce such for all time.

The emphasis on Eastern spirituality, although useful in making Arabs feel good about themselves compared with "materialist" Americans, still left Arabs in America with little cultural heritage to offer their American-born children. The result often was to ignore their Arab heritage and, especially beginning in the 1920s, to emphasize almost full assimilation in American society. As the children grew up immersed in American society and culture while simultaneously exposed to a smattering of Arabic words at home and some Arabic food and music, they often found themselves experiencing an identity crisis of some kind, mainly resulting in rootlessness, ambiguity, and a fractionalized personality.[56] These were the reactions of some of the Arab-American literati of the post-World War II period. The very culture of their own country denied them the privilege of being openly proud of their heritage. They sometimes dealt with this awkward situation by complaining about American prejudice and discrimination against Arabs and by simultaneously denigrating their own people and heritage—if only to ingratiate themselves with their readers, their fellow Americans.[57]

The 1967 war changed the situation radically. Israel, in the short period of seven days, defeated the Arab armies. The Arab people generally felt let down and humiliated. Arabs in America, both newcomers and third-generation descendants of the early pioneers, deeply resented the extreme partisanship America and Americans (especially the U.S. government and people) showed toward Israel and the occasional hostility toward Arabs. The consequence was for Arab Americans to shake off their malaise and to organize. Their first goal was to fight against the negative stereotyping of Arabs. Their second was to help modify American policy toward the Middle East and make it more balanced. In the process, sectors of the well-established older community de-assimilated. They began openly to call themselves Arab and to join political groupings set up to defend Arab and Arab-American causes.[58] Arab Americans also began to organize conferences and publish journals and books in defense of their cause. They wrote fiction, poetry, and memoirs declaring pride in and solidarity with Arabs and the Arab community in America.

Open Arab-American pride in their heritage and activism on behalf of their cause does not, however, mean that prejudice against them ceased. On the contrary, many in the community feel that prejudice and discrimination have increased. Different reasons have been advanced to explain the prejudice and discrimination that Arabs encounter in North America, and different individuals and groups have emphasized what they believe to be the main cause or the one most pertinent to their situation.

The most popular explanation for the negative stereotypes Americans hold about Arabs is that they are ignorant of the truth because they have not read or have read inaccurate and false reports about Arabs and have not come into contact with Arabs. According to this view, the stereotypes are mainly the result of propaganda by and on behalf of Zionist and pro-Israeli supporters. The primary objective of this propaganda has been to deprive Arabs, especially Palestinians, from presenting their case to the American public and the American political leadership.[59]

In this view, the attempt to deny Arabs and Arab Americans a public voice also extends to the political arena. In this way, it becomes a "politics of exclusion" in an attempt to prevent debate on any issues that reflect poorly on Zionists or Israel. It also smears and defames Arab candidates for political office to defeat them and exclude them from effective participation in political decision making. This "political racism" is presumed to be ideological in nature and not necessarily directed against Arabs or Arab Americans as a people or as an ethnic community.[60]

Another view sees hostility and violence against Arabs and Arab Americans as anti-Arab racism. This hostility is seen as part of the native racist attitudes and is believed to be present in all sectors of American society, not just among fringe groups. Somewhat related to this view is "jingoistic racism," which is directed at whatever foreign enemy is perceived to be out there.[61] Because of the many recent conflicts in the Middle East in which the United States directly or indirectly became involved and where incidents of hijacking and hostage taking occurred, many Americans reacted negatively against a vaguely perceived enemy next door, often not distinguishing between Arabs and Muslims or between Arabs and any foreigner who "looks" Arab.[62]

Still another view of negative Arab stereotypes, at least in the United States, argues that these ideas are "rooted in a core of hostile archetypes that our culture applies to those with whom it clashes."[63] According to this argument, most of the elements that constitute the Arab image in America are not unique to Arabs but also have been applied to other ethnic groups, especially blacks and Jews in the form of racism and anti-Semitism. These negative stereotypes have been transferred to a new group, the Arabs or Arab Americans.

Part of the negative stereotyping and hostility many Americans harbor toward Arabs is based on the latter's alleged mistreatment of their women. It is rather ironic, therefore, that Arab-American women find themselves the subject of prejudice, discrimination, and hostility at the hands of American men and women. This is often the result of hostility based on race, color, or religion.[64]

Arab-American women have had more problems than their male counterparts in defining an acceptable or comfortable identity. The problem is multifaceted and affects different sectors differently. Women who have come from the most traditional countries of the Arab world have experienced a greater restriction of their freedom in the United States. This is primarily the result of an inability on the part of traditional husbands, fathers, and brothers to deal with the nearly complete freedom accorded to women in American society. Just as important is the inability of the women to participate fully in the United States because they do not know the language, lack the necessary education, and are unfamiliar with American customs. They are not psychologically ready to countenance, let alone internalize, certain mores pertaining to the public display of affection and male-female interaction. Because many cannot drive and probably do not have a car, they find themselves much more isolated than they were back home, where they often had a vibrant and full life, albeit within the confines of the family and female friends.[65]

Among middle-class, first-generation Arab-American women, there is perhaps not much adjustment necessary. They usually follow the somewhat liberal mores they brought with them from the old homeland. On the other hand, Arab girls reaching their adolescence in the United States are likely to experience more problems as a result of the potential clash between traditional child-rearing practices and the freer atmosphere found in North America.[66]

Among better-educated, young Arab-American women, the issue of identity is both more subtle and more openly discussed. Like their male Arab-American counterparts, these women suffer from and are offended by the hostility against Arabs and Arab Americans. They also find American views of how women are allegedly treated in the Arab world to be inaccurate and grotesque. Nevertheless, they would like to expand the rights of Arab women and to improve the quality of their lives. They resent and reject any attempt on the part of Arab-American men to define what their role should be in maintaining Arab culture and mores in North America. In particular, they want to reject the notion that family honor resides in women and that the way a woman behaves, especially concerning her modesty and sexuality, can bring honor or dishonor to the family. They do not wish to be the conveyors or transmitters of tradition and culture—at least not as these are defined by men or as they prevail in the old homeland.[67]

Women and men in the Arab-American community of the 1990s find that the "white" racial classification that the early Syrian-Arab community worked so hard to attain is flawed. In practical daily interactions, Arabs in America are often treated as "honorary whites" or "white but not quite."[68] In reaction to this situation, at least four different orientations have been advocated. For the majority, especially among the older and well-established Christian community, there is some disgruntlement but general passivity about the discrimination and the prejudice that accompany their "white but not quite" status, and they work to remove these negative attitudes. Others, especially the Arab American Institute, have argued for a special designation of Arabs in the United States as a minority (e.g., the Hispanics) or as a specific census category encompassing all peoples of the Middle East.[69] Still others, especially some young, educated Arab-American women, have expressed a preference for the designation "people of color."[70] This would place them as part of a larger category that includes most of the federally recognized minorities in the United States. There are also those who resent being boxed into one category. Their sense of identity is multifaceted; they are men or women; Arab, American, Muslim or Christian; white or dark skinned; and so on. They think of themselves in different ways at different times or in different contexts, and they argue for getting rid of such categories or for the use of more descriptive categories that recognize different aspects of their background, culture, or physical appearance.[71]

The search for an adequate or comfortable identity for Arabs in America has been guided and perhaps complicated by the need to feel pride in their heritage and simultaneously avoid prejudice and discrimination in their new homeland. For most, the search is neither successful nor final. They continue to experience marginality in American society and politics, and they try to overcome this in various ways. Some resort to ethnic denial; they de-emphasize their Arab or Islamic background by claiming a connection with what they believe is a more acceptable appearance in America. Instead of proclaiming their Arabism, for instance, they claim that they are Lebanese or Egyptian. Some may even deny their heritage altogether, claiming to be Greek or Italian. Some new arrivals instead choose ethnic isolation. They are unwilling to change themselves and do not believe they can change the host society.

Among those who want full integration or assimilation into American society, especially middle-class Arab Americans, many emphasize the strong cultural link between Arabs and Americans. They refuse to give up and continue to work hard to show where the dominant American view is wrong. For most, accommodation is the easiest and most comfortable stance. These men and women consciously or subconsciously act in ways that reduce their difference from the American dominant group. They attempt "to pass."[72] Others, especially those who seek material success, especially those who are in public professions (e.g., television, radio, movies), often give in and convert to the prevailing view. Not infrequently, the very individuals who are looked down on by the Arab-American community are selected to speak for and represent the Arabs in America.[73]

The Arab-American Community in the 1990s

After more than a century of immigration, it is clear that the basic reasons Arabs came are no different from those that drove or attracted other groups to come here. They came because of the promise of a quick fortune and a sense of adventure; the threat of war or economic disaster; education, training, technology; and the thrill of living in a free democratic system. Whatever their reasons, true integration and full assimilation have eluded them. In part, this is the result of the many developments leading to the debunking of the notion of a melting pot and the greater tolerance of a multicultural society. The more important reason, however, has been the hostility the host society has shown toward Arab immigrants.[74]

Nevertheless, Arabs in America have done very well. Since the 1960s, there has always been at least one representative of Arab background in the U.S. Congress (e.g., James Abourezk, Mary Rose Oakar, Mark Joe [Nick] Rahall II). Others have served as state governors (e.g., Victor Atiyeh, OR) or on the White House staff (e.g., John H. Sununu). Similarly, individuals of Arab descent have been elected to the Canadian parliament (e.g., Mac Harb, Mark Assad) and to provincial legislatures. Many of these individuals have faced difficulties in attaining their positions because they were of Arab background. Some have found it useful to de-emphasize or deny that background to get or maintain their positions. Most also have not been strong or vocal supporters of Arab or Arab nationalist causes. Nonetheless, ethnic pride is more openly displayed by an increasing number of political candidates at local, state, and national levels.[75]

Arab Americans have done well and fared better economically than the general population average in many areas. The 1980 and 1990 U.S. census data show that Arab Americans reach a higher educational level than the American population as a whole. According to the 1990 census, 15.2 percent of Arab Americans have "graduate degrees or higher"—more than twice the national average of 7.2 percent. Household income among Arab Americans also tends to be higher than the average. Arab Americans have also done well in professional, management, and sales professions.[76]

Although many Arabs in America have reached the highest level of their profession in almost all professions,[77] the American media primarily highlight the negative achievements of Arabs and Muslims. Quite often, the media announce the Arab or Islamic origin or affiliation of anyone accused of a terrorist act—even before they know whether the perpetrator is Arab or Muslim. In the case of positive role models such as Michael DeBakey or Ralph Nader, the media often never mention their Arab background. One reason is that "some [too many] have found it necessary to hide their origins because of racism."[78] Lists of prominent Arab Americans occasionally are published in the press to inform the public about the community's accomplishments, but the fact that such lists are compiled indicates that Arab Americans feel the sting of negative stereotyping and try to correct the bad publicity. Despite the fact that Arabs have lived in America for more than a century and despite their major successes, they are still struggling to be accepted in American society. Full integration and assimilation will not be achieved until that happens.[79]

Notes

1. See William E. Leuchtenburg, "The American Perception of the Arab World." In George N. Atiyeh, ed., *Arab and American Cultures* (Washington, DC: American Enterprise Institute for Public Policy Research, 1977), p. 15.

2. Although it is possible to speak of several waves of Arab immigration to North America (e.g., 1880s to World War I, World War I to World War II, 1945 to 1967, 1968 to the present), there have been two main waves: from the 1880s to World War II and from World War II to the present. The major differences in the character and composition of the immigrant populations can be detected primarily between these two groups.

3. Unless otherwise indicated, references to the Arab community include the Arabs in Canada and those in the United States. Because of the much smaller numbers of Arabs in Canada, leadership on major issues usually has come from the Arab community in the United States.

4. See appendixes 1 and 2 in Gregory Orfalea, *Before the Flames: Quest for the History of Arab Americans* (Austin, TX: University of Texas Press, 1988), pp. 314–15. There were about 11,000 Arabs in Canada in 1931. For more on the subject of Arab immigration to Canada, see Baha Abu-Laban, *An Olive Branch on the Family Tree: The Arabs in Canada* (Toronto: McClelland and Stewart, 1980).

5. This is the official U.S. government figure cited in Philip Hitti's "The Emigrants," published in the 1963 edition of the *Encyclopedia of Islam* and reproduced in *Al-Hoda, 1898–1968* (New York: Al-Hoda Press, 1968), p. 133. A much larger estimate of 800,000 (Lebanese) was given by Ashad G. Hawie, *The Rainbow Ends* (New York: Theo. Gaus' Sons, 1942), pp. 149, 151.

6. This figure does not include the Arab community in Canada, which has fewer than 400,000 persons today. For estimates of Arab immigration to Canada, see Baha Abu-Laban, *An Olive Branch on the Family Tree: The Arabs in Canada* (Toronto: McClelland and Stewart, 1980) and Ibrahim Hayani's chapter in this book. Philip M. Kayal gave the low estimate in 1974 for Arabs in the United States but provided a revised estimate much closer to the generally accepted figure in 1987. See his "Estimating Arab-American Population," *Migration Today* 2, no. 5 (1974): 3, 9, and "Report: Counting the 'Arabs' Among Us," *Arab Studies Quarterly* 9, no. 1 (1987): 98–104.

7. See Philip K. Hitti, *The Syrians in America* (New York: George H. Doran, 1924), p. 48; Alixa Naff, *Becoming American: The Early Arab Immigrant Experience* (Carbondale, IL: Southern Illinois University Press, 1985), p. 83; Samir Khalaf, "The Background and Causes of Lebanese/Syrian Immigration to the United States before World War I." In Eric J. Hooglund, ed., *Crossing the Waters: Arabic-Speaking Immigrants to the United States before 1940* (Washington, DC: Smithsonian Institution Press, 1987), pp. 17–35; and Charles Issawi, "The Historical Background of Lebanese Emigration: 1800–1914." In Albert Hourani and Nadim Shehadi, eds., *The Lebanese in the World: A Century of Emigration* (London: I.B. Tauris, 1992), pp. 13–31. See also Baha Abu-Laban, "The Lebanese in Montreal." In Albert Hourani and Nadim Shehadi, eds., *The Lebanese in the World: A Century of Emigration* (London: I.B. Tauris, 1992), pp. 227–42.

8. Charles Issawi, "The Historical Background of Lebanese Emigration: 1800–1914." In Albert Hourani and Nadim Shehadi, eds., *The Lebanese in the World: A Century of Emigration* (London: I.B. Tauris, 1992), p. 22.

9. Philip K. Hitti, *The Syrians in America* (New York: George H. Doran, 1924), pp. 49–50. See also Akram Fouad Khater, "'House' to 'Goddess of the House': Gender, Class, and Silk in 19th-Century Mount Lebanon," *International Journal of Middle East Studies* 28, no. 3 (1996): 325–48.

10. For an informed and intelligent discussion on this and related issues, see Louise Seymour Houghton's series of articles entitled "Syrians in the United States," *The Survey* 26 (1 July, 5 August, 2 September, 7 October, 1911), pp. 480–95, 647–65, 786–803, 957–68.

11. For an early account of Arab immigration to the United States and to North America in general, which cites religious persecution as the reason for migration, see Basil M. Kherbawi,

"History of the Syrian Emigration," which is part seven of Kherbawi's *tarikh al-Wilayat al-Muttahida* (*History of the United States*) (New York: al Dalil Press, 1913), pp. 726–96, published in Arabic.

12. See Leila Tarazi Fawaz, *An Occasion for War: Civil Conflict in Lebanon and Damascus in 1860* (Berkeley, CA: University of California Press, 1995). See also, Mikha'il Mishaqa, *Murder, Mayhem, Pillage and Pluder: The History of Lebanon in the 18th and 19th Centuries.* Translated by Wheeler M. Thackston, Jr. (Albany, NY: State University of New York Press, 1988).

13. See Louise Seymour Houghton's series of articles entitled "Syrians in the United States," *The Survey,* 26 (1911), pp. 480–95; and Alixa Naff, *Becoming American: The Early Arab Immigrant Experience* (Carbondale, IL: Southern Illinois University Press, 1985), pp. 128–200. For Canadian statistics, see Baha Abu-Laban, *An Olive Branch on the Family Tree: The Arabs in Canada* (Toronto: McClelland and Stewart, 1980).

14. *Kawkab America* (15 April 1892): 1, English section. The English titles of Arabic newspapers cited here are provided as originally used. The titles in parentheses are the transliterations used by the Library of Congress.

15. Even though *Kawkab America* was published for about seventeen years, only copies of the first four years are available, the others have been lost.

16. See Motaz Abdullah Alhourani, "The Arab-American Press and the Arab World: News Coverage in Al-Bayan and Al-Dalil" (master's thesis, Kansas State University, Manhattan, KS, 1993).

17. For a history of the organizational and political activities of Arabic-speaking groups in the United States during this period, see James Ansara, "The Immigration and Settlement of the Syrians" (master's thesis, Harvard University, Cambridge, MA, 1931).

18. Among these, the most important journal was *The Syrian World,* published and edited by Salloum Mokarzel. A useful publication is the *Annotated Index to the Syrian World, 1926–1932* by John G. Moses and Eugene Paul Nassar (St Paul, MN: Immigration History Research Center, University of Minnesota, 1994).

19. See Philip M. and Joseph M. Kayal, *The Syrian-Lebanese in America: A Study in Religion and Assimilation* (Boston, MA: Twayne Publishers, 1975).

20. A good account of the most prominent of these writers is provided by Nadira Jamil Sarraj, *Shu'ara' al-Rabitah al-Qalamiyah* (Poets of the Pen League) (Cairo, Egypt: Dar al-Ma'arif, 1964), published in Arabic.

21. See, for instance, Ameen Rihani, "To Syrians in the [American] Armed Forces," *As-Sayeh (al-Sa'ih)* (16 September 1918): 2, published in Arabic.

22. Advertisements and editorials in support of American Liberty bonds were found in most Arabic publications of that period, including *Al-Hoda* and *Meraat-ul-Gharb.*

23. See, in particular, *Syria Before the Peace Conference* (New York: Syrian-Lebanese League of North America, 1919).

24. This was the view often voiced after French entrenchment in Syria and Lebanon in the late 1920s and the 1930s.

25. For a summary of these views, see "Editors and Arabian Newspapers Give Opinions on Zionism," *The Jewish Criterion* (5 July 1918): 16–17.

26. Among the more active participants in public lectures and writings on this issue were Ameen Rihani and F. I. Shatara. The Arab National League was established in 1936, and members spoke out on Palestine and other issues. For coverage of these and other activities related to the Palestine issue, see *Palestine & Transjordan* for that period. See also "A Communique from the Arab National League," *As-Sayeh* (6 August 1936): 9.

27. On the occupations of emigrant Arabs, especially in North America and specifically about those engaged in commerce, see Salloum Mokarzel, *Tarikh al-tijara al-Suriyya fi al-mahajir al-Amrikiyya* (The History of Trade of Syrian Immigrants in the Americas) (New York: Syrian-

American Press, 1920), published in Arabic. On peddling activity, see Alixa Naff, *Becoming American: The Early Arab Immigrant Experience* (Carbondale, IL: Southern Illinois University Press, 1985), pp. 128–200.

28. The Arabic press of the period was replete with such advice.

29. Edna Bonacich, "A Theory of Middleman Minorities," *American Sociological Review* 38 (1973): 591.

30. Prejudice against Arabs in America was widespread, and there was also some discrimination, especially in the southern United States. See, for instance, Nancy Faires Conklin and Nora Faires, "'Colored' and Catholic: The Lebanese in Birmingham, Alabama." In Eric J. Hooglund, ed., *Crossing the Waters: Arabic-Speaking Immigrants to the United States before 1940* (Washington, DC: Smithsonian Institution Press, 1987), pp. 69–84.

31. See, for instance, H. A. El-Kourie, "Dr. El-Kourie Defends Syrian Immigrants," *Birmingham Ledger* (20 September 1907) and "El-Kourie Takes Burnett to Task," *Age-Herald* (Birmingham, AL) (20 October 1907): 6.

32. In 1908, Canada issued the Order-in-Council, P.C. 926, which severely restricted Asiatic immigration. Negative attitudes about "Syrians," mistaking them for "Turks," also were a factor in reducing the level of Arab immigration to Canada. See Baha Abu-Laban, "The Lebanese in Montreal." In Albert Hourani and Nadim Shehadi, eds., *The Lebanese in the World: A Century of Emigration* (London: I.B. Tauris, 1992), p. 229.

33. See Kalil A. Bishara, *The Origins of the Modern Syrian* (New York: Al-Hoda Publishing House, 1914), published in English and Arabic.

34. See *Ex Parte Dow*, 211 F. 486 (E.D. South Carolina 1914) and *In Re Dow*, 213 F. 355 (E.D. South Carolina 1914).

35. *Dow v. United States et al*, 26 F. 145 (4th Cir. 1915).

36. See Joseph W. Ferris, "Syrian Naturalization Question in the United States: Certain Legal Aspects of Our Naturalization Laws," Part II, *The Syrian World* 2, no. 9 (1928): 18–24.

37. *In Re Ahmed Hassan*, 48 F. Supp. 843 (E.D. Michigan 1942).

38. *Ex Parte Mohriez*, 54 F. Supp. 941 (D. Massachusetts 1944).

39. See the Arabic edition of *Al-Hoda, 1898–1968* (New York: Al-Hoda Press, 1968).

40. *The Syrian Voice* changed its name to *The Syrian and Lebanonite Voice* in the late 1930s.

41. See M[ichael A.] Shadid, "Syria for the Syrians," *Syrian World* 1, no. 8 (1927): 21–24, and see "'Syria for the Syrians' Again: An Explanation and a Retraction," *Syrian World* 3, no. 4 (1928): 24–28.

42. For an excellent early study of New York Arabs, see Lucius Hopkins Miller, "A Study of the Syrian Communities of Greater New York," *Federation* 3 (1903): 11–58.

43. This was the message often presented in *Al-Akhlaq (al-Akhlaq)* (Character) in the 1920s.

44. See the various articles in the Arabic press by Afifa Karam and Victoria Tannous.

45. This issue occupied the Arab community for a long time and was almost a weekly subject in the main newspapers until peddling activity dwindled in the late 1920s. See, for instance, Afifa Karam's (untitled) article about women peddlers and the *Kashshi* in *Al-Hoda* (14 July, 1903): 2.

46. See, for instance, Habib I. Katibah, "What Is Americanism?" *The Syrian World* 1, no. 3 (1926): 16–20; W. A. Mansur, "The Future of Syrian Americans," *The Syrian World* 2, no. 3 (1927): 11–17, and see "Modern Syrians' Contributions to Civilization," *The Syrian World* 4, no. 5 (1930): 7–14.

47. The question about whether to teach Arabic to their children was a controversial issue in the 1920s and hotly debated in two main journals, *The Syrian World* and *Al-Akhlaq*.

48. See Michael W. Suleiman, "A Community Profile of Arab-Americans: Major Challenges and Concerns," *Arab Perspectives* (September 1983): pp. 6–13.

49. See Ibrahim Abu-Lughod, ed., *The Arab-Israeli Confrontation of June, 1967: An Arab Perspective* (Evanston, IL: Northwestern University Press, 1970).

50. Michael W. Suleiman, "Arab-Americans and the Political Process." In Ernest McCarus, ed., *The Development of Arab-American Identity* (Ann Arbor, MI: University of Michigan Press, 1994), pp. 37–60.

51. See "Dictionary of Races or Peoples." In *United States Reports of the Immigration Commission* (Washington, DC: Government Printing Office, 1911).

52. The details of these appeals are discussed in Michael W. Suleiman, "Early Arab-Americans: The Search for Identity." In Eric J. Hooglund, ed., *Crossing the Waters: Arabic-Speaking Immigrants to the United States before 1940* (Washington, DC: Smithsonian Institution Press, 1987), pp. 37–54.

53. C. P. Snow, *The Two Cultures and the Scientific Revolution* (Cambridge, England: Cambridge University Press, 1961).

54. This became a popular theme among many Arab-American writers. See, for instance, Abraham Mitry Rihbany, *A Far Journey* (Boston, MA: Houghton-Mifflin, 1914).

55. Abraham Mitrie Rihbany, *The Syrian Christ* (Boston, MA: Houghton-Mifflin, 1916).

56. See Evelyn Shakir, "Pretending to Be Arab: Role-Playing in Vance Bourjaily's 'The Fractional Man,'" MELUS 9, no. 1 (1982): 7–21. See also Vance Bourjaily, *Confessions of a Spent Youth* (New York: Bantam Books, 1961).

57. See, for instance, William Peter Blatty, *Which Way to Mecca, Jack?* (New York: Bernard Geis Associates, 1960).

58. See Ali Shteiwi Zaghel, "Changing Patterns of Identification among Arab Americans: The Palestine Ramallites and the Christian Syrian-Lebanese" (Ph.D. diss., Northwestern University, 1977).

59. Much has been written in this vein. For a lengthy bibliography, see Michael W. Suleiman, *The Arabs in the Mind of America* (Brattleboro, VT: Amana Books, 1988). For a Canadian-Arab activist's view, see Sheikh Muhammad Said Massoud, *I Fought as I Believed* (Montreal: Sheikh Muhammad Said Massoud, 1976).

60. Helen Hatab Samhan, "Politics and Exclusion: The Arab American Experience," *Journal of Palestine Studies* 16, no. 2 (1987): 11–28.

61. Nabeel Abraham, "Anti-Arab Racism and Violence in the United States." In Ernest McCarus, ed., *The Development of Arab-American Identity* (Ann Arbor, MI: University of Michigan Press, 1994), pp. 155–214.

62. For documentation, see, for instance, *1990 ADC Annual Report on Political and Hate Violence* (Washington, DC: American-Arab Anti-Discrimination Committee, 1991). For Canadian statistics, see Zuhair Kashmeri, *The Gulf Within: Canadian Arabs, Racism and the Gulf War* (Toronto: James Lorimer & Co., 1991).

63. Ronald Stockton, "Ethnic Archetypes and the Arab Image." In Ernest McCarus, ed., *The Development of Arab-American Identity* (Ann Arbor, MI: University of Michigan Press, 1994), p. 120.

64. See the various essays and poems in Joanna Kadi, ed., *Food for Our Grandmothers: Writings by Arab-American and Arab-Canadian Feminists* (Boston, MA: South End Press, 1994).

65. See Louise Cainkar, "Palestinian Women in the United States: Coping with Tradition, Change, and Alienation" (Ph.D. diss., Northwestern University, 1988).

66. See Charlene Joyce Eisenlohr, "The Dilemma of Adolescent Arab Girls in an American High School" (Ph.D. diss., University of Michigan, 1988).

67. For an excellent study on Arab-American women, see Evelyn Shakir, *Bint Arab: Arab and Arab American Women in the United States* (Westport, CT: Praeger, 1997).

68. Joseph Massad, "Palestinians and the Limits of Racialized Discourse," *Social Text* 11, no. 1 (1993): 108.

69. The attempt has failed, at least so far. See the 16 September 1997 letter to Katherine K. Wellman of the Office of Management and Budget sent on Arab American Institute (AAI) stationery and signed by Helen Hatab Samhan (AAI), Samia El Badry (Census 2000 Advisory Committee), and Hala Maksoud, American-Arab Anti-Discrimination Committee.

70. Lisa Suhair Majaj, "Two Worlds: Arab-American Writing," *Forkroads* 1, no. 3 (1996): 64–80. See also different entries in Joanna Kadi, ed., *Food for Our Grandmothers: Writings by Arab-American and Arab-Canadian Feminists* (Boston, MA: South End Press, 1994).

71. See, for instance, Pauline Kaldas, "Exotic." In Joanna Kadi, ed., *Food for Our Grandmothers: Writings by Arab-American and Arab-Canadian Feminists* (Boston, MA: South End Press, 1994), pp. 168–69.

72. See Nabeel Abraham, "Arab-American Marginality: Mythos and Praxis." In Baha Abu-Laban and Michael W. Suleiman, eds., *Arab Americans: Continuity and Change* (Belmont, MA: AAUG Press, 1989), pp. 17–43.

73. See Michael W. Suleiman, "American Views of Arabs and the Impact of These Views on Arab Americans," *Al-Mustaqbal Al-Arabi* 16 (1993): 93–107, published in Arabic.

74. Milton Gordon states that the absence of a hostile attitude on the part of the host society is a key factor in the integration and assimilation of immigrants. See his *Assimilation in American Life: The Role of Race, Religion, and National Origins* (New York: Oxford University Press, 1964).

75. These attitudes were evident in a 1998 survey of Arabs active in U.S. politics, an analysis of which I plan to publish.

76. For analyses of some of the 1980 and 1990 U.S. census data, see John Zogby, *Arab America Today: A Demographic Profile of Arab Americans* (Washington, DC: Arab American Institute, 1990), and Samia El-Badry, "The Arab-American Market," *American Demographics* (January 1994): 22–27, 30. See also "CPH-L-149 Selected Characteristics for Persons of Arab Ancestry: 1990," U.S. Bureau of the Census, 1990 Census of Population and Housing, C-P-3-2, Ancestry of the Population in the United States: 1990.

77. Examples include Michael DeBakey in medicine (heart surgery); Elias Corey in chemistry (1990 Nobel Prize winner); Casey Kasem, Danny Thomas, and Paula Abdul in entertainment; Helen Thomas in journalism; Doug Flutie in sports (1984 Heisman Trophy winner); and Ralph Nader in consumer advocacy.

78. Casey Kasem, "We're Proud of Our Heritage," *Parade* (*Kansas City Star*) (16 January 1994): 1.

79. See Lisa Suhair Majaj, "Boundaries: Arab/American." In Joanna Kadi, ed., *Food for Our Grandmothers: Writings by Arab-American and Arab-Canadian Feminists* (Boston, MA: South End Press, 1994), pp. 65–84.

Part I

Profiles of Specific Communities

May Seikaly

I   Attachment and Identity: The Palestinian Community of Detroit

Although Arab Americans constitute relatively new communities in the United States, a fair amount of literature on their history and development has been generated. Interest in recording the social, economic, and political experiences of these immigrants has grown in tandem with the expansion of their numbers and their visibility on the American scene. Since the late 1960s, the upsurge in the literature has reflected a growing sense of ethnic identity among the members of these communities (e.g., the Muslims in America) and a closer link to their countries of origin.[1] It also has been a response to western attitudes toward Islam and U.S. official policy about the homelands of these communities.[2] Another area of scholarly interest that has produced prolific writing is Arab and Muslim women. This field of study sheds light on the social and cultural dynamism within these societies in the Middle East and the diaspora. These many sources have informed the historical background of the Arab-American experience provided in this chapter.

Although the earliest Arab immigrant communities congregated initially in the northeastern states close to their ports of entry (i.e., New York and Boston), they gradually filtered to areas of economic pull such as Detroit, Los Angeles, and Houston. Arab migration has been primarily to and from urban centers, although it has attracted many rural Arabs. The earliest waves of immigration to the United States occurred at the close of the nineteenth century, predominantly from Syria and Lebanon but with a small number from Palestine. The preponderance of these immigrants were Christian, although Muslims also immigrated at this time.[3] The ratio of Christian to Muslim immigration for the period until the mid-twentieth century has been estimated at 90 to 10 percent. Some writers claim that this ratio has drastically changed since 1948, following the expulsion of Palestinian Arabs from their homeland and the influx of Asian Muslims to the United States. Since 1948, Palestinians have been trickling in to join the other, larger Arab immigrant communities, and proportionately many more Muslims came with those waves of migration. Although there are no reliable statistics on the current number of Arab Americans or Palestinians, estimates by observers and experts put the total of Arabic-speaking communities at approximately three million, with the Palestinians averaging 12 to 15 percent of that number.[4]

Like other Arab immigrants, Palestinians came in direct response to economic and political "push factors" in their home country. However, in the Palestinian case, these factors were punctuated by dramatic civilian dislocations and flight. The first of these waves in 1948 was followed by another in 1967, when the whole of Palestine fell under Israeli military control. The next wave of migration occurred in 1970, after the Palestinian-Jordanian debacle and its aftermath of strained relations. Emigration again increased in 1982 in response to the deteriorating conditions of Palestinian life in Lebanon after the Israeli occupation, the expulsion of the Palestine Liberation Organization, and the Sabra and Shatila massacres.[5] The final link in this chain of misfortunes was the Gulf War and the resulting expulsion of Palestinians from Kuwait and most of the Gulf states. Since 1948, immigration to the United States has attracted Palestinians suffering from the economic and societal upheavals brought about by contraction of local options for refuge.

Until the 1960s, Arab immigration to the United States was motivated by economic factors and limited by legal restrictions. Thereafter, immigration was sought for various other reasons by Arabs, including Palestinians. Although economics remained a significant attraction, education, technical opportunities, and a more liberal political atmosphere became important reasons for people to immigrate.[6] At a time when the older communities had almost become acclimatized to the U.S. social and political scene, a more youthful generation of Arab immigrants who were socialized and politicized in the Arab world of the 1950s and 1960s joined their ranks. Among the new waves of immigrants were students seeking technical and professional training and families looking for better opportunities and a more liberal atmosphere. These newcomers brought energy and zeal into the established Arab-American communities and reinvigorated the ethnic features of that community with political and social orientations that reflected the changes the Arab world had experienced since World War II.

A major issue that caught the imagination and emotions of all was the Palestine War of 1948 and the dispersal of the Palestinian people. It was the first event that directly touched most Arab Americans and involved them in activities that went beyond the charity to their families and villages back home. After 1967 these events came to their sitting rooms through media coverage, and their lives were affected by the recognition of American pro-Israeli policy and a vocal anti-Arab public expression.

Palestinians were prominently represented among the new waves of Arab additions to the ethnic communities of the United States. By the late 1960s, Palestinians came in families and as individuals, as legal immigrants to join family members, and as students, many of whom ultimately settled in the country. They came from all social strata, from rural areas seeking economic opportunities and a refuge, and from middle-class families seeking education and professional opportunities. Among them were the highly qualified professionals and intellectuals, as well as those with minimal formal education.

Detroit was the destination of many because it offered the largest concentration of ethnic Arabs, providing family and friends and a familiar way of life. Already-settled Arab and Palestinian communities provided primary group support to help initiate new immigrants into the American system. Whether Muslims or Christians, these primary channels supplied newcomers from the same families, from among friends, or from the same village with the facilities to settle, find work, and adjust.[7]

The Detroit auto industry and allied economic opportunities had attracted Arab immigrants since early in the twentieth century. A community had grown there, becoming a primary group that attracted other immigrants. Christian and Muslim Palestinians have lived and worked in Detroit since the early 1930s. However, their numbers had grown significantly only after 1948, and by the 1960s, their community had swollen to include all social strata and a large number of politicized and educated newcomers.[8] Although it is impossible to gauge the exact number of Palestinians living in the Detroit metropolitan area, research in the early 1980s has estimated their number to be 12.5 percent of the total Arab-American population of 200,000.[9] This number seems to have grown because of protracted Israeli policies in the West Bank and the results of the Gulf War. This approach explains the suggested number of 25,000 to 30,000 Palestinians living in Detroit. Observers also suggest that the ratio of Muslims to Christians for this group of residents is nearly equal.

All sects of this community initially settled within the boundaries of Detroit, and a pattern of differentiated settlement among Christians and Muslims gradually developed. Like all immigrant communities, the features of Palestinian immigration followed the pattern of family chain and primary group attraction. The most common form of immigration was through the sponsorship of family members among whom they set roots at first. The socioeconomic background of the immigrants dictated the areas of settlement and their later mobility. Muslims initially congregated in Highland Park and the south end of Dearborn, and with improved economic conditions, they moved northward into Dearborn and on to the closest western and southern suburbs. The Christians settled initially in Detroit and then moved to the western suburbs of Westland, Livonia, and Farmington Hills, often going by way of Dearborn in their climb economically. Although Palestinian presence in Detroit today is minimal, except for few families at the borders of Dearborn or the few in the wealthiest residential pockets (e.g., Grosse Pointe) and in some left-over retail stores, many Palestinians, especially Christians, started their immigrant lives there. Nevertheless, there are Palestinians of both sects scattered in most parts of metropolitan Detroit, especially in the wealthier suburbs to the east and north.

Like other Arab immigrant communities, Palestinian settlement patterns were modeled on the life they had left behind: homogeneous communities grouped by family, religion, sect, and village. They also reproduced, in as far as possible, the lifestyle they had been accustomed to in terms of social contacts and linkages, celebrations of joy and sorrow, and leadership "za'ama" alliances. In the United States, wealth and financial success replaced lineage and family names as the criteria of social status and leadership. Education and professionalism as means of economic advancement and respectability became goals among the second generation.

Relationships among the early immigrants were based on sectarian, economic, and village affiliations, not on political association. This approach was challenged, especially among the middle class, by the changed political atmosphere in the city from the 1970s through the early 1990s. The waves of immigrants since the late 1960s

influenced the local Palestinian communities with new ideologies and new political concepts. The students and immigrants of the 1960s and 1970s brought radical political
views bonding their nationalist feelings into their ethnic identities while at the same
time expecting to function within the U.S. democratic system. The centrality of the
Palestinian problem in the Arab political discourse was reflected in the political scene
locally, providing Palestinians of all strata with an atmosphere that touched their deepest commitment. When political developments after 1990 put their ideologies and the
whole nationalist movement on hold, Palestinians in a more fundamental fashion than
other Arab Americans faced questions about their social and political identity and their
relationship to America.

Research Design and Data

The data on and conclusions about the profile of the Detroit Palestinian community,
particularly its social and political identification today, are drawn from my research on
a sample of Palestinians, representative of the whole community, who have been residing in Detroit for a minimum of fifteen years. These findings are based primarily on
formal, open-ended life history interviews that were confirmed and verified by interview comparisons and documented records, as well as my observation and participation in community affairs and conduct.

This study sought to define the community's perception of itself through the words
and lives of its members, to hear "their truth" as Ronald Fraser calls it, combining fac-
tual and subjective elements in this assessment.[10] Based on the conviction that the past,
in all its nuances and flavors, colors and defines the present human experience, these
life histories give meaning to the current conflicts and dilemmas of the community
when viewed within the spectrum of its past. In addition to finding the present through
the past, oral history is an excellent medium to translate the personal into the public
and the political.

The Palestinian community of Detroit is a composite community, with cleavages
along economic, social, and religious divides, which were taken into consideration in
the choice of respondents. Fifty interviews were administered in Arabic, English, or a
combination of both languages. Respondents from Ramallah and the Jerusalem district
made up the largest group in the samples of Christian and Muslim participants. The
Ramallah Christian community is the largest single ethnic group among the Palestinians, with an estimated number of 5,000. Among the Muslims, the Beit Hanina and Bireh
community are next in size, but their numbers have dwindled through outward migration, mainly to Ohio, in the last decade. Attention was given to sample selection to
ensure a fair representation of all socioeconomic milieus, of women of all strata and
sects, and of some active second-generation members to provide insight and analysis
of their parents' experience and its effect on their lives. The first priority was to select
elderly, clear-minded respondents whose lives spanned the longest period of the Palestinian experience. This group was represented by 13 interviews of persons older than
70 years of age and a similar number who were 60 years or younger and who had a
clear, youthful memory of the period before 1948.[11]

By using oral interviews to study the Palestinian community of Detroit, a wide range of possible research topics opened up for future investigation. Although the life history interviews collected for this study provide many research topics, only some of the information was used for this essay; I focused on the major theme of Palestinian community identity and the challenges of today.

Analysis: Method and Results

The most difficult task in the analysis of the oral interviews was interpreting the inner intent of the narration and understanding its complexities. Interpretation becomes the mediator, the bridge, between the academic, theoretical concepts about society and social change and the experiences, recollections, and passions of the individuals interviewed. By viewing the whole matrix of society in an integrated form, the individual experience makes sense on the level of its broad association with the ethnic community in terms of ideology and political beliefs.

Although the retelling of life histories added significant dimensions to the Palestinian story and made sense of that experience, the interview was an event in itself, imparting other aspects of the life being told. A few interviews included more than one respondent, and these gave a more vivid picture of intercommunal relationships, the persistence of traditional values and behaviors, the respect for age, and conformity to the traditional norms. Subtle rivalries, competitions, and differences of opinion added spice to the meetings, suggesting deeper differences and serious malaise within the established social group.

Soon after starting the interviews, it became clear that the Palestinian community as a whole was in a state of crisis, characterized by paralysis and inertia of all political activities. Narrow social, sectarian, and village identification was pervasive. Social and ethnic introversions among the Palestinians were clear indications of the community's frozen political stance and disarray. In this situation the Palestinians found themselves the most vulnerable and the worst hit. They witnessed retractions in the political platforms they had supported. They felt betrayed, with even fewer options for a homeland.

In these interviews, which recounted life histories from birth through adulthood, the experience of betrayal had started early. This was expressed in the words of many of the interviewees:

> I became aware of injustice early on, when as a child of eight I encountered an Israeli soldier who mistreated my best friend because she was Muslim. This awareness was endorsed when I experienced the wrenching sorrow of a cousin's death, burnt by Israeli soldiers, and also when my father was beaten up in our house in front of us, his kids, for having opened the front door during an imposed curfew.

Another participant put it clearly: "All Palestinians feel betrayed by the international powers and by Arab leaders." Yet another person saw the situation in a historical depth that reflected her personal experience:

> There was nothing to enjoy! We grew up in an atmosphere of misery: this one died, the other killed or arrested. It was continuous—first the British, then the Jews mistreated the people.

There were no human rights; no one cared about what happened [to the people]. To whom should one complain? This Palestinian catastrophe still goes on.

Even though the respondents came from varied socioeconomic and religious backgrounds, all those who experienced the dramatic events of 1948 gave similar impressions and related deep, trenchant memories. The sense of loss, dislocation, fear, panic, misery, and betrayal were remarkably similar and continued to color the interviews in varying intensity. These early experiences had influenced the later lives of all respondents. Even for those who learned about these events from their parents, 1948 stood as a landmark in their lives.

The memories of the period before 1948 and of the event itself released a flood of enlightening information. Men and women from villages and towns who recalled that period had clearly relived it often during the intervening years. Names of victims, descriptions of incidents, and personal contributions, reactions, and analyses were vivid and cathartic. The dispersal of 1948 and the communal misery and degradation that accompanied it seem to be the basis for development of a pervasive ethnonational identity among disparate people. Subsequent history and a legacy of hardship and injustice were also relayed in continuum that strongly suggests the psychological basis for the development of a Palestinian ethos, characterized by adamant attachment to ethnicity despite all odds. The personal memory, which had become that of the group, has had climactic influence on the path their lives took and their quality of life. It is an experience etched in their memory and persona, and whether consciously or otherwise, it affected all future dealings, as was made clear in their accounts. Their words stand witness to the intensity of those events:

When an old man [Abu Musa] was shot while sitting in a corner of the street, our whole neighborhood panicked and sought refuge in another quarter.

We scrambled, afraid and uncertain, trying to take valuables with us, but finally, barely made it with our lives.

Even though a child then, I still remember the dead bodies in the streets of Jaffa on our way out.

Snipers were all around us, but the men begged them [the attacking Jewish force] to let them bury the dead woman properly.

The many tales I know of the 1948 flight will make you cry; death, burial, humiliation, and loss. So many people lost loved ones as well as their homes.

The Social Dimension

Like other Arab-American communities, attachment to cultural ethnicity is a defining feature of the Palestinian group. However, Palestinians have promoted this definition to an entrenched nationality, an overpowering commitment that is continuously fed by political events and remains at the back of their consciousness. They have created a badge of differentiation. It is reminiscent of early ethnic group behavior in the United States, particularly of communities that had come from embattled environments and societies and that had experienced isolationist biases, such as the Irish and Jewish early immigrant communities. Among the Palestinians, the sense of injustice and beleaguerment is active and seems never ending: "Life under occupation jarred and strained my sense of justice and human dignity. I found it hard to remain silent in face of these transgressions."

In view of such a history, a certain political ideology emerged that reflected Palestinian world and life view. It was an emphatic attachment to the primary unit of political identity, the ethnic culture, and the structures that support its perpetuation. All respondents emphasized the reproduction of culture with its ethnic particularities. It is the constant, the refuge in a world of flux. The condition of homelessness, exile, harassment, and defeatism is offset by finding refuge in one's ethnic setting. Social, religious, and political structures that ensure the survival of this group identity become paramount. However, the vehemence of this attachment was expressed in various levels of intensity among the sample interviewed, reflecting socioeconomic, sectarian, and generational cleavages in the community.

On a scale differentiating the stance of the various strata of the community, Muslim men who are older, of humble economic means, with little education, and mostly of village origin express the most traditional or conservative viewpoint, followed by older women of the same socioeconomic level. The attitudes of most Christians and the majority of middle-class, better-educated Muslims (elderly and middle aged) are comparably more moderate and flexible. However, this stratum is generally moved by traditional value-based social behavior. Those who have shown the least tradition-bound social attitude are mostly the better-off (although not necessarily only those), cosmopolitan strata of Muslims and Christians; they are mainly second generation, better educated, and attuned to Arab and American politics. Throughout the study, these variant attitudes and emphases were reproduced on the same scale specified here.

Palestine, the homeland and the nostalgic village, is alive in Palestinian memories and viewed as the utopian solution. On the whole, this community sees itself as transplanted, forced into exile by conditions beyond its control. To mitigate the effect of this alienation, Palestinians in America transplant the lifestyle of the old country, with its habits, traditions, beliefs, and physical environment. They surround themselves with the artifacts of the culture: embroideries, the mounted religious drawings and scripts, the sounds of Arabic music and language, and the smells of Arab food.

I am an American of Palestinian origin. I feel the solutions to my ethnic group are to be sought within mainstream American political structures. The process needs patience and hard work.

I am Arab Palestinian, and I feel guilty for abandoning my country.

I am strongly attached to Palestine and Jerusalem. This is where I was born, where my childhood memories formed, and the center of my family. My history is there.

The yearning for return seems more philosophical than practical, even though many express their intention to do so in the long run and have already bought real estate in anticipation. Some of the older men explained their need to return as the only method left to safeguard against dilution of their ethnicity in America. Palestinian resistance to acculturation and assimilation is explained in this persistent attachment to the dream of return, regardless of obvious handicaps. However, Arab conditions under the Likud government do not encourage strong commitment to such an option, which was expressed by a cautious, undecided stance of many. A significant portion of the sample who, coming from areas under occupation since 1948 and being well established financially in Detroit or having fully adapted to the American setting, have excluded that option.

All Palestinians have been socialized within the patriarchal system to some degree. Patriarchal values of male dominance and parental rights and expectations are formally accepted by some and inherently accepted by almost all. This principle and its implementation are more dominant within the Muslim traditional family structure. Christians also view the patriarchal system as their cultural form of social relations, although its application by middle-class Muslims and Christians is flexible and rationalized.

The whole community agrees on the need to perpetuate tradition to protect ethnic distinctiveness and ensure survival. Tradition is a defense and a refuge from alien values, habits, and behaviors. The family or home is the reproducer of cultural authenticity and offers the solution to the social dispersion of the community. A system of dual expectations and roles for males and females is a part of this social tradition that puts pressure on women to be cultural guardians and educators. Among members of the conservative stratum, this has produced a more conscious binding to ethnicity and tradition by women but not necessarily by men. The condition of women within this stratum in Detroit and the social expectations about their dedication and service to the culture are similar to the traditional behaviors among Chicago Muslims in terms of gender issues and women's cultural roles.[12]

Most of the women interviewed for this study had been active in political and charitable organizations until recently and had contributed significantly to gender-related concerns within the community. The women respondents of all socioeconomic strata and educational levels appeared to be socially and politically conscious, perceptive of the social ills of the community, and active as the reproducers of Palestinian culture among the young. Women were as deeply and strongly affected as men by the moral injustice of their nation's case and up to date with its latest events. Whereas older women, similar to men, were agitated by what was perceived as the threat to tradition and its survival by a nonconformist youth, younger women were much less alarmed.

Second-generation women had much in common in terms of their adaptability to change, absorption of western culture, and genuine commitment to cultural preservation. However, they were also in a state of inaction because of the political inertia that had beset the community as a whole. Nevertheless, many among them had not abandoned their involvement in community affairs, especially in issues concerning women, and they felt adjusted to the American way of life. Although women are burdened by society's conservative demands on their behavior, they seem to cope adequately with the tensions that surround their everyday life.

These issues and those of the future generations of Palestinians had become the major subjects of debate in conservative circles. At a time when the political environment had contracted, a more introverted attitude prevailed, and the smallest social and family concerns became major disputes. More than before, members of these circles, especially the men, ponder the significance of family and women as vehicles of cultural ethnicity. When it comes to women, who are the symbols of male authority within the patriarchal system, the barometer of family honor, and the reproducers of ethnic culture, conservatives dread the impact of American values and fear a disintegration of traditional ethnic culture. Within the community, the growing economic and social independence of women is deplored and considered to be a reason for the alarming rise in divorce rates. This issue was raised more by older-generation Muslim than Christian conservative respondents and seems to occupy their minds and govern their concerns about the future.

Most members of the community also were concerned about the next generation and its future identity. With the many attractions the United States offers and the consequent weakening of family and cultural ties, they feared that the next generation of Palestinian Americans would be lost to the culture. They thought this situation would be worse among the young men, who are afforded more freedom and whose lapses into the American lifestyle are accepted, making them more prone to acculturation than women. The problems of the younger generation were placed at the door of Americanization, loose morality, and the effects of television, freedom, and weak social and economic paternal and parental control.

Christian attitudes about most of the serious concerns of the society are similar to those of the Muslims. Whether it pertains to tradition and the preservation of the culture in terms of gender relations and parental expectations or the patriarchal system and its ethos of male and female roles and their definitions, these attitudes and practices are less intense among the Christians and the wealthier Muslim stratum. Wealth, education, and longer residence in the United States, which are more characteristic of the Christians in Detroit, explain their flexible social approach to these issues. However, even they bemoan the loss of traditional social standards. Members of these strata are also worried about the future cultural identity of their children and the gradual weakening of their attachment to the ethos they have lived by.

Although Muslim and Christian Palestinians were equally involved in political activities in previous years, the current absence of such opportunities has affected their contact and relationships. Both communities are more involved with internal social affairs, economic pursuits, and respective religious activities. Both sides seem to gradually revert to old attitudes of traditional stereotyping of one another, shown by mild tensions and suspicion. These attitudes are more obvious among the lower middle class and the geographically separated communities and much less apparent among the upper middle class and the wealthier, educated strata.

Loneliness is a common condition among the Palestinians. Loneliness is explicitly expressed by many. It is mentioned particularly by the old, and it is an undercurrent among those who feel isolated from the larger Palestinian concentrations. Although some Christians of the Jerusalem villages attach themselves to the Ramallah community, they feel discriminated against by a clannish attitude of that old, established group. Similarly, some Muslim groups attach themselves to larger communities such as Bireh and Beit Hanina. Nevertheless, this leaves unattached those who cannot find their ethnic niche among the many little ethnicities the Palestinians have retreated into. This feeling is strongest among those with few immigrants from their own towns and villages, such as Gaza, the Hebron district, and the north of Palestine. The personal feeling of loneliness is magnified by the general sense of isolation the community is experiencing.

The Political Dimension

The clearest and loudest message of all participants in this study has been their political identity as Palestinians. Although many hyphenated their designations with Arab or American, their identity was clearly focused on the roots of the early socializing and politicizing process in their lives. Social and cultural concerns were expressions of their political concerns. At every turn, Palestinians found cause to link their present status with the legacy of a painful past. As one respondent commented, "We are a nation who labors under feelings of suffering and a central heroic theme that has colored our view of ourselves." Another one said, "The story of Palestine is the cruelest one [of all other people], and no one cares, and it still goes on. . . . It is distressing to think of 'Al-Shattat' [the dispersion] of the Palestinian people, the loss of land, and degrading of [our] identity."

As relayed in the interviews, they persisted in confirming their commitment to their culture and their homeland despite injustice and overwhelming odds. By repetitive expressions, they all try to impress and confirm the strong attachment to an identity that even the young, who have spent all or most of their lives in the United States, recognize.

The political status of the homeland—Palestine—has influenced the way Palestinians identify and view their own status in the United States. Most of the respondents defined their lives as a series of events and junctures correlated with the history of the Palestinian problem. The events of 1948 left a deep wound in the Palestinian psyche, and those of 1967 had a similar impact on the people interviewed. The life experiences recorded in every interview were organized in stages punctuated by events related to Palestinian history. "I recall that my father came home the day after Deir Yasin." "When Nasir died, I felt lost because an anchor of the Palestinian cause was lost." "Sabra and Shatila converted me." "When Sadat went to Jerusalem, I could not study for my exams."

The period before 1967 was recalled by some as a time of rebellion, of struggle to construct an identity squashed by Jordanian or Syrian coercive and alienating policies. Many who had lived during that period in the Arab countries had been embittered and became more Palestinian oriented. "As a teenager I was arrested by the Jordanian police along with other students for expressing my views on Palestine and I was jailed—this on top of our loss; it was endless," said one participant.

The events of 1967 constituted a watershed in Palestinian and Arab politics. In Detroit, they were a catalyst that ignited the political atmosphere and brought together intellectuals, student activists, and various community members. In the decade that followed, a number of developments swept the Arab and Palestinian communities into an era of closer links with the Arab countries and among themselves. This period redefined Arab perceptions of themselves and of the United States political system. It was also during this period that the main Arab-American organizations—Association of Arab-American University Graduates (AAUG), American-Arab Anti-Discrimination

Committee (ADC), Arab American Institute (AAI), National Association of Arab Americans (NAAA)—were established,[13] as well as local organizations for social services such as ACCESS. Many Palestinians were active participants in this process and saw in it a fulfillment of their Arab and Palestinian nationalist leanings. The generation of immigrants who came to Detroit in the 1970s and 1980s were quite distinct from the earlier ones. They came with self-views defined as Arabs, as nationalists, and as activists of political orientations, some from within Palestinian structures.

Palestinianism was not necessarily the only identity that they assumed during all stages of their lives. During these politicized eras, activists were exposed to various ideologies that shaped their political development and identity. Most have expressed adherence and commitment to pan-Arab feelings as part of this identification. However, this idea was defined by particular partisanship imported from the Arab countries. Further party alliances, defined by Palestinian organizational divisions, found echos locally, leading to many cleavages among the Palestinians. This rapid proliferation of orientations was a prelude to the process in which political life, bound to the events of state and party politics outside the American scene, disintegrated in the local communities along the same lines that Arab politics abroad did. Because much of Arab politics involved Palestinian affairs, such as the civil war in Lebanon, the Israeli occupation of south Lebanon, the Sadat initiative, the Gulf War, and the Oslo accords, local Palestinians were directly and deeply affected. For the activists among them, the results of these political events were interpreted as another betrayal; others absorbed it and accommodated to what remained, and still others began to search for alternative solutions to those presented in the political arena. The outward signs of this state of disorientation and confusion have been the paralysis and inertia the community has experienced for the last five years.

Various levels of identifications have operated simultaneously among Palestinians. Although a sense of overall nationalism as culturally Arab and ethnically Palestinian was experienced by all and sharing the feelings of loss and anxiety is loosely felt by most, some have given priority to political ideologies and their Palestinian dimension to define the parameters of that identity. Others expressed their sense of identity in religiocultural terms, an Arab-Muslim identity that has become stronger in the diaspora as a result of the failure of all nationalist and socialist ideologies. This search for identity has had paradoxical effects. On the one hand, it pushed them to belong to an entrenched ethnic group, with whom they shared a familiar cultural legacy and history. On the other hand, it made them aware of their image and that of Arabs in the political and social setting around them.

Despite that awareness, Palestinians in Detroit have lived on the periphery of the American political system. Most respondents recognize the community's inadequate use of the political system to promote their aims, which is one reason for the impasse they find themselves in. Their attitude toward the United States and its political system can be measured by the small number of people who vote. Only 30 percent of the sample said they voted in U.S. elections, and for most of these, the choice of candidate is based on his or her stance on Arab causes and the Palestinian issue. One politically active respondent said, "We need to understand and work within the American system, building bridges and contacts." Another expressed his exasperation with that system: "After

1967 and the tremendous loss then, I concentrated on the Palestinian cause and Arabism; I made less American friends." Another well-established, long-term resident said, "I like America and living in America; however, I do not like this country's foreign policy. It is influenced by lobbyists and special interest groups." Nevertheless, second-generation American Palestinians have become more involved in local American politics and see that path as the means for effective community recognition and the safeguarding of its rights.

Even though the community is weighed down by recurring unfavorable conditions, the debates within its circles are lively and reflect its gradual adjustment to change and political realities. The most positive and optimistic stance is offered by the more educated members of the younger, second-generation Palestinian Americans who, while identifying with their ethnic origin, see their future in mainstream American politics. They were critical of Arab political divisions and resented their reflections locally. In this situation of crisis, they seemed to be the least stunned and disoriented.

Conclusion

Fifty Palestinians in Detroit were generous and willing to relive on record the experiences of their lives, enriching our understanding of their special experience and their sense of identity and its significance to the wider arena of diasporal communities in the United States. Through their memories, they reweaved the experience of Palestinian hope and despair and have shown its impact on their thoughts, actions, and identifications today.

The continuous contraction of a Palestinian refuge is potent and painful. The amputations of 1948, 1967, 1970, 1973, and 1982 and the events of the 1990s have affected the local community to various degrees and in diversified forms. Some impart a feeling of resignation tinged with desperation, but some still cling to their roots—the village and the family to go back to. Others, especially the educated youth, visualize the creation of alternative channels in the diaspora, a bridge constructed by their own lives to again connect with the old. There are also those who see their future in becoming an effective ethnic community within the American community of the many.

There is a general sense of confusion and anguish about the future among the community as a whole. This situation has been generated by the course of events dealing with the fate of a Palestinian solution, particularly after the Gulf War and in the convoluted peace process. This community, which has bound its identity with the fate of its homeland, has been on a roller coaster of euphoria, expectations, and disappointments leading to the current state of uncertainty and anguish. Ethnic communities are not static, and changes that affect their members are reflected in their perception of themselves and their relations to the broader society. The Palestinian community of Detroit seems to be undergoing a crisis accelerated by events within it and political conditions beyond it that ultimately mold its identity.

Notes

Acknowledgment: Special appreciation goes to Wayne State University, College of Liberal Arts, for the summer of 1997 fund that made this research possible.

1. E. C. Hagopian and A. Paden, eds., *The Arab-Americans: Studies in Assimilation* (Wilmette: Medina University Press, 1969); Barbara Aswad, ed., *Arabic Speaking Communities in American Cities* (New York: Center for Migration Studies, 1974); S. Y. Abraham and N. Abraham, *Arabs in the New World: Studies on Arab-American Communities* (Detroit: Wayne State University–Center for Urban Studies, 1983); Ernest McCarus, ed., *The Development of Arab-American Identity* (Ann Arbor: University of Michigan Press, 1994); Jamal N. Adawi, *Al-Hijra al-Filastiniya ila Amrika [Palestinian Migration to America]* (Nazareth: Beit al-Sadaqa Press, 1993); *Al-Mustaqbal Al-Arabi (file on Arab Communities in the West)* (no. 209, July 1996), pp. 56–88.

2. E. H. Waugh, S. M. Abu-Laban, and R. B. Qureshi, eds., *Muslim Families in North America* (Edmonton: The University of Alberta Press, 1991); B. Aswad and B. Bilge, eds., *Family and Gender Among American Muslims* (Philadelphia: Temple University Press, 1996).

3. My own grandfather had emigrated from Haifa in Palestine to New York with my father and two other children in 1911 and 1912. He came to join his uncles, who had already established themselves in the peddling business. The aim was economic improvement and evasion of possible military induction of his sons and himself. Among these early Palestinian immigrants was Abdul Hamid Shoman from Beit Hanina, near Jerusalem, the business entrepreneur and future owner of the Arab Bank.

4. These estimates were compiled from statistical estimates of Arab communities in the United States and from members of these communities interviewed for this research, all admitting the difficulty of providing concrete reliable data. See Alixa Naff, "Arabs in America: A Historical Overview." In S. Y. Abraham and N. Abraham, eds., *Arabs in the New World: Studies on Arab-American Communities* (Detroit: Wayne State University–Center for Urban Studies, 1983), pp. 9–27; also see Sameer Abraham, "Detroit's Arab-American Community: A Survey of Diversity and Commonality." In S. Y. Abraham and N. Abraham, eds., *Arabs in the New World: Studies on Arab-American Communities* (Detroit: Wayne State University–Center for Urban Studies, 1983), pp. 88–91.

5. Yvonne Y. Haddad, "Maintaining the Faith of the Fathers: Dilemmas of Religious Identity in the Christian and Muslim Arab-American Communities." In Ernest McCarus, ed., *The Development of Arab-American Identity* (Ann Arbor, University of Michigan, 1994), pp. 61–63; and Michael W. Suleiman, "Arab-Americans and the Political Process." In Ernest McCarus, ed., *The Development of Arab-American Identity* (Ann Arbor, University of Michigan, 1994), pp. 45–46.

6. Yvonne Y. Haddad, "Maintaining the Faith of the Fathers: Dilemmas of Religious Identity in the Christian and Muslim Arab-American Communities." In Ernest McCarus, ed., *The Development of Arab-American Identity* (Ann Arbor, University of Michigan, 1994), pp. 62–63; and Michael W. Suleiman, "Arab-Americans and the Political Process." In Ernest McCarus, ed., *The Development of Arab-American Identity* (Ann Arbor, University of Michigan, 1994), pp. 37–46; S. Abraham, "Detroit's Arab-American Community." In S. Y. Abraham and N. Abraham, eds., *Arabs in the New World: Studies on Arab-American Communities* (Detroit: Wayne State University–Center for Urban Studies, 1983), pp. 90–91; Louise Cainkar, "Palestinian Women in American Society: The Interaction of Social Class, Culture, and Politics." In Ernest McCarus, ed., *The Development of Arab-American Identity* (Ann Arbor: University of Michigan Press, 1994), pp. 90–96.

7. For a thorough analysis of these relations and their historical background, see chapters by Barbara Aswad, Charles L. Swan, Leila Saba, and Laurel Wigle in Barbara Aswad, ed., *Arabic Speaking Communities in American Cities* (New York: Center for Migration Studies, 1974); chapters by Alixa Naff, Sameer Abraham, Nabeel Abraham, and Barbara Aswad in S. Y. Abraham and N. Abraham, *Arabs in the New World: Studies on Arab-American Communities* (Detroit: Wayne State University–Center for Urban Studies, 1983); and Louise Cainkar, "Palestinian Women in American Society: The Interaction of Social Class, Culture, and Politics." In Ernest McCarus, ed., *The Development of Arab-American Identity* (Ann Arbor: University of Michigan Press, 1994), pp. 90–92

8. Detroit and particularly the south end of Dearborn have been researched because they are considered the largest geographic concentrations of Arab settlement. See chapters about Detroit and its Arab community in S. Y. Abraham and N. Abraham, eds., *Arabs in the New World: Studies on Arab-American Communities* (Detroit: Wayne State University–Center for Urban Studies, 1983); in this book (p. 90), Sameer Abraham reports the first Palestinian presence in Detroit to have been in 1908 through 1913.

9. Sameer Abraham, "Detroit's Arab-American Community: A Survey of Diversity and Commonality." In S. Y. Abraham and N. Abraham, eds., *Arabs in the New World: Studies on Arab-American Communities* (Detroit: Wayne State University–Center for Urban Studies, 1983), pp. 88. This estimate was based on projections of respondents to this research who have direct access to their communities and who gave cautious estimates.

10. Ronald Fraser, *Blood of Spain: The Experience of Civil War, 1936–39* (New York: Penguin, 1981), p. 32.

11. The sample included 20 Muslim males, 7 Muslim females, 14 Christian males, and 9 Christian females. Two of the respondents came from Israel, and most of the others came from West Bank towns and villages or from Jordan, Syria, or Lebanon. Many Palestinian towns could not be represented, and these interviews were administered only once with no returns. For the sake of accuracy and thoroughness, some of the interviews need to be repeated and expanded.

12. Louise Cainkar, "Palestinian Women in American Society: The Interaction of Social Class, Culture, and Politics." In Ernest McCarus, ed., *The Development of Arab-American Identity* (Ann Arbor: University of Michigan Press, 1994), pp. 85–105.

13. Michael W. Suleiman, "Arab-Americans and the Political Process." In Ernest McCarus, ed., *The Development of Arab-American Identity* (Ann Arbor, University of Michigan, 1994), pp. 45–46.

Richard T. Antoun

2   Jordanian Migrants in Texas and Ohio: The Quest for Education and Work in a Global Society

The subject of this chapter is the experience of transnational migration in its personal and humanistic aspects and in its various multicultural contexts. The research is part of a larger case study focused on migration from the Jordanian village of Kufr al-Ma to seventeen different countries in Europe, Asia, North America, and Arabia.[1] The students traveling the farthest, spending the longest periods abroad, and encountering the hardest cultural shocks are those in the United States. It is only in the United States that students are subject to continuous change in numerous aspects of their lives: schools attended, professional goals, place of residence, place of work, women dated, and cars bought and sold. This chapter compares and contrasts the experiences of four Jordanian men who spent five to thirteen years seeking higher education and work in the highly mobile and heterogeneous cities of Dallas–Fort Worth, Galveston, and Midland, Texas, and Cincinnati, Ohio, in the 1980s and 1990s.[2] Their education and work, the mechanism of acculturation to American society (i.e., family, friends, wives, or girl friends), their degree of acculturation to American society, their view of their own village tradition, and the attitudes they held toward important social questions are discussed.

The migrants shared some experiences. Three of the four came to the United States for a higher education, and the fourth has studied on his own to upgrade his occupational status. Until they finished their formal education, three of the students worked during almost all their spare time while pursuing their studies. As a result, they took a long time to finish their degrees; the two who finished took seven and ten years, respectively, to finish a four-year degree; a third has been here 11 years and has the equivalent of a junior college degree; and the fourth has dropped out of college after two and one-half years and has little intention of returning. The common experience has been that of running out of money, having to work to support themselves, cutting back on studies because of limited resources, and extending the period of study in the United States. This experience has led to an unusually prolonged period of acculturation in the United States.[3]

All the migrants received a green working card and subsequently obtained citizenship through marriage with Americans. Three of the four are still happily married, but one is divorced and intends to return to Jordan to marry, although not necessarily to work. All live in small apartments, with three of four in one-bedroom apartments. All are hard-working, working fifty to eighty-four hours each week. All the migrants are nonpracticing Muslims, but all have a Muslim identity, and they wish to pass that identity or at least their cultural identity on to their children. All see a good part of their working lives as being spent in the United States with their families. Two of the four intend to return permanently to Jordan in the future. As a result of their long exposure, all the migrants have been acculturated in dress, language, idiom, and politeness formulas, and three of the four entered the dating game with the zest of young men coming from rural Arab societies in which cross-sex interpersonal relations outside the family were relatively closed.

Dan

Dan is the oldest migrant (forty-three years old) and was the first to arrive in the United States.[4] He received his higher education in Dayton and Cincinnati, Ohio, in business management and accounting after being trained in the Royal Military College in Amman and the Pakistani Naval School in Karachi and after serving eleven years in the Jordanian Army, during which time he was for some period the chief of guards at the Jordanian embassy in London. It was not uncommon for Jordanian migrants to the United States and other countries to have had a multicultural experience such as Dan's before arriving in their host country (e.g., Abu Dhabi, Greece, Egypt, Turkey, Pakistan, Saudi Arabia, England). Dan was befriended in Cincinnati by a Jordanian family who ran a restaurant in which he worked; he was always at their home and ate their food, and they helped him finance his car. He had a difficult time in school while working. For three years he worked eighteen hours each day at two jobs, as restaurant manager and in the college commissary. In the restaurant, he cooked chili, cut meat, and cleaned and shined the chili machines, which reached an internal temperature of 140 degrees. He went home from work bursting with tension. He was estranged from his father, and during his thirteen-year stay in the United States, the son never received help from or corresponded with him.

In 1984, the year he graduated, an American professor, who had taught him and with whom he had become friendly, encouraged him to enter into a partnership with him and open up a restaurant called the Pasta Palace. They received a loan from the bank, and Dan acted as manager, trouble-shooter, and jack-of-all-trades in the restaurant. However, Dan's role as co-owner and manager was cut short by the professor's heart attack. In 1985, Dan left Ohio and went to Dallas to live with two Jordanian friends from the same region as his home village.

Early in his stay in Ohio, however, an event occurred that affected his view of American women and the direction of his acculturation thereafter. He married a college freshman, an American.

Let Dan speak for himself: "She was eighteen years old; she was after me. I treated her as a sister; she changed her mind and became romantically inclined. I loved her, but there was too much of an age difference. I was pure and innocent [then]." It was a different tradition and culture. They fought at breakfast. "Over what," I asked? He didn't want to eat bacon; she talked about "that stupid religion [that wouldn't permit a man to eat bacon]." She said Muslims put veils on their wives. "She approached me one day, saying she wanted to become a Muslim. She was scared." She divorced him. She was a student at the University of Dayton; she had just finished high school. Her mother paid for the divorce because he could not afford it. They had been married just six months. I asked what he thought the basic problem was? He was strongly Arab and was unable to accommodate to the new society. "When someone said, 'Hi' to her [when they were walking on the campus] I became suspicious," he said. She smiled at her former boy friends. I told her, "You shouldn't say 'Hi' to anyone."

Dan had grown up in a Jordanian village in a religious and tribal milieu where, as he said, "I can't remember looking at a girl's face [when we passed in the street]; we used to look down at the ground [out of modesty]." He said he was too shy to ask a girl out in Dayton or Cincinnati; they came and took him out. He liked the company of women and entered the dating scene with a vengeance. He considered himself Americanized. But marrying an American? "I had a really bad experience," he said. "All they [American girls] care about is having fun and getting drunk, not living a respectful life." He resented the fact that American women wanted to go out and have fun with their girl friends (without their husbands or boy friends) and that his girl friend always wanted to see an American movie and never an Arabic videotape. Thereafter, while living in Texas, Dan dichotomized all his relations between women, dating many women whom he considered not to be respectable.

At the end of this thirteen-year period in the American diaspora, he summarized his feelings about his identity: "I don't want anyone to put my country down. I'm not very religious, but I want my kids to be Muslims. I want to meet one of my own people. I want to marry someone who won't cheat on me. If I have a child I want him to be mine and not gone after five years [as happened to his Jordanian friend after divorce]." I asked him if he was going back to Jordan to marry. He said he was returning for a visit and keeping his options open. I asked, "Are you going to stay in Jordan and work?" "No, this is my country. I am a citizen [of the United States]."

Dan continued his frenetic working patterns in Dallas, eventually becoming night auditor of the Dallas–Fort Worth airport while daylighting as manager of a 7-Eleven store. He previously worked as a telemarketer for American Airlines for three years and won the prize for the highest sales representative for one year; the job familiarized him with various accents of American English. He spent his money on cars, food, and women. He said that he had no savings. There is no doubt that he had become acculturated to American society and was economically integrated within it, albeit in an incomplete manner, because no one job was sufficient to make a living and raise a family.

Although he interacted for most of his waking hours with Americans, 99 percent of his friends were Arab Americans. Once or twice each week, he got together with other Arabs at Denny's for coffee. I asked him whether he ever suffered from discrimination. He replied, "Here you are an Arab or a Muslim." He almost got in a fight a few days before at Denny's because he and his friends were speaking Arabic. A man was sitting with his girl friend in the next booth and moved away, saying to the waitress that they should speak English or get out. Dan got mad and told him off, saying, "You're neither civilized nor educated."

On his only nonworking day, Sunday, he got up late and often asked his Jordanian friends over for coffee and sometimes for a meal. I spent one such Sunday with him. Although the television was broadcasting the NFL football game, nobody was paying attention to it. The meal he prepared was a strictly Jordanian dish (*maqluba*), and all the conversation was in Arabic. During the afternoon, Dan received twelve telephone calls, all in Arabic. He said that he liked Americans but that "you had to get out of yourself to match their personality." When he went to an American bar, he suffered. He ended the conversation by saying, "You have to feel at home with your own people."

It was clear to me that Dan's reference group and his imagination remained tied to Jordan and to his own village. He spent a good sum every month on telephone calls to Jordan, and he had not spent all his money on cars, food, or women! Besides saving for education, he had saved a substantial sum and spent it on the purchase of land and a new house in his home village. Dan wanted to retire to Kufr al-Ma and to die there.

I asked Dan what his view of his own village upbringing was. "It was a good thing I was brought up to be a good child, to respect [others]; [I was taught] to be a good person, religious, encourage education. On the negative side, I never had a chance to be a child at home; [the upbringing] was too disciplinary, too strict; they didn't give a boy the chance to make his own decisions. My father wanted me to study, and it was my dream to be an army officer."

I then asked Dan a series of questions about the 1991 Gulf War. "Did the war lead to any changes in your relations with Americans?" "No." "With other Arabs?" "I lost my respect for Saudi Arabia, but that doesn't mean I won't go and work there. They never gave the Arabs a chance to solve their problems first. Iraq was willing [to have an inter-Arab solution], but it did exactly what the United States wanted them to do [provoke a war]. The greatest disgrace was that if they [Saudi Arabia] are so rich, why not do it on their own? Why, they are the richest country in the world! All they had were mercenaries [*murtaziqa,* meaning American troops]. I'm not for Iraq occupying Kuwait. But what happened there was a crime."

"Did the war lead to any changes in your own feelings about yourself, your country, the Arab World, or the Middle East?" "I lost confidence in the Arab World. I believe they will never be united. They've never been [united]. We should work to create a new leadership to take care of the people before they [the leaders] take care of themselves."

"What do you think of all the American flags and yellow ribbons?" "It was foolish. You are a superpower plus thirty-two countries [are on your side]. Who are you fighting? An out-dated army. [It's] like you fight a little child and beat him up and make him a hero."

'Isam

The last migrant to arrive is the youngest (twenty-three years old) and the one who has been in the country the shortest time (five years). 'Isam graduated from a high school in Abu Dhabi, where his father, after emigrating from Jordan, had been a junior high school principal for fourteen years. 'Isam, following his older brother who had emigrated six years before him, went to San Antonio, where he registered at a local non-denominational college, taking mainly science subjects after studying English for one year at a Catholic college. He dropped out of college after two and one-half years to work full time. From the beginning, two attributes marked his style of living in San Antonio: his workaholic habits and his avoidance of Middle Eastern students. In his first year of schooling, he simultaneously held two jobs: cashier and dish-washer. Subsequently, he became a manager at Pizza Hut, a waiter at TGI Fridays, a manager at an Italian restaurant, a manager at an Iranian restaurant, and finally, the manager of the Red Lobster restaurant in Midland, a city in the oil country of Texas, 300 miles west of Dallas. Each new job provided a salary increment. When I met him in 1991, he was involved in a one-man advertising-board business and a one-man marketing enterprise that brought together manufacturers and suppliers. His wife told me that he derided his older brother, Samir, for becoming and remaining economically dependent on an American school principal who had befriended him and provided Samir a free room in his house and lent him one semester's tuition. 'Isam was the proverbial self-styled, self-made young man with a burning ambition. He told me that he planned to be a millionaire by the age of thirty! A programmed decision-maker, he planned to set aside 10 percent of his income for his parents each year and to retire in seven years! Although he disassociated himself from his brother's lifestyle, he too had been dependent for one and one-half years on the same high school principal for a room and for valuable advice in adjusting to American life in San Antonio.

'Isam said that he did not like many of the Middle Eastern students in San Antonio because "they are a bunch of socialists; they are always talking politics; they aren't here to learn, mostly to discuss." They talked about Karl Marx and solving political problems. Samir got him to room with a Palestinian student, but 'Isam got tired of the constant discussions, of watching TV, and of smoking and playing cards, and he left the apartment after a few months. He said to his wife at this time, "Those are the Arabs that give us a bad stereotype." Whereas Samir avoided Arab students for pragmatic reasons, 'Isam avoided them for ideological reasons as well.

It was clear early on that 'Isam put himself on an assimilation track. He told his parents in Abu Dhabi when he left that he was not coming back, and before he married his future wife, an American girl of Hispanic origin on her mother's side and a doctor's daughter, he repeated his resolve. He had entered the dating scene with a vengeance. He said that one day in Midland he was going through his address book and discovered the names and addresses of twenty-eight women and decided that was too many. He said he got tired of the wild girls who would "be here today and gone tomorrow." He diligently courted a woman whom he described as "nonparty, family bred, and traditional American." She never came to the restaurant with her girl friends, only with her parents.

His role as an "assimilator" of American culture and not just an acculturator (i.e., someone who accepted American values and not just American ways) did not mean that 'Isam cut himself off from his own family. He calls his brother in Abu Dhabi two or three times each month, and at his father's behest, he sent several thousand dollars to his brother to ransom him out of army service in Abu Dhabi during the Gulf War. A collage of his immediate family sits in a prominent place in his Midland apartment.

Because his wife was Roman Catholic, I asked 'Isam whether they had discussed how to bring up their children. They talked about raising their children in a religious tradition. 'Isam said that he had no hang-up about bringing up their children as Catholics. He said to his wife, "I'll go with you [to church] some of the time, though I don't believe in it. I'll raise them [children] with the same ethics I grew up with." I had asked 'Isam earlier what his feelings about Christianity and Islam were? He said, "I respect both; neither is wrong; [there are] people who misuse religion. I'm an atheist." His wife regarded this statement with some skepticism, telling me later, "'Isam says he's an atheist, but there's more Muslim in him than he realizes." 'Isam drinks alcohol, but they are both against drugs.

They were married by a Lutheran pastor. Brian, the school principal with whom he lived, was a Lutheran. They decided to be married at Brian's church in a small chapel. It was a private marriage; there were only eleven persons there including 'Isam's brother, but not his wife's parents, who disapproved of the marriage. His older brother counseled 'Isam against the marriage, but he disregarded his brother's advice. The reception was at Brian's home.

"What is your view of your own upbringing?" I asked. "I had a great time in Kufr al-Ma. It was fun: going around school, playing marbles, going with my dad. I loved social gatherings and *mansaf* [the Jordanian national dish of rice and lamb meat always served in a collective social setting]! My dad always treated us as adults. We sat next to him in the *sidr* [place of honor in the guest house] and drank coffee. [As a result] I can stand in front of 30,000 and talk."

"Did the Gulf War lead to any changes in your life here in Midland?" "I was afraid my last name or looks would turn people off—you know, Red Necks. In San Antonio, I knew a lot of people." In Midland, 'Isam was referred to as, "This guy, Ali." He was harassed at the Dallas airport. Too many questions were asked, and the authorities went through his suitcase thoroughly. They went through his shoes. "I was mad. 'Can I speak to your supervisor?' I asked." When the baggage search persisted, he finally said to the baggage inspector, "I'm going—if you want to keep the baggage, stuff it!"

"Did the war lead to any changes in your view of Americans and American society and culture?" "Not in any way. I didn't have a problem with the war. The idea was good. The purpose was good: protect your oil. I love what's going on with the Kurds. They destroyed civilian places and didn't get Saddam. Now they're fixing it [by intervening on the Kurds' side]. If there had been more involvement by the UN, it would have been better." 'Isam put a yellow ribbon on his car, and when supporters of the war came to his restaurant and asked permission to put up a sign saying, "Free Kuwait," he said, "Sure, put it up," and he left it up for a week.

Samir

Samir was the pioneer migrant to Texas from Kufr al-Ma, arriving in 1979. After going to an English-language school in Houston, he entered San Antonio college in 1980.

He received an associate's degree in applied science and economics in 1985, but in 1991, when I interviewed him, he still needed 123 hours to finish a bachelor's degree in electronics. In 1989, he moved with his wife to Dallas and gained employment as a biomedical technician. His wife worked full time as an executive secretary.

During his student days, unlike his brother, Samir shunned manual labor. He was not about to work his way through school. He said with satisfaction, "I've never taken jobs in restaurants. I've avoided that like the plague, thank goodness." He did tutor students in English and worked for a brief period as a tourist guide.

From the beginning, Samir wanted to live with an American family. Samir rented a room with an American family with four children, but he had little privacy. Through an American friend he met Brian, the school principal who discovered one day that Samir sat for long periods in his apartment in a bathtub filled with cold water to cool off in the 120-degree temperature. Brian lived alone in a big, air-conditioned house in one of the nicer sections of San Antonio and offered to rent Samir a room in the house. Samir accepted. They became good friends. After Brian took a trip to the Middle East with Samir in 1985, visiting Samir's family in Jordan and Abu Dhabi (as well as Egypt), where he received gracious hospitality, Brian refused to charge Samir any rent. Samir lived in Brian's house till he was married in 1989.

Samir's predilection for socializing with Americans was not accidental. I asked him how often he visited co-villagers (there were four others in Texas), Jordanians, Palestinians, and Arabs in Texas? He replied that since coming to Dallas his only contact with them was with Dan, whom they saw in Arlington once every three months. Dan and his wife did not have much time for socializing because their daughter had been born five months earlier. Samir had never socialized with members of the sizable Arab community in San Antonio. His father had told him before he left Abu Dhabi, "Try not to be anti-social, but stay away from Arabs; become friends with Americans; you'll learn faster." Early on he had roomed with a Syrian and a Jordanian, but he left after a brief period. I asked, "What are the good and bad points about Palestinians, Syrians, Jordanians, and Arabs?" He replied that association with Arabs was detrimental to students here to learn the language; "one must push oneself to interact with society."

Brian's kinsfolk thought he could do no wrong; he was extremely well liked, was regarded as a nephew in Brian's home, and was taken along on family visits and outings. This meant a lot to Samir: "I was befriended and treated as one of the family. It was a warm group."

The other avenue of acculturation and eventual assimilation that Samir pursued was through the San Antonio Coronation Association in which Brian played a key role as organizer and designer. The association put on an October pageant every year; it was held in the municipal auditorium and was one of the leading social events of the year in the city. Although it was sponsored by the Lutheran church, it was ecumenical in its composition and organization. Brian encouraged Samir's participation, and Samir became rapidly and intensely involved in its activities to the degree that he became the main organizer of the yearbook, the main publicity person for the pageant (soliciting ads from local merchants and organizations), and a participant in building the floats. In addition to developing his artistic, organizational, and commercial skills, Samir met his future wife in the pageant; she participated as a Scottish bagpiper.

Like 'Isam's wife, Samir's wife, V, came from a mixed ethnic and religious background. She counted seven different ethnic strands in her family. Her father had been raised a Catholic and her mother Baptist, but they had not imposed a religious orientation on her, and she was brought up in the Lutheran church. When I raised the question of how they would bring up their children, V said that she loved Arabic food and that she made hummus and baked kibbie and tabooli; she would love to take a trip to the Middle East and live there for a while. On the rare occasions when they visited Dan during a Sunday gathering at Arlington, she was the only woman present and did not resent the fact that all the men were speaking Arabic and listening to Arabic tapes. She was reading about bilingual education and supported it. She encouraged Samir to speak to their daughter in Arabic and said that she would support Samir taking their daughter to the mosque and teaching her the Qur'an. She could take her daughter to the Lutheran church and let her choose when she grew up. I asked Samir, "Will you educate your daughter in anything she chooses?" He nodded affirmatively, but added that, if she had musical talent, he would support her but not to go to Broadway or Hollywood. Samir had told me earlier that he had gone to both Catholic and Lutheran churches in San Antonio because it was a Christian country (and Brian was a Lutheran). He asked many questions about Christian ceremony and belief, but he did not wish to convert. He said he was not a good Muslim but that religion was an ancient thing and could not be shaken off. He had agreed to the baptism of their child but didn't want Islam to be relegated to a secondary thing. Samir would not allow me to photograph his "Lutheran Coronation" T-shirt (he had given one to me as a gift), because he thought that the people in Kufr al-Ma might think that he had converted to Christianity.

With only a few close friends attending, Samir and V were married by a Lutheran minister, a friend of Brian's, who lived in New Orleans. In the context of V's multicultural background and Samir's multicultural exposure in San Antonio, the marriage and its form were not points of controversy. However, as an indicator of his desire to transfer his cultural identity to his daughter, Samir and V gave her an Arabic first and middle name.

I asked Samir to explain his views of birth control. "I think I'm for it." "By what methods?" "Birth control as a practice is an excellent idea, especially in the Middle East—families with so many kids. I'm not planning to have so many kids. I want to provide college. It's a necessity and an obligation to feed and care for a child but also to provide a college education, especially at this time. Without a degree, where would they be? I don't want to produce someone who will be a public charge. Education will determine your socioeconomic status. You'll associate with a higher class. They won't have to be a liability to everyone. For a girl [education] is more necessary than for a boy; she needs to be independent. It's no longer that a man is the provider; she will be as well. What if she married someone who doesn't treat her well? She does not have to take it."

This egalitarian perspective toward gender differences and a complementary division of labor is applied in the every-day cooperation of Samir and V in raising and attending to their infant daughter. The baby wakes up at 6:00 A.M. Samir feeds her and puts her in the car seat. He gets ready for work while V takes the baby to the sitter. Then she goes to her work as an executive secretary, seven miles away. Samir leaves for work at 8:00 A.M. and stays at work till 4:30 or 5:00, but sometimes he has to stay till

10:00 P.M. After work, Samir picks up his daughter at the baby-sitter's home and feeds her. On Saturday, he takes care of the baby while V does the grocery shopping. V does the laundry on Sunday.

"What is your view of your own upbringing?" I asked. "It was an excellent upbringing. My father exposed me—knowing so many people. You know how he socializes with masses of people. He used to take me with him on an 'uzuma [meal invitation] to Irbid or Amman. He put me in a play in the village [his father was schoolmaster]. I played the role of Omar ibn al-Khattab [an Arab hero] in the school play. The master of ceremonies introduced me in a booming voice, 'Now that lion-cub, Samir.' I had memorized my lines." "And he's still doing it," Brian interjected. "My father was the school principal and he pushed me. . . . My mother provided the love. Negatively, I think I was spoiled. My father was the eldest male. They were making sun-dried clay for building [one day] and stamping on it outside to prepare it. I went inside and put water on my mother's dough and stamped on it. They laughed it off and didn't punish me." When he was threatened with punishment he ran off to his grandmother, and she protected him.

"Did the Gulf War lead to any changes to your life here in Dallas?" "None." "Did it lead to any changes in your relations with Americans?" "None. At work they know me as an Arab but trust me as an individual." V interjected that people in the street do not recognize Samir as an Arab. "There was one red-necked engineer [at work]. He asked me what I thought about the war. He asked, 'Why don't they give Palestinians Iraq?'" Samir replied, "Get educated first [and then I'll answer your questions]."

"Did the war lead to any changes in your relations with other Arabs?" "No, I wasn't in contact [with them]. I stay away from discussions about religion and politics. They [Americans] have a prefabricated opinion [about the war] here."

"Did the war lead to any changes in your own feelings about yourself, your country, the Arab world, or the Middle East?" "No, not really. I was thankful I wasn't an Iraqi or Kurd. I've heard about the Kurds. The war made me more empathetic, not sympathetic: the mother who dove into the grave with her child; the old men and women running for their lives. Why should dictatorship do that? It makes you feel good about the coalition. They stopped him, but stopped short."

"What do you think of all the American flags and yellow ribbons?" "It was symbolic of patriotism. Schwartzkopf as a hero—all that is falsehood. It was not a real war. The guy didn't desire to be called a hero."

"What was the most surprising thing to you about the way Americans reacted to the war?" "The big hoopla. Families have their sons and all [to think about]. I did not condemn it [the hoopla]. I'd welcome back a brother [from the war]. I wouldn't blame the military men. They're sheep. They don't vote on what war they're going to."

Bahhar

Bahhar's story provides a familiar example of chain migration. Bahhar followed his elder brother who was studying medicine in Salonika, Greece. After studying Greek for six months at the university, he studied for two years at the Merchant Marine Academy, graduating in 1975 with a radio officer's license. For the next four years, he worked as chief mate and radio officer in the Greek merchant marine. He traveled all over the Mediterranean and Europe, all around Africa, and all around the Indian Ocean. They frequently stayed many days or a week at particular ports, and he liked going ashore every day, mixing with the natives and enjoying their customs.

In 1979, he met an American undergraduate from Texas, R, in the port of Aqaba, Jordan, on her way back to the United States by way of Europe. The merchant ship on which she chose to return happened to be Bahhar's, and because the ship was small, she ate in the officer's dining room. Bahhar convinced her to stop in Greece and visit his brother there. After she returned to the United States, they corresponded for one year. When he found out that the shipping company for which he worked had ships that sailed to North America, he asked for and was granted a transfer to ships that sailed around the Gulf of Mexico. Thereafter, for more than a year, R traveled around the Gulf of Mexico, meeting him every few weeks at various ports for a few days when he came ashore, and occasionally he met her in Galveston, where she was studying and living with her mother and brother, who was a pathologist at the University of Texas. One day when she broke down in tears because Bahhar's ship could not come into Galveston harbor because of the fog, her brother decided that it was time to bring the courtship to a conclusion, and when the fog lifted and Bahhar came into port, the brother arranged for them to have a blood test and brought a justice-of-the peace and had them married on the spot. Because Bahhar had to leave port the very next day, they celebrated their wedding a few weeks later off the coast of Venezuela with the ship's crew as the guests! That summer, Bahhar and R went back to Kufr al-Ma, Jordan, and the village preacher drew up a Muslim marriage contract.

Bahhar's acculturation to American society was facilitated by his brother-in-law, who arranged his marriage, provided him housing (in an apartment house he owned), and found him a job as an officer on a geodetic research ship run by the University of Texas, and by his mother-in-law, in whose apartment he and R lived for many months after he moved to Galveston. Bahhar's acculturation was also facilitated by the fact that he came to Galveston and not to Houston or San Antonio, where many other Arabs lived. Although he talked occasionally to Samir over the phone, he had only seen him and 'Isam once when they visited him in Galveston, and he had never seen Dan, although he had talked with him on the phone a few times. Bahhar's acculturation was also facilitated by his cosmopolitan attitude. I asked him, "Does nothing shock you about American life?" He replied, "On the ship, we were coming to different places all the time. I was all over Europe. When the ship came into port, I used to get excited. It doesn't mean that much to me anymore. When we arrive in a new country, I sit and relax on the ship's deck the whole day." On another occasion he told me, "I've traveled so much that I must accept people the way they are."

Bahhar's accommodative attitude to other cultures was matched by R's enthusiasm for travel and exotic cultures. She had visited Kufr al-Ma three times, the last time with their toddler son without Bahhar, who was out to sea. During her studies at the University of Texas, where she received a bachelor's degree in science, radio, and television film, she took courses in Middle Eastern studies and had read the book I had written about her husband's home village in the Ajlun district of Jordan. She looked forward to returning to Jordan to live.

When I asked Bahhar and R if they had talked about how the children would be raised, Bahhar said that he wanted the children to be Muslims and have Arabic names. R said that was okay as long as she raised them properly (according to her values), they had her maiden name in their name as well as Bahhar's, and they had a Christmas tree and an Easter basket.

Although Bahhar was thoroughly acculturated to American ways through his wife and affines, he was not assimilated into American culture. This fact was revealed by his comparison of sailing with Greeks and Americans. The Greek sailors were happy—they liked sailing; they regarded it as a fortunate profession. The American sailors always seemed to have problems that they brought on board with them. One had to be careful how one treated them; they were friendly one day and standoffish the next; they were temperamental. Bahhar observed that the American sailors used their shore leave to go to the nearest bar and get drunk instead of enjoying the customs of the new country, and when they returned to their ship after several months' leave, they were invariably in debt. The Greek shipping company reserved most of the Greek sailor's salary while he was at sea and released it to his wife and family to live on. One incident in particular chagrined and amazed Bahhar. When the geodetic ship was in Japan, one American sailor (who went on shore every day and got drunk) asked Bahhar to pick up a kimono for his wife. When Bahhar asked, "What kind of kimono?" the sailor replied, "Any kind." When Bahhar asked the sailor his wife's size, the sailor didn't know or care! Whereas most of the Greeks were older career sailors, the American seismic specialists on the geodetic ship were "young kids trained in computers" (and not seamanship); they came straight out of their computer labs and were put on the ship. As a result, there was a high turnover of personnel on all the geodetic ships he served on. This was not a situation in which camaraderie could grow.

"What is your view of your own upbringing?" I asked. Bahhar said, "It was simple. I didn't have much. My father and my family raised us as good children—respectful of them and everyone else. We were quiet—not like other kids, fighting." "Was there anything bad about your upbringing?" "We didn't have much to show. We were not open to the other world. I always, when I was a kid, had a dream. I wanted to get out of Jordan one day [to know] what's going on outside. My [oldest] brother left [for Arabia]. Even my [next oldest] brother left [for Greece]. [I thought to myself] I'd probably do the same thing. If they had stayed in Jordan, I'd probably have done the same—maybe joined the army or gone to a university in Jordan. Other relatives went. My family said, 'Go to your brother [in Greece].' It was cheaper to send me there than elsewhere."

"Did the war lead to any changes in your relations with Americans?" "No, not on ship. We always talked there, but I never argued with them. There was no point in talking to someone who doesn't know what's going on. I just watched the news. If someone understood, I'd talk. People didn't distinguish between Iraqis, Jordanians. I tried to avoid all that."

"Did the war lead to any changes in your own feelings about yourself, your country, the Arab World, or the Middle East?" "Right now I have a job. It's okay; no problem. If I start looking for another job [as he was anticipating doing], I don't know how they'll look at me. As an Arab? People look at you in a different way [when you're an

Arab]. They don't want to get to know you at first. Because you're an Arab you lose a lot of points—unless they need your body."

"What was the most surprising thing to you about the way Americans reacted to the War?" Bahhar said, "Americans were with Saudi Arabia [as allies], but they talked as if they were waging a war against all Arabs. Americans take one leader and extend [the animosity] to all nationals. They assumed all Jordanians are pro-Saddam. All Iraqis are seen as guilty."

Reflections on Transnational Migration

Kufr al-Ma is only one Jordanian village among hundreds that are the source of transnational migration because of Jordan's paucity of agricultural and industrial wealth and opportunity. The four Jordanian migrants described are only a few of more than 150 transnational migrants from Kufr al-Ma on whom I have information. The capsule profiles presented are a selection of only four of more than forty in-depth interviews conducted by me in 1986, 1989, 1993, and 1998.[5]

The outstanding fact about the migration from Kufr al-Ma is its diversity. I have not been able to capture the variety of experiences and modes of personal transformation of these migrants, because they diverge into three separate streams: those who pursue transnational migration for work (mainly to Arabia), for higher education (mainly to Pakistan, Greece, Europe, and the United States), and for military training (migrants sent abroad by the Jordanian Army to the United States, Britain, and Pakistan). Not only do the experiences of migrants differ substantially depending on the culture, social structure, and economy of the host country, but they also differentiate with the particular locale to which they migrate. New York City is not Dallas, Athens is not Salonika (most Jordanian migrants went to northern Greece), and Karachi (a teeming multi-ethnic entrepôt is not Feisalabad (a more homogeneous city in the heart of the agricultural Punjab)—the latter two are sites of universities Jordanians attended in Pakistan. All migration, then, is local, and the implications of that locality are important for different degrees of migrant acculturation or assimilation. In some locales, such as Arabia and Pakistan, migrants are encapsulated and have little interpersonal contact with members of host societies outside the work and study milieu; in other locales, they come into intimate contact with host country nationals through work, residence, propinquity, and marriage. I have described and analyzed these matters in detail in another work.[6]

The profiles of these four migrants do reflect certain themes and conclusions found to be general among those interviewed and with whom considerable participant observation has taken place over the years. Most migrants spent long periods abroad and developed more than a passing acquaintance with host societies and cultures. All underwent some degree of acculturation; they gained a facility with language, dress, and local custom. Most worked hard during their sojourn abroad, whether as professionals, semi-professionals, students, or skilled or semi-skilled traders and craftsmen. In the process of these long study and work lives abroad, they often underwent considerable physical and psychological stress and were led to reflect on their own identities and customs in relation to their host societies.

My study of transnational migration from the village of Kufr al-Ma, Jordan, to seventeen different countries does not confirm the view that migration leads to social disorganization and anomie or to "crippled cultures ... besieged traditionalists or ... deracinated modernists."[7] Neither does it support the opposite view that migration has led to the development of transnational social networks, cultures, and ideologies.[8] Most transnational migrants from Kufr al-Ma have chosen to return to Jordan after educational and work experiences abroad. Although they have been exposed to multicultural contexts in locations as different as Houston, Texas; Jidda, Saudi Arabia; Karachi, Pakistan; and London England, they have rejected assimilation as an option while at the same time becoming acculturated to their host societies, often rapidly. They have maintained the attitude of sojourners abroad rather than emigrants or exiles (from Jordan) or immigrants to the United States or Arabia. In that sense, the assimilators in Texas, 'Isam and Samir, are atypical. Dan, on the other hand, is atypical in the intensity of his rejection of certain aspects of American society. My research among transnational migrants from Jordan to four continents has impressed me not with the prominence of assimilative or exile attitudes, but rather with the resiliency of migrants in coping with their problems through effective localized social networks and the occasional use of home visits and modern transnational communications. They have used these mechanisms to reinterpret their traditions to incorporate much of the new while retaining much of the old in a scenario encompassing both worlds.

Why have these Jordanians chosen to be "sojourners" and "acculturators" rather than "exiles" or "assimilators"? My tentative answer is that they have come from the tribal culture of Transjordan in which ties to one's kinsmen and one's native village exercise a powerful hold on the imagination. Rarely did I find a person who spoke in pejorative terms about his or her upbringing in the native village or about the poverty of the village and the past hardships endured in the pre-1970 period, including absence of piped water or of water at all, because cisterns ran dry in July in drought years, and absence of paved roads, electricity, and solid housing. They instead spoke of the rich social life of the village; the constant visiting of kinsmen, neighbors, and friends; and the internal resolution of disputes by the leaders of the community in their own guest houses (*madafas*) without resort to state courts. Although this social structure and culture has to a considerable extent disappeared, it still resonates in their imagination as a force for return, undermining the drive for assimilation to a new and what they consider impoverished way of life in the diaspora.

Notes

1. I have conducted anthropological field work in Kufr al-Ma on nine separate occasions over thirty-nine years, the longest being the initial year of dissertation field research in 1959 and 1960 and the shortest and last of four days' duration in 1998. The research has focused on the social structural (*Arab Village: A Social Structural Study of a Transjordanian Peasant Community*, Indiana University Press, 1972), political (*Low-Key Politics: Local-Level Leadership and Change in the Middle East,* State University of New York Press, 1979), and religious (*Muslim Village in the Modern World: A Jordanian Case Study in Comparative Perspective,* Princeton University Press, 1989), life of the community.

2. A fifth student in Texas has been discussed in another publication. See Antoun, "Sojourners Abroad: Migration for Higher Education in a Post-Peasant Muslim Society," in Akbar Ahmed and Hastings Donnan, eds., *Islam, Globalization, and Postmodernity,* Routledge, London, 1994.

3. Acculturation is the process of taking on cultural traits of the host society without a change in the basic values of the borrowing individual. For a discussion of the anthropological and sociological literature on acculturation and assimilation and the differences between these processes see Raymond Teske and H. Nelson Bardin, "Acculturation and Assimilation: A Clarification," *American Anthropologist* 1 (1974): 351–67.

4. All names used for migrants are pseudonyms.

5. Although the numbers of migrants studying or working abroad have declined substantially, on my most recent field trip to Jordan in March 1998, I continued to be astonished by the range and variety of the experiences of transnational migrants from the village. One retired Air Force officer, an engineer, had just returned to Kufr al-Ma after serving a year as volunteer with the United Nations Peacemaking Force in Bosnia, Croatia, and Macedonia. Another, a professor of linguistics at Yarmouk University, had returned two years before from South Korea where he had spent four years setting up an Arabic Studies Program!

6. I am readying a manuscript for publication entitled, "Transnational Migration in the Post-Modern World: A Jordanian Case Study in Comparative Perspective."

7. See Harold Isaacs, *Idols of the Tribe: Group Identity and Change,* Harvard University Press, Cambridge, 1989, p. 106 *ff.* for this view.

8. See Linda Basch, Nina Glick, and Cristina Szanton-Blanc, *Schiller's* Nations Unbound: *Transnational Projects, Post-Colonial Predicaments, and Deterritorialized Nation-States,* Gordon and Breach, New York, 1994, for the elaboration of this view.

Linda S. Walbridge

---

3   **A Look at Differing Ideologies Among Shi'a Muslims in the United States**

The immigrant Muslim community in the United States contains a disproportionate number of Shi'a Muslims. As is common among immigrant groups in America, these people are "refugees," whether or not that term is legally proper. They hail from the southern regions of Iraq and Lebanon, old strongholds of Shi'a populations, where warfare, occupation, and persecution have made their homelands intolerable. The revolution in Iran caused the flight of many thousands of Iranians who disagreed with the new government over a wide array of issues.

It is the Arab Shi'a Muslims—particularly those from Lebanon and Iraq—who have established themselves in the forefront of institution building and leadership in the United States.[1] The Iranian Shi'a in this country are far more likely to be secular or at least at odds with the sort of Shi'ism being put forth in the Islamic Republic of Iran. Iranians in the Los Angeles area, for example, although expressing a desire to build a communal religious life, generally wish to do so without including the *ulama* in their activities. The Los Angeles Iranians who attend traditional Shi'a mosque activities gravitate to mosques built and led by Iraqi *ulama*.

The political situation in the Middle East, particularly in Iran and Iraq, which are centers of Shi'a learning, has had a direct impact on Shi'a religious leadership. As a response to these political conditions, new ideologies have arisen that attempt to influence the direction of Shi'ism. In both countries are contenders among the highest ranking *ulama* (*mujtahids*) for leadership (*marja' taqlid*) of the Shi'a world. This struggle for leadership reflects and affects the type of religious ideology and institutions found in the Arab Shi'a community in North America.

In this chapter, based on anthropological fieldwork, I focus on two approaches to activist Islam that can be found among younger Shi'a in the United States and Canada and how these approaches relate to political and ideological struggles in the Middle East. I discuss the views of Seyyid Muhammad Fadlallah of Lebanon, who has been the principal figure advocating the modernization of Shi'ism since the death of the Iraqi philosopher cleric, Baqir as-Sadr. His views and theories are contrasted with those of individuals and groups who identify with Ayatollah Khomeini and who consider themselves aligned with the Hizbullah movement.

The differences between the groups discussed are not highly visible ones. Disagreements among them are not about issues involving alcohol or dating nor about the importance of prayer and fasting. They instead disagree about the role of the *ulama* and, to some extent, about issues of nationalism.

When speaking about "activists," I am not talking about people who are necessarily militant or deeply involved in political activities. I am speaking about people who have a deep conviction that Islam holds the key to improvements in the social order and that the practice of this religion is ultimately a communal affair. Although they constitute a minority among the Shi'a residing in the United States, they are still an important minority because of their high level of motivation. They tend to be the ones organizing conferences and other events where they may vent their views.

This study had several purposes:

1. It demonstrated that Arab Shi'a activists are not a monolithic group and that differences among them, although often subtle, are important for understanding the adaptation of Shi'ism to American life. The two groups discussed are referred to as Da'wa and Hizbullah, but I use these labels to suggest sympathy or identification with the two ideologies, rather than membership in the organizations.
2. It showed that religious activism among Shi'a in the United States has more to do with internal reforms of religious institutions and religious practices than it does with political protests.
3. It explained how the younger generation of Arab Shi'a express their differences in viewpoints about their regular activities and daily lives.

The *Ulama* Among the Shi'a

The paramount difference that divides Sunni and Shi'a is that of leadership of the umma. Although the death of the Prophet signaled an immediate controversy over leadership, it was not until the death of the Prophet's grandson Hussein in Karbala, Iraq, that a true split in the community began. Those who believe that it is among the *Ahl al Beit* that the rightful successors to the Prophet should be found are called Shi'a. Within the Shi'a, those who believe that there is a continued inheritance of leadership in the Prophet's family and that it began with the Prophet's son-in-law, the Imam Ali, and concluded (for the time being) with the occultation of the Twelfth Imam are called *Ithna Ashari* or Twelver Shi'a. These are the Shi'a to whom I refer in this chapter.

In Twelver or *Ithna Ashari* Shi'ism, the *ulama* have played an essential role in community life. The *ulama*, through the Shi'a courts, are traditionally involved in family matters such as disputes between husbands and wives and accusations of incest and adultery.[2] They have a ranking system that reflects their level of knowledge and indicates the degree of social prestige that they have achieved in the community. Many of the *ulama* have only a limited education and become mullas ministering to the needs of a local community. Some receive special training in preaching and often lead the ritual mourning services related to the suffering of the imams. The *mujtahids* are at the top of this social and religious hierarchy. They are the ones who, having completed all three levels of their *howza* education and having gained distinction for their learning in the process, are qualified to interpret the law and to act as representatives of the imam. The *marja' taqlid* is at the pinnacle of this hierarchy.[3]

A major rift developed in Shi'ism in the seventeenth century related to the role of the *ulama* between the followers of the Usuli school and the followers of the Akhbari school. The latter were opposed to the ever-increasing power of the *mujtahids* and their use of rationalist principles (Usul) of jurisprudence in ijtihad. They believed instead that jurisprudence should be based on the Traditions of Islam. The Usulis won out, but Akhbaris can still be found in the Gulf region. Some of their ideas seem to have been revived, although the Akhbaris are never given credit for them.

Central to Shi'a theology is the concept of being *muqallid* to a *marja' taqlid*. Ideally, there is a consensus that one *mujtahid* has risen above all the others in learning and in justice and becomes recognized as such among Shi'a throughout the world. In reality, it rarely works like this. Frequently, one *mujtahid* does develop a very large and widespread following, but he always has contenders for the position, and these contenders always have some *muqallid*. The *muqallid* pay their religious taxes (*khums*) to their *marja'* and are required to follow the teachings of the *marja'* on matters of law and ritual. Among those who have lived more on the periphery (i.e., far away from the centers of Shi'a learning) are Shi'a who have never heard of the *marja' taqlid,* although people became more familiar with the term after the Iranian Revolution. Khomeini, himself considered a *marja'* (although not the sole one), was instrumental in raising people's awareness of the institution of the *marja'iyya*.

Although the apolitical Abul Qasim Khu'i, who resided in Najaf for many years, had a far larger following worldwide than Khomeini ever had, those *muqallid* to Khomeini, by virtue of their politicized approach to religion, gained far more attention. Lebanese Shi'a, who were aligned with the militant Hizbullah movement that wished to establish an Islamic government in Lebanon, generally were *muqallid* to Khomeini during his lifetime.[4] Shi'a are supposed to follow a living *marja',* although this is an issue under debate. Some Shi'a continue to follow a deceased *marja'* on all the issues on which he has adjudicated but turn to a living *marja'* with new questions. Since the death of Khomeini, those aligned with the Hizbullah movement in Lebanon (and their sympathizers in the West) have tended to follow the person that the Iranian government has supported: Ali Khamenei. Although Khamenei supporters are a minority among the Shi'a in North America, they are an outspoken group. Being more ideological than those who wish to have a depoliticized Shi'ism, they are more likely to take action to assert their positions, such as putting up posters of Khomeini and Khamenei and insisting on stricter adherence to Islamic or specifically Shi'a regulations in the mosques.

Arab Shi'a who believe that national politics should be separate from religion followed Abul Qasim Khu'i, who died while under house arrest after the Gulf War. Many of the leading *ulama* residing in Iraq were put to death or disappeared while in prison under Saddam Hussein's government. The most famous and outstanding of these *ulama* was Baqir as-Sadr, a rising star in the *marja'iyya* and the leading clerical figure in the Da'wa movement.[5] He is often referred to as "Iraq's Khomeini," although this title is somewhat misleading. The intelligentsia among Iraq's Shi'a, many of whom had drifted away from religion, became ardent Shi'a again because of the influence of Baqir as-Sadr. His execution in 1980 left a vacuum for those who subscribed to his thinking about the role of Shi'ism in the modern world. Baqir as-Sadr saw the *marja' taqlid* as an institution with tremendous potential to lead the Shi'a, but one that would necessitate major reforms.[6] To a broad spectrum of young Shi'a in the West, Baqir as-Sadr is a hero. To a select group, his writings are the guiding force for the reformation of Shi'ism.

Today, most Shi'a outside of Iran say they are *muqallid* to the person they view as being Khu'i's successor in Najaf: Ayatollah Ali Sistani. How he gained such a position in a relatively short period is complicated. Part of the answer is that he represents a moderate and traditional view of Shi'a practice and does not involve himself in dangerous political interests. It is Sistani's picture that hangs in the Khu'i Foundation mosques in Queens, New York, and in London. The fact that the Khu'i family has acknowledged Sistani as the grand *marja'* of the Shi'a world has served Sistani well.

There are other contenders for the position of *marja'*. However, most of these have been neutralized by the Iranian government or done away with by Saddam Hussein. There is one, however, who has largely remained outside the domain of either government: Seyyed Muhammad Fadlallah of Lebanon. He is seen as an activist and a model for many Shi'a youth, and he is viewed as an alternative to the Iranian model of Shi'a activism. Although his position as a contender for the *marja'iyya* remains ambivalent, it is apparent to those who know the signs of someone who has a quest for the *marja'iyya* that he is indicating his desire for the position. Fadlallah was closely linked with Baqir as-Sadr and to a large extent continues as-Sadr's legacy. Many of those who were supporters of Da'wa now see Fadlallah as Baqir as-Sadr's successor. For this reason and for reasons of convenience, I refer to Fadlallah's followers and sympathizers as "Da'wa."

The Council of Shi'a *ulama* in North America has come up with its own list of *maraji'* (plural of *marja'*), which includes the three contenders previously cited: Sistani, Khamenei, and Fadlallah. Although this list is subject to change, the idea that a group of *ulama* (none of them *mujtahids*) from various nationalities came together on American soil and made such a decision is quite extraordinary and could have far-reaching implications.

In this chapter, I limit the discussion to the general contrast between those Arab Shi'a in the United States who are *muqallid* to Khamenei and those who are *muqallid* to or ardent admirers of Fadlallah. However, the dividing lines are not as clear as they may seem. For example, those formerly *muqallid* to Khomeini could object to Khamenei's claim for leadership on the basis that he is only a political figure and does not have the religious qualifications to be a *marja'*. Others who are *muqallid* to Fadlallah today may have been *muqallid* to Khu'i, Khomeini, or another contender for the *marja'iyya*. Fadlallah, although viewed as the archetype of the politicized *alim* and the right arm of Iran in Lebanon, openly supported Khu'i even before Khomeini's death. People close to *ulama* circles say that he was afraid that, had he supported Khomeini and Khamenei as *maraji'*, the *marja'iyya* would have been centered in Iran and been under the control of the Iranian government. If he was ever to rise to the position of a widely recognized *marja'* who could influence the Shi'a world, he knew that having the *marja'iyya* in Iran would ultimately work against him and his plans. He therefore remains somewhat ambiguous about his own position. He has come out in support of Ayatollah Sistani, angering the Lebanese Hizbullah. (Before the deaths of Khomeini and Khu'i, he acted as a representative for both of these grand *maraji'*.) At the same time, he has written a book, *Masa'il Fiqhiyya*[7] (in English known as Fiqh Questions), an indication of his own desire to be a *marja'*.

The ambiguities of the institution of the *marja'* make it possible for someone to be muqallid to a *mujtahid* who is not universally recognized as a *marja'*. This was the case with Baqir as-Sadr and now with Fadlallah. However, just because someone does not have wide recognition as a *marja'* does not mean that he lacks the influence and potential to guide. As long as he has followers to spread his word and his writings, he can wield much influence.

Finding Fadlallah

While visiting a mosque in San Diego, I was introduced to an erudite Shi'ite in his late thirties who grew up in southern Iraq. Although his father was religious, most of the people around him were not particularly concerned with religion, having been affected by the modernist trends in Iraq. They were concerned with economic prosperity and wished to disassociate themselves from what were considered outmoded religious restrictions. They were not likely to be paying religious taxes to the *marja'* nor to follow his guidance. The man in question came to the United States twenty years earlier to be educated and remained, but he had already been affected by the writings of Baqir as-Sadr. In the courtyard of the San Diego mosque, he praised Baqir as-Sadr, happy to find someone to share his interest in his work. However, he soon told me that Fadlallah, who had been a friend of Baqir as-Sadr's, can be considered his successor. He said that Fadlallah was the most influential person among intellectual Shi'a and was interested in seeing Shi'ism address issues of the modern world.[8]

In a mosque in Los Angeles, I spoke to a woman in her thirties. Originally from Baghdad, she was working on a Ph.D. in one of the physical sciences. She had been drawn to the Islamist movement at least in part because of the influence of Baqir as-Sadr and his illustrious sister, known as Bint al-Hoda, who was executed with her brother. Dressed in a modified *hijab* and extremely articulate, especially about her ideas regarding women and their equality with men, she was *muqallid* to Fadlallah. She was well versed in his opinions and believed that Fadlallah presented "the true Islam," an Islam highly compatible with the modern world. According to her, "Fadlallah, I think, is giving the correct view of Islam, although we have never heard this before. Marriage, divorce, the form of the hijab are all issues that he addresses. We don't have to wear traditional *hijab*, just things that meet the qualifications of modesty."

In Detroit, a woman in her forties from an old, highly prestigious *ulama* family, spoke glowingly of Fadlallah. This woman, although to all outward appearances a traditional Najafi woman, is university educated and a defender of women's rights—at least to the point that she argues strongly for the equality of men and women. Although she is not *muqallid* to him, Fadlallah, in her eyes, does present a way for women to become more active in the world.

Fadlallah has been branded as a terrorist in the United States and is associated with the most oppressive and backward form of religion, but among these followers, he is a hero and a feminist! In addition to being receptive to the concerns of women, he also is more sensitive to the problems facing the youth in the West than are the other *maraji'*, who do not seem to have an appreciation of what it is like living in a society dominated by non-Muslims. In this regard, Fadlallah has had an advantage over the other *mujtahids*. He has been in the United States. (While he was in the United States, Muslim students took him on the tourists' tour of the White House.) He has kept in touch with the younger Shi'a residing here. These are university-educated people who are devout in their religion but not inclined to blind obedience. Their influence on Fadlallah—and as a consequence, Fadlallah's influence on at least a certain class of believers in the West—has led to some interesting developments.

Fadlallah and "the Youth"

Ohio has been a center of Muslim activity in the United States for Sunnis and Shi'a. In the 1970s, there were some joint activities among Sunni and Shi'a students who were more or less united in the Muslim Student Association. However, as has been the pattern in the United States, this joint endeavor did not last. The Iranian students broke away from the Muslim Student Association to form their own *anjoman* because of their political orientation. They were anti-Shah, and their main concerns were nationalistic.

Another Shi'a youth group that formed in the 1970s is referred to simply as the Muslim Group. Its founders were mostly from the Gulf and from Iraq. They were followers of Ayatollah Khu'i and of Baqir as-Sadr who had decided that they wanted their own, Shi'a-oriented group. Although the original founders of the Muslim Group have since become adults, they continue to be active and see themselves as youthful innovators in the community. They attempt to serve as a unifying force among Shi'a Islamists in North America, although this is not always an easy task.

One of the tasks that the Muslim Group assigned itself was to send questions to Ayatollahs Khu'i, Khomeini, and as-Sadr. These *mujtahids* had published books, but with the exception of Baqir as-Sadr, they tended to write in a medieval style that shed little light on the problems of twentieth century American society. The questions put forth by the Muslim Group necessitated that the *mujtahids* write about issues relevant to the concerns of these North American Shi'a. The questions and answers were subsequently published.

Fadlallah, perceiving the needs of this intelligent, younger population of Shi'a, wrote his own book. Rather than following the usual model of the *risala,* his book (*Masa'il Fiqhiyya*) is written in far simpler and more accessible language and is based on the kinds of questions that had been put to the earlier ayatollahs. Since then, Khamenei followed this lead and published a similar book, such that in a very short period the Muslim students in North America began having an impact on the institution of the *marja'*.

It was not just the clarity of Fadlallah's answers that was appealing to many of these younger Shi'a. Although this is not the place for a serious analysis of the philosophy of Seyyed Fadlallah, a few of his ideas should be presented. One of the striking features found in the *risalas* of the *maraji'* is the focus on the *nijasa* of *kafirs* (i.e., the ritual impurity of nonbelievers). However, there is no textual basis for rulings that limit a Muslim's interactions with nonbelievers. The restrictions that are prescribed are based on a "precaution" (*ihtiyat*), which is to say that it is better to err on the side of caution by following the rules that differentiate the ritually pure from the impure. Fadlallah disagrees with this argument. For him, everyone is at least physically *tahir* (pure) because there is no textual proof to decide otherwise. Such an opinion is especially significant for those who live among large numbers of non-Muslims.

Fadlallah's opinions also lead in the direction of permeable borders between Shi'a and other Muslims. Fadlallah has ruled as having "no historical basis" stories that have been told for generations and that perpetuate Sunni and Shi'a antagonisms. One example is the story of Omar and Abu Bakr allegedly pushing Fatima and causing her to miscarry. Fadlallah, while not saying the story is untrue, states that it lacks historical documentation, leaving the door open for doubt. For Shi'a living in the West, where they may find good reasons to wish to bridge the gap with non-Shi'a Muslims, this sort of opinion is extremely liberating.

Fadlallah follows in the footsteps of other Najaf-educated *ulama* in that he is a legalist.[9] Unlike Khomeini, who mixed *irfan* (mysticism) with jurisprudence,[10] Fadlallah avoids *irfan* and is what one might consider "ultra rationalistic." However, he differs from other *mujtahids* in that he prefers a simpler, less burdensome approach to legal and ritual matters. He wishes to do away with the concept of precaution, for example, signifying that he wishes to have a more straightforward approach to the texts. For Fadlallah, all opinions should have a textual basis. His followers in the West sound very much like Sunni "fundamentalists" who place a high premium on using the Qur'an as the basis for their religious beliefs and practices. By placing so much emphasis on the Qur'an, they are thereby diminishing the importance of centuries' worth of opinions by the *ulama*. His followers tend to be educated men and women who take their religion and religious education very seriously. They are not reluctant to challenge the opinion of an *alim* when they disagree, whether that *alim* is the sheikh of a local mosque or a *marja' taqlid*. This attitude is what sometimes leads them into conflict with their Hizbullah brethren.

In fairness, I should also comment that objections to Fadlallah's teachings are as strong as the words of praise. For example, one Iraqi *alim* from an influential Karbala family has expressed outrage over the ideas put forth by Fadlallah. Among other things, he is critical of Fadlallah's ruling that he can find no legal reason to forbid female masturbation. Such pronouncements, this *alim* feels, can only have deleterious effect on the community. However, a member of the family of another *marja' taqlid* told me that he could understand the appeal of Fadlallah to Shi'a living in the West and believes that other *mujtahids* should follow his lead, at least to some extent.

Hizbullah Versus Da'wa Youth

The Hizbullah movement, which developed in Lebanon and Iran, is very *ulama* centered. In interviews I conducted among Lebanese Shi'a in the Detroit area, those who identified themselves with Hizbullah were most likely to see the *marja' taqlid* as infallible. They stated that, if a *marja'* said something, it must be true. If it sounds strange or incorrect, the problem was caused by the faulty understanding of the laymen. They believe that clerics are qualified to lead the government in all matters and that their knowledge of the Shari'a provides sufficient guidance for them.

The differences between Hizbullah and Da'wa believers can be exemplified in the case of the dispute over the direction of the *qiblah*. However, before embarking on this story, I must make it clear that, regardless of whether people are aligned with Hizbullah or Da'wa, they were likely to have recognized the late Ayatollah Khu'i as being the greatest *mujtahid* of his time. Even those who had been ardent admirers of Khomeini and were proponents of his political agenda might have followed Khu'i on religious and ritual matters. A person associated with Da'wa was not necessarily *muqallid* to Baqir as-Sadr. Even his activist sister was *muqallid* to Khu'i. When Ayatollah Khu'i said that the believers in the United States should face southeast when praying, most Shi'a in the United States paid attention, and most of them also obeyed.

It was the highly rationalistic, independent Da'wa people who questioned this pronouncement. Among this group were many engineers and scientists who firmly and clearly stated that the *marja'* was incorrect and that one should face due northeast to pray. Ayatollah Khu'i's son, the late Mohammad Taqi, in helping to design the Khu'i mosque in Queens, insisted that the niche in the mosque marking the direction of the *qiblah* face southeast in keeping with the teachings of his illustrious father. The Shi'a who were aligned with the Da'wa movement and with Fadlallah's philosophy were adamant that this niche did not face the direction of the *qiblah,* and when they visited the mosque in Queens, they prayed facing northeast while others faced southeast! Their message was clear: the *marja's* domain of expertise did not extend to scientific matters, and because his opinion went contrary to the scientists, it was to be ignored.

For anyone who has listened to devout Shi'a speak about the *marja' taqlid,* especially sympathizers of Hizbullah, such opinions are startling. They are very likely to claim that the *marja'* is infallible and that, if the *marja'* took an opinion on any issue, that opinion would be considered true and legally binding. For Hizbullah, the *ulama* define what is right and wrong based on their knowledge of the Shari'a. Lower-ranking *ulama,* following the "infallible" *marja',* would necessarily be guided correctly. Although it is necessary to be vigilant and find an *alim* who is a staunch follower (and perhaps even a representative) of a *marja' taqlid,* after you have faith in him, you do not question his opinions.

In contrast, advocates of Fadlallah want explanations and sound, rational, scientific thought. They are not afraid to challenge the *ulama,* insisting that they do not want a local sheikh's opinion but that of the *marja'* himself, often placing the layman and the *ulama* at odds with one another.

This is an interesting development among the Shi'a. Michael Gilsenan, writing about *ulama* in Lebanon, pointed out the close relationship between sheikhs and young men.[11]

It is these young men who so often surround the sheikh and attend his sermons and participate in the rituals he leads. In Iran, the *ulama* were closely linked to young men and were seen as their leaders—spiritually and militaristically. However, the "young people" who follow Fadlallah (many of whom are now responsible adults but still see themselves as a new generation of believers) are not so dependent on the *ulama*. Because they are educated and feel capable of making their own judgments, they set a high standard for their *ulama* and do not tolerate haughtiness or condescension from them. Just as they would judge a scientist, a physician, or an engineer by his abilities, they judge an *alim* by the keenness of his mind, the breadth of his knowledge, and his humility in listening to the opinions of others—even laymen.

Some of the founders of Da'wa had been affected by the Ikhwan, a Sunni organization founded in Egypt that is not *ulama* based and has an anti-*ulama* element.[12] However, considering that Da'wa was founded by *ulama* and that it is so closely associated with Najaf, one of the great centers of Usuli Shi'ism, it is remarkable that the prestige of *ulama* did not rise in this group.

The disgruntlement with the *ulama* by the Da'wa extends beyond such issues as the direction of *qiblah* and exact times for fasting. They feel that the reverence given to the *marja'* and to the *ulama* in general can lead to corruption, to a lack of initiative on the part of the average believer, and to a lack of accountability. Their tendency to question the *ulama* about the reasoning behind a decision or an opinion has angered and alienated some of the *ulama* from the Da'wa followers. The *ulama* find it startling to have their opinions and those of the *marja'* challenged. One person who was visiting the Detroit area described to me a situation in which he was sitting with other like-minded friends and was asking an *alim* for one of the *marja's* opinions on a certain topic. The *alim* gave an answer, but his audience insisted that he clarify whether this was his opinion or that of the *marja's*. Stunned, the *alim* chastised the men for what he considered to be arrogance on their part. Although the *ulama* are interested in winning over this group because of its high educational level, potential for influence, and money-earning capacity, they are also leery of them because of their independent mindedness and candidly expressed views. A Hizbullah audience is less challenging because they look to *ulama* of all levels for leadership. They only ask that their *ulama* be interested in enforcing the Shari'a and take an active role in bringing people closer to the legalistic approach to Islam.

Because the Muslim Group spans a fairly wide spectrum of Shi'a, the meetings must be balanced so that the *ulama* and non-*ulama* intellectuals are represented. At times, the balance is not easily achieved. For example, at one specifically religious gathering that was hosted by Pakistani Shi'a, a visiting non-*alim* Islamist was selected to speak to the audience, although there were a number of prominent *ulama* in the room. The Islamist is active on the political front in his work to promote the rights of the Shi'a in Iraq. The Iraqi *ulama* have more or less conceded this political role to such people. However, they do express some resentment at being superseded in the purely religious sphere.

Hizbullah and Da'wa sympathizers also differ in other respects. Those associated with Hizbullah, by following Khamenei, are asserting their desire to Islamize government and society. For these people, Khamenei is the symbol of the victory of Islam over Western secularism. Alienated from Western values and traditions, they feel no discomfort with supporting someone who is so clearly at odds with the U.S. government. Da'wa supporters, although they have been involved in some anti-Western activities, by and large have a broader and more realistic perspective. They are well aware of the need to work with others to implement change. Of major concern to them is the fate of Iraq and its large Shi'a population. Although highly critical of U.S. policies in Iraq, they recognize that the United States must play an important role in ridding Iraq of the current Ba'thist regime and establishing a safe environment for the beleaguered Shi'a.

Although it may seem as if there is a division between Lebanese and Iraqis, with the former being associated with Hizbullah and the latter with Da'wa, this is an oversimplification. There are strong links between the Lebanese and Iraqi Shi'a in the United States that reflect the ties established between these two nationalities in the Middle East. These two nationalities tend to share mosques to an extent that other national Shi'a groups do not. Iraqi *ulama* are likely to serve as mosque leaders or commonly as *khatibs* for the recitation of the mourning ceremonies during Muharram. There is a fair degree of interaction between the two groups, with the Iraqis, because of their links to the shrine cities, enjoying considerable prestige among the Lebanese.

Defining and Preserving Identity

In the United States, Twelver Shi'a have maintained a strong separate identity. Although Sunnis and Shi'a occasionally attend each other's mosques for Friday prayers, it appears to be more common for Sunnis to pray in Shi'a mosques than vice versa. In New York, for example, Sunnis can be found at the Khu'i Mosque—most definitely a Shi'a institution—in Queens on Friday afternoons. This fact only became known to me because I found women dressed in Palestinian dress among the participants. When asked, they shrugged off the difference between Sunni and Shi'a. The Shi'a *Ithna Ashari* Khoja women around them agreed that "there is no difference." However, the rituals and some of the beliefs of the Shi'a make it difficult for all differences to be ignored. In a small mosque on Atlantic Avenue in Brooklyn, the sheikh, who originates from the shrine city of Karbala, said that he ministers to the needs of many African-American converts to Islam who are not at all concerned with Shi'a-Sunni differences. However, this is not the usual pattern for Islamic communities. Whenever possible, the two groups go their separate ways in terms of communal ritual life.

Because the Da'wa sympathizers and others who are influenced by the writings of Fadlallah de-emphasize the differences among Shi'a and all others, it may seem that they are actively bridging the gulf between Shi'a and Sunni. Da'wa was strongly influenced in its beginnings by the Ikhwan of Egypt, which is Sunni. However, this has not been the case. The fact that the Shi'a students broke away from the Muslim Student Association is one indicator.

There are many reasons why the Shi'a may not be eager to join with the Sunnis in the United States—reasons that have little to do with close-mindedness and more to do with the reality of trying to keep alive a rich religious tradition in a society that tends to homogenize religions. The combination of Sunnis and Shi'a in regular mosque affairs would almost certainly entail the Shi'a having to make the compromises. They are the ones who would have to suspend the distinctive rituals, particularly relating to the Imam Hussein, that are so much a part of their religious lives. In seeking a common denominator with the Sunnis, these rituals would suffer. Even Da'wa supporters, eager for a return to fundamentals, are not willing to relinquish the mourning ceremonies of Muharram and other rituals. They may not feel that the wailing and extreme forms of remorse sometimes practiced are appropriate, but they certainly would not forgo the commemoration of the events at Karbala. Although too much veneration of the twelve imams offends their rational approach to religion, dismissing the imams as not being central to their religious system is not part of their agenda.

The real issue in the American Shi'a community is to define the type of religiosity that is going to prevail. The *marja' taqlid* is central to this endeavor. Whether a *marja'* is recognized, which *marja'* is followed, and how much influence he has largely determine a host of other issues. The *marja'* is generally the preserver of a strict and conservative view of religion. Only rarely is this role challenged. The challenge can come from a radical, antimodernist, political front that is exclusive in its approach as was put forth by Khomeini and carried on by Khamenei. Alternatively, the challenge, although perhaps political, can strive to attain a modus vivendi with modernism and promote a belief system with more permeable boundaries. Baqir as-Sadr's approach, now elaborated by Fadlallah, falls in this category.

Understandably, these differences sometimes produce tensions. For example, a mosque referred to as the "Lebanese mosque" in Los Angeles was almost devoid of decoration during a visit there in March 1996, except for a picture of Ali Khamenei alongside of a picture of Khomeini, suggesting that those who frequent this mosque are aligned with Hizbullah or at least sympathetic to that cause. However, with further questioning, I found that the congregants at the mosque were more likely to be followers of Sistani than Khamenei. A substantial number of followers of Fadlallah also attend services at this mosque. Because of the diversity of opinion over the issue of the *marja'*, it had been decided that no pictures would be hung. However, the Khamenei supporters went ahead and hung Khamenei's picture. After it was up, people felt reluctant to take it down. Such an act would have been considered unforgivably disrespectful to a *"marja'."*

Conclusions

Since the Iranian revolution, the institution of the *marja'iyya* has gained increasing attention among academics and Shi'a themselves. The *marja'* has traditionally been a religious figure who instructs the community in terms of religious and ritual obligations. However, since the Iranian revolution, the potential for the *marja'* to play a larger role in leading the Shi'a spiritually and politically has been at the forefront of debates in the Shi'a Muslim community. Although most Shi'a clearly do not wish for a politicized Islam, including a politicized *marja'iyya,* even those who view Islam as a political force have differing views about the role of the *marja'*.

The two groups discussed in this chapter, one of which I refer to as Da'wa because it is inspired by the writings of Imam Baqir as-Sadr, a founder of Da'wa, and the other as Hizbullah because they were followers of Khomeini during his lifetime and now are followers of his successor, Khamenei, are at odds about the role the *marja'* should play in the lives of the people. To Hizbullah, who are religiously conservative, the *marja'* is an infallible leader who must be obeyed in all things, whether these matters are religious or secular. To a person related to Da'wa, the *marja's* role is far more narrowly defined. The *marja'* is supposed to issue fatwas (i.e., religious opinions) only on religious law and not in matters requiring expertise in other areas of specialization. The *marja'* is respected by this latter group for his leadership in socioreligious reform, such as enhancing the rights of women, harmonizing science and religion, and finding commonalities between Shi'a and Sunnism.

The different ideological views regarding Shi'a leadership have important implications for the Shi'a in the United States. In this country, there is potential for the Shi'a to unify around one *marja'* helping the people eventually to overcome ethnic and national divisions, much as Roman Catholics eventually did in the United States. However, the Shi'a must decide how much of a role the *marja'* has in defining the religious dimensions of the various communities. Will the *marja'* be one who is turned to in all matters of personal and communal life, or will he be more of a figurehead and a symbol of Shi'a unity? Will he address political matters, or will he be isolated from the turmoil of the world and be confined only to purely religious and ritual matters? The answers to these questions are being worked out in the Shi'a communities.

Notes

Acknowledgment: I would like to express my deepest gratitude to Dr. Talib Aziz for his critique of this study.

1. The Lebanese and Iraqi Shi'a residing in the United States live in more or less isolated religious and ethnic enclaves. The Lebanese Shi'a may participate in broader Arab affairs in the community, but most of their activities are among their co-religionists of Lebanese background. For a discussion of Lebanese in the United States, see my book, *Without Forgetting the Imam: Lebanese Shi'ism in an American Community* (Detroit, MI: Wayne State University Press, 1997). Iraqi Shi'a have only come in relatively large numbers to the United States since the 1991 Gulf War. These refugees are extremely isolated. For a discussion of Iraqi Shi'a in the Detroit area, see my chapter, "After Karbala: The Iraqi Refugees in Detroit." In Nabeel Abraham and Andrew Shryock, eds., *From Margin to Mainstream: Arab Detroit Comes of Age* (Detroit, MI: Wayne State University Press, in press).

2. See Fuad I. Khuri, *Imams and Emirs: State, Religion and Sects in Islam* (London: Saqi Books, 1990), pp. 179–88.

3. Abbas Amanat, *Resurrection and Renewal: The Making of the Babi Movement in Iran, 1844–1850* (Ithaca, NY: Cornell University Press, 1989), pp. 33–69; Juan R. Cole, "Imami Jurisprudence and the Role of the *Ulama*: Mortaza Ansari on Emulating the Supreme Exemplar." In Nikki R. Keddie, ed., *Religion and Politics in Iran* (New Haven, CT: Yale University Press, 1983), pp. 33–46; Hamid Dabashi, *Theology of Discontent: The Ideological Foundation of the Islamic Revolution in Iran* (New York: New York University Press, 1993); Moojan Momen, *An Introduction to Shi'i Islam* (Oxford: George Ronald, 1985); and Ahmad Kazemi Moussavi, "The Institutionalization of *Marja'-i Taqlid* in the Nineteenth Century Shi'ite Community," *The Muslim World* 84, no. 3–4 (1994): 279–99.

4. Linda S. Walbridge, *Without Forgetting the Imam: Lebanese Shi'ism in an American Community* (Detroit, MI: Wayne State University Press, 1997).

5. Hanna Batatu, "Shi'i Organizations in Iraq: al-Da'wa al-Islamiyah and al-Mujahidin." In Juan R. I. Cole and Nikki R. Keddie, eds., *Shi'ism and Social Protest* (New Haven, CT: Yale University Press, 1986), pp. 179–200; and Elie Kedourie, "The Iraqi Shi'is and Their Fate." In Martin Kramer, ed., *Shi'ism, Resistance, and Revolution* (Boulder, CO: Westview Press, 1987), pp. 135–57.

6. See T. M. Aziz, "The Role of Muhammad Baqir al-Sadr in Shi'i Political Activism in Iraq from 1958 to 1980," *International Journal of Middle East Studies,* 25, no. 2 (1993): 207–22; and Chibli Mallat, *Renewal of Islamic Law: Muhammad Baqer as-Sadr, Najaf and the Shi'i International* (Cambridge: Cambridge University Press, 1993).

7. Seyyed Muhammad Fadlallah, *Al-Masa'il al-Fiqhiyyah* [Fiqh Questions], 4th ed. (Beirut: Dar al-Malaak, 1995), published in Arabic.

8. Interview with an Iraqi Shi'ite, April 1995.

9. For Seyyed Fadlallah's views, see *Min Wahy al-Qur'an* (Beirut: Dar al-Zahra, 1983); *Ta'amulat Islamiyyah hawl al-Mar'ah* (Beirut: Dar al-Malaak, 1994); and "Al-Manhaj al-Istidlali," *Al-Murshid,* 3–4 (1995): 257–9.

10. Ervand Abrahamian, *Khomeinism* (Berkeley: University of California Press, 1993).

11. Michael Gilsenan, *Recognizing Islam* (New York: Pantheon Books, 1982).

12. Gilles Kepel, *Muslim Extremism in Egypt: The Prophet and Pharaoh.* Translated by Jon Rothschild. (Berkeley: University of California Press, 1986).

Part II

Arabs and the American Legal System

Fatima Agha Al-Hayani

4   Arabs and the American Legal System: Cultural and Political Ramifications

Racism and discrimination against various groups have been prevalent in American society. The extent varies and so does its impact. During certain periods in our history, prejudice and discrimination seem to diminish; however, it would be naive to presume that they have been eliminated. Instead, it would be a fair assumption to accept the fact that prejudice and its consequences, although latent, do exist and affect the lives of many people in different forms and in varied degrees.

Many works and studies have addressed the problems faced by Arabs in the United States and the vilification practices against them.[1] Such vilification is detrimental to the psychological and emotional well-being of all Arabs. In some cases, this negative attitude may transmit to the work place and produce injurious results, but does the problem run much deeper than that?[2] Aside from suffering the humiliation of name calling, the emotional trauma resulting from some form of harassment, and the fear of attack, there may be other, more serious repercussions that affect the Arab in various situations and circumstances. Cultural differences along with the political occurrences relating to the Middle East have adversely affected the Arab community. Moreover, one must ask whether a correlation exists between the barrage of negative stereotypes triggered by the involvement of the United States in the Middle East and the rendering of justice in American courts.[3] How do other areas dealing with the law, such as child custody, domestic violence, the police, and insurance coverage, affect the rendering of just and equitable practices for Arabs?

How do Arabs contribute to this situation themselves? Does the behavior of some of them affect other Arabs as they face the law? Does the legal system affect them the same as it does non-Arabs who face the same problems? How much do they understand the laws and the mechanics of the legal system, the welfare system, the cultural and societal practices in this country? It is true that injustice sometimes knows no color, race, or creed. It can happen to all, but does it affect the Arab more harshly than the average American?

This chapter concentrates on the Arabs in the Detroit and Toledo areas. I sought information from lawyers who represent Arab clients, social workers who deal with an Arab population and other ethnic groups, insurance agents and their perspective on issues pertaining to Arab clientele, and civic and religious leaders of both communities. I also investigated the concerns within the schools where students with Arabic backgrounds attend and the programs offered to help such students in solving their particular problems.

Background

There are approximately 200,000 Arabs in the Greater Detroit and Toledo area.[4] They come from various countries in the Middle East, with a large number coming from Iraq, Lebanon, Syria, and Yemen. The biggest concentration is in Dearborn, Michigan, where the major population is Arab. Although there are second- and third-generation Arabs there, many are first-generation immigrants. Whereas the first immigrants tended to assimilate and adopt some aspects of the American culture and language,[5] the new immigrants tend to congregate with their own groups and feel reluctant to integrate and assimilate, because they believe that to assimilate is to lose one's culture and one's identity.[6] Many only speak Arabic and understand very little English, even though they have lived in the United States for many years. This may not seem important to some, but such situations have created problems for the Arabs and for those involved in the legal system, the insurance agencies, the social services, and the schools.

The Court System

In the administration of justice in the courts, many Arabs and their lawyers believe that adverse publicity in the media that portrays Arabs and Muslims in a negative way has hindered a fair judgment in jury trials. In many cases of sexual assault when Arab men are the accused and the accuser is not, the chances of a conviction are much higher than the average. Although no documented statistics based on ethnicity are available, many Arab lawyers agree that they prefer to plea-bargain a case or revert to a bench trial in most situations rather than risk a conviction.[7]

According to some lawyers and some Arab leaders in the Dearborn and Detroit area, Arabs receive harsher sentences than non-Arabs for similar crimes. The higher percentage of convictions of Arabs during the Gulf War testifies to the presence of punishment based on ethnic lines as a result of prejudice and not as a result of proof without a doubt. This pervasive attitude is not limited only to cases of assault, but it also includes cases dealing with custody, domestic violence, and basic civil rights.[8]

Such a situation does not exist uniformly in every area. Judges in the Dearborn area, according to some lawyers, have been more sensitive to the issue of prejudice based on ethnicity and have attempted to instruct juries to do the same.[9] This happened as the result of many discussions between Arab civic leaders and the authorities to sensitize the latter to the problems facing Arabs and to acquaint them with the prevailing feeling among them concerning those in authority. However, according to Mr. Mosabi Hamed, who works with a large Arab clientele, Oakwood and McComb county judges are not as sensitive and tend to be harsher in their judgment on Arabs in that area than those presiding in Dearborn. Some lawyers disagree with this statement and state that the situation depends on the lawyer who is handling the defense, but they do agree that the degree of justice sometimes depends on the location of the trial and the presiding judge. They added that these factors affect all defendants: Arabs and non-Arabs.[10]

Aside from the negative stereotype and prejudice, there exists another dimension that weighs heavily in the administration of justice in the Detroit and Dearborn areas. This factor is the existing tension between African Americans and Arabs. If an Arab is charged and is being tried, a trial by jury presents the worst scenario for receiving a just verdict. According to many lawyers, the hostility from the African Americans does not stem from bias or prejudice based along ethnic lines; rather, it is bias based on resentment between those who are financially well off and those who are not.[11] With many African Americans living in the area and serving on the jury, the effect of such tensions and hostilities between Arabs and African Americans creates a bias against Arab defendants.

This problem has existed for some time and has been addressed by Judge Shakkoor and other Arab personalities to diffuse some volatile situations.[12] One incident occurred when an Arab gasoline station owner shot an African American during a robbery. In this situation, there were no charges made because, according to the police, the evidence showed that the shooting took place when the proprietor of the station was defending himself. However, the African-American community felt otherwise, and many of its members threatened the owner of the station until he was forced to sell his station. As expected, no other Arab would buy the station at any price, let alone at a reasonable price. One solution was to sell the station to an African American, but those who were mediating could not find a buyer, and the man had to close the station. In this situation, the law supported the Arab American but could not prevent his losses nor could it prevent the hostility between the two groups, hostility that does affect an outcome in a jury trial.

Although the legal system must rely on facts and proof in presenting a case, there are cases for which this procedure is not always followed in a fair and equitable manner. In some cases, circumstantial evidence has been admitted only because of certain assumptions pertaining to the behavior of Arab males. In many incidents, it is the defendant's word against that of the plaintiff. According to some lawyers and some Arabs, the jury almost always accepts the plaintiff's testimony over that of the defendant if he happens to be Arab.[13] The same could be said for non-Arab defendants, but many Arabs and Arab lawyers feel that they are more targeted as a result of the negative images of the Arab males portrayed in the media.[14] Moreover, the same number of lawyers believe that as the Gulf War accelerated so did the hostility toward Arab defendants.[15]

If a large number of Arabs live in the Detroit and Dearborn area, why are they not called in as jurors, which would help to alleviate the problem of prejudice and help in rendering fairer and unbiased judgments? Unfortunately, not many Arabs are registered as voters, and their names therefore are not available for jury duty. Some of the lawyers stated that many Arabs who are called for jury duty do not want to serve because they could not afford to be away from their jobs.[16] Some Arab jurors find all types of excuses to disqualify themselves, such as their inability to understand English. As a result, many lawyers representing Arabs avoid jury trials in most cases.

To prove this point, Mr. Hamed cites a case tried in 1993 in Wayne County Court. A young Arab man who arrived with a political asylum visa developed a relationship with an older woman. Later, the young man decided to get married to a young lady from his home town. As soon as the older lady became aware of his intentions, she went to the police and charged the man with sexual assault and rape. His lawyer studied the case and discovered that the police had already arrested and charged the young man, claiming that they had sufficient evidence. The evidence turned out to be anything but sufficient. Because the lady in question did not report the assault for two days, there was no chance to examine any evidence that rape actually occurred. The fact that this young man had no record of violence, had no problems with the police, did not demonstrate a violent temper, and had no history of sexual violence was not given enough consideration. He did not understand the social rules, nor was he aware of the appropriate behavior in such situations. The charge was made. It was the lady's testimony against the young Arab's testimony, and he was found guilty and sentenced to three years. In this case, the judge was very understanding and fair, but the jury found the defendant guilty.[17]

In 1992 in Oakland County, another Arab was accused of raping his girlfriend who already had a child and was living on welfare. One day, she invited him to a picnic in Birmingham. During the picnic, he noticed that she was stealing money from his pocket. This infuriated him. He left her in the park and decided to end the relationship. Soon after, she accused him of raping her. Although there were no signs of rape, the charges were made. The lawyer tried to plea-bargain; but the prosecutor refused. When the case was tried, the jury had three women jurors who should have been disqualified but were not, even though their daughters had been raped. The verdict was guilty, and the sentence was three years in jail.[18]

Another typical case dealt with a young Yemeni male who was eighteen years old and worked in his family's grocery store. One day, a young girl, who used to work for the family but was fired for stealing, walked in the store when the young man was working alone. The young man asked her to leave, but she refused, a situation that led him to hold her arm and push her outside the store. Soon after, a charge was made that the young man had assaulted her. There were no witnesses and no physical proof of any type presented to the court. However, the charge was made, and the feeling of the lawyer was that the young girl's word would be accepted as evidence over that of the young man's.[19] A jury trial could have condemned the young man to a twenty-year sentence. Instead, by pleading no contest to a crime he did not commit, the young man was sentenced to two years, and because he had no prior convictions, he was placed on probation for those two years, provided he attended counseling sessions.

To circumvent a biased jury in this geographic area, some lawyers prefer a bench trial, a process by which the case is presented to the judge, who alone decides the case. Such trials do not require a jury, and according to some lawyers in the Dearborn area, they tend to be fairer to Arab defendants. In most cases, lawyers representing Arabs felt that the judges usually were less biased.[20] They also felt that, despite the villainous propaganda against the Arabs, most judges tend to weigh the evidence more seriously and more objectively and rule according to what the evidence shows. Many of them seem to be less emotionally influenced in weighing such evidence. The judges in the Dearborn area have shown more sensitivity toward Arabs, but in the suburban and more affluent areas of Detroit, some lawyers stated that the judges tend to be resentful and more biased against Arabs.[21] Because of negative experiences with members of the Arab community, some judges hold some prejudice and are negatively biased. Nevertheless, compared with a jury trial, bench trials present a better chance of a fair verdict.

Other problems exacerbate the situation. Many immigrants cannot speak or understand English at all, or they barely speak it but understand only enough to manage some basic conversation.[22] However, the questions in court are sometimes asked in such a manner that many misunderstand their intent and their meaning, a situation that could easily jeopardize a case. There are also some who refuse to ask for an interpreter, stating that their English is very good although it is not. In some situations, even when there is an interpreter, the answers to the questions as strictly interpreted are an exact translation from the Arabic, a situation that in some cases makes the answer detrimental to the witness or the defendant.[23]

In one case, the lawyer of an Arab on trial explained to the court that his client was innocent and asked for a lie detector test. His request was rejected on the grounds that the defendant did not speak English. When the lawyer suggested that an interpreter could translate for the defendant, the court rejected this request, saying that this process is not permissible, although it is.[24] The implication according to the defense lawyer is that an Arab interpreter may in some way vary the question or the answer to help the defendant. Some police detectives believe that some defendants pretend that they do not understand English to avoid answering questions or to exonerate themselves from intentionally breaking the law.[25] In certain situations, whereas the lawyer is an Arab and understands what is being said in the testimony, the translations of the interpreter were not totally correct. Part of the problem in such situations is the varied colloquialisms used in different Arab countries. *Mabsoot* in Lebanese means content or happy, but in the Iraqi colloquial use, it means physically beaten.[26]

Sometimes, mannerisms stand in the way of justice. In one case, an Arab was accused of assaulting a young girl. The lawyer felt that, by means of a bench trial instead of a jury trial, he had a good chance to clear this young man, because the lawyer was convinced that the evidence was clear and would prove that his client was innocent. He was certain that the judge would rule favorably for his client. However, that was not the case. The defendant was found guilty of assault and battery, placed on probation, and ordered to attend counseling sessions about violence. The judge explained that his reasons were based on the attitude of the defendant. According to the judge, the defendant did not show any sympathy or remorse; instead, he acted in a very arrogant manner. This situation demonstrates a lack of cultural understanding and mannerisms of the defendant who, knowing that he was innocent, did not show any apprehension or worry during the trial, a behavior misconstrued by the judge as that of an arrogant and unfeeling man.[27]

In other situations, some statements may be completely ignored or dismissed as untrue, or in some cases, an alibi furnished by an Arab is not considered as valid as one given by a non-Arab. In one case, an Arab young man was accused by his girlfriend of assaulting her. He had an alibi furnished by a friend, an Arab, at the time of the alleged beating. Later, the girlfriend admitted in front of two policemen that she lied to punish her boyfriend because he wanted to end the relationship. She admitted again to two policemen that she lied about her accusations. Her denial was ignored. The police claimed that the reason they did not believe her the second time was that many women deny the initial charges for many reasons. It was possible that the girl was afraid or that her boyfriend had appealed to her to drop the charges and change her statement. However, even though the man had an alibi and even though he insisted that he was innocent and that he only wanted to end the relationship, he was still charged with assault and battery, and as a result of a plea-bargain, the young man received a lighter sentence.[28]

Domestic Violence and Law Enforcement Agencies

Almost all lawyers have admitted that cases of domestic violence among Arabs are on the rise.[29] According to some of them, when the police officers are called to an incident of domestic violence, they address the situation by ignoring it or by overreacting. In the first scenario, the police do not take seriously the wife's complaint that her husband has been abusive based on their experience with some Arab women who change their story later. This, according to the police, happens to all groups and is not limited to Arab women. However, it is the attitude of the police toward what they consider Arab cultural practices that makes them take such a situation lightly. From the negative information concerning the Arabs, wife beating is portrayed as an acceptable Arab behavior and custom; therefore, the police ignore the complaint and fail to see the problem. The lawyers acknowledge the fact that, in many typical instances, the police are reluctant to be involved in domestic violence. The problem that concerns the Arabs lies in the rationale taken by some members of the police force that Arab culture permits abuse of women, a statement cited in many cases as the reason for the police not to become involved. In some situations, the detectives are justified in their feelings.[30]

A typical case, presented on 22 November 1996 in the 19th District Court in Dearborn, concerned a charge of assault. It was a case against an Arab man (Mr. S.) whose wife had called the police. A detective was sent to investigate the situation. Both husband and wife were present in the court and so was the detective. The couple came together without a lawyer. To begin with, the Arab man pleaded guilty to the charge but did not understand the meaning of the word "provocation" that the judge used during the questioning. This was another example of problems faced by Arabs who refuse to have a lawyer, believing that they understand enough English during the questioning. The wife, who was not Arab, did not want to prosecute, citing as a reason the emotional difficulties that her husband was facing. Therefore, no questions were asked, and the detective did not need to testify. Such incidents frustrate the police who must answer such calls and tend to harden the attitudes of police detectives when the same situation recurs.[31]

On the other hand, some members of the police overreact and play the part of a vigilante. If they find any bruises on the wife or the children, the whole family is placed in a shelter to protect them from the abuse of the father and husband. When the husband tries to explain his position, the common statement given by the police is that "you are not back home now; you are in America." The implied meaning is that beating women and children is not an acceptable behavior in American society nor would it be tolerated as it would be "back home." There are many cases pending in which the husband has lost touch with his family as a result of a protective custody law for the wife and children.[32] One case goes back four years, during which time the husband has not seen his family and has hired a lawyer to help him find them.[33]

In some cases of wife abuse, the wife calls the police and receives no help, but she incurs the wrath of her husband, his family, and quite possibly her own family. She feels humiliated and probably would never attempt to seek help from the police again. In other cases, the shame of being taken to a shelter with the children and dishonoring the family outweighs any benefit derived from calling the police, regardless of the latter's good intentions. As a result, many women try to find solutions through arbitration by family members or religious leaders if possible.

Another reason for the increase of wife abuse is the welfare system. As some families qualify for welfare, some husbands, according to lawyers, come to depend on the welfare check, and rather than find work, they spend most of their time in coffee shops, or they gamble and drink. They also become abusive when the wife refuses to give them more money to waste. Such situations have forced the wife to seek divorce, and the records show that there has been a notable increase in the number of cases dealing with domestic violence and in divorce cases initiated by women within the Arab community.[34] The laws pertaining to the welfare system have opened the door for many women to become more independent. This economic independence gives them more freedom and diminishes the husband's control over his wife and his children, creating a volatile situation.[35]

There exist several theories to explain this situation: the education women receive from the media and the law concerning their rights and readily available legal help and information; the changing attitudes of the police force toward such violence; and the realization by Arab women that American society does not dwell on the concept of saving face nor does it consider a woman's behavior a dishonorable act when she fights for her rights in a violent or abusive relationship.

Another factor in such situations is the financial aid afforded many families through the welfare system. Public assistance laws (e.g., Aid to Families with Dependent Children) have opened the door for women to seek divorce and become eligible for such assistance. This economic independence gives women more freedom and has contributed to a weakening of the husband's status and control over his wife and family. Mr. B., an Arab businessman, stated that Arab women visit with each other and tend to teach one another what to do in case they encounter problems with their husbands. What compounds the problem for the husband in domestic violence situations (and which the police use against him as a result) are statements that the husband may make when agitated and angry and that, when literally translated, may project an image of a violent and a dangerous man.[36] Such expressions as "I'll kill them" or "I'll cut short their life," when used in Arabic and when literally translated into English, sound extremely dangerous, but Arabs know that they are not taken literally. Similar statements occur in the English colloquial usage with statements such as: "I'll break every bone in your body

if you do that." Do most people literally mean that? However, during a domestic violence scene, these statements, when said in anger and heard by the police, take on gar-
gantuan proportions and often hurt the man.[37]

Other factors that contribute to the increase in domestic violence are beyond the scope
of this chapter. Suffice it to say that there exists a common situation that generally results
in domestic violence. Mr. B., a Lebanese who has had much experience with the
Lebanese community in particular and the Arab community in general, believes that
much domestic violence stems from certain situations. The first is an older man who
has been working in the United States most of his life when he marries a much younger
woman. He works long hours and would like to come home at the end of the day to
rest. The wife has been alone throughout the day and waits for her husband to enter-
tain her. Friction and antagonism erupt when he declines, and the problems begin,
problems that may end in violence. Another major problem develops when some women
choose to work outside the home but are not allowed to do so or may be limited by
the husband concerning the type of work they are permitted to undertake.[38] In another
situation, the wife at home and alone for long periods befriends a male young neighbor who is closer to her age, a situation resulting in dire consequences that sometimes
lead to acts of violence or murder.

In other situations in which the victims are Arabs, the consensus among most lawyers
and Arabs living in this area is that the police are insensitive to their complaints and
are very slow to act to rectify a problem. For example, a young Arab Muslim girl
befriended another young girl in the school who happened to be a non-Arab Christian
fundamentalist. The latter, aided and encouraged by her family, felt it her duty to save
her "heathen" friend by taking her away from her own family. The young girl was
reported missing. Her parents went to the police and reported that their daughter had
been technically abducted. The police did not take their complaint seriously and did
not follow up on the case. When the family retained a lawyer to press the issue, their
daughter had already been taken across the state line to Ohio. Although the police were
informed of this move, which constitutes a bigger offense, they still ignored the parents' complaint. The case is not closed yet.[39]

There are cases of abuse by the police. In one situation, an Arab man and his family were returning from a campground in Dearborn when he was stopped for speeding.
When the officer decided to send him to jail instead of issuing a ticket, the man pleaded
with him not to do so because his mother was ill and his wife did not drive. The officer ignored him and prohibited him from going to the campground, stating, "We don't
want your kind of people there [the park]; we would really like it if you go back where
you came from."[40] Other abuse does occur, and as a result of many complaints and of
consultations and mediations by Arab leaders and interfaith organizations, the Dearborn police department became sensitive about the issue of bias. However, suspecting
that some Arabs are using the issue of prejudice to their advantage, the police department has installed in all police cars cameras and audio apparatus that can pick up conversations from 100 feet away to monitor every episode and to curtail any type of
harassment. This plan has helped the police and the Arab community. If there is abuse
by the police, it will be recorded, and those who fabricate negative stories about the
alleged aggressive and biased behavior of the police know there is a record of the event.

This procedure has helped to curtail unfounded claims of abuse.[41] Such situations explain the reluctance of any police officer or detective to give an opinion on any of the cases dealing with Arabs in Dearborn.

The Welfare Situation

Representatives of the welfare agencies indicated that many Arab families have mastered the legal process pertaining to their rights in the welfare system.[42] According to those who work for the welfare system, some have taken advantage of the programs offered by these agencies to the point of abuse, which has made matters worse for the families in need of such help.[43] The general feeling from some members of these agencies is that many Arab families abuse the welfare system and, by doing so, create another type of negative stereotype. They cite many cases to support their statements.

The prevalent situation is that of the so-called married-unmarried couples who seek help.[44] The mother usually files the claim for herself and the children and states that the father has left her and that his whereabouts are unknown. The claim usually is accepted, and payments begin. The next year, the same lady comes to add a newborn to the list. When the social worker, who in this case happens to be an Arab, asks her about the father of the newborn, the answer is usually a typical one: "My husband came back for a few weeks to try and work out our problems but to no avail." As a result he is alleged to have disappeared again, leaving her with another child. In another situation, a lady came for the second year to register a second child for welfare benefits. When asked about her husband, she stated that they were not married but were living together on a trial basis. The relationship did not work out for them the first time, but they tried again. Because the woman had another newborn, the social worker retorted with "do you try this every year?"[45]

The social workers, some of whom are Arabs, know quite well that living with someone, even though he or she may be another Arab, is not and would not be condoned by Arab society without a legal marriage. This problem is sometimes circumvented by having what some consider a Muslim marriage without the benefit of legal registration in the court system.[46] In some divorce cases, some partners go through the divorce in the courts but remain married through an imam; the divorcee's husband "rents" a room in the same household, and both receive welfare checks.[47] For some couples, such so-called religious marriages have created many problems for the husband and the wife. In one situation, the wife could not go to the local authorities to establish a legal marriage and to demand child support from her husband, nor could she stop him legally from remarrying, because her marriage to him was never recorded in the courts.[48] In another, the wife was divorced by the imam, remarried, took her children, and moved to another state, and the husband had no control in the matter. The latter situation is being fought in the courts to establish that the man is the father and to apply for his paternal rights and joint custody.[49]

In Toledo, Ohio, the Methodist church that handles welfare cases for the needy received a large number of Arab applicants seeking financial help. Unable to accommodate all of them, the church contacted the Islamic Center of Greater Toledo for help.

Imam Abd al-Munim al-Khattab suggested a solution for the problem. He asked the Methodist Relief Agency to refer all the families to him to determine their need, after which he would send them back to the Methodist agency accompanied by a letter ascertaining such need. Not one family has come forward, but this does not mean that there are no bona fide families who are in need and deserve to receive help. Many are in need of housing or assistance of one type or another and should receive it.

Other factors force some families to seek public assistance. In many situations, the reasons for being on welfare is not to receive welfare checks and food stamps but to receive medical benefits for the family, benefits they could not afford on the salary they were earning.[50]

Custody

In the area of custody, Arab culture and tradition are very much child oriented. It could be said that Arab children tend to be more spoiled and pampered, more loved and more nurtured, as evidenced by the endearment terms used when parents address their children. However, in some cases, the general Arab attitude about discipline may be misconstrued in American society as too physical or too violent when some parents believe it to be part of rearing and disciplining children.[51] Some Arab children, subjected to films and educational programs concerning abuse, have capitalized on this point and used the law as a weapon or as a means to gain more freedom. Parents become frustrated when faced with such situations. Several lawyers have stated that some children have even threatened to report their parents to the social agencies for child abuse, and these children have also manipulated the counseling services at their schools. However, some of the counselors have not been receptive to the complaints of parents when they sought help for themselves and for their children.[52]

Many Arab parents do not participate enough in school activities involving their children. One major deterrent is the language barrier, but schools have tried to work with Arab children. They have bilingual teachers and have been sensitive to the Muslim dietary rules and to other cultural and religious differences.

Cultural and language misunderstandings are exemplified by a case in which a fourteen-year-old boy was forbidden by his father to go out with a group of boys who were into drugs and other illegal activities. The young man refused to listen to his father and went out at night while the parents were sleeping. The father asked the school counselor to help or to recommend a person or agency that could help him in reaching his son. The counselor dismissed his complaints and failed to see any problem with the young man, believing that the father was far too strict. Not being able to monitor his son during the night or to prevent him from sneaking out at night, the father tied his son to the bed. The following day, the son reported to the counselor in school that he was tied to the bed with a rope during the night. What transpired was a nightmarish experience for the family. The young man was taken away from the family, and the father was charged with child abuse. It took a few weeks of discussion and a sympathetic lawyer before the situation was rectified, and the father and son began attending counseling sessions to bridge their differences.[53]

Another situation resulted from a lack of communication because the parties involved did not speak or understand English and because an uninformed and seemingly biased physician believed the negative stereotype about these "Third World people." The case involved a young daughter of an Arab family who developed a terrible rash after she had her bath. The parents took her to the hospital emergency room. Immediately, the doctor in charge called the social agency and reported a case of child abuse. The parents were not aware of what was happening. The young girl was taken away from her family, and the other children were also placed in foster homes. An Arab lawyer, after spending several weeks explaining and presenting positive evidence concerning the family, was able to convince the social service that the rash was the result of the soap that the mother used in the tub, a soap to which the young girl was allergic; the mother ignorantly used a detergent.[54]

In placing Arab children in foster homes, the Muslim dietary laws are rarely considered. The children in foster homes have been forced to eat pork and pork products, because the agency was not aware of these laws or because they did not deem them important. Some lawyers feel frustrated in such situations and complain that Arab families never sign up as foster parents. It is also a complaint that the social service agencies make as they try to find suitable placement for children in foster homes.[55]

Insurance

Stereotypes also affect the legal rights of Arabs in Dearborn in the cost of insurance coverage and paid claims. For some lawyers and many Arabs, premium fees are higher in districts where Arabs live than in other areas. In other areas, insurance premiums must follow the law. If an area is designated a high-risk area, the premium becomes higher. Whether Arabs have a higher rate of claims than other groups is questionable. One report claimed that 8,788 cars had been stolen from the Dearborn area. All these claims were paid by the insurance company, but it is not clear whether the cars belonged to Arabs only. The Dearborn area is surrounded by ghetto-type districts whose inhabitants find it easy and profitable to steal cars from Dearborn, because many of the Arabs living there have expensive cars. Mr. Mosabi Hamed, an Arab lawyer, stated that three of his cars were stolen in 1995. The tendency of the insurance companies, he stated, is to deny all claims, but in his situation, the claims were paid immediately.

Claims of fire damage and theft are also high, resulting in higher premiums.[56] Mr. Attalla and Mr. Harb, both practicing lawyers in Dearborn, think that insurance practices are generally fair and nondiscriminatory. Others such as Mr. Mashhour disagree, stating that in cases dealing with Arabs, the insurance companies demand 100 percent positive proof in cases of accidents, fire, or any type of claim before a claim is paid.

In some cases, even the testimony of policemen has not been accepted because they were Arabs. When an Arab reported a lost boat after Labor Day, the insurance company found a witness who stated that she saw the boat abandoned in her driveway two months before it was reported missing. The two Arab policemen testified that this was not the case, because they saw the man use his boat throughout those two months.

However, the insurance company refused to pay the claim. The case was taken to court, and the claimant won the case. This example testifies to the fact that, although there is some illegitimate abuse and fraud of insurance claims, not all of them are fraud. Many lawyers stated that fraud knows no ethnic boundaries, but according to some, the Arab community is targeted by the insurance companies.[57]

Conclusion

It is fair to assume that the law can be and is sometimes negatively biased against Arabs. Such bias affects the administration of justice in a fair and equitable manner in jury trials, bench trials, and cases in which lawyers opt for a plea-bargain. Many lawyers tend to shy away from jury trials, because they feel most juries are affected by the negative depiction of Arabs. They also think that, if more Arabs become eligible to serve as jurors and are elected for jury duty, the problems of discrimination could be alleviated.

Another source of discrimination is police behavior and attitudes. In the Dearborn area, many Arabs feel targeted by the police. They also complain of lack of support and negligence because, in their own estimation, the police do not respond to their concerns or their problems.

Most Arabs feel that the welfare system deals with them fairly, although lending itself to some manipulation by some. Domestic violence seems to be on the rise for various reasons, such as availability of economic independence for the wife through public assistance, a situation that diminishes the husband's control over his wife and family and creates friction and discord within the family. Another area that adversely affects Arabs is the role played by the social services whose employees have a tendency to judge Arabs on the basis of negative stereotypes and without understanding the cultural and social traditions. In some custody cases, children are taken away from their parents without a thorough investigation of the problem, and negative assumptions are made about Arab parenting practices.

Another sensitive situation is the relationship between African Americans and the Arab community in Dearborn. Arabs also feel that they are unfairly treated and targeted as high-risk clients by insurance companies.

There have been many successful attempts to sensitize the court system and the police to the problems that Arabs are experiencing. Religious and civic leaders and interfaith participants have been working to facilitate a positive interactions among the concerned parties and to alleviate the tension. However, the Arabs themselves need to assess the problems they face to devise a plan of action to counteract such bias and unfair treatment. It is not enough to know that the law, in some situations, is negatively biased against them; Arabs must pinpoint these problems and address them as other minority groups did throughout the history of the United States. In the past few years, community efforts have gained impetus, and efforts to educate the Arab community have achieved some success. Unfortunately, the problems continue to affect the lives of Arabs in this area. The Arab community must acknowledge that it is not only paramount to become aware of the problems it faces, but also must become politically and socially active in combating such problems.

Notes

1. See, for example, earlier works by Abdo Elkholy, *The Arab Moslems in the United States* (New Haven, CT: College and University Press, 1966); Elaine C. Hagopian and Ann Paden, eds., *The Arab Americans: Studies in Assimilation* (Wilmette, IL: Medina University Press International, 1969); Barbara C. Aswad, ed., *Arabic Speaking Communities in American Cities* (Staten Island, NY: Center for Migration Studies, 1974); Baha Abu-Laban and Faith T. Zeadey, eds., *Arabs in America: Myths and Realities* (Wilmette, IL: Medina University Press International, 1975). Also see later works by Baha Abu-Laban and Michael W. Suleiman, eds., *Arab Americans: Continuity and Change* (Belmont, MA: AAUG Press, 1989); Sameer Y. Abraham and Nabeel Abraham, eds., *Arabs in the New World* (Detroit, MI: Center for Urban Studies, Wayne State University, 1983); Eric J. Hooglund, ed., *Crossing the Waters: Arabic-Speaking Immigrants to the United States before 1940* (Wash., D.C.: Smithsonian Institution Press, 1987); Michael W. Suleiman, *The Arabs in the Mind of America* (Battleboro, VT: Amana Books, 1988); Yvonne Yazbeck Haddad, ed., *The Muslims of America* (New York: Oxford University Press, 1991); and Barbara C. Aswad and Barbara Bilge, eds., *Family and Gender Among Muslim Americans* (Philadelphia, PA: Temple University Press, 1996).

2. See Michael W. Suleiman, "The New Arab-American Community." In Elaine C. Hagopian and Ann Paden, eds., *The Arab Americans: Studies in Assimilation* (Wilmette, IL: Medina University Press International, 1969), pp. 37–49; and "American Mass Media and the June Conflict." In Ibrahim Abu-Lughod, ed., *The Arab-Israeli Confrontation of June 1967: An Arab Perspective* (Evanston, IL: Northwestern University Press, 1970), pp. 138–54.

3. See "ADC Releases Hate Crime Report: Anti-Arab Incidents up 300% in 1991," *ADC Times* 13, no. 2 (1992): 1, 10.

4. Telephone interview with Ismael Ahmed, Executive Director, Arab Community Center for Economic and Social Services (ACCESS), September 1996.

5. Sameer Y. Abraham and Nabeel Abraham, eds., *Arabs in the New World* (Detroit, MI: Center for Urban Studies, Wayne State University, 1983); Ernest McCarus, ed., *The Development of Arab-American Identity* (Ann Arbor, MI: University of Michigan Press, 1994).

6. See Yvonne Y. Haddad and Jane I. Smith, "Islamic Values among American Muslims." In Barbara C. Aswad and Barbara Bilge, eds., *Family and Gender Among Muslim Americans* (Philadelphia, PA: Temple University Press, 1996), pp. 19–40; Sameer Y. Abraham and Nabeel Abraham, eds., *Arabs in the New World* (Detroit, MI: Center for Urban Studies, Wayne State University, 1983); and Baha Abu-Laban and Michael W. Suleiman, eds., *Arab Americans: Continuity and Change* (Belmont, MA: AAUG Press, 1989).

7. Interview with Mohsin A. Mashhour, an Arab lawyer practicing in Dearborn, Michigan, August 1996.

8. Interviews with Adel Harb, an Arab lawyer practicing in Dearborn, Michigan, October 1996, and with Chuck Olowan, a Muslim civic leader in Dearborn, September 1996.

9. Interviews with Mosabi Hamed, an Arab lawyer practicing in Dearborn, Michigan, and working as legal specialist for ACCESS, and with Tim Attalla and Adel Harb, Arab lawyers practicing in Dearborn, Michigan, October 1996.

10. Interview with Tim Attalla, October 1996.

11. Interview with Mohsin Mashhour, August 1996.

12. Interview with Judge Shakkoor, April 1995.

13. Interviews with Mohsin Mashhour, August 1996, and with Mosabi Hamed, October 1996.

14. See Michael W. Suleiman, *American Images of Middle East Peoples: Impact of the High School* (New York: Middle East Studies Association of North America, 1977).

15. Interviews with Chuck Olowan, a Muslim civic leader in Dearborn, September 1996; with Mosabi Hamed, October 1996; and with Mohsin Mashhour, August 1996.

16. Interviews with Mosabi Hamed and with Tim Attalla, October 1996.

17. Interview with Mosabi Hamed, December 1994.

18. Interview with Mosabi Hamed, December 1994.

19. Interview with Mosabi Hamed, December 1994.

20. Interviews with Tim Attallah, Mosabi Hamed, and Adel Harb, October 1996.

21. Interviews with Mosabi Hamed, December 1994, and with Mohsin A. Mashhour, August 1996.

22. See, for instance, Barbara C. Aswad and Barbara Bilge, eds., *Family and Gender Among Muslim Americans* (Philadelphia, PA: Temple University Press, 1996); and Albert Hourani and Nadim Shehadi, eds., *The Lebanese in the World: A Century of Emigration* (London: I.B. Tauris, 1992).

23. Interview with Mosabi Hamed, October 1996.

24. Interview with Mosabi Hamed, October 1996.

25. Members of the police department would not comment on any issue, opinion, or facts. They had strict orders to withhold their opinions on all cases.

26. Members of the police department had strict orders to withhold their opinions on all cases.

27. Interview with Mohsin A. Mashhour, August 1996.

28. Interview with Mohsin A. Mashhour, August 1996.

29. Interviews with Mosabi Hamed, Tim Attalla, and Adel Harb, October 1996.

30. Interviews with Mosabi Hamed, October 1996, and with Mohsin A. Mashhour, August 1996.

31. Telephone interview with the detective dealing with the case, December 1996.

32. Interview with Mosabi Hamed, October 1996.

33. Interview with Mosabi Hamed, October 1996.

34. Interviews with Mosabi Hamed, Tim Attalla, and Adel Harb, October 1996.

35. Interviews with Mosabi Hamed, Tim Attalla, Adel Harb, and Mr. B., a Lebanese businessman who has lived in Dearborn for many years, October 1996. See, for example, Louise Cainkar, "Immigrant Palestinian Women Evaluate Their Lives." In Barbara C. Aswad and Barbara Bilge, eds., *Family and Gender Among Muslim Americans* (Philadelphia, PA: Temple University Press, 1996), pp. 41–58; and Yvonne Y. Haddad and Jane I. Smith, "Islamic Values among American Muslims." In Barbara C. Aswad and Barbara Bilge, eds., *Family and Gender Among Muslim Americans* (Philadelphia, PA: Temple University Press, 1996).

36. See, for example, Baha Abu-Laban and Michael W. Suleiman, eds., *Arab Americans: Continuity and Change* (Belmont, MA: AAUG Press, 1989).

37. Interviews with Mosabi Hamed, October 1996, and with Mohsin A. Mashhour, August 1996.

38. See, for example, Jane I. Smith. "The Experience of Muslim Women: Considerations of Power and Authority." In Yvonne Yazbeck Haddad, Byron Haines, and Ellison Findly, eds., *The Islamic Impact* (Syracuse, NY: Syracuse University Press, 1984).

39. Interview with Mosabi Hamed, December 1994.

40. Interview with Mohsin A. Mashhour, August 1996.

41. Interviews with Tim Attalla, Adel Harb, and Mosabi Hamed, October 1996.

42. Interview with Nabiha Charara, June 1996.

43. Telephone interview with Dr. Radwan Khoury, Arab American Chaldean Council (AACC), June 1996.

44. This situation is not a *mut'a marriage*. For more information on this type of marriage, which is applied only among the Shi'a sect, see Linda S. Walbridge, "Sex and the Single Shi'ite:

Mut'a Marriage in an American Lebanese Shi'ite Community." In Barbara C. Aswad and Barbara Bilge, eds., *Family and Gender Among Muslim Americans* (Philadelphia, PA: Temple University Press, 1996), pp. 143–54.

45. Interview with Nabiha Charara, June 1996.

46. Interviews with Nabiha Charara, June 1996, and with Mosabi Hamed, October 1996.

47. Interview with Imam Abd al-Munim al-Khattab, Director, Islamic Center of Greater Toledo, July 1996.

48. Interviews with Imam Abd al-Munim al-Khattab, July 1996, and with Mosabi Hamed, October 1996.

49. Interview with Mosabi Hamed, October 1996.

50. Interviews with Mosabi Hamed, October 1996, and with several families on welfare who did not wish to be identified.

51. Interview with Mohsin A. Mashhour, August 1996.

52. Interview with Mosabi Hamed, October 1996, and with Mohsin A. Mashhour, August 1996.

53. Interview with Mosabi Hamed, December 1994.

54. Interview with Mosabi Hamed, December 1994.

55. Interviews with Tim Attalla, Adel Harb, and Mosabi Hamed, October 1996.

56. Interviews with Tim Attalla and Adel Harb, October 1996.

57. Interviews with Mohsin A. Mashhour, August 1996, and with Mosabi Hamed, October 1996.

Kathleen M. Moore

---

5   **A Closer Look at Anti-Terrorism Law:** *American-Arab Anti-Discrimination Committee v. Reno* **and the Construction of Aliens' Rights**

Recent legislation entitled the Anti-Terrorism and Effective Death Penalty Act[1], signed into law on April 24, 1996, seems to a number of its critics to represent a perversion of justice within which constitutional rights have been sacrificed in the name of national security. The legislative debates show that members of Congress constructed this law, and the legal classification of "alien terrorist"[2] on which it turns, for apparently irreconcilable ends: first, to combat terrorism by removing so-called aliens[3] and fining[4] permanent residents and citizens who support or are affiliated with a "terrorist organization,"[5] and second, to preserve a modicum of due process guarantees, including very limited summary disclosure of classified information, for "alien" targets of deportation proceedings. Under the terms of this law, the government may deport an immigrant even if she or he has not committed any crime. Aliens will not be given sufficient opportunity to defend themselves in deportation hearings and, on losing their cases, must leave the United States, forfeiting any opportunity to petition the government for redress or to make an appeal.[6] Congress effectively has created a new class of persons who are defined as deportable merely because of their association with a disfavored group, not because they personally committed a terrorist act.

A provision of the anti-terrorism law creates a new court, called the removal court, which hears the government's deportation cases against immigrants behind a cloak of secrecy.[7] This is expected to facilitate the deportation of suspected terrorists because it allows the government to present evidence against suspected alien terrorists in secret, nonadversarial sessions in which the defendant is not present and does not have a chance to respond to the evidence presented by the government. The government argued that it needed the secret removal court because deportation proceedings until now have been conducted as public hearings, and the government is constrained in using classi-fied information when it pertains to national security concerns for fear of revealing the identity of intelligence sources. Under the current law, if the removal court accepts the government's case against a suspected alien terrorist, the defendant receives an unclas-sified summary of the evidence against her or him, without showing the identity of informants, to be used in preparing a defense. The new law requires only that the unclassified summary be specific enough to permit the alien to "prepare a defense" against the noncriminal charges in deportation hearings, a standard that is lower than the one prevailing in criminal cases in which classified evidence is used. In criminal cases, the government's unclassified summary must "provide the defendant with substantially the same ability to make his defense as would disclosure of the specific classified infor-mation."[8] The removal court judges and the government in effect are playing with a full deck of cards, but the defendant in a removal court proceeding has only one-half of the cards, and a few of the aces are missing.[9]

The creation of the removal court increases the use of secrecy in American jurispru-dence, which in itself is a disturbing trend. It also raises constitutional questions about what sort of due process guarantees the United States is required to provide before kick-ing suspected terrorists out of the country and how far the First Amendment goes in protecting the free speech and associational rights of immigrants and others who may provide material support to what the government considers to be unpopular or threat-ening causes.

The anti-terrorism law is infirm for several reasons,[10] not the least of which is that it fails to accomplish the disparate purposes for which it ostensibly was intended. It neither combats terrorism nor provides adequate procedural guarantees for persons accused of associating with blacklisted terrorist groups and are thereby subject to depor-tation. Any attempt to reflect on the implications of this law for the members of groups that are affected by it, who are most likely to be subject to its provisions and to be silenced by them, must raise a host of questions. How does this law distinguish between "insiders" and "outsiders" in a normatively defensible way? Does it attempt to secure or undermine a sense of full membership in the social and political life of society for all individuals within that society? Can it keep allegiance to the political community durable in the face of mounting pressures, both external and from within?

In this chapter, I investigate the ways in which the anti-terrorism statute furthers par-ticular definitions of citizenship and "alienness" and defines the major status relation-ships constituting our society. The first task is to render explicit what is at issue in the constructed differences between citizen and alien and to trace the shift from persons, things, and actions as legal subjects to the creation of legal fictions of identity. Although the Anti-Terrorism and Effective Death Penalty Act of 1996 is ostensibly about terror-ism, it should not be viewed in isolation from the enactment of a companion law about immigration, the Illegal Immigration Reform and Immigrant Responsibility Act (IIRIRA).[11] Together these laws are changing current immigration practices by creat-ing new secret procedures for the removal of suspected alien terrorists, by shifting the authority to make "expedited removals" to immigration inspectors at ports of entry, and most significantly, by setting unprecedented limits on judicial review. A provision of the new immigration law, the constitutionality of which has been affirmed by the

Supreme Court in *Reno v. American-Arab Anti-Discrimination Committee* (hereinafter *Reno v. ADC*),[12] strips the federal courts of jurisdiction to hear legal challenges to the deportation process, at least until the final deportation order has been issued. The burden of this falls most heavily on immigrants whose origins are located in nations or regions considered a serious threat to American national security.

The second task of this chapter is to consider the implications of the Court's interpretation of IIRIRA in *Reno v. ADC*. I consider the language of the 1995 Ninth Circuit ruling in *American-Arab Anti-Discrimination Committee v. Reno* (hereinafter cited as *ADC v. Reno*),[13] which affirmed the aliens' freedom of association rights and spoke of a "tolerance of difference," in contrast to the language of the Supreme Court decision in *Reno v. ADC,* which excluded the eight alien defendants from the constitutional standards applied to citizens. These decisions must be understood in light of social conditions and indicators of public unease with immigration such as California Proposition 187, the Official English movement, the recently reduced levels of legal immigration, and the proposed constitutional amendment to deny birthright citizenship to children of undocumented aliens. As the means of control increase, the more pressing becomes the question of who is legally part of the American civil community. The answer to this is more problematic than may appear at first glance.

The Rise of the Alien as a Legal Fiction

The individual becomes an alien through a legal construction—through the practice of jurisprudence. The actions she or he takes and others take with regard to the individual are mediated through law. In the words of theorist J.G.A. Pocock, "acts of authorization, appropriation, conveyance, acts of litigation, prosecution, justification"[14] define the significance of citizenship. A citizen is someone who is "free to act by law, free to ask and expect the law's protection, a citizen of such and such a legal community of such and such a legal standing in that community."[15] Citizenship implies a certain form of human association and a claim to being recognized as fully human. In an ideal modern sense, rights are understood as universal, but everywhere we see them being differentiated. One's right of appeal to the privilege and protection of the law, to claim rights and immunities, is determined by one's status as a citizen.

Attached to citizenship are a legal status (e.g., standing to sue in certain courts) and rights to certain things under the law (e.g., property, immunities, protections). These by definition are not available to the alien. A distinction is made through the law between the citizen and the alien, which turns on access to a certain status and rights. The individual alien is not seen so much as the bearer of a singular character or culture, but the collectivity of aliens, in the plural form, amounts to a conceptual category of persons distinctive for what they lack under the law. The legal fiction of alienness has contributed to the persistence of the identity of the citizen.[16] As an artifact of the legal construction of the identity of citizen, the rights of the alien as noncitizen came to be determined as less than equal to those recognized as belonging to the citizen.

In past decisions, the Supreme Court has recognized that aliens' rights are less than citizens' rights under the Constitution. In *Mathews v. Diaz,* the Court in 1976 held that "in the exercise of its broad power over naturalization and immigration, Congress regularly makes rules that would be unacceptable if applied to citizens."[17] With respect to the case of the "L.A. 8," former FBI Director William Webster told Congress in April and May of 1987 that had the eight defendants been U.S. citizens, "there would not have been a basis for their arrest."[18] In the final disposition of this case, in *Reno v. ADC*, the Supreme Court offered what is perhaps the strongest opinion yet limiting the rights of immigrants. On the First Amendment question, Justice Scalia wrote for the Court in *Reno v. ADC*, "As a general matter . . . an alien unlawfully in this country has no constitutional right to assert selective enforcement as a defense against his deportation."[19] The Court's holding bars anyone who is subject to deportation from trying to defend herself by asserting that she is being targeted for her controversial political beliefs that any legal citizen would be free to embrace. Throughout the country, in the discussions over measures such as California's Proposition 187, the rights of "aliens" (whether labeled "lawful" or "undocumented"), in kinds and degrees, have been hotly contested in an era of growing hostility toward the presence of noncitizens.

What explains this growing hostility toward the presence of noncitizens and, in particular, the strong bipartisan support on Capitol Hill for the passage of the anti-terrorism act? It seems too easy to say that America is in search of a new enemy to replace the fallen Soviet Union as a means of reconstituting the image of an insecure world to justify the continuing hegemonic role of the United States as global superpower. Several significantly titled recent works suggest the connection between the end of the Cold War and the rise of new global threats to civilized life as we know it. Francis Fukuyama's *The End of History*[20] and Samuel P. Huntington's "The Clash of Civilizations?"[21] are just two examples. The risks to national security described in these works render seemingly rational and "apolitical" a *very* political process of differentiation—of establishing a morally defensible way of distinguishing between insiders and outsiders, allies and adversaries. Similarly, the new anti-terrorism act makes legal a means of exclusion based on political beliefs and affiliations of a class of persons, creating a legal classification that ultimately will have serious political consequences. That it may silence voices, quell public activities, and arouse suspicions based solely on a person's surname is not farfetched. The forced incarceration of Americans of Japanese ancestry in U.S. internment camps during the Second World War is a case in point.[22] Now fear of terrorism surfaces in the airlines passenger profiling of Arab Americans started in the aftermath of the Oklahoma City bombing and the TWA 800 disaster. Judgment is based on the identities of individuals, rather than their actions.

The distinction between insiders and outsiders, which is made to appear to be morally defensible, turns not on an assessment of risks posed by unstable regimes "out there," but on the definition of citizenship "at home," its connection with the language of rights, and the validation of particular claims on an array of resources widely considered to be increasingly scarce even in a peacetime economy. The wedge issues of welfare, affirmative action and immigration reform are more fitting concomitants to the appearance of the recent anti-terrorism legislation than foreign policy concerns. Understood in this context, the law can be seen as a political invention meant to affirm that "we" are citizens and full members of the civil community and succinctly to arrive at a leaner, meaner understanding of what constitutes that community. The broad class of noncitizens are "the new enemy, the new objects of legislative war."[23] The fiction is continued that there is an essential difference between those on either side of the distinguishing criteria of the law.

Although the argument that the demise of the Cold War explains the recent trends toward nativism and xenophobia in American politics is compelling, I argue that there is another reason intrinsic to self-determination and politics that is enduring. The issue of exclusion is not seen by lawmakers, judges, and the general public simply as a legal or doctrinal question. Instead, it is embedded in complex relationships, the social and economic conditions within which people live, the goals of public policy and the more general perennial debates over the proper role of the branches of government, and the distribution of resources and power in American society. Not only does it represent "new" nativism,[24] it is also a new *federalism*, focused on the level of government to be entrusted with the power of self-determination in an era of displaced suspicion. The public vilification of suspect aliens through law should be interpreted not only as a means to ease domestic insecurities by creating the specter of an enemy, but also as a way of defining civil society. In this demarcation of insider or outsider status, there is a definite shift away from communism and toward terrorism as the quintessential "un-American activity."[25]

Narrowing of the Civil Community

Exclusion based on political beliefs in immigration and citizenship law is nothing new. American experiences with immigration and citizenship bear the imprint of historical trends and continue to be shaped by current conditions and evolving political pressures toward exclusion. The standards for admissions into the United States and for naturalization have become ever more sensitive to an alien's professed political beliefs and political behavior. The rights associated with status relationships (e.g., aliens, citizens) concerning membership in the civil community have taken on new meanings with the passage of time.

Congress began to set standards for admissions in the first comprehensive immigration law of 1882 and to exclude from entry anyone who failed to meet these standards. Lunatics, idiots, and convicts were the first classes of persons to be excluded from the nation. A racial classification also became salient that year, with the adoption of the Chinese Exclusion Act of 1882.[26]

The federal immigration law was amended in 1903 to add for the first time explicitly political grounds for exclusion. Persons believing in the violent overthrow of the U.S. government were excluded, and anarchists were the intended subjects of the law.[27] After World War I, communist parties and other radical associations formed in the United States, and their presence produced the Red Scare. Thousands of radical aliens were seized in 1919, and hundreds were deported to Russia in that year.

Anti-communist sentiments rose after World War II and national security legislation received high priority in Congress. The impact of the Cold War could be felt on the home front and abroad. Spanning more than four decades, approximately from the end of World War II to the collapse of the Soviet Union in 1991, the Cold War fostered a pervasive sense of crisis that justified the use domestically of undemocratic measures (distinguishing between alien and citizen, but also significantly compromising the rights of the citizen) as means to save the nation.[28] The Internal Security Act of 1950[29] expressly excluded communists from entry into the United States, and in broadly defining the excluded group, the law barred anyone "likely to" engage in "subversive activity." In domestic battles against communism, the Federal Bureau of Investigation (FBI) and the Central Intelligence Agency (CIA) systematically infiltrated groups and spied on American citizens.[30] The FBI's counterintelligence program (COINTELPRO) was designed as a surveillance operation directed at individuals and groups opposed to the Vietnam War.[31] In the words of one federal court, its purpose was to "expose, disrupt, misdirect, discredit, or otherwise neutralize the activities" of leftists in the United States.[32] The CIA opened more than 215,000 letters to or from the Soviet Union between 1952 and 1972 and maintained a watch list that singled out certain groups for special attention.[33] In 1978, Congress created the Foreign Intelligence Surveillance Act Court, a body of judges that authorizes the government's wiretapping of suspected "foreign agents," which serves as the model for the removal courts created by the Anti-Terrorism and Effective Death Penalty Act.[34]

Congress passed increasingly stringent immigration laws designed to keep out undesirables. Legislative action removed virtually all constraints on the executive branch's power to assess and counter national security threats by excluding unwanted immigrants. Historically, immigration law has not been subject to judicial scrutiny, in part because it is linked to foreign policy and considered a "political question," governed exclusively by the so-called political branches of the federal government, and legislative power to exclude and deport immigrants has been largely unchecked by the courts.[35] Ironically, for the sake of democracy, Congress suspended some of the essential tenets of democratic rule in decision-making by giving to the executive branch (wherein the Immigration and Naturalization Service [INS] resides) nearly unimpeded power to act in foreign policy[36] and limiting individual civil liberties to combat a designated menace to the survival of democracy.[37]

In the early days of the Cold War, Congress passed the McCarran-Walter Act of 1952,[38] which focused on the immigrant's political beliefs as grounds for making judgments about suitability. The Act was designed to restrict the entry of communists, but it also contained a provision that allowed for the expulsion of an alien on the basis of confidential information without a hearing.[39] The rights of aliens against deportation were much narrower than the rights of immigrants after they had acquired American citizenship. With no statute of limitations in it, the Act allowed for the deportation of an alien at any time after a prohibited act (e.g., membership in a subversive organization) had been committed. On the other hand the expulsion, or expatriation, of naturalized citizens required the government to show proof of objective intent—in other words, that the individual voluntarily relinquished citizenship—which may be implicated by one of the following acts: an act of treason or subversion, including membership in a blacklisted radical group advocating the violent overthrow of the U.S. government; naturalization in a foreign country; an oath of allegiance in a foreign country; and military service in a foreign country.

It was under the McCarran-Walter Act that the defendants in the L.A. 8 case (seven Palestinians and one Kenyan) were initially arrested in 1987 for supporting the Popular

Front for the Liberation of Palestine (PFLP) and affiliating with an organization "that advocates ... doctrines of world communism." However, because the McCarran-Walter Act was repealed in 1991, the government claimed that the L.A. 8 were still deportable under the "terrorist activity" provisions of the Immigration Act of 1990[40] or on the "nonideological" grounds that they violated certain technical immigration rules (i.e., by overstaying their visas or failing to register for enough credits to maintain full-time student status).[41] The Court of Appeals for the Ninth Circuit held, in November 1995, that the government could not "selectively enforce" the immigration rules, singling out these defendants while not prosecuting others who engaged in the same conduct. Such selective enforcement, it was ruled, is ideologically motivated. Moreover, the government in this case tried to use secret information to justify deportation of the two defendants who were resident aliens, charging that they were involved in the advocacy of terrorism, but the appeals court rejected this secrecy, saying classified information may not be used in deportation proceedings. Selective enforcement and classified information produce a chilling effect on speech, reasoned the Ninth Circuit, and immigrants have basic free speech rights.

American law, however, has been ambivalent on the question of the rights afforded to noncitizens. The status of alienness affects the allocation of rights and benefits in our society, and the law is deeply divided about the significance of that status.[42] In some decisions, the Supreme Court has treated alienness as irrelevant and an illegitimate basis for the less favorable treatment of persons.[43] For instance, in *Graham v. Richardson* (1971), the Court held that "classifications based on alienage, like those based on nationality or race, are inherently suspect and subject to close judicial scrutiny."[44] In this case, alienness is a legal status that is presumptively illegitimate as a justification for discriminatory treatment. In a subsequent case, Justice John Paul Stevens wrote, it is "habit, rather than analysis, [that] makes it seem acceptable and natural to distinguish between ... alien and citizen."[45] In other cases such as *Plyler v. Doe* (1983), the Court has rejected even illegal or undocumented status as a basis for making distinctions between aliens and citizens with respect to constitutional and statutory rights.[46]

The Supreme Court has held that some constitutional protections apply to aliens, but in other contexts, the Court has treated alienness as an appropriate basis for establishing a scale of rights.[47] The government has provided an "ascending scale of rights [to the alien] as he increases his identity with our society," which in the view of the Court is in accordance with the government's prerogative as a sovereign nation, defending the integrity of its national borders.[48] Differential treatment has become a prerogative of sovereign power. Aliens matter because citizenship matters. The Court once provided a tautological definition of citizens and aliens: "citizens are full members of the national community, while aliens are 'by definition those outside of this community.'"[49] Social and legal inequalities are legitimated by construed differences between citizen and alien.

Politics of Inclusion and Exclusion

By examining the distinction between citizens and aliens, we can see how images of the self and politics make elusive the sense of full membership in the social and political

life of the community. In the post-Cold War era, we see public anxieties about an indeterminate and incorrigible enemy in responses to instances of terrorism on American
soil. News media interpret for us the meaning of public opinion polls, taken immediately after events such as the World Trade Center bombing in 1993, the Oklahoma City
bombing in 1995, and the TWA Flight 800 tragedy and knapsack bomb in Olympic
Park in Atlanta, both in the summer of 1996, to indicate that Americans are increasingly worried about personal safety.[50] The consequences of such widespread feelings
are rarely considered in such accounts, but the effect is to cast the American public as
distrustful of the unfamiliar, the unknown alien or outlaw presumed to be responsible
for these attacks. Linkage between the Oklahoma City bombing and international terrorism was immediate. In the hours and days after the blast, news organizations and
law enforcement officials rushed to speculate that investigation of the crime would
focus on "Middle Eastern looking" suspects. After it had been realized that the source
of the attack was domestic, not international, *Newsweek* summarized the prevailing
mood as follows:

> Had "they" been responsible, as so many suspected, the grief and anger could have been
> channeled against a fixed enemy, uniting the country as only an external threat can do. We
> might have ended up in war, but what a cathartic war it would have been! Or so it felt, in
> brief spasms of outrage, to more Americans than would care to admit it. And if we could-
> n't identify a country to bomb, at least we could have the comfort of knowing that the
> depravity of the crime—its subhuman quality—was the product of another culture unfath-
> omably different from our own.[51]

The analysis described here leaves the impression that, if "we," the full members of society, could ascertain that "they," aliens or just terrorists, have fixed, immutable biologic
or cultural traits, the drive behind exclusion would be justified, and making effective
policies of admission and deportation would be much easier.

Portrayed as vulnerable and fearful of future terrorism, the public has been responded
to by lawmakers, who are seen as having authority to do something about national
security. The White House reacted to the Oklahoma City bombing by announcing the
President's strong support for a counterterrorism measure already making its way
through Congress and urging its speedy passage, although the bill attempted to target
international, not domestic, sources of terrorism.[52] During debates on the Senate floor,
emphasis on the need to pass the counterterrorism measure with dispatch in light of
the Oklahoma City bombing was bipartisan.[53] Some concern for the costs of urgency
were also expressed, although with much less vigor; Senator Orrin Hatch urged careful deliberation so civil liberties would not be sacrificed unnecessarily.[54]

The institutional bias evident in Senate debate, to rely on Congress and the Executive to provide solutions to terrorist attacks from unidentified fronts, supports the
notion that ordinary folks, constituting the public, are a significant threat to public life.
Simultaneously, threats are seen as emanating from the people who are terrorists—most
especially from aliens but also, with the revelation of the arrests of Timothy McVeigh
and his associates as suspects in the Oklahoma City bombing, from outlaw citizens—
and from the knee-jerk reaction of people to curtail the civil liberties of a broad range
of persons potentially affected by the adoption of a counterterrorism statute. Pressures

on Congress to eliminate the due process rights of aliens subject to deportation because of their alleged affiliation with terrorist organizations, as defined by the Secretary of State, are portrayed by a small number in Congress as rash.

This response tends to present a portrayal of the public, rather than the institutions of the state, as a threat to democracy. More commonly, however, congressional debates elicit discourse that perpetuates a duality between "us" and "them," the citizen and the alien, with a suspicion of the outsider. Consider the comments of Senator Judd Gregg (R-New Hampshire), in the days after the Olympic Park bombing in Atlanta: "The fact is, we have stepped out of the Cold War into a very hot war, and it is a hot war that involves people who have targeted Americans and American institutions with the intention of bringing physical harm to those institutions and to our citizens."[55] Gregg makes an important essentialist distinction between members of and outsiders to the American community:

> We should not be naive about this. We are a nation which has some wonderful characteristics. One of the great characteristics of our Nation is that we always believe in the best in people. We always give people the benefit of the doubt. We are an optimistic and upbeat country. It is our nature to think positively, not only about ourselves but about our neighbors throughout the world. This is a wonderful characteristic, and, hopefully, nothing will ever cause us to lose that better nature which makes up the American personality. But it is time, also, for us to be realistic. *There are evil people out there* [emphasis added] . . . There are people out there whose intention it is to kill Americans, to destroy American institutions simply because we are Americans.[56]

Gregg continues by stating a duality between domestic and international sources of terrorism. Domestic terrorism, he argues, is containable because of our institutions that are "well structured to address [it] already. The FBI and the various State agencies which do law enforcement are well-tooled and well-experienced in how to address, to meet, to obtain intelligence on and to respond to, domestic terrorism. . . ." However, it is not the core threat to the United States, which Gregg defines as international terrorism, sponsored by nations such as Iran, and the question remains: "How do we address this new international threat, this new cold war which is now a hot war for us?" For Gregg, the appropriate response is in the hands of federal agencies such as the State Department, the CIA, the Defense Department, and the Justice Department and in Congress' ability to delegate its authority to these agencies to create a response to the threat of international terrorism. All this Gregg states in response to an incident, the bombing during the 1996 Summer Olympics in Atlanta, which is not suspected to be linked to international terrorism.[57]

Analysis of Aliens' Legal Rights

In its brief before the Ninth Circuit Court of Appeals, the Justice Department said that, although the L.A. 8 defendants had not been accused of committing a crime, their fundraising and distribution of literature on behalf of the PFLP constituted "concerted acts of an international terrorist conspiracy." In the view of the Justice Department, the PFLP is defined as "one of the world's most notorious international terrorist organizations," responsible for airline hijackings in the 1970s and still opposed to any Israeli-Palestinian peace accord. The Justice Department's brief points to Court decisions that have established a gradation of rights in society, applying constitutional protections differently to aliens than to citizens. Deportation hearings are a special case, the Department of Justice opines, with no corollary among the citizen population.

However the appellate bench in *ADC v. Reno* rejects this limitation on constitutional rights. The language of the judicial decision is revealing. The decision holds, "Contrary to the government's suggestion, the foreign policy powers which permit the political branches great discretion to determine which aliens to exclude from entering the country do not authorize those political branches to subject aliens who reside here to a fundamentally different First Amendment associational right."[58] The three-judge panel found that in times of crisis, "[a]liens, who often have different cultures and languages, have been subjected to intolerant and harassing conduct in our past, particularly in times of crises. . . . It is thus especially appropriate that the First Amendment principle of tolerance for different voices restrain our decisions to expel a participant in that community from our midst."[59]

To determine whether the government could limit the due process rights of the L.A. 8, the Ninth Circuit used a three-pronged balancing test. With this test, the court must first weigh the private interest of the individual; second, the risk of an erroneous deprivation of that interest; and third, the government's interest. The court ruled that due process concerns are paramount and will almost always require the government not to use classified information against aliens if it refuses to disclose the information. "Only the most extraordinary circumstances could support [a] one sided process," writes the appeals court. "We cannot, in good conscience find that the president's broad generalization regarding a distant foreign policy concern or related national security threat suffices to support a process that is inherently unfair because of the enormous risk of error and the substantial personal interests involved." The First Amendment right to associate freely cannot be impaired for foreign policy concerns.

The appellate decision in *ADC v. Reno* constructs a vision of a political community that is tolerant and multicultural. It constructs out of the Framers' intentions a recognition that "aliens within this country participate in a reciprocal relationship of societal obligations and correlative protection."[60] About the applicability of the First Amendment to deportation hearings, the decision states that the same standard applies to deportation as to other kinds of procedures. "Because we are a nation founded by immigrants, this underlying principle is especially relevant to our attitude toward current immigrants who are part of our community."[61]

Taken as a whole, this decision is committed to the idea of a heterogeneous public, an idea that arbitrary classifications subvert. The government denies that the anti-terrorism act is a response to *ADC v. Reno,* but officials admit that the case of the L.A. 8 is a prime example of the sort of trouble the government has been having in deporting suspected terrorists without the use of secret removal courts.[62] We have to be sure to understand fully how significant this political invention is. "Immigration law has been structured in light of wartime considerations, therefore these laws pitted U.S. citizens against enemy aliens. Despite changed fears, immigration law is still based on these premises, thereby resulting in modern day xenophobic laws."[63]

After the Ninth Circuit held in *ADC v. Reno* that aliens' rights to free speech and associational activity were constitutionally protected, the case of the L.A. 8 was remanded to the lower court, where U.S. District Judge Stephen V. Wilson (Central District of California) later ruled that the defendants had been targeted impermissibly by the INS for "selective enforcement" of immigration laws because of their fundraising activities on behalf of an international terrorist organization.[64] This decision was then appealed by the Justice Department and was argued in 1997 before the same Ninth Circuit Court of Appeals panel that had upheld the constitutional rights of the L.A. 8 in 1995. The Justice Department argued that the passage of the IIRIRA of 1996 made Judge Wilson's ruling invalid because, according to the new law, judicial review of INS deportation proceedings before they are completed (i.e., with the issuance of a final order of deportation) is barred, even in cases involving free-speech claims. Justice further argued that IIRIRA could be applied retroactively to cases pending in the courts at the time of the statute's enactment in 1996. In July 1997, the Ninth Circuit Court of Appeals again held in favor of the L.A. 8, ruling that prompt judicial review of their First Amendment claims is required because the injury done by the government is irreparable if the Constitution is violated and cannot be vindicated by "post-deprivation remedies." In other words, the clock cannot be turned back, and limits placed on constitutionally protected rights *while* deportation cases are pending—in this case, for twelve years—are impermissible. Rights abridged, even temporarily, can never be fully restored, and such limits have a chilling effect on the expressive activities of the defendants and on those of other aliens who fear they may become the next targets of INS deportation proceedings. In June 1998, the U.S. Supreme Court agreed to hear the case of the L.A. 8 with respect to one question: whether, in light of IIRIRA, the lower courts have the jurisdiction to hear a challenge to deportation proceedings prior to the entry of a final order of deportation when a continuation of those proceedings will chill the aliens' First Amendment rights.[65]

The U.S. Supreme Court handed down its decision in the *Reno v. ADC* case in February 1999. Instead of limiting its review to the single question about lower-court jurisdiction, the Court also decided the merits of the selective enforcement defense raised by the L.A. 8. In a two-pronged decision, the Court held in the first part of its decision, with a vote of 8 to 1, that the limitation placed on judicial review before the completion of deportation hearings was constitutionally valid. Congressional intent in passing IIRIRA, the Court reasoned, was to streamline the process of deporting or denying entry to aliens who had broken the law. The Court also held that, by barring immigrants' access to the courts during the deportation process and limiting them to a single appeal at the end of the process, the statute is simply putting an end to the long delays created by aliens who demand judicial intervention in the administrative deportation process. In the second part, decided by a vote of 6 to 3, the Court rejected the eight activists' claims that selective enforcement of the law had a "chilling effect" on their First Amendment rights. Justice Scalia, writing for the Court, held that making a selective enforcement claim would be very difficult to do in court because "such claims invade a special province of the Executive, its prosecutorial discretion." The Court further reasoned that, because of sensitive foreign policy and foreign intelligence considerations, about which the Executive branch has special knowledge, "the Executive should not have to disclose its 'real' reasons for deeming nationals of a particular country a special threat—or indeed for simply wishing to antagonize a particular foreign country by focusing on that country's nationals—and even if it did disclose them a court would be ill equipped to determine their authenticity and utterly unable to assess their adequacy."[66]

The claims of selective enforcement, even if true, do not make the arrests invalid because the government may have its reasons for singling out these particular defendants—reasons it does not have to reveal, much less defend.

In deciding against the eight activists in the case of the L.A. 8, the Supreme Court may have crafted a ruling that will have far-reaching effects on the rights of all immigrants. By severely limiting aliens' access to courts when facing charges leading to deportation and, more generally, by limiting the scope of protection offered by the Constitution, the Court has reinforced the division between citizen and alien. This in effect redefines the major status relationships that constitute our society—citizenship and alienness—in ways that further disable the alien.

Laws such as the Anti-Terrorism and Effective Death Penalty Act (AEDPA)and IIRIRA and the concomitant narrowing of the civil community result from the heightened sense of insecurity required to maintain a restructured, wartime regulatory state after the primary security target disappears. The transition to a peacetime economy after the Cold War, with its touted "peace dividend," reveals a significant rupture between the means (e.g., statutes, surveillance, exclusion) and the rationale of regulation. The regulatory state perpetuates essentialized understandings of the self (as citizen) and the other (as alien) and will continue to distribute rights and therefore power hierarchically as long as a heightened sense of insecurity persists. Political discourse operates to structure expectations at two levels, to address the international and domestic sources of terrorism, with the former being acted on every time the latter threat rears its head.

Notes

1. AEDPA, Public Law No. 104-132, 110 Stat. 1214.

2. AEDPA, Public Law No. 104-132, 110 Stat. 1214.

3. By statute, the word "alien" means any person not a citizen or national of the United States. See U.S.C. section 1101(a)(3) (1987).

4. Penalties range up to ten years' imprisonment and civil fines of $50,000 and more.

5. The law gives the Secretary of State, an executive official appointed by the U.S. President, full discretion to define terrorist organizations. Provisions of the law state that a terrorist organization may be any group deemed by the Secretary of State to be "engaged, or which has a significant subgroup which engages, in terrorism activity, regardless of any legitimate activities" of the organization or the subgroup. This means that the government can assess fines or initiate deportation proceedings against anyone who gives money to humanitarian or charitable projects of organizations designated by the Secretary of State to be "terrorist organizations." In the words of Michael Vatis, the Deputy Director of the Justice Department's Executive Office for National Security, this is because "[m]oney is fungible. If a person gives money to a terrorist organization intending that the terrorist group is going to use it for one of its hospitals, we have no way of ensuring that the terrorists aren't actually going to use it to buy bombs." This statement was cited

in Benjamin Wittes, "Immigrants, Civil Libertarians Unite: Clinton Anti-Terrorism Bill Angers Rights Groups," *Legal Times* (March 13, 1995): 2. An outspoken critic and immigration expert, Professor Deborah Anker of Harvard University, believes the law will become a political weapon to silence unpopular voices. She states, "A terrorist organization is a group that the United States, for political reasons, is not supporting at the moment." This statement was cited in Wittes, *Legal Times* (March 13, 1995): 2. However, one year after the law's enactment, the State Department had not yet designated any foreign organization as a terrorist group, "the necessary first step in triggering the law's ban on domestic fund raising for foreign terrorists" (Benjamin Wittes, "Feds Move Slowly on Terror Law . . . ," *New Jersey Law Journal* (June 9, 1997): 9. This led the Anti-Defamation League of the B'nai B'rith, one of the main supporters of the legislation, to complain that the government was moving too slowly. President Clinton, by issuing executive orders, has named some Middle East organizations terrorist groups in order to freeze their assets in this country, and Secretary of State Madeleine Albright eventually invoked her authority to do so in accordance with the 1996 Anti-Terrorism and Effective Death Penalty Act.

6. Persons outside the borders have fewer legal rights than those within the United States, and it is difficult for someone outside of the territorial boundaries of the United States to present a case.

7. In September 1996, Chief Justice William Rehnquist appointed the five federal judges who sit on the removal court for terms ranging between one and five years. The court will authorize deportation of noncriminal aliens who allegedly are members of terrorist organizations.

8. The Classified Information Procedures Act is cited in Benjamin Wittes, "Secret Deportation Panel Raises Due Process Issues," *The Recorder* (April 25, 1995): 1.

9. The image of playing cards is taken from a statement by James Dempsey, deputy director of the Center for National Security Studies, a civil liberties group, cited in Wittes, *The Recorder* (April 25, 1995): 1.

10. One might think the law's fatal flaw would be its shift from personal guilt to guilt by mere association. However, the Supreme Court repeatedly has held that Congress may enact legislation allowing for deportation on ideological grounds and for association with groups advocating violence, rather than criminal activity. See, for instance, *Fong Yue Ting,* 149 US 698 (1893); *US ex rel Turner v. Williams,* 194 US 279 (1904); and discussion in H. R. Henthorne, "Resident Aliens and the First Amendment: The Need for Judicial Recognition of Full Free Speech and Association Rights," 39 *Catholic University Law Review* 595 (1990). For a departure from prior cases, see *Bridges v. Wixon,* 326 U.S. 135, at 163 (1944) (J. Murphy, concurring), where guilt by association is a violation of the fundamental principles underlying American law. This concurrence is noteworthy in that no distinction is made between the rights of citizens and the rights of resident aliens under the law. However, a few years after the Bridges decision, the Court returned to the position that aliens have fewer rights than citizens in *Harisiades v. Shaughnessy,* 342 U.S. 580 (1951).

11. IIRIRA, Public Law No. 104–208.

12. *Reno v. American-Arab Anti-Discrimination Committee,* 525 U.S. (1999); 1999 U.S. LEXIS 1514.

13. *American Arab Anti-Discrimination Committee v. Reno,* 70 F3d 1045 (9th Cir. 1995). David Cole, Georgetown University Law Center professor and attorney for the defendants, said of this ruling that it is "the clearest ruling yet that aliens have the same [due process and] First Amendment protection as US citizens." Cited in *National Law Journal* (November 27, 1995): A11.

14. "The Ideal of Citizenship Since Classical Times," in Ronald Beiner, ed., *Theorizing Citizenship* (Albany, NY: SUNY Press, 1995), p. 35.

15. Beiner, *The Ideal of Citizenship,* p. 36.

16. As legal scholar Martha Minow puts it, the problem in such legal fictions, which create dichotomies (e.g., alien/citizen), requires that we expose the "rigidity and limitations of patterns

of thought that force perceptions into dualities: good/bad, same/different, white/black, male/female. Becoming adept at recognizing how each half of a given duality depends on the other half in self-definition and how crudely each duality divides varieties and ranges of perceptions and experience can help people challenge the seeming inevitability of dualisms in social practice." *Making All the Difference: Inclusion, Exclusion, and American Law* (Ithaca: Cornell University Press, 1990), p. 236.

17. 426 U.S. 67, 79–80 (1976).

18. Webster made these remarks at confirmation hearings when he was considered for the head of the Central Intelligence Agency. He testified to Congress that the eight defendants "were arrested because they are alleged to be members of a world-wide Communist organization which ... makes them eligible for deportation." See *Hearings before the Senate Select Committee on Intelligence on the Nomination of William H. Webster, to be Director of Central Intelligence,* 100th Congress, 1st sess. 94, 95 (April 8, 9, 30, 1987; May 1, 1987). See *National Law Journal* (November 27, 1995): A11.

19. *Reno v. ADC,* 1999 U.S. LEXIS 1514, p. 28 (Lexis pagination is subject to change with final publication of the decision).

20. *The End of History and the Last Man* (New York: Free Press, 1992).

21. *Foreign Affairs* 72 (Summer 1993), pp. 22–49.

22. During World War II, seventy thousand Japanese-American citizens and thirty to forty thousand Japanese aliens, but not German Americans, were relocated to internment camps based on wartime suspicions. See Juan F. Perea, ed., *Immigrants Out! The New Nativism and the Anti-Immigrant Impulse in the United States* (New York: New York University Press, 1997), p. 2. The current anti-terrorism statute may lead to Arab Americans and immigrants from the Arab world feeling the legal and social discrimination Japanese Americans suffered during World War II, when they were interned for the sake of "public safety." See Kathleen M. Moore, *Al-Mughtaribun: American Law and the Transformation of Muslim Life in the United States* (Albany: SUNY Press, 1995), p. 104, 115–16. Such fears may not be unfounded. In an article in the *Detroit Free Press,* the INS was reported to have prepared a 31-page document called "Alien Terrorists and Undesirables: A Contingency Plan," in which details for surveillance and detention of certain people are developed. Iranians and Arabs are the only examples explicitly cited as possible suspects. The plan states that the government would "concentrate its counter-terrorism efforts against particular nationalities or groups known to be composed of certain nationalities, " cited in "Aliens Face Jail in Plan," *Detroit Free Press* (7 July 1987).

Concerns about internment and other forms of war-related discrimination were reflected in statements by Arab Americans interviewed during the Gulf War ("Desert Storm") of 1991. See, for example, "FBI Quest Leaves Many Arab-Americans Fearful," *Los Angeles Times* (24 January 1991); "Inquiries on Arab-Americans by FBI Raise Concern," *New York Times* (12 January 1991); and "U.S. Moslems Say Crisis Distorts Peaceful Faith," *Boston Globe* (22 September 1990). In 1988, Congress officially apologized to Japanese Americans for the harm inflicted on them and their relatives in the internment camps and noted that judgments based solely on *identity* are a violation of civil liberties. See Public Law 100–383, section 1 (1988), 102 Stat. 903 (1990).

23. Perea, *Immigrants Out!*, p. 2.

24. Nativism has been defined by immigration scholar John Higham as "intense opposition to an internal minority on the grounds of its foreign (i.e., "un-American") connections (cited in Perea, *Immigrants Out!* note 22:1)." It is designated here as new because periods of nativism have come and gone in American history. The question is what social conditions are concomitant with, and therefore may indicate, the onset of nativism.

25. Examples of alleged instances of terrorism that have occupied public attention recently include the "Unabomber" Ted Kazynski, the World Trade Center bombing in New York City in

1993, the bombing of the Federal Building in Oklahoma City in 1995, the downing of TWA 800 and the explosion at the Atlanta Olympics in 1996, anti-abortionist gunfire and bombings at womens' health clinics, and anonymous threats of anthrax.

26. Public Law, Ch. 117, 22 Stat. 58. For discussion of exclusion of the "unwanted" through these laws, see Moore, *Al-Mughtaribun*, pp. 28–29, 32–42.

27. Anarchists became the subject of exclusionary efforts after the assassination of President McKinley in 1901.

28. Examples include the anti-communist witch hunts of the HUAC hearings, the surveillance activities of the COINTELPRO and the CIA, and President Truman's seizure of the nation's steel mills during the Korean conflict in the name of national security (see successful constitutional challenge in *Youngstown Sheet and Tube Co. v. Sawyer,* 343 U.S. 579 [1952]).

29. Public Law 831, Ch. 1024, 64 Stat. 987.

30. See *Commission on CIA Activities Within the United States, Report to the President* (1975), cited in Jill Elaine Hasday, "Civil War as Paradigm: Reestablishing the Rule of Law at the End of the Cold War" in 5 *Kansas Journal of Law and Public Policy* 129 (1996), p. 139.

31. The FBI, under J. Edgar Hoover's direction, conducted this operation in the name of combating terrorism. See Curt Gentry, *J. Edgar Hoover: The Man and the Secrets* (New York: Norton, 1991), pp. 412, 442, 682–83.

32. *Hobson v. Wilson,* 737 F2d 1, 10 (D.C. Cir. 1984), cited in Hasday, "Civil War as Paradigm."

33. See Hasday, "Civil War as Paradigm."

34. See Wittes, "Secret Deportation Panel."

35. See Peter H. Schuck, "The Transformation of Immigration Law," *Columbia Law Review* 84 (January 1984): 1–90.

36. The judiciary has long deferred to Congress and the Executive in foreign policy making, calling it a "political question." The Supreme Court has also declared that the power to exclude or deport aliens flows from the inherent power of a sovereign nation to conduct international relations (*Fong Yue Ting,* 149 U.S., at 705–7) and consistently has given Congress and the Executive broad power over immigration as an adjunct of foreign policy.

37. See historian Paul Kennedy where he writes that the United States may be handicapped as a global superpower by its constitutional doctrine of separation of powers because the President is often called on to "make swift decisions vis-à-vis countries which enjoy far fewer constraints." See *The Rise and Fall of the Great Powers* (New York: Random House, 1987), pp. 524–25.

38. Public Law 82-414, 66 Stat. 166.

39. The McCarran-Walter Act of 1952 contained twenty categories of deportable aliens, but because of the large numbers of subcategories within each category, there are roughly 700 grounds for deportation. Generally, aliens may be deported for acts committed at, before, or after entry.

40. Public Law 101-649, 104 Stat. 4978 (1990), codified as amended at 8 U.S.C. section 1251(a)(4)(B)(1994), rendering deportable any "alien who has engaged, is engaged, or at any time after entry engages in terrorist activity."

41. Technical violation charges regarding visas were brought against the six defendants who were temporary residents. Two defendants were granted permanent resident status after the lawsuit began and were not deportable for visa status violations. The INS charged them with the anti-terrorism provision of the Immigration Act of 1990, which allows deportation of permanent residents if it is proven that they advocate terrorism (e.g., killing or injuring government officials, destruction of property). None of the eight defendants were charged with violence but were charged with fund raising and distribution of PFLP literature.

42. Linda S. Bosniak, "Membership, Equality, and the Difference that Alienage Makes," *New York University Law Review* 69 (December 1994): 1047–1149.

43. Bosniak, *New York University Law Review* 69 (December 1994): 1054.

44. 403 U.S. 365, 372 (1971).

45. *Cleburne v. Cleburne Living Center, Inc.*, 473 U.S. 432, 453, n. 6 (1985).

46. For example, *Plyler v. Doe*, 462 U.S. 725 (1983); the Court invalidated on equal protection grounds a Texas state law that withheld funds from school districts for the public education of children who were illegal aliens. See also Bosniak, "Membership, Equality and the Difference."

47. For instance, see *Johnson v. Eisentrager*, 339 U.S. 763, 769 (1950), in which the Court held that there are "inherent distinctions recognized throughout the civilized world between citizens and aliens."

48. *Johnson v. Eisentrager*, 339 U.S. 770 (1950).

49. Bosniak, "Membership, Equality and the Difference," citing *Cabell v. Chavez-Salido*, 454 U.S. 432, 439–40 (1982).

50. For instance see Gerald Seib, "Terrorism Fear Running Deep, U.S. Poll Says," *Wall Street Journal* (27 April 1995): A4. The author says a poll taken after the Oklahoma City bombing indicates that 6 of 10 Americans fear that terrorists will carry out acts of violence in the United States. This is an increase from the 48 percent of Americans who felt very concerned about a terrorist attack in the aftermath of the World Trade Center bombing.

51. Jonathan Alter, "Jumping to Conclusions," *Newsweek* (1 May 1995): 55.

52. Clinton "prodded Congress to act swiftly on the [Comprehensive Terrorism Prevention] bill: 'We must not dawdle or delay; Congress must act, and act promptly.'" *Congressional Quarterly* (11 May 1995): 1180.

53. See remarks of Senators Hatch, Dole, Specter, Lieberman, and Daschle, 141 *Congressional Record* S7585, S7596, S7599, S7608 (May 26, 1995). See also the comments of Senator Dianne Feinstein: "I'm going to vote for everything [in the bill] because I think we need to take an unparalleled step in our society to put an end to this." See *Congressional Quarterly* (11 May 1995): 1180.

54. See *Legal Times* (17 July 1995): 1, in which Hatch is quoted as saying, "We'd be better bringing [the bill] up next year . . . where we have some time to really consider it."

55. 104th Cong., 2d sess., 142 *Congressional Record* S94-0-9480, S9482 (2 August 1996).

56. 104th Cong., 2d sess., 142 *Congressional Record* S94-0-9480, S9482 (2 August 1996).

57. 104th Cong., 2d sess., 142 *Congressional Record* S94-0-9480, S9482 (2 August 1996).

58. *ADC v. Reno,* supra note 13, at p. 1056.

59. *ADC v. Reno,* p. 1064.

60. *ADC v. Reno,* p. 1065.

61. *ADC v. Reno,* p. 1064.

62. See comments of Justice Department official, Nicholas Gess, cited in Wittes, "Secret Deportation Panel."

63. "Terrorism: The Problem and Solution—The Comprehensive Terrorism Prevention Act of 1995," by Melissa A. O'Loughlin, *Journal of Legislation* 22 (1996): 110.

64. The L.A. 8 argued that the charges were filed against them in retaliation for their association with the PFLP and demonstrated to the lower court that the INS had not brought similar deportation proceedings against other alleged terrorist groups whose views the government might favor.

65. This case was filed as *Janet Reno, Attorney General, et al., Petitioners, v. American Arab Anti-Discrimination Committee, et al., Respondents* (No. 97-1252).

66. *Reno v. ADC,* 1999 U.S. LEXIS 1514, p. 32.

Mohamed Mattar

6   Legal Perspectives on Arabs and Muslims in U.S. Courts

An estimated five to eight million Muslims live in the United States. This chapter is devoted to a discussion of cases in which Islamic law issues have been debated in American courts. The number of these cases has grown with the increase in commercial relations between the United States and other states in which Islam plays a role in shaping their legal systems. The increased number of disputes involving Islamic law in the United States also reflects the rising number of immigrants from the Arab world and other predominantly Muslim countries, as well as the relatively large numbers of Muslim African Americans. The chapter focuses on religious discrimination in prison and in the work place and on issues related to marriage, divorce, and child custody.

Ethnic and Religious Discrimination

In *Michigan v. Saad Bahoda,*[1] prosecutorial misconduct was an issue, and the court had to decide whether use of a reference to the terms "Arab," "Arab connection," and "Iraqi" at a trial conducted during the Persian Gulf War had deprived defendant of a fair trial. The rule is that injection of racial or ethnic remarks into any trial may arouse the bias of jurors against defendant and lead to a decision based on prejudice rather than on the guilt or innocence of the accused. American courts are open to aliens and citizens alike, and any attempt that arouses prejudice of jurors to curtail this right is a departure from the proper privilege of counsel and, when carried to the extent indicated by the language quoted, is sufficient to justify reversal of the case.

In the case under review, references were made by the prosecution to the defendant's Arab ethnicity during the opening statement and during the questioning of prosecution witnesses. Moreover, in his closing argument, the prosecutor stated, "this man comes from the Middle East, and he's not content to make his money from the gas station. He needs more; he gets into the cocaine, nontaxable income lifestyle." When the defendant was indicted by a grand jury for conspiracy to possess with intent to deliver cocaine, he appealed his conviction, claiming that he was denied a fair trial. The Court of Appeals held that all references to the defendant's Middle East background and Arab ethnicity were improper, especially because the trial occurred during the Gulf War. The Supreme Court of Michigan disagreed and concluded that the statements were not intended to inflame the jury and not of a degree that prejudiced the defendant's right to a fair trial. The Court added, "Simply because these references occurred during the Persian Gulf War does not mean that reversal is required. It must be remembered that we were fighting with, as well as against, those of Arabic heritage during the Persian Gulf War. Hence, prejudice by use of Arabic ethnicity does not automatically follow."

In *O'Lone v. Estate of Shabazz*,[2] the U.S. Supreme Court held that the prison regulations that prevented Muslim inmates from attending Jum'ah services did not violate the inmates' right to free exercise of religion. The inmates concerned were low-security prisoners who were assigned to outside work details. Because permitting the inmates to attend Jum'ah services proved to be burdensome and posed something of a security risk, prison officials issued a policy memorandum that prohibited inmates assigned to outside work details from returning to the prison during the day except for emergency reasons. The U.S. Supreme Court, balancing the constitutional rights of prisoners against the legitimate objectives of incarceration, stated that the prison regulations alleged to infringe constitutional rights are judged under a reasonableness test less restrictive than that ordinarily applied to alleged infringements of fundamental constitutional rights. It concluded that the policy directive, as implemented, was neither arbitrary nor irrational and that it did not violate the plaintiffs' constitutional rights.

In another case, *Cleophus Khalid Abdur-Ra'oof and Abdul-jail Danfodio v. Department of Corrections*,[3] the issue was whether the Department of Corrections' policy, which denied Muslim prisoners the right to attend Friday afternoon Jum'ah prayer services and the congregational services of Eid-al-Fitr and Eid-al-Adha, impermissibly infringed on their constitutional rights under the free exercise clause of the first amendment of the U.S. Constitution. The policy directive provided in part that "[b]eyond the state observed holidays institutions shall not make provisions for the observance of religious holidays. Because the working day in institutions is intended to approximate that of the work world outside prison, released time from work assignments for personal interest activities including religious services or other activities will not be permitted." The Circuit Court found that the policy directive as implemented was arbitrary and irrational and ordered the Department of Corrections not to enforce it in such a way as to prevent attendance at the services.

In *Muhammad Rasheed v. Chrysler Motor Corporation*,[4] the claim involved discriminatory termination of employment brought under the Michigan Civil Rights Act. To successfully bring a religious discrimination claim under the Michigan Civil Rights Act, a plaintiff must make a prima facie showing of religious discrimination by demonstrating disparate treatment or intentional discrimination. To establish disparate treatment, the plaintiff must show that he was a member of a protected class and that he was treated differently from persons of a different class for the same or similar conduct. The employer then has the burden of establishing a legitimate reason for the treatment, which the Chrysler Motor Corporation failed to do in this case.

The plaintiff had been employed by the defendant, Chrysler Motors Corporation, since 1967. In 1978, he became a member of the American Muslim Mission. In 1981, he transferred from Chrysler's Hugo Foundry plant to its Trenton plant. After that, the plaintiff asserted he was subjected to daily harassment relating to his religious beliefs from coworkers and his supervisor. His supervisor informed him of his dislike for those who adhere to the plaintiff's religion, and he often participated in or encouraged the religious harassment. Guards at the plant allegedly attempted to stop the plaintiff from taking an Islamic newspaper into the facility because it was "subversive." He was called "Ayatollah cockamania," and numerous remarks were made about how Muslims should stay in Detroit. Pork was put near his work station during the holy month of Ramadan. His supervisor told a coworker to give him some "American food."

Shortly before being discharged, the plaintiff was subjected to several disciplinary actions. One involved his attempt to participate in the fast of Ramadan. During this holy month, Muslims are required to fast from sunrise to sunset. The plaintiff could not break his fast during his regularly scheduled dinner period (8 P.M. until 8:30 P.M.). Although his supervisor would not accommodate his need to take a later dinner break, the plaintiff was able, when his supervisor went on vacation, to make arrangements with the substitute supervisor to take a later break. When his supervisor returned, he revoked this privilege and suspended the plaintiff for one day for abuse of dinner privileges. The plaintiff prevailed in his action of religious discrimination, and the jury awarded him damages in the amount of $61,300.

Application of Islamic Law in American Courts

A typical dispute involving a debate of an Islamic law issue may arise in two different sets of cases. First, Islamic law may be applied as foreign law in accordance with the rules of conflict of law. Second, Islamic law issues may be addressed and decided by an American judge before the rules of American law may be applied. In these cases, the application of American law requires the judge to interpret issues of Islamic law.

Although different types of problems are addressed in these two types of cases, the application of Islamic law in American courts poses common difficulties resulting mainly from the religious nature of Islamic law (i.e., the fusion of law and religion in Islamic law) and the absence of a contemporary Islamic legal system.

First, unlike the American legal system, which is secular, Islamic law is of a religious nature. Islam is a religion and a social order. As such, it comprises devotional obligations and rules regulating the relations among individuals, and these two types of rules are sometimes inseparable. In the civil legal terminology, civil law is defined as a collection of rules of social conduct, enacted by a competent authority and accompanied by sanction. Legislation, promulgated by an official law-making body, is the main source of law in a civil law system. In the common law system, law is mainly the product of court decisions. In contrast, Islamic law is of divine origin. Its very source is the Qur'an, a creation of God, the ultimate authority, and an expression of His will.

The fusion of law and religion is reflected in the structure of the Islamic legal system in several ways. The scope of the law in Islam is more expansive than that of the positive laws of various legal systems. In an incomparable theory of liability, Islamic law does not merely categorize human acts in terms of what is lawful and unlawful, as in other legal systems. In Islamic legal theory, acts may be classified in different circumstances as mandatory, permissible, recommended, reprehensible, or forbidden. Islam enumerates various legal injunctions in the different aspects of law such as marriage, divorce, wills, inheritance, contracts, torts, property, crimes, and punishment. Because the basic religious premise underlies all these areas, understanding one specific issue in a particular subject requires an examination of other branches of the law. For example, rules of interference with contract and inducement of breach by a third party are best illustrated in the rules of marriage in Islamic law. In another example, the theory of abuse of rights is explained in the area of wills and inheritance. Whereas a study in the common law or the civil law systems presents common social, economic, and political problems that are comparable to the American system, Islamic law has its distinct language, vocabulary, norms, and concepts that are totally different from Western laws.

The second reason for the difficulties of applying Islamic law in American courts is the absence of a contemporary Islamic legal system. An American judge dealing with common law or civil law systems finds no difficulty in applying various rules of foreign legal systems that are part of these two systems of the legal family. The English law, for instance, presents the common law system, and the German law and the Italian law are two examples of the application of the civil law system. What is the legal system that applies Islamic law and exclusively presents its rules and structures in their entirety? The Shari'a law, in its purist doctrine, as a legal system, is comprehensive, exclusive, and immutable.[5] Shari'a law, however, is no longer the comprehensive, exclusive, or immutable system in any of the legal systems of the Muslim world today. Although Islamic law once had great influence on the legal systems of the Arab countries of the Middle East, many of the traditional rules of Islamic law have been replaced by rules derived from the European legal systems. During the last century, the codification movement predominantly rested on the secular Western model of law, not the religious texts of Islamic law. In the field of private law, a Muslim code of obligations, called the *Majallat-al-ahkam-al adliyah*, was enacted in 1877 in the Ottoman Empire, but it was later abandoned in favor of the Western-style codes. Even the family laws of marriage and divorce were amended and modified in the name of reform. Shari'a courts were abolished and replaced by secular courts, and in the process, these codes became the primary source of law, while the Qur'an and the Sunnah were relegated to the status of historical and remote sources of law.

Even Saudi Arabia, which remains faithful to the Islamic principles, has not fully implemented Islamic law in the legislative enactments of the kingdom. Faced with the rapid growth of commercial activities and the oil industry in the mid-1950s, the Saudi legal system had to enact various regulations. The Saudi approach to legal reform, however, was piecemeal. In an attempt to fill in the legislative gap, the Saudi legislator supplemented the existing Shari'a law with decree regulations and statutes. Instead of searching for substitute Islamic rules and revising the Islamic jurisprudence with its distinct concepts and terminology, the Saudi legislator incorporated Western-style codes. Although the Saudi legislative enactments did not contradict the established principles of Islamic law, Islamic law was not the guiding force for these legislative enactments. The Saudi legislator was satisfied with incorporating Western-style law and insisting on a few Islamic-law rules whenever it was felt there was a need to protect an Islamic value or to include an Islamic prohibition.

A few examples can illustrate this approach. Although the Saudi labor law was totally based on the Egyptian labor law, an additional principle was embodied in article 160 that provided that "in no case should men and women commingle in the place of work or in the accessory facilities or other appurtenances thereto." The Commercial Paper Regulation incorporated the Geneva Uniform law of bills of Exchange of 1930 and of Checks (1931), but it omitted the provisions dealing with interest, a practice that is prohibited under Islamic law. Furthermore, the Statute of Registration of Trademarks was careful to rule out registration of a trademark that contradicts morality or undermines Islamic decency or religious practices. The Copyright Act of 1990, to conform with the Shari'a notion of *bia-al-jahala,* limited the scope of copyright protection to works that have already been realized. Under the law, an author cannot claim copyright protection for "prospective intellectual production."

Although Shari'a courts in Saudi Arabia constitute the judicial body that has general jurisdiction over all civil, criminal, and domestic relations cases, various quasi-judicial bodies or decree judiciaries were created to decide various private disputes. Members of these bodies are not all judges, although they render judicial judgments. The Shari'a courts' jurisdiction under the present Saudi judicial system does not include commercial cases. Even in criminal cases, only *hudud* cases are within its jurisdiction. The Board of Grievances is the judicial authority empowered to decide cases of crimes such as forgery and bribery.

The adequacy of quasi-judicial forums in Saudi Arabia was addressed by an American court in *Jeha v. Arabian American Oil Co.* (ARAMCO),[6] in which a non-Saudi employee's wife was treated in Saudi Arabia by doctors employed by ARAMCO who failed to properly diagnose cancer in her breast. Applying the forum non conveniens rule, which states that courts should decline to hear cases that are more adequately decided by tribunals of another country, the court ruled that the plaintiff had an adequate judicial forum in the Saudi Arabian legal system. The court was convinced that Saudi law recognizes a cause of action for medical malpractice and that such claims are handled by a quasi-judicial special commission called the Legal Medical Commission, the decisions of which are appealed to the Board of Grievances.

Even when Islamic law principles are applied to commercial activities and business transactions, they cause much debate and are sometimes the source of great confusion. For instance, the United Arab Emirates' Civil Code of 1985 addressed interest agreements in Article 714. The Article outlawed such arrangements by stating that "if the contract of loan provides for a benefit in excess of the essence of the contract otherwise than a guarantee of the rights of the lender, such provision shall be void but the contract shall be valid." The banking community was troubled by this rule, and the legislator, in an attempt to resolve obvious uncertainty in commercial transactions, enacted Law No. 1 of 1987 to amend article 1 of the Civil Code. The new law limited the application of the Code to civil, not commercial, transactions. It reads: "The text of Article 1 of the Federal Law No 5 of 1985 ... is hereby replaced by the following text: the attached law shall apply in respect to civil transactions in the state of the United Arab Emirates, but commercial transactions shall continue to be governed by the laws and regulations in force in that regard until the Federal Commercial Code is enacted." Similarly, United Arab Emirates courts, confronted with the adaptation of the Islamic rules to the modern world of trade and business, held in the context of prohibition of interest that "this court has been consistent in holding that banking law, in its present structure, which is related to the world banking laws, is an economic necessity. Consequently, although interest is prohibited as a general rule in Islamic law, it may be permissible as an exception to further a public policy of the state. Such interpretation must prevail until an alternative is adopted. It does not contradict Islamic law, and a contracting party may not avoid payment of the interest on the ground that it is prohibited under Islamic law."

Basic Premises in the Application of Islamic Law in American Courts

A few basic premises guide the application of a foreign law in American courts. First, foreign law is considered, under the modern rule, as a question of law, not a question of fact. According to the Federal Rules of Civil Procedure, Rule 44.1, courts are allowed to take judicial notice of foreign law. Any form of reasonable notice to the court is sufficient to raise foreign law questions. Second, courts usually rely on the stipulations of the parties, as introduced by expert witnesses on the rules of the foreign law. Under the federal rules of Civil Procedure, courts may consider any relevant materials or sources of foreign law, whether or not submitted by the party. Third, under the common law doctrine of forum non conveniens, a court may dismiss an action, even though it has jurisdiction and venue is proper if, in its discretion, it determines that justice and convenience warrant dismissal. The court must decide whether an "adequate" alternative forum exists that possesses jurisdiction over the case (i.e., whether the plaintiff will be deprived of any remedy or otherwise treated unfairly). The following are examples of the applications of these rules and procedures to cases involving Islamic family law.

Islamic law marriages have been recognized by American courts. In *Ohio v. Phelps,*[7] the state appealed the trial court ruling that a common law marriage existed between defendants. The state contended that the trial court's ruling destroys its murder case against the defendant (the husband) by preventing the state from compelling his wife to testify against him under the espousal privilege doctrine. The defendants were indicted for aggravated murder. The state made clear its intention to introduce numerous statements made by the wife that directly implicated the husband in the murder.

Although common law marriages were prohibited in Ohio by statutory amendment after 10 October 1991, common law marriages that occurred before that date continued to be recognized. Three conditions had to be met: an agreement of marriage, cohabitation as husband and wife, and a holding out by the parties to those with whom they normally come into contact, resulting in a reputation as a married couple in the community.

Mr. Phelps testified that he had been married to his wife in the Islamic faith on two occasions. He stated that they were first married in May 1980 before an imam or

Islamic minister. A marriage contract in their Muslim names was registered with the mosque. Witnesses signed the contract. Vows were taken at the ceremony, and they had two children. They lived together and had joint checking and savings accounts. Their mail was received at a common address. The two were formally divorced on 9 September 1988. Mr. Phelps testified that, 23 January 1991, they were married again. Another Islamic certificate was filed, and the same steps were taken as after the first marriage. The defendants were remarried, and the ceremony was conducted in a manner consistent with Islamic tradition. The marriage certificate in question displayed the signatures from witnesses at the ceremony. The imam who conducted the ceremony signed the certificate. It was a formalized ceremony designed as a right to hold couples out in the community as being married. There was no evidence that the two did not intend to stay married. The Court of Appeals affirmed the trial court's holding.

American courts have also recognized the enforceability of the mahr (dowry) agreement between Moslem couples. In *Shaukat Aziz v. Patina Aziz,*[8] the plaintiff (husband) and defendant (wife) were married against a mahr under Islamic law, which called for a $32 prompt payment by the plaintiff at the time of the marriage and a $5,000 deferred payment, to which defendant is entitled in case of divorce. The plaintiff contended that the mahr is a religious document and therefore not enforceable as a contract. The court upheld the agreement, stating that the mahr conformed to the requirements of the General Obligations Law 5-701 (a) (3), and its secular terms, which called for payment of $5,000, are enforceable as a contractual obligation, notwithstanding that the mahr was entered into as part of a religious ceremony.

The courts have also upheld the nonexistence of the concept of community property in Islamic law as applied in various Middle East countries. In *Nationwide Resources Corp v. Massabni,*[9] both parties were Christians from Syria. They moved to Lebanon, Morocco, and in 1978, the United States. The husband started a series of businesses and invested in various projects. Although the presumption in American law is that all property acquired by either spouse during marriage is community property, the Syrian and Lebanese laws state otherwise. According to article 39 of the law of personal status for the Catholic communities (Syrians and Lebanese), spouses may each keep ownership of movable and immovable properties. The article in *Majmu'at al-Qawanin al-Lubnaniyah* states that "[a] married couple may each keep ownership of movable and immovable properties and the right to manage them, to benefit from them, and keep the proceeds of such worth unless they have agreed in writing to the contrary." The court therefore said it is obvious that the concept of community property as a result of marriage does not exist in Syria.

Immovable property, including property of a married woman, must be registered in the Real Estate Register. The law also requires that any document that may establish any right to a property must be recorded. Consequently, any community property must be designated as such by either one of the spouses at the time of purchasing any real property and by registering the other party as co-owner. Without such registration, neither the wife nor the husband has a claim against the other. The court concluded that the wife in a Syrian Catholic marriage does not share her husband's properties, nor does she have an ownership interest in her husband's earnings unless he has specially registered part of his property to her in the public record. There was no evidence that the husband did so. The investment was his separate property unless it was transmuted to community property by agreement, gift, or commingling. None of these instruments were proven.

However, American courts have denied the enforceability of Islamic family law in various contexts on the basis that its rules contradict public policy. While holding that the dowry agreement that was entered into according to Jordanian law[10] was enforceable, the court said "prenuptial agreements which facilitate divorce or separation by providing for a settlement only in the event of such an occurrence are void against public policy." In another case,[11] the court stated that, "based on the testimony of wife two's expert, the trial court could have found that Islamic law simply allows a non-Muslim to convert to Islam by pronouncing a short phrase, and then divorce his wife through the ex parte procedure of *talak* (divorce). The harshness of such an action to the non-Muslim divorced wife runs so counter to our notions of good morals and natural justice that we hold that the Islamic law in this situation need not be applied."

Child custody law in the United States and the Islamic legal system differ widely. Under Islamic law, a divorced or widowed mother has custody of her children for a period of time. In Saudi Arabia, which adopts the Hanbali branch of Islamic law, a divorced mother has the right to custody of her son until he reaches seven years of age. The father then takes custody of the boy. The mother also has the right to custody of her daughter until she reaches nine years of age or puberty, whichever comes first. The mother, however, may lose custody by marrying a man related to the child within a certain degree, if she becomes physically or morally unfit, or if she renounces Islam.

The law of the United States in the area of child custody is not based on a sex-based presumption of fitness. It instead adopts a balancing test to determine the best interest of the child and modifies the traditional common law rule or the "tender years" doctrine prevalent in the early twentieth century. Gender-based presumption has been replaced by the best interest of the child analysis. Whereas the first approach focuses on the rights of the parents, the second is concerned with the needs of the child, and the court takes into consideration a variety of factors that determine the totality of the child's situation.

A U.S. court applies the Islamic law of child custody only when it serves the child's best interests. In *Abdul-Rahman Omar Adra v. Clift*,[12] the court applied American law to a child custody case, although all the concerned parties were Muslims. In this case, the father tried to regain custody of his daughter when she reached the age of nine in accordance with the Lebanese law. The mother fled to the United States with her daughter. The father brought a lawsuit. The court recognized that Lebanese law entitled the father to custody of his daughter. The court, however, applied the American law and reached the conclusion that the daughter had to stay with her mother. The court took into consideration the fact that they were living in the United States although they were following the Islamic faith.

The same approach was adopted by the court in *Ali v. Ali*[13], in which the plaintiff (wife) was born in New Jersey and was an American citizen. The defendant (husband) was a Palestinian national. They were married in 1983 in Gaza in a Muslim ceremony and had a son, Nader. The married couple lived together in Gaza between 1986 and 1991. In June 1991, after the outbreak of the Gulf War, the plaintiff and her son returned to New Jersey to be with the husband and father. On 28 July 1993, the defendant obtained a divorce form the Shari'a court in Gaza that granted him custody of Nader.

The defendant asserted that he was entitled to the custody of his son based on the Shari'a court's decree and based on the doctrine of comity under which an American court should recognize a judgment of a foreign court subject to two conditions. These are that the foreign court had the jurisdiction of the subject matter and that the foreign judgment will not offend the public policy of the American state. In such cases, notice must be sent to all affected persons, and the party asserting the foreign judgment must file a certified copy of the custody decree with court clerk so that it may be enforced. In this case, the defendant failed to file a certified copy of the Shari'a court's order that he sought to enforce, and the wife was never personally served with the ex parte order. Moreover, the defendant did not provide a copy of the Shari'a decree awarding him custody. The American court had no knowledge of whether the Shari'a court made specific findings about what was in the son's "best interest."

The defendant submitted proof in support of his request for comity, which indicated that, under Muslim law, a father is automatically entitled to custody when a boy is seven (art. 391 of Islamic Shari'a law), and the mother can apply to prolong custody until the boy is nine (art. 118 of the law of family rights). There is no question, however, that under Shari'a law, the father or the paternal grandfather is irrefutably entitled to custody. The court said "such presumptions in law cannot be said by any stretch of imagination to comport with the law of New Jersey whereby custody determinations are made based on the 'best interests' of the child and not some mechanical formula." According to New Jersey law (9-2-4), "in any proceeding involving the custody of a minor child, the rights of both parents shall be equal." The court further stated,

> There is no mechanical presumption that either the father or the mother is entitled to custody at a fixed age. The defendant seeks to have this court place its imprimatur on a decree that is diametrically opposed to the law of New Jersey and which is repugnant to all case law concerning factors to be considered in making a custody determination. Thus, for the foregoing reasons, the Shari'a court custody decree cannot be enforced or recognized by the New Jersey courts under the doctrine of comity ... this court cannot sanction the Islamic law imposed by the Shari'a court. Shari'a law in regard to custody determinations offends the public policy of New Jersey ... the law of the Shari'a court is undeniably arbitrary and capricious and cannot be sanctioned by this court, which uses the "best interests of the child" as the overriding concern.

In *Al-Silham v. Al-Silham*,[14] a Saudi Arabian, while residing in the United States for pursuing a master's degree in Industrial Safety, married Lori (a Christian) and had Layla, a daughter, on 26 August 1990. On 7 September 1991, they separated, and on 28 April 1992, they divorced. At trial, the court considered the reasons for the breakup of the marriage to determine which parent would be better suited to be designated as custodial parent. The court found that, after marriage, the parties experienced a serious clash. The appellant, because of his Islamic faith, considered that the appellee (wife) was to provide services to the family and was not to have outside relationships or an active voice in family affairs. He became physically and verbally abusive to the appellee and was dictatorial, controlling, and jealous of the appellee's family and friends.

The court concluded that the appellant's motion for shared parenting was not in the best interests of the child, because it found that the parties had not demonstrated an ability to cooperate or to make decisions jointly and that the appellant had attempted to assert his authority in disregard of the appellee's rights. The court also stated its concern about the potential for kidnaping by the appellant, the dramatic cultural differences between the Muslim religion and Christian religion, and the lack of a legal process to secure the return of a minor child once he or she is removed to Saudi Arabia. The court granted reasonable visitation rights to the appellant, although under the supervision of the appellee or an adult approved by appellee. The court concluded: "We do not find that the trial court denied appellant his constitutional rights under the equal protection clause of the U.S. Constitution or the Ohio constitution."

Conclusions

This chapter addressed a variety of issues that result from the interaction of different cultures and religions as they are practiced by citizens and immigrants to the United States. These include ethnicity and race, religious discrimination in prison and the workplace, and most importantly perhaps, the determination about whether Islamic law is admissible in American courts.

Although this is only a preliminary survey of an emerging area, some tentative conclusions may be stated. For instance, use of ethnic or racial references is permitted as long as such references do not jeopardize the right to a fair trial. Freedom of prisoners to exercise their religion may be limited so long as prison policies and practices are not deemed arbitrary or irrational. In the workplace, intentional discrimination and harassment are clearly unconstitutional. In the application of foreign law and more specifically of Islamic law in American courts, certain principles guide judicial decisions. Cases more conveniently decided by tribunals of the foreign country should be declined. Islamic law in the matter of marriage and dowry is recognized by American courts. However, where Islamic law contradicts public policy, it is deemed inapplicable. The discussion of these cases clearly shows that the differences in culture, practices, and religious beliefs between Muslims and non-Muslims must be appreciated and recognized in the application of Islamic law in American courts.

Notes

1. 448 Mich. 261, 531 N.W. 659 (1995).
2. 482 U.S. 342, 107 Sup. Ct. 2400 (1987).
3. 208 Mich. App. 626, 528 N.W. 2d 840 (1995).
4. 196 Mich. App. 196, 493 N.W. 2d 102 (1992).
5. See N. J. Coulson, "Law and Religion in Contemporary Islam," *Hastings Law Journal* 29, no.6 (1978): 1447–57.

6. 741 F. Sup. 122 (SD Tex 1990).
7. 100 Ohio App. 3d 187, 652 N.E. 2d 1032 (1995).
8. 127 Misc. 2d 1013, 488 N.Y.S. 2d 123 (1985).
9. 143 Ariz. 460, 694 P. 2d 290 (1984).
10. *In Re Marriage of Dajami,* 25 Cal. Rptr. 871 (Cal. App. 4 Dist., 1988).
11. *Seth v. Seth,* 694 S.W. 2d 459 (Tex. Civ. App. 2 Dist. 1985).
12. 195 F. Sup. Ct. 857 (D. Md. 1961).
13. 279 N.J. Sup. Ct. 154 (1994).
14. Case No. 93-A-1770 (Ohio App. 1994).

Part III

Youth and the Family

Sharon McIrvin Abu-Laban
and Baha Abu-Laban

7 Teens Between: The Public and Private Spheres of Arab-Canadian Adolescents

Adolescence, to paraphrase Charles Dickens, may be the best of times and the worst of times. The angst of the young is documented in literature, film, social science research, and hand-wringing conversations between middle-aged adults. In adolescence, biological changes are omnipresent as the body alters, sometimes dramatically, along the journey from childhood to adulthood. It is during adolescence and the young adult years that families often exert considerable pressure to retain the earlier compliance of childhood and mold (or hammer) the young person into making appropriate choices. The crush of necessary decisions in pre-adulthood, involving such issues as dating, marriage, education, and occupation, have critical implications for adult opportunities, life trajectories, and the vested interests of the larger family unit. At the same time, to be a member of the youth generation—to be a teenager, adolescent, or young adult—is often associated with personal concerns about acceptance and sense of place beyond the circle of the family. The concern with age-peers is heightened. Being "different" is not often perceived as a badge of honor by the young.

What then are the experiences of the young in North America who are descendants of recent immigrants? What pressures face second-generation youth whose parents are defined as foreign, newcomers, or outsiders trying to make it to inside? What pressures are faced, particularly by children of the Arab diaspora, whose ethnocultural heritage is often devalued by the larger society?[1] How do youth of Arab descent perceive, address, submit to, or resist the assemblage of cross-cutting pressures from immigrant parents, age peers, and a largely majoritarian school system? How do these young negotiate their youth, their growing-up, their movement from child to adult, from the family of their childhood to the family of their adult creation in a climate where their parents are less culturally knowledgeable, where they and their parents may share a devalued ethnicity, and where the expectations of their family may seem very different from the expectations that govern their friends and classmates?

This chapter describes the result of a study that is part of a larger research project on youth and family dynamics. It focuses on a group of early and late adolescents and young adults of Arab-Canadian descent. Collectively, these young people experience the afflictions and annoyances of adolescence in the North American context but with degrees of difference. They have parents who experienced their own youth in countries in the Arab Middle East. Canadians of Arab descent are officially members of a "visible minority," a designation used in federal policy pronouncements and legislation to buttress programs aimed at promoting equity and multiculturalism. Visible minorities are defined as "nonwhite" or "non-Caucasian." There is a variation in the way or extent to which these Arab-Canadian youth are recognizable as being visible, officially or unofficially.[2] However, in Canada, at the third millennium, being of Arab descent is a form of "stigma" as the term is used by Erving Goffman.[3] It is an attribute that may be hidden, but if revealed in the right (or wrong) time or place, it has the potential to be deeply discrediting.[4]

This analysis examines the perceived consistencies and inconsistencies across two major areas in the lives of these Arab-Canadian youth: the sphere of family and home and the sphere of school and community. It raises questions concerning the degree of fit between these spheres, the areas of overlap, the points of opposition, and the significance of gender differences.

The analysis that follows begins by situating these Arab-Canadian youth in the larger sociohistorical context of the Arab-Canadian immigration experience and contrasting this with the current demographic characteristics of the community and the characteristics of the young informants in this study. The chapter next examines two major influences on the lives of youth in the Arab diaspora, the more private world of parents and kin in contrast to the more public world of school and age peers. It queries the extent to which and ways in which these influences affect the North American adaptation of teens from immigrant families and specifically the ways in which gender plays an important role in shaping the adaptive encounter.

The Community in Sociohistorical Context

Immigration to Canada from countries of the Arab Near East began late in the last century. Historically, Arab immigrants have experienced an ebb and flow in Canada's receptivity to them. Around the turn of the century, there were fears that these Arab-origin immigrants, along with immigrants from Asia and Eastern and Southern Europe, would negatively affect Canada's Anglo-Saxon heritage and white European master project. Consequently, Arab immigrants faced serious barriers to their admission, were characterized harshly by ranking officials of the time, and were viewed as difficult to assimilate into the Canadian ideal.[5]

In the post–World War II period, Canada's immigration policy was liberalized, and many barriers against the admission of so-called undesirable immigrants were removed, particularly after 1967. In consequence, by census day 1991, there were 151,125 Canadians who claimed Arab single origin and an additional 52,820 who claimed Arab multiple origins (e.g., Arab and Italian, Arab and Ukrainian), for a total of 203,945 of

Arab descent throughout the country.[6] Given the large influx of Arab immigrants and refugees since the 1991 Canadian census, it is estimated that by 1996, there were about 300,000 people of Arab origin (single and multiple) in Canada. Of the total Arab-origin population, about 75 percent are foreign born (i.e., born outside Canada), reflecting the predominance of immigrants in this ethnocultural group. Lebanese, at about 49 percent of the total, constitute the largest Arab-origin group, followed by Egyptians (13 percent), Maghrebis (6 percent), Syrians and Somalis (5 percent each), Palestinians (3 percent), and Iraqis (2 percent). The remaining 17 percent are recorded in the census as "Arab" with no reference to the country from which they came. Almost six of ten are Christian (Catholic, 29 percent; Eastern Orthodox, 20 percent; and Protestant, 9 percent); and four of ten are Muslim.

Eighty-five percent of Arab-origin Canadians are residents of Ontario and Quebec (about equally divided between these two provinces); about one in ten live in Alberta (mainly in Edmonton and Calgary); and the balance are to be found in British Columbia and the maritime provinces. Occupationally and educationally, Arab-origin Canadians are fairly well placed in Canadian society. In a ranking of groups designated as "visible minorities" in managerial and professional occupations in Canada in 1991, West Asian and Arab Canadians tied with Korean Canadians as having the second largest proportional representation (27 percent) in these occupational categories.[7] (Japanese-origin Canadians rank highest with 36 percent, according to age-standardized data in 1991). In a ranking of the yearly average incomes of visible minorities, Statistics Canada (1989) notes that Arab origin men ranked second highest of fifteen visible minority ethnocultural groups earning an average of Cn. $24,172 in 1986. In contrast, in a similar ranking of "visible minority" females from the same fifteen categories, Arab women ranked eighth in terms of their average yearly income ($12,086). At a collective level, Arab Canadians have a large number of religious institutions and secular organizations that help them to maintain their linguistic and cultural heritage. Nevertheless, the Canadian-born generations have moved further along the continuum of acculturation and assimilation than the immigrant (parental) generations.[8]

A Sociohistorical Effect: Situational Vulnerability and Compromised Identity

Although statistical evidence suggests that the economic integration of Arab Canadians is progressing, Arab Canadians do not fare as well at the level of popular imagery and perceptions. In a 1977 national survey of Canadian attitudes, for instance, Arab Canadians were ranked near the bottom by the numerically dominant Anglo and French populations.[9] In a list of 27 ethnic groups, Arab Canadians were ranked 24 by Anglo-Canadian respondents and 23 by French-Canadian respondents. At least at the survey level, majority Canadians do not feel close, socially or attitudinally, to Canadians of Arab heritage. In some ways the hostile attitudes of the early twentieth century appear to fester, awaiting an opportunity to erupt. To the extent that this is the case, being Arab Canadian is a *compromised identity*.

Research evidence indicates that Arab Canadians (like Arab Americans) have been and continue to be victims of prejudice, discrimination, and stereotyping.[10] In certain situations, they become victims of racial violence and physical attacks threatening life,

person, or property, as was the case during the Gulf War. A Canadian journalist documented a number of attacks against Arab and Muslim Canadians during the Gulf
War.[11] In a similar vein, a 1991 study provides a detailed account of how the Canadian
media in general were slanted in their coverage of the war and its Canadian impact and
how Arab and Muslim Canadians were harassed:

> In various parts of the country, people whose last names were similar to that of Saddam
> Hussein were reporting harassment. For some people, even using a credit card or giving their
> name to a delivery person presented the potential for a hostile response. Crank phone calls,
> hostility and anger from neighbors and work associates, vandalization of Arab-Canadian
> businesses, death threats, "Go Home" signs in some areas of immigrant concentration, the
> harassment of children and the verbal abuse of women wearing traditional Muslim attire
> were reported and whispered about.[12]

While recognizing the uniqueness of the Gulf war, in many ways it was an exacerba-
tion of the vulnerability of Arab Canadians to fall-out from the geopolitical realm. The
Oklahoma City bombing, various airplane hijackings, explosions in Israel, and charges
of terrorist plots combined to point to Arab Canadians as suspect. This vulnerability
affects young and old, and compromises their Arab ethnic identity. This may be particularly the case for young people who find themselves between two cultures, with divergent values and divergent institutions that compete for their loyalty and sense of identity. On one side are Canadian cultural values and institutions and, on the other, are the
culture, values, and institutions that the Arab immigrant generation brought with them
to the host society. This in-between position can be a weakness and perhaps a strength.

The Study Group: Youth in Edmonton, Alberta

The study conducted in the fall of 1992 focused on the adaptive experiences of Arab-
Canadian youth, an under-researched segment of the Arab diasporic minority. A non-
probability sample of 62 young people of Arab ancestry residing in Edmonton, Alberta,
was covered in the study. The respondents were identified partly with the help of Arab-
Canadian community members, including teachers and local leaders, and partly with
the help of the respondents themselves by using a snowball technique. Special attention
was given to obtaining a sample, representative in terms of sex, religion, and Arab country of origin. The trained interviewer, a woman of Arab descent, conducted in-depth
interviews lasting one to two hours. The interview schedule covered the respondent's
background; school experience; relationships with teachers; relationships with peers;
relationships with parents; exposure to and attitudes toward the mass media, and ethnic identity.

The respondents were about equally divided between males and females, and six of
ten were born in Canada. Slightly less than one-half of them were of Lebanese descent,
and slightly less than one-half were about equally divided between Palestinian, Iraqi,
and Egyptian descent. About 47 percent of these respondents were between seventeen
and twenty years of age; about 37 percent were sixteen years of age or younger; and
the remaining 16 percent were twenty-one years of age or older. All were unmarried.
Six of ten were Muslim (mostly Sunni, but also Druze and Shi'i), and four of ten were

Christian (including Catholic, Antiochian Orthodox, and Coptic). For 64 percent of these respondents, Arabic was their first language and, for most of the rest, English or both Arabic and English were their first languages. The respondents came from solid middle class backgrounds; more than 80 percent of their fathers and mothers who were gainfully employed were in professional, managerial, business, white collar, or technically skilled occupations. About nine of ten respondents were students at the time of the survey, and about 10 percent had full-time or part-time jobs.

The Community and School Sphere

Typically, school absorbs a massive amount of the time and energy of the young. The school-age peer realm is seen as a major influence on North American youth. In terms of teens' reported adaptation to school, the results of this survey indicate that seven of ten Arab Canadian youth are "happy" or "very happy" at school; two of ten are "moderately happy"; and the balance are "neutral" or "moderately unhappy" (none were "unhappy" or "very unhappy"). When looking at gender differences, although 86 percent of males report themselves in one of the "happy at school categories," only 58 percent of females report so favorably on the school experience. Most Arab-Canadian youth continue to attend school beyond the legislated age of 16.

To assess attitudes toward school, the respondents were asked two relevant questions: "What do you feel is (was) the *most fun* about attending school?" "What do you feel is (was) the *least fun* about attending school?" The answers to the first open-ended question suggest that the greatest pleasure in attending school revolved around being with friends, the presence of nice teachers, meeting new people, and learning. Responses to the second question indicate that the less enjoyable aspects of school revolved around dislike for certain subjects, examinations, homework, waking up early, and coping with negative or racist attitudes of teachers or peers (mentioned by as many as eight respondents).

In response to another open-ended question about things the respondent would like (have liked) to see changed at school, most responses related to quality and attitudes of teachers, issues of crowdedness, course offerings, and similar factors. Three respondents mentioned issues of discrimination and racism against Arab students.

Teachers as Interpreters of Ethnicity

The respondents' relationships with teachers were assessed by a series of questions that were phrased in the present tense for those who were going to school and in the past tense for those who were not going to school. In response to a question ("Do [did] you have any favorite teacher[s] at school?"), 70 percent of the respondents indicated that they did have a favorite teacher. The qualities most frequently reported for favorite teachers included good teaching and communication skills, sense of humor, ability to relate to students, patience and helpfulness, friendliness, and interest in what they teach.

On the opposite side, respondents were asked, "Are (were) there any teachers that you don't (didn't) like or feel comfortable around?" Forty-eight percent of the respondents answered in the affirmative. The qualities most frequently reported for the least favored teachers were failings such as poor teaching skills, bad attitude, strictness, arrogance or racism, picking on students, and playing favorites.

With specific reference to ethnic origin, the respondents were asked the following question: "Has it ever happened that a teacher commented (positively or negatively) on your ethnic origin or behaved toward you in a certain way because of your Arab origin?" The respondents were asked to describe these situations and give positive or negative comments, as appropriate. Of the fifty-eight who responded to the question, exactly 50 percent answered the question in the affirmative. Positive examples (nineteen) outweighed the negative (eleven) by almost two to one. The positive and negative comments given were interesting:

Positive Comments

They mentioned how beautiful Lebanon was (like Paris), and it is ruined now.

That we Lebanese have a good history and he [teacher] wishes he were Lebanese.

My social studies teacher was interested in the political situation in Lebanon and used to ask me about it. He was objective about it.

They are interested in the Muslim religion and ask me questions about it.

She [teacher] comments on the Egyptian culture, because she thinks that Egypt is interesting.

Comments on my last name that it's interesting.

On the other hand, negative comments from teachers reflect insensitivity and cultural ignorance:

Negative Comments

In elementary [school] I was told that I'm incompetent and that my name sounded like a pig.

One teacher walked in once after I got 80 percent [in a science test] and said, "You know why he got 80 percent? So that he can make bombs and blow up people."

One of my elementary teachers told my mom that I couldn't take part in the communion because she didn't consider me Christian.

One teacher said to me that all Iraqis are stupid.

When I was going to Lebanon, [the teacher] automatically said "oh, you're going to get married."

I would be walking down the hall, and one would say, "Walk like an Egyptian" . . . the song.

Some Lebanese students got into a lot of fights, so teachers became prejudiced towards us all, and thought we like to fight all the time.

During the Gulf War some used to call me Saddam-lover, because I was opposed to them.

Teachers can act as filters for ethnicity. Given that they are usually the primary adult contact outside the home and that they are sanctioned by the larger community to instruct youth, their power is considerable. To the extent that teachers function as the authority center of the school, their pronouncements can take on normative proportions. How they handle the local playout of global upheavals such as the Gulf War is part of the cauldron in which the sense of ethnocultural identity of Arab-Canadian youth is shaped into adult form.

Peers as Interpreters of Ethnicity

The adolescent peer group is acknowledged to exert much influence on North American youth. No less than teachers, age peers act as filters for ethnicity. Given North American teenagers' strong desire for acceptance by peers, ethnic identity is often shaped in relation to the context in which these teenagers operate. For Arab-Canadian youth, the age peers' context provides mixed signals. For example, Arab ethnicity does not go unnoticed among the majority peers. More than one-half of the respondents reported receiving comments from classmates or coworkers regarding their ethnic heritage. On the positive side, many respondents reported that others were curious to learn more about Arabs, showed curiosity and good-will about Arab customs and rituals, or showed appreciation for Arab food and strong family ties. On the negative side, there is intermittent status devaluing reflected in sports talk (e.g., calling a basketball game the "mother" of all games), comments concerning surnames or overly strict (or "not with it") parents, or being called a terrorist or accused of hiding a gun. The negative comments accelerated during the Gulf War, and then, for some, receded.

> In the tenth grade a friend of mine said all Iraqis should be shot during the war. But after the war, there was no change in our relationship.

> Discussions during the Gulf War in front of me, basically saying that Saddam is evil and that Arabs are trouble makers.

> I had a different point of view than them, which made them resent me at the time of the war, but everything went back to normal after the war.

> They'd say all these Arabs are [expletive deleted].

> Some would make fun of Arabs in the Gulf War in front of us in class.

The responses of the students reflect the pattern observed earlier with regard to one of the sociohistorical effects of being of Arab descent in Canadian society—a sense of being at risk or somewhat vulnerable. Ethnic identity may expose youth to unforeseen consequences for which they are ill prepared. Events on the scale of the Gulf War brought home situational vulnerability and compromised identity to many Arab Canadians, young and old.

Several questions were used to look at the friendships that Arab-Canadian youth have established with age peers. Who are these peers? From where are they drawn? Is there a structural difference between peers at school and peers outside the school? To assess relationships with peers, the respondents were asked, "Considering your closest friends *in school or at work*: Are any of them of *Arab origin*? Are any of them from the *same religion*? Are any of them *blood relatives*?" Five response categories were provided under each question: "Yes, only a few of them," "Yes, some of them," "Yes, most of

TABLE 7-1. Close Friends Within and Outside of School: Percentage Distribution by Sex

Characteristic	Male			Female		
	Yes	No	Total %	Yes	No	Total %
Within School						
Are any of them						
of Arab origin	69	31	100	50	50	100
of same religion	72	28	100	58	42	100
relatives	28	72	100	19	81	100
Outside of School						
Are any of them						
of Arab origin	66	34	100	68	32	100
of same religion	69	31	100	83	17	100
relatives	39	61	100	38	62	100

them," "Yes, all of them," "No, none of them." The same set of questions and response categories were repeated, this time focusing on closest friends *after school hours or work hours*. The preceding response categories were dichotomized by combining all the "yes" responses and comparing them with the "no" responses. Table 7-1 shows how peer relations are structured within and outside of school for males and females.

Seven of ten young Arab-Canadian males include among their close friends at least some who are of the same ethnic background within and outside of the school. Similarly, seven of ten of these respondents report that at least some of their friends are of the same religious background within and outside of the school. In contrast, five of ten Arab-Canadian female students include among their close friends at school at least some who are of the same ethnic background; and six of ten female students include at least some who are of the same religious background. Within the school setting, young Arab-Canadian females, although close to their ethnic group and kin, are nevertheless much less prone than their male counterparts to be tied to friends who are of the same ethnic or religious background. Differences in friendship patterns between males and females tend to disappear outside of school, except that females (83 percent) are more likely than males (69 percent) to be tied to friends who are of the same religion (see Table 7-1).

Despite some striking differences between males and females, these findings confirm earlier research as they emphasize that ethnicity and religion count in the formation of peer groups among Arab-Canadian youth. This conclusion is reinforced by responses to the following question: "Do you feel more comfortable being around *Arab* or *non-Arab* peers?" Although 66 percent of the respondents reported that it made no difference, 29 percent reported that they were more comfortable around Arab peers, and 5 percent felt more comfortable around non-Arab peers. There were some noteworthy gender differences. For example, 38 percent of the male respondents reported that they were more comfortable around Arab peers, compared with only 22 percent of the female respondents making that assertion, and none of the male respondents reported that he was more comfortable around non-Arab peers. In contrast, 10 percent of the females stated that they were more comfortable around non-Arab than Arab peers.

Several reasons were given for being more comfortable around Arab peers:

We understand each other because we have the same background.

Because you're protected. They support you against other groups. You feel strong among them.

Because you speak the same language, and they understand you better.

I feel I can trust them ... because their home is like my home and vice-versa as if we were one family.

I guess you don't feel embarrassed to do some things in front of them, because you share the same common customs.

The reasons for some females to actually state a preference for non-Arab peers seem linked to a sense of personal freedom and individuality. In the words of one young woman: "My own people aren't quite developed yet. It's hard to deal with them. As an Arab woman, I can only do so much. They can't accept the fact that I am liberal." Another young female student gave a less categorical answer, stating that "it makes no difference being around Arab peers as long as they are not fundamentalist and ask about religion and why I act differently from what Islam says."

An important finding from this study is that age peers and family overlap in a way not typically expected in North American families. James Coleman's pioneering study of North American youth, for example, reported no overlap between the adolescent peer group and family.[13] In contrast, one study of Arab youth in Lebanon showed that the adolescent peer group is also, at least in part, a kinship group.[14] In the Edmonton survey, within school, 28 percent of male respondents and 19 percent of female respondents are embedded in peer groups that include at least some relatives. Outside of school, nearly four of ten respondents, male and female, report that their peer groups are at least partially kinship groups. This area of overlap may have important implications for ethnic identity retention and transmission (see Table 7-1).

The Family and Home Sphere

Arab-Canadian family life reflects traditional patterns common to family life in the Arab world and acculturative changes resulting from the impact of the Canadian environment on this immigrant group. In Arab culture, the traditional value system is collectivist in orientation, emphasizing the group, hierarchical relationships, harmony, and conformity. The traditional Arab family system is one in which sex roles are sharply defined, men possess more power and status than women, and the father has the highest authority within the family. In Canada, the prevalent value system is individualistic in orientation, emphasizing the individual, privacy, the value of personal fulfillment, independence, and egalitarianism. Typically, Canadian family life reflects attributes that stand in contrast to the ones characterizing a traditional collectivist culture.[15]

The generational factor is most critical in influencing family structure and the nature of family life among Arab Canadians. Family life among the immigrant generation, particularly in the early years of settlement, more strongly reflects patterns prevailing

TABLE 7-2. Time Spent with Father and Mother: Percentage Distribution by Sex

Amount of Time Spent	Sons with		Daughters with	
	Father	Mother	Father	Mother
Considerable	59	69	28	63
Moderate	24	24	47	31
Little	17	7	25	6
Total %	100	100	100	100

in the country of origin than does family life among second and subsequent generations. Parenting in the diaspora reflects the considerable challenge. In either case, the family is a central unit of organization in the life of Arab Canadians.

Gender and Family Embededness

A common observation about teenagers in North America is that they do not spend much time with parents or engage in a wide range of activities with them. The situation characterizing Arab-Canadian youth appears to be different, as evidenced by responses to the following questions: "On the average, how much time would you say you spend with your father?" "On the average, how much time would you say you spend with your mother?" Four response categories were provided in each case: "considerable time," "a moderate amount of time," "little time," and "not at all." Table 7-2 shows the responses by sex to these questions.

With reference to time spent with father, 59 percent of sons and only 28 percent of daughters checked the category "considerable time," and 24 percent of sons and 47 percent of daughters checked the category "a moderate amount of time." About two of ten respondents, male and female, checked the category "little time" (and none checked the category "not at all"). On the average, time spent with mother is more than with father. About two-thirds of sons and daughters say that they spend considerable time with mother; about one-fourth (slightly more in the case of daughters) say that they spend a moderate amount of time with her; and only 7 percent say that they spend little time with mother. Sex differences in time spent with parents are noticeable. Although most sons spend a considerable amount of time with father and mother and most daughters spend a considerable amount of time with mother, only a minority of daughters spend considerable time with father.

Shared Activities and Desire for Increased Contact. To assess the frequency of doing certain activities with parents, the respondents were asked the following question: "How often do you do the following activities with *one or both of your parents?*" Six activities were singled out for the respondents' consideration: "visiting friends or relatives," "watching TV," "traveling," "attending public events or public places," "shopping," and "doing work around the house." Four response categories were provided for each of these activities: "often," "sometimes," "seldom," and "never." For the purpose of the analysis, the first two categories ("often" and "sometimes") were combined to read

TABLE 7-3. Shared Activities with One or Both Parents: Percentage Distribution by Sex

| | Frequency of Joint Participation | | | | | |
| | Sons | | | Daughters | | |
Activity	Often	Less Often	Total	Often	Less Often	Total
Visiting friends/relatives	52	48	100	44	56	100
Watching TV	48	52	100	47	53	100
Traveling	31	69	100	45	55	100
Attending public events/places	34	66	100	53	47	100
Shopping	31	69	100	66	34	100
Working around the house	62	38	100	81	19	100

"often," and the last two categories ("seldom" and "never") were combined to read "less often." (None of the respondents checked the "never" category in relation to any of the activities under investigation.) The statistical results are provided in Table 7-3.

By far, the activity that Arab-Canadian teenagers do most often with one or both of their parents is working around the house (mentioned by 81 percent of daughters and 62 percent of sons), followed by shopping (66 percent of daughters; 31 percent of sons), visiting friends or relatives (44 percent of daughters; 52 percent of sons), watching TV (47 percent of daughters; 48 percent of sons), attending public events (53 percent of daughters; 34 percent of sons), and traveling (45 percent of daughters; 31 percent of sons) (see Table 7-3).

The amount of time spent with parents is a function of individual preferences or opportunities involving teenagers and parents. How satisfied are the respondents with the time they spend with parents? About two of three respondents reported that they were satisfied; however, almost 32 percent stated that they would like to spend more time with parents, and only 3 percent reported that they would like to spend less time with parents. The responses of males and females were similar.

Trust and Confiding. One important measure of the strength of Arab-Canadian family is the trust that children may have in their parents. This was assessed by the following question: "In general, do you confide in or talk to one or both parents about your personal life or problems?" In response to this question, about nine of ten said "yes," and only one of ten said "no." Remarkably, about nine of ten respondents stated that they talk "often" (35 percent) or "sometimes" (56 percent) with parents about personal life or problems. Not surprisingly, 52 percent of the respondents talk more with mother than father about these personal problems; 36 percent talk equally with father and mother; and a minority of 13 percent talk more with father than mother about personal matters. It is clear from these results that Arab-Canadian youth are not isolated from their parents.

Gender and the Family Burden

Despite their experience with what appears to be a strong and trusting family situation, nearly one-half of Arab-Canadian youth report that they often or sometimes face disagreements with or criticisms by parents. Most commonly, these disagreements or criticisms revolve around the expectation of spending more time on school work, staying out late, choice of friends or amount of time spent with friends, trying to learn Canadian ways and fit in with Canadian peers, maintaining heritage (e.g., culture, language, religion), loyalty to and respect for parents, spending money, the way things are done around the house, and girls going out on dates (i.e., the double standard in the treatment of boys and girls).

Parents as a Resource. The extent and nature of problems faced by young Arab-Canadian men and women were assessed by two questions: "Do you think that young Arab-Canadian women face *more* problems, *less* problems, or about the *same* number of problems as young Arab-Canadian men?" "Do you feel that there are sex differences in the *kinds* of problems faced by young Arab-Canadian men and women?" (If yes, "what are these differences?") In response to the first question, 58 percent of the respondents felt that Arab-Canadian women face more problems than Arab-Canadian men, and 8 percent felt that women face fewer problems than men. About one-third of the respondents felt that Arab-Canadian men and women face an equivalent number of problems. However, when sex differences were considered, we found that 49 percent of the sons saw more problems for females than males, and 70 percent of daughters reported more problems for females than males.

The issue of sex differences in the kind of problems faced by young Arab-Canadian men and women looms large. Seven of ten respondents affirmed that there were differences in the kinds of problems faced by men and women. The differences principally revolved around a wide range of restrictions applied to women compared with men. In the words of male and female respondents,

> Everybody thinks of us as weaker and vulnerable, that we need to be protected all the time.

> Parents think it's OK for a guy to go out, and they condone it. Girls can't do that.

> The man can do anything, the girl is being watched all the time. If she is with a male friend, people would talk about her.

> Men have more freedom; women are more restricted from going out.

> The culture restricts them [women] more ...

> Women face more pressure and a limited amount of freedom. It looks bad for a girl to be seen in a bar ... her reputation is always on the line.

> Men can get away with everything, as if there were two books written, one for men and one for women. Women are constrained.

> We're expected to follow two different standards, Arab and Canadian. It is almost impossible to bring them together because they're totally different.

Although the overwhelming majority of the comments were made about restrictions on the freedom of Arab-Canadian women, there were a few comments about the kinds of problems faced by men:

> Canadians pick more on young Arab men than Arab women.

> Men are more involved in the larger society, which creates more problems for them, like getting into fights with others more than women.

TABLE 7-4. Attitudes Toward Intermarriage and Male-Female Relationships: Percentage Distribution by Sex

Topic of Question[a]	Males' Attitudes				Females' Attitudes			
	Unfavorable	Neutral	Favorable	Total %[b]	Unfavorable	Neutral	Favorable	Total %[b]
A young Arab-Canadian man								
Staying out late with his friends	10	10	79	99	9	25	66	100
Going out on dates	28	10	62	100	25	22	53	100
Marrying a non-Arab	38	14	48	100	34	22	44	100
A young Arab-Canadian woman								
Staying out late with her friends	55	14	31	100	22	22	56	100
Going out on dates	59	14	28	101	44	16	41	101
Marrying a non-Arab	52	21	28	101	44	12	44	100

[a]How strongly do you disagree or agree with the following?
[b]Percentage totals may be less or more than 100 due to rounding.

The girls don't go out as much, so they don't have to face some problems and pressures from parents, such as taking the car or staying out late.

Curfews, dating, and possible marriage are familiar issues to parents of young adults. Respondents' attitudes toward these issues and their perceptions of their parents' attitudes were assessed by a series of six statements, each of which was to be rated on a scale ranging from 1 to 7 (1 = strongly disagree; 4 = neutral; 7 = strongly agree). In the first round of rating, the respondent was asked to indicate how strongly he or she disagreed or agreed with the statements, and in the second round, the respondent was asked to indicate how strongly he or she thought his or her parents disagreed or agreed with the statement. In this analysis, the scale was collapsed to a trichotomy because of the small size of the sample: "unfavorable," "neutral," and "favorable." Self-ratings are reported in Table 7-4, and parental ratings are reported in Table 7-5.

Table 7-4 shows that 79 percent of young Arab-Canadian male respondents are favorable to the scenario of "a young Arab-Canadian man staying out late with his friends"; 62 percent are favorable to "a young Arab-Canadian man going out on dates"; and 48 percent are favorable to the scenario of "a young Arab-Canadian marrying a non-Arab." A similar trend is observed for the three scenarios among female respondents, but the percentage associated with each scenario is slightly less for female than male respondents. When the scenario changes to "a young Arab-Canadian woman staying out late with her friends" (or "going out on dates" or "marrying a non-Arab"), larger percentages of female than male respondents tend to be favorable to the three scenarios.

Sex differences are also noticeable in Table 7-5, which shows how sons and daughters perceive parental attitudes toward the same three scenarios. For example, 38 percent of sons and 34 percent of daughters perceive their parents to be unfavorable toward "a young Arab-Canadian man staying out late with his friends"; toward ". . . going out on dates" (45 percent of sons; 41 percent of daughters), and toward ". . . marrying a non-Arab" (72 percent of sons; 56 percent of daughters). When the scenarios are couched in terms of "a young Arab-Canadian woman . . ." (see lower half of Table 7-5), the

TABLE 7-5. Perceptions of Parental Attitudes Toward Intermarriage and Male-Female Relationships: Percentage Distribution by Sex

Topic of Question[a]	Sons' Responses				Daughters' Responses			
	Unfavor-able	Neutral	Favor-able	Total %[b]	Unfavor-able	Neutral	Favor-able	Total %[b]
A young Arab-Canadian man								
Staying out late with his friends	38	10	52	100	34	16	50	100
Going out on dates	45	10	45	100	41	31	28	100
Marrying a non-Arab	72	3	24	99	56	19	25	100
A young Arab-Canadian woman								
Staying out late with her friends	76	10	14	100	59	9	31	99
Going out on dates	79	7	14	100	69	9	22	100
Marrying a non-Arab	79	4	18	101	63	19	19	101

[a]How strongly do you think your parents disagree or agree with the following?
[b]Percentage totals may be less or more than 100 due to rounding.

findings reflect the daughters' and the sons' perceptions of a double standard in the treatment of men and women. A larger proportion of male than female respondents (correctly) perceive the rules to be stricter for daughters than for sons. Hence, some Arab-Canadian women complain about the double standard that exists in Arab culture.

Conclusions

Three strands seem useful to pursue: the areas of overlap between the family and kin sphere and the school and peer sphere and the implications of these for ethnocultural adaptation and retention; the major discrepancies in adaptation between daughters and sons; and the identity issues (personal, ethnic, and national) as daughters and sons progress further along the traditional milestones of adult life.

Areas of Overlap

The overlap between the family and kin sphere and the peer and school sphere is particularly interesting when age peers are also kin and when they are of common ethnic background. These situations can be conceptualized as partially overlapping spheres. At the points of common space lie synergistic opportunities to capitalize on the familiar and address the unfamiliar. These points may be a real strength for the immigrant family. The commonalties also may be seen to aid the negotiation of the youth and parents in terms of family adaptation to the larger environment and to justify or validate parental family and cultural practices.

Gender Discrepancies

Judging from self-reports, ethnicity plays a variable role in the lives of teenagers. The Arab-Canadian students under study reflect differences in their perceptions of peer and school support or opposition. The evidence suggests a sizable gap between parents and youth in conduct codes. This group of Arab-Canadian youth appears to be structurally tightly embedded in the family unit, but a major point of tension is related to issues of gender. In the perceptions of males and females, gender makes a major difference in their own expectations and their perception of their parents' expectations. Although sons report awareness of this, it is nothing like the reports of daughters. Compared with sons, daughters report less happiness with school, less involvement with parents, less television viewing, more household work, more traveling, and more attendance of public functions with parents (or being accompanied by parents). The latter burst of activities reflects the controls over daughters that restrict them from unchaperoned activities. The specter of difference is stronger for adolescent girls than for adolescent boys. The girls' fit into the larger culture appears to be shaped by parental behavior and the perception of parental behavior. The net effect of this is that daughters' ethnocultural "difference" may be less amenable to concealment.

Unfolding Identity Issues

The numbers can only be suggestive at this point, but daughters are more likely to report feeling more comfortable with Canadian than Arab peers; more likely to feel that being Arab is a problem; more likely to have hidden their Arab identity at one time or another; and more likely to identify as Canadian than Arab.

What of the future? British research on young English Sikh males suggests a recommitment to ethnicity when marriage occurs, indicating acceptance of parental choice and acquiescence to adult status. On the other hand, in the view of some Arab-Canadian women, marriage can be a form of emancipation, a way of gaining greater freedom to navigate within the culture. This raises questions concerning the reciprocal effects of gender and marriage and their implications for the maintenance and transformation of ethnocultural identity among second-generation families.

Notes

1. The term diaspora, from the Greek meaning dispersion, was once used in North America to refer singularly to the Jews. In an era of globalization, extensive migration, and transnational connections, diaspora is used in a far broader way to refer to groups of people who once shared commonalities and homogeneities and are now dispersed, scattered, or displaced and relocated into new settings that may involve changed power dynamics, a more complex sense of personal and collective identity (e.g., identifying with the new and the old locale), and often the experience of being expected to represent those in the ancestral lands to the majority population in the receiving countries. A range of peoples outside their ancestral homelands have been characterized as diasporic, including Arabs, South Asians, and Chinese. See Avtar Brah, *Cartographies of Diaspora* (London: Routledge, 1996); Iain Chamber, *Migrancy, Culture, Identity* (London: Routledge, 1994); and Rey Chow, *Writing Diaspora* (Bloomington: Indiana University Press, 1993).

2. Anthony Synnott and David Howes, "Canada's Visible Minorities: Identity and Representation." In Vered Amit-Talai and Caroline Knowles, eds., *Re-Situating Identities: The Politics of Race, Ethnicity, and Culture* (Peterborough, Canada: Broadview Press, 1996), pp. 136–60.

3. Erving Goffman, *Stigma* (Englewood Cliffs, NJ: Prentice-Hall, 1963).

4. West Asians and Arabs compose one of the ten designated categories. The other nine are Japanese, Pacific Islanders, Filipinos, Koreans, Chinese, Blacks, South Asians, South East Asians, and Latin Americans. First Nations (aboriginal) peoples are excluded from this categorization.

5. For a detailed discussion of this period, see Baha Abu-Laban, *An Olive Branch on the Family Tree: The Arabs in Canada* (Toronto: McClelland and Stewart, 1980).

6. Compare Baha Abu-Laban, "Arab Canadians." In *The Canadian Encyclopedia* (Tornoto: McClelland & Stewart, 1996).

7. Karen Kelly, "Visible Minorities: A Diverse Group," *Social Trends* 37 (1995): 2–8.

8. See Sharon McIrvin Abu-Laban, "The Co-existence of Cohorts: Identity and Adaptation among Arab-American Muslims," *Arab Studies Quarterly* 2 (1989): 45–63.

9. J. W. Berry, R. Kalin, and D. M. Taylor, *Multiculturalism and Ethnic Attitudes in Canada* (Ottawa: Ministry of Supply and Services, 1977), pp. 94–97.

10. For details, see Baha Abu-Laban, *Olive Branch;* Farid E. Ohan and Ibrahim Hayani, *The Arabs in Ontario: A Misunderstood Community* (Tornoto: Near East Cultural and Education Foundation, 1993); Karim H. Karim, *Images of Arabs and Muslims: A Research Review* (Ottawa: Policy and Research, Multiculturalism Sector, Multiculturalism and Citizenship, 1991); Margaret Cannon, *The Invisible Empire: Racism in Canada* (Toronto: Random House of Canada, 1995); and Tamer Anis, *A Profile of Anti-Arab Racism and Discrimination in Canada* (Ottawa: National Council on Canada-Arab Relations, 1996). For U.S. attitudes, see Michael W. Suleiman, *The Arabs in the Mind of America* (Brattleboro, VT: Amana Books, 1988).

11. Zuhair Kashmir, *The Gulf Within: Canadian Arabs, Racism and the Gulf War* (Toronto: James Lorimer & Co., 1991).

12. Baha Abu-Laban and Sharon McIrvin Abu-Laban, "The Gulf War and Its Impact on Canadians of Arab and Muslim Heritage." In Baha Abu-Laban and Ibrahim Alladin, eds., *Beyond the Gulf War: Muslims, Arabs and the West* (Edmonton, Canada: MRF Publishers, 1991), pp. 125–26.

13. James S. Coleman, *The Adolescent Society* (Glenco, IL: Free Press, 1961).

14. Baha Abu-Laban, "The Adolescent Peer Group in Cross-Cultural Perspective," *Canadian Review of Sociology and Anthropology* 7 (1970): 201–11.

15. For further details on the collectivist and individualistic value systems, see H. C. Triandis *et al.,* "Individualism and Collectivism: Cross-Cultural Perspectives on Self-Ingroup Relationships," *Journal of Personality and Social Psychology* 54 (1988): 323–38; and H. C. Triandis, C. McCusker and C. H. Hui, "Multimethod Probes of Individualism and Collectivism," *Journal of Personality and Social Psychology* 59 (1990): 1006–20.

Kristine Ajrouch

8   Family and Ethnic Identity in an Arab-American Community

Ethnic identity in the United States emerges through the confrontation of two driving forces: the immigrant culture and the host culture. These two forces push against one another, with each striving for domination. Eventually, the two forces negotiate a relationship in which both cultures have a place. The interaction between the immigrant and host culture produces the developing characteristics of an ethnic identity in America.[1]

A critical source of the immigrant culture is found within the family. This chapter addresses the Arab family and how it contributes to the formation of an ethnic identity among the second generation. Also important in this discussion is the environment of American society, or the host culture. The weaving of immigrant and host cultures creates a unique situation for the second generation. Family relations become embedded in the host society with immigration and play a role in the development of an ethnic identity.

The social processes that constitute the designation of "peoplehood"[2] among the ethnic group commonly referred to as Arab are examined through an in-depth study of Muslim Lebanese families living in Dearborn, Michigan, which is home to the largest Arab Muslim community in the United States.[3] In particular, this chapter examines the interpretations those of Arab descent produce regarding their ethnic identity. Several questions are raised at the outset. What does it mean to be Arab, and what does it mean to be American? Which identity do they take for themselves and why? How do they arrive at these identities?

These questions were generated after I had begun observing Arab-American adolescents in a middle school located in Dearborn. After three months of observing and ultimately participating in the daily activities of the school I arranged to meet a group of eight students after school over three days to discuss their experiences of growing up in America. One year later, I arranged for two more focus groups, each with eight to ten students to elaborate on the discussions of the year before. I then organized two focus group discussions with parents of adolescents, each consisting of six to eight parents, with the intention of having them discuss the experience of raising their children in America. All of the focus groups met during two-hour periods.

Gender became a primary aspect of Arab identity, as did religion. Gender is the focal point of conversation, particularly for the adolescents. Their interpretations of what it means to be Arab and what it means to be American revolve around female behavior. My work with these adolescents led me to propose that gender is a critical variable in the formation of ethnic identity. Religion, on the other hand, is the dominant theme in the parents' conversations when they discuss Arab identity. It represents the system of meaning that the parents rely on to justify the behaviors they expect from their children and to demonstrate the significance of their cultural identity. There is a relationship between gender and religion, but there is a distinct generational difference in which aspect is stressed.

Ethnic Identity and Arab Family:
Responsibility and Honor

Abdo Elkholy writes about the immigrant Arab family and the tensions that exist between the immigrants and the children they raise in America. A cultural clash arises when the opposing life views held by each generation confront one another. According to Elkholy, the parents are products of the traditional, agrarian culture of the Middle East, where the past is revered, there is emphasis on stability and conformity, and the elderly are held in high esteem because of their life experiences. Their children are growing up in the technological, industrial culture of America. For them, the focus is on the future, not the past. Youth have higher status than the elderly, and emphasis is placed on personal achievements, rather than accumulated life experiences. Growing up in America, the children are faced with both worlds and both cultures. Elkholy states, "The second generation plays a transitional role between the old and the new cultures and is often the victim of both."[4]

I begin with the premise that the foundation of ethnic identity derives from the home and the family. In so far as the home socializes children to a particular identity, there emerge expectations based on that identity. According to Mindel and Habenstein, "The maintenance of ethnic identification and solidarity ultimately rests on the ability of the family to socialize its members into the ethnic culture, and thus to channel control, perhaps program future behavior."[5] The family teaches ethnic identity, and through that instilled identity, the older generations attempt to control the actions of their offspring.

The structure of the Arab family exhibits two prominent qualities that demonstrate its ethnic quality; it is patrilineal and extended. The patrilineal structure of the Arab family "refers to a system of descent whereby an individual is entitled to certain rights through his or her father, and automatically belongs to a group defined through the father."[6] Within this type of family organization, all persons know to which group they belong. It is assigned at birth. A feeling of security results from this membership, a theme that consistently emerged through my focus group discussions with adolescents and parents. Family members assume a responsibility for one another. Men and women have definitive rights and duties. The actions of individuals in the family come to represent the entire family. Whether someone in the family acts positively or negatively, the entire family is implicated, and in this manner, the family name is established.

Aswad writes that often, in discussions of the Arab family, their patrilineal organization is mistaken for Western patriarchy. She makes a clear distinction between the two. Patriarchy refers to power and dominance by senior male family members. Although patriarchy may exist in Arab families, it also may not be present in the Arab family structure. Patriarchy is a phenomenon found in family relations across cultures; it is not the underlying, definitive factor that organizes the Arab family. Patrilineality better defines family organization in the Arab culture.

The connection between family members in this patrilineal structure delineates certain responsibilities for one another that are levied on family members, and therefore families tend to take on an extended form.[7] The extended family is conventionally defined as a family form that may include parents, children, grandparents, uncles, and aunts dwelling in one household. However, it is more useful to apply this term as a sensitizing concept that represents an ideal. In actuality, the extended family form has rarely been found to exist among Middle Eastern families during this century.[8] I use the term "extended family" to conceptualize a set of relationships among individuals in which a household composed of parents and children maintains close contact with their relatives and kin. These relationships are important for many reasons, including financial, social, and emotional support.

Within an extended family organization, a communal quality is present. The family name and reputation are important aspects of identity for individuals.[9] Feelings of security and solidarity arise through the identity of family affiliation, because members within the family network take care of one another. For example, males usually are responsible for supporting the family economically, whereas females are in charge of and virtually embody family honor. This responsibility carried by the female makes her important in the maintenance of social order. Social order is represented by family honor, which represents a core aspect of Arab culture. The female is therefore a valued element of the family and society. Her esteemed value becomes something to guard.

Many researchers who examine Arab culture suggest that the main reason for a girl's restricted activity has to do with the concept of honor. The notion of family honor is directly linked to the chastity of its female members.[10] Specifically, it is her sexual conduct which must be guarded. Because of the patrilineal nature of the Arab family, it is important for family honor and for family responsibility; responsibility and group membership derive from the paternity of a child. Chastity and honor become imperative qualities for the female. I posit that, because of these factors, the female is a fundamental and valued element to the creation and maintenance of an Arab ethnic identity.

Adolescents: Issues of Gender and Ethnic Identity

The perception that gender differences exist between how males and females are treated within families and the community became apparent at the outset of the discussions. The focus group discussions elicited cultural knowledge, which allowed for an understanding of family relations in the Arab-American community and its impact on ethnic identity formation among the adolescent children of immigrants.

The adolescents in my focus groups, most noticeably the girls, made constant comparisons between how they perceived boys were treated and how they were treated. The girls incessantly brought up the different behaviors tolerated by their families and community and were often torn between expected behavior and how they desired to act. They referred more often to social differences than to material differences. The girls did not perceive that the boys acquired more material objects than they did; they instead complained about the permissiveness the males acquired to do such things as simply going out.

When asked to define what it means to be Arab and what it means to be American, it was the behavior of the females that emerged as the defining characteristic. To summarize, the American girl is perceived as immoral, whereas the Arab girl is respectful. The essence of being Arab was most sharply expressed by the behavior of the females. Discussions initiated by the adolescents within the focus group most often centered on the issue of dating, which is a sensitive issue among adolescents in the first place but has far-reaching implications with regard to the preservation of an Arab identity.

The Arab-American girls are the ones who seem to feel more tension between the two pertinent cultural forces. They feel pressure from their families to act honorably, yet are lured by the perceived autonomy possessed by "American" girls. In the focus group discussions, the girls were vocal about this tension:

Adolescents—Focus Group 1:23

H: . . . but most girls, just because they're American, yeah, they think they can do whatever they want. Like they can wear short shorts and daisy dukes.

L1: They sleep around with guys. They're allowed to have a boyfriend.

H: It seems to me their parents don't care.

L2: I mean all you hear about is an American pregnant and then they put it on national TV. Oh yeah, I'm pregnant at the age of twelve, and I'm proud of it.

L1: Like us, the Arab. If a girl slept with a guy, there goes her reputation. But if an American girl slept with a guy, it's like OK to do it.

The focus group narrative demonstrates to some degree the inner struggle that most females in this community experience. Their observations of "American" girls around them and as portrayed through the media reveal a lifestyle void of restrictions. However, at home and in their community, restrictions and limits are the norm for the female. The girls in the discussion seem to be criticizing the "American" girls, but they do not state that they themselves are morally superior, only that if an "Arab" girl were to engage in the same kinds of behaviors, she would then incur a bad reputation. One of the girls even makes a reference to the parents of "American" girls, stating that she senses "American" parents are not bothered by the scandalous actions that are described.

The importance of family is also demonstrated as the girls talked about their brothers. Their brothers were the individuals most often scolding or threatening their sisters if they "misbehaved" or acted in a manner that could tarnish the family name. The consensus, however, is that boys or brothers acquire this attitude after they begin to associate with other Arabs. One participant stated that she believes "Arabs change Arabs." She told the story of how she used to live in Detroit in an area in which not many Arabs lived. During this time, she had quite a bit of autonomy. She was allowed to go out and, according to her, do whatever she wanted. However, she believes that since her family moved to Dearborn her brother has changed. She states that he no longer lets her answer the phone, and when his friends come over, she and her sisters are not allowed to sit in the same room. She believes that he has become more strict than her father.

This group pressure described by the female adolescents where Arab boys change their attitudes after they are in the company of other "Arab" males materialized during another focus group discussion. In an earlier focus group, one of the male participants stated that he had a younger sister but did not really care one way or the other if she talked to boys or had a boyfriend. In this focus group, which included three more boys, the teenagers were again discussing the different behaviors expected from males and females. The boys said that if they ever found out that their sisters were going out with boys, they would be extremely upset and take action. The same boy who in the earlier focus group said he did not care was now talking like the other boys. One of the female participants became perturbed as she remembered his comments from the week before and abruptly announced that his sister was going out with a boy—a piece of information about which she later insisted he knew. The boy's reaction was one of shock. He stopped talking, put his head down, and began to cry. The other adolescent males began to comfort him, saying, "It's all right, man," acknowledging the hurt they feel when somebody talks about their sister.

It seems that the adolescent boys have learned about family honor and feel a responsibility to uphold that honor by regulating the behavior of their sisters. It also seems that this feeling is intensified when they live in an Arab community. Arab identity is notably significant for these adolescents in the context of female behavior.

Gendered differentiation in social activities also produces another characteristic cited by the adolescents as part of being "Arab": the emergence of a communal feeling among the adolescents. Although female behavior is restricted and closely monitored, a resulting outcome is a strong feeling of solidarity. The girls especially talk about how they watch out for one another and how the boys watch out for them and act in the girls' best interest. The boys tell the girls when they're doing something wrong, whether it is flirting with a boy, going out too much, or hanging around with the wrong crowd. One of the participants put it nicely:

Adolescents—Focus Group 1:46

H: Like you've got everybody watching out for you, taking care of you. It's like, it's like we're a family, but if you're American, they don't care about you, you know.

The teenagers feel a communal bond through the instilled behaviors each gender is expected to uphold.

The data gathered from the focus groups with these adolescents suggests that, in the case of Arab ethnicity, female conduct is the locus or site of that identity. Although the Arab female has traditionally embodied respect and honor, restrictions on her activities become exaggerated in an environment of perceived threats. American society, which fosters feelings of independence, autonomy, and freedom, surrounds the ethnic community of Dearborn, Michigan. America's pluralistic society allows for optional behaviors not normally sanctioned in homogeneous societies. When an arena exists in which to participate in activities that traditionally were not a part of one's culture, the original or immigrant culture loses its tacit characteristics and becomes explicit. It is when options arise outside of the traditional societal structure, as is the case found in the United States of America, that an intensified threat appears. This is demonstrated through the gender conflicts expressed by these adolescents.

Parents: Issues of Religion and Ethnic Identity

When a teacher explained to the students in her class, 90 percent of whom were of Arab descent, that I was present in their classroom because I wanted to research Arab ethnicity, one of the girls turned around and poignantly inquired if I intended to write about how they forget their religion when they come to school. This statement was a clue to what would ensue in the focus group discussions with the immigrant parents of these adolescents. Religion was an underlying theme in the immigrant parents' descriptions of raising their child in an Arab fashion.

All of the parents in these focus groups are immigrants from south Lebanon, and all are Muslim, as were the adolescents. The period they have lived in the United States varies from fifteen to twenty-five years. The most striking theme that emerged from the focus group discussions was the pervasiveness of religion as a major underpinning of ethnic identity. Sossie Andezian writes about how Islam helps the Arab immigrant to define himself or herself by opposition to the non-Muslim. The interaction of the immigrant and host society, along with the struggle within the community to maintain its members' identity, sparks the revival of religious customs and beliefs that in the country of origin are reserved for the more "religious" believers. Religious practices enable the Arab immigrants to maintain social rules that might otherwise disappear outside of their native country.[11]

Occasionally, when a parent described religious characteristics for defining the Arab identity, another parent challenged these descriptions, stating that they were supposed to talk about Arab, not Muslim, characteristics. However, when discussing the work of raising their children, the conversation reverted to religious precepts and beliefs. The parents echoed the behaviors observed and articulated by the adolescents when asked about the differences practiced in raising their daughters and sons. When questioned directly about whether they raise their sons and daughters differently, the immediate response was an acknowledgment of allowing significantly different social behaviors.

Ethnic identity has religious undertones. The significance of this finding is that none of the participants was prompted to talk about religion; it was not a topic introduced by the focus group moderator. Instead, it emerged as the parents discussed their experiences raising children in America, and it appears as a central theme in the participants' attempts to define Arab identity. Abu-Laban states that religion provides a chief impetus for the development of social identity,[12] and ethnicity is a social identity. The major form that religion takes in these parents' articulation of Arab ethnicity is that it provides a solid foundation for coping with life in America. For example, it was often stated that the Muslim religion, Islam, provides a moral code for children growing up in America.

A father illustrated this point as he told a story in the focus group discussion. He told the other parents about how his eldest son, at the age of twelve, had asked if he could go with his class after a school event to a fast food restaurant. This father agreed, but having never been faced with this situation, he decided to follow his son to see what exactly happens when a group of adolescents go out together. He saw some behaviors that he did not approve of, but he also observed that his son was not participating in those activities. When his son returned home, the father asked his son to tell him about the evening. The son told his father where they went and what he ate. The father asked what else happened. The son said that some people went outside to smoke and drink, but that he had not been part of that group. The father explained that it was the religious upbringing that contributed to his son's refrain from joining the kids who were smoking and drinking.

Parents—Focus Group 1:54

F3: But in, when he was little, I put fear of God in him. I say we're Muslim: we're against this; we're against that. Muslim, it's *akhlaq* (moral code), it's a gift from God. If you teach, if anybody in the face of the Earth teaches his kids the Muslim way, there wouldn't be no evil in the face of the Earth.

The parents also remark on how they must make a concerted effort to teach their children who they are by invoking the teachings of Islam. They all agree that in Lebanon there was no effort exerted by families to take them to the mosque or to set out explicitly to learn about religion. It just happened in the course of everyday living. In America, efforts must be made to teach the children to guarantee that they will not become "too" American—so they will not acquire American characteristics considered undesirable. All of the participants believe that Islam is central to their children's identity. As one participant stated,

Parents—Focus Group 2:24

M2: Islam is a way of life. It teaches you how to deal with society and people and relate to other people. Of course, you know, if you teach your kids religion, it helps; it builds in your personality.

Another mother, when prompted to describe what qualities her son has that show that he is Arab, answered directly,

Parents—Focus Group 2:78

M1: Well, it's back to the religion; we try to explain to him since he was a little kid, you know ... even our American next door, his friend, he's teaching him the same way; he's doing it, you know. Outside. He can't steal with him. He can't, that's *haram* (not allowed, against religion); even he (the American boy) started saying *haram, wallah* (I swear to God).

It was stated repeatedly that Arabs have the fear of God, that the religion teaches that fear, and that it is that quality they strive to pass on to their children.

Parents use this fear of God to instill expected behavior in their boys and girls so that they act as appropriate, respectful individuals, especially with regard to the different social behaviors tolerated by the parents. One father recounts a story of the time his daughter accused him of practicing double standards. His son was allowed to have boys and girls visit the house. His daughter, on the other hand, was only allowed to bring girls home. He proudly announced that his daughter never talked about boyfriends.

Parents—Focus Group 1:36

F3: ... she knows she's a Muslim. She knows that. She's a Muslim; if anybody wants to meet her, and this when she was five or six years old, it was whispered in her ears, you do not ever talk to boys, you do talking, never a boy put his hand on your shoulder, never, except me—I'm the only one. Your uncle even wouldn't kiss you. I'm the only one who can kiss you on here, on the forehead, and this was brought up with her as a Muslim way.

In another instance, the parents discussed how their children prefer for the most part to choose other Arab children as friends. Their reason is elaborated in the following discussion as "American" girls are criticized:

Parents—Focus Group 2:8

M3: They just, I feel that, they don't understand that type of ...
M4: Yeah.
M3: Even Lisa, in high school. "Ma, they come home the next day; they brag about being drunk or the boys they slept with."
M?: Oh yeah.
M3: ... or what they did, and so to them, that's just ...
M4: That's why it depends on how you raise your kids, you know, especially in our culture.
M3: Right.
M4: You raise them the Islamic way.

Religion is an underlying factor in teaching their children what behaviors are tolerated, and it serves to give their children an identity. Arab ethnicity is intertwined with religious foundations. A reason for this may be that in Lebanon, along with family affiliation, religion is a major component of one's political and social identity. This becomes evident in examining the political structure of Lebanon. By political arrangement, quotas are set for the number of members serving in the political establishment, and positions of leadership are designated according to religious status. For example, the President of Lebanon must be a Maronite Christian, the President of the Parliament is Shi'a Muslim, and the Prime Minister of the country is a Sunni Muslim. Whereas civil, commercial, and criminal laws are the same for all citizens (i.e., the administration of such laws is carried out by state courts), family matters concerning marriage, divorce, and inheritance are left up to religious courts officially recognized as part of the Lebanese judiciary. Religion and sect have to be designated on all legal identifications, regardless of personal wishes.[13] In the immigrant parents' country of origin, religion is a major component of their identity, and much of ethnic relations in Lebanon is based on religious affiliation.

Family law has not yet been tempered by Western or secular forces. Therefore it represents the realm in which to develop and maintain an ethnic identity. Family matters are the context in which social relations maintain a sanguine sense of identity. Because religious law is that which governs family matters in Lebanon, it is interesting to consider the implications for behavior in America—particularly the differences in social permissiveness allowed by the parents between their sons and daughters.

The sacredness of family does not exist with males alone. The female is a vital part of this institution and therefore an important aspect to consider. The importance of the female arises in the discussions of the adolescents and parents. The divergent ways in which parents view and treat male and female children were discussed openly by the adolescents and parents. The major conflict faced by these families is found in the looming ideal of freedom and autonomous choice that pervades the fabric of American life while the parents strive to maintain the importance of the family unit.

Girls see freedom all around them and wish to acquire it, just as it is granted to their brothers. The issue of dating is that situation in which this discrepancy becomes most evident. All of the parents state how they treat their children the same except when it comes to dating. The basic explanation is that girls and boys are different. As one mother stated,

Parents—Focus Group 2:43

M3: Well, we just feel the boy can take care of himself, and if a boy goes out with a girl, nobody's gonna point a finger at him. If a girl's seen dressed [the wrong way], they start talking about her. And her reputation is ruined for life. So that's our culture.

The parents, however, also understand that the restrictions on girls are exaggerated by living in America, especially because they are afraid of "what's out there." They see and hear about the actions of American teenagers and fear for their daughters' reputations. One mother sums up a major reason that underlies their fears in a discussion about why they are afraid:

Parents—Focus Group 2:44

M3: You know why, because here we, you believe in boyfriend and girlfriend. And if you let this loose, then the girl is gonna say it's why you have to keep a tight rope. You can't let them know what's going on out there. Or if they do, you just have to keep an eye on them.

The fact that dating and having a boyfriend or a girlfriend is considered normal and even desirable in American society prompts Arab parents to maintain a stronger hold on their daughters, whom they explain have much to lose from such situations. They also mention that in Lebanon, although boys sometimes date, it is not openly accepted; whereas here in America, families are beginning to accept the fact that their sons date and even have the girls to their house. Boys have little to lose from dating, and so it is not considered to be as threatening to the family.

The same standards and expectations that are levied on Arab girls are not applied to the non-Arab girls that the boys date. They do not own membership in an "Arab family" and therefore do not assume the same responsibility and same codes of conduct that derive from a patrilineal family organization. The parents' opinions of the girls their sons date vary. They understand that these girls do not live by the same rules that they apply to Arab girls, and initially they may be considered undesirable as future wives. On the other hand, there were at least two participants who had sons who married non-Arab girls, and these parents expressed an overall positive experience with their non-Arab daughters-in-law.

This polarization of how male and female children are treated in America by their families and community has led to the proposition that, within this Arab-American community, ethnicity is a gendered process. Boys take on more of the social characteristics of the dominant American society, whereas anti-assimilation pressure is exerted on the girls through careful monitoring of social activities.

Conclusions

The ethnic community found in Dearborn, where these immigrants and their children live, offers two worlds. One is made up of a predominantly homogeneous Arab population, and the areas outside of that ethnic community in Dearborn are more diverse, offering anonymity and encouraging autonomy. A traditional culture thrives within a modern, industrial culture. This dual existence encourages a stricter practice of the traditional culture than found in its native lands. Religious precepts are invoked by immigrant parents to convince their children of the right manner in which to behave, along with the wrong behaviors to avoid to ensure that they act as respectful Arabs. Although families may use religion selectively, such as means to convey specific behaviors over others, it nevertheless proves to be a potent instrument, allowing parents to raise children in an Arab fashion.

The threat of losing the Arab heritage surfaces as the interaction between the two cultures progresses. This process plays out in the gender relations of this ethnic group. The boys are encouraged to enter the new world, while the girls are restricted from displaying behavior that the community may interpret as too liberal.

I have suggested that an ethnic identity in America emerges through the interaction of the host culture and the immigrant culture. An Arab ethnic identity is being created as a dialectic emerges that includes a disdain for the American culture but includes a desire to acquire those attributes deemed desirable. I propose that these immigrant families hold onto their Arab ethnicity through their daughters and strive to attain the American dream through their sons.

Some scholars have made arguments about the centrality of women to the maintenance of Arab culture and women as the embodiment of ethnic heritage.[14] Perceiving gender as a critical variable in the lives of Arab immigrants in the United States has recently surfaced in the literature.[15] Cainkar, for example, puts forth a firm argument on the gender issues surrounding assimilation and acculturation among Palestinian immigrants. However, there is no blatant assertion that ethnicity tends to be a gendered process among Arab Americans. My research suggests that females face fervent anti-assimilation pressure in America and come to bear almost the entire weight of maintaining an Arab identity for their families and community. In these Arab-American families, the female seems to anchor the group's sense of identity. Further research must address the issue of gender as a mediator for ethnic identity formation and the importance females hold for a future Arab identity in the United States.

Notes

Acknowledgment: This work was funded in part by NIA grant T32-AG0017.

1. M. P. Erdmans, "Immigrants and Ethnics: Conflict and Identity in Chicago Polonia," *The Sociological Quarterly* 1 (Winter 1936): 175–96.

2. Milton Gordon, *Assimilation in American Life: The Role of Race, Religion, and National Origins* (New York: Oxford University Press, 1964).

3. John Zogby, *Arab America Today: A Demographic Profile of Arab Americans* (Washington, DC: Arab American Institute, 1990); and Linda S. Walbridge, *Without Forgetting the Imam* (Detroit, MI: Wayne State University Press, 1997).

4. Abdo A. Elkholy, "The Arab American Family." In Charles H. Mindel and Robert Habenstein, eds., *Ethnic Families in America: Patterns and Variations* (New York: Elsevier, 1981), pp. 154–55.

5. Mindel and Habenstein, *Ethnic Families in America,* pp. 6–7.

6. Barbara C. Aswad, "Strengths of the Arab Family for Mental Health Considerations and Therapy." In Ismael Ahmed and Nancy Gray, eds., *The Arab American Family: A Resource Manual for Human Service Providers* (Lansing: Eastern Michigan University and ACCESS, 1988), pp. 93–101.

7. Baha Abu-Laban, *An Olive Branch on the Family Tree* (Toronto, Canada: McClelland & Stewart, 1980).

8. E. T. Prothro and L. N. Diab, *Changing Family Patterns in the Arab East* (Beirut: American University of Beirut, 1974), p. 62. See also Mary C. Sengstock, *The Chaldean Americans: Changing Conceptions of Ethnic Identity* (New York: Center for Migration Studies, 1982), p. 24.

9. Barbara C. Aswad, "Arab American Families." In Mary Kay DeGenove, ed., *Families in Cultural Context* (Mayfield, CA: Mayfield Publishing, 1997).

10. Abu-Laban, *Olive Branch;* Elham-Eid Alldredge, "Child-Rearing Practices in the Homes of Arab Immigrants: A Study of Ethnic Persistence" (Ph.D. dissertation, Michigan State University, 1984); Aswad, "Strengths"; and Sana Al-Khayyat, *Honor and Shame: Women in Modern Iraq* (London: Saqi Books, 1990).

11. Sossie Andezian, "Women's Roles in Organizing Symbolic Life: Algerian Female Immigrants in France." In Rita James Simon and Caroline B. Brettell, eds., *International Migration: The Female Experience* (Totowa, NJ: Rowman & Allanheld, 1986), pp. 254–65.

12. Abu-Laban, *Olive Branch.*

13. Kamal Salibi, *A House of Many Mansions,* (Berkeley, CA: University of California Press, 1988).

14. Andezian, "Women's Roles"; and Evelyn Shakir, "Arab Mothers, American Sons: Women in Arab American Autobiographies," *MELUS* 3 (Fall 1991): 5–15.

15. See Louise Cainkar, "Palestinian Women in American Society: The Interaction of Social Class, Culture and Politics." In E. McCarus, ed., *The Development of Arab-American Identity* (Ann Arbor, MI: University of Michigan Press, 1994), pp. 85–105.

Baha Abu-Laban and
Sharon McIrvin Abu-Laban

---

9   Arab-Canadian Youth in Immigrant Family Life

This chapter examines the issue of Arab-Canadian immigrant integration from the perspective of the family, with a specific focus on adolescents in the newcomer family. We argue that members within the same family unit may differentially integrate and settle into a new community. Uniformity should not be assumed among family members, and the fact of potential variation in their settlement presents a researchable opportunity that may enrich our understanding of the immigrant experience.

What is meant by immigrant or immigrant family integration? A dominant theme in contemporary ethnic studies is the issue of immigrant integration into the host society. This is as much true of Canada and the United States as of countries of the European Union.[1] Researchers agree that integration is a complex, multifaceted process, but there is no universal agreement on what this concept means. In the Canadian context, integration officially refers to the encouragement of "newcomers to adapt to Canadian society and to be received by Canadians and their institutions without requiring newcomers to abandon their cultures to conform to the values of the dominant group, as long as the adherence to immigrants' cultures does not contravene Canadian laws."[2] In a similar vein, a 1990 report of the Commission of the European Communities endorses the principle of elimination of discrimination and adds "Integration respects the other's culture and terms of religion and of language, while enabling [the individual] to partake in the social, economic, and institutional structures of the host society."[3]

Research indicates that the immigrants' capacity to access desired economic and cultural goods, such as jobs, housing, health, education, justice, and political participation, is positively related to integration. In this sense, the term integration refers to the degree to which a minority group approaches parity with the dominant group.[4] Progress toward integration is often hindered by racial discrimination and poor racial relations. As a multidimensional process, integration may progress in varying degrees of success and intensity in the economic, educational, social, cultural, and political domains. Generally, successful economic integration of immigrants is related to knowledge of the language of the host society.[5]

The larger society's receptivity to the integration and settlement of newcomers may vary. How does this play out in the context of the family? At the outset it should be remembered that there is variability *within* families. Family members do not experience life in a uniform way; they may hold differing, sometimes contradictory views, and engage in differing, even opposing practices. The common imagery surrounding the notion of family implies a sameness and constancy that is belied if by nothing else but the passage of time and the aging of its members. Children grow older, grow up, and become adults while their parents age and, with good fortune, become old. Families in which power, influence, and resources are distributed along lines of age can experience power shifts—sometimes dramatically. In North American society, adolescence often signals shifts in family power. This period of incipient adulthood can present challenges to parents in general. For immigrant parents, the challenges may be exacerbated.

This chapter attempts to provide a sociological perspective on the impact of the generational factor on Arab immigrant family life. The discussion focuses on how Arab-Canadian youth link with Canadian society and what can be learned from the experience of youth and families that may be instructive in facilitating immigrant family integration. After an analytical explication, the paper uses evidence from interviews with youth in Edmonton, Alberta, to suggest the importance of attending to the factors that promote or hinder adaptation, including factors inherent in parent-child relationships and the perceived degree of openness and inclusivity in the larger environment toward Canadians of Arab descent.

Factors in the Family Developmental Cycle

It has been suggested that parents are the bone on which children sharpen their teeth. This may have been said by the parent of an adolescent. The changes involved in parenting an adolescent or young adult, in contrast to parenting a child, can be dramatic.

> Parents can no longer maintain complete authority. Adolescents can and do open the family to a whole array of new values as they bring friends and new ideas into the family arena. Families that become derailed at this stage may be rather closed to new values and threatened by them and they are frequently stuck at an earlier view of the children. They may try to control every aspect of their lives at a time when, developmentally, this is impossible to do successfully.[6]

In many ways, youth and parents in Arab immigrant families are in an even more difficult situation. The young, in the context of schooling, are intensely exposed to the socializing influence of the institutions of the larger society and, theoretically at least, they can more readily acquire new modes of thinking and experience that may be more sharply at odds with what they learn at home.[7] In the process of integration into the larger society, young Arab Canadians may experience conflict with their immediate family and with peer group and institutional representatives of the host society.[8]

Typically, Arab-Canadian youth are embedded in a strong web of relationships within the family and in the larger community. However, there are contrasts between the parent generation and the youth generation that set the stage for disagreements.[9] There are invariant differences:

1. *Birth Cohort Disparities*

   Parents and children were born in different eras. They can never share the common experience of being from the same historic period. For example, the parent who was ten years old in 1958 has had a very different childhood from that of the youth who was ten years old in 1988. For immigrant families, these differences in epoch are often compounded by differences in culture. They cannot share the same childhood experience as ten-year-old children.

2. *Differing Historical Influences*

   Historical periods present unique contexts for the experience of being a teenager or adult. For all parent-youth dyads, the elder and the child reach critical chronological milestones at different points in history. To be a young person in times of war may be very different from being a teen in times of peace. A parent who experienced her or his sixteenth birthday in 1981 in Tal el-Za'ter camp has had distinctive experiences that are not replicated in the experience of the child. Hence, there are distinctive characteristics in the experience of the parent that are not replicated in the experience of the child and vice versa. The first day of school, driving a car, and exercising the vote can all count as significant milestones in a life. Parent and child may pass through similar milestones, but the adolescence of the parent cannot replicate the adolescence of the child. Although all parents have experienced adolescence, not all of their knowledge is relevant and transferable to their child. For immigrant families, differences in historical periods can be significant; being a teenager in Palestine in 1948 going through the Arab-Israeli war is different from being a North American teenager of Arab descent in 1995 observing the media effects of the Oklahoma City bombing.

3. *Physiological Disparities*

   Parents and youth will always be in *different phases in biological time.* One is growing up, and the other is growing old. Differences in strength, stature, and energy are common. When the adolescent is reaching peak power, the parent of the adolescent typically is experiencing declining reserves. One may have energy to burn; the other may need to conserve energy, apportioning it out with measurable care. These biological differences are constants that can impede understanding between the generations.

4. *Differential Velocities of Change*

   Parent and child face different social pressures. Schools push toward change, and socialization is accelerated for youth; cultural pressures promote changes between childhood and adolescence. For the adult, the world of work and family may provide less pressure or opportunity for change. For youth, demands for change also may be found in the peer culture.

   These four factors are constant, inevitable differences that can contribute to a cumulative gap between immigrant parent and young adult child. Such factors are confounded and conflated in the settlement process of the immigrant parent with an adolescent child. Possible discrepancies in culture and a range of other variables such as gender and class add to the contrasts. Such differences can increase the difficulties that young adults may feel in adopting parental role models for tackling the culture in which they live. A number of researchers argue that the relationship between parent and child in the immigrant family has a heightened potential for tension. If we look at the inevitable contrasts between all parents and teens and how these may compound with families undergoing settlement, we also need to look at characteristics in the host society that may affect parent-youth distancing.

Arab-Canadian Families in Societal Context

To place the issues facing Arab-Canadian families in context, it is important to underline a few facts about the Arab-Canadian community's settlement experience, together with the implications of this experience.[10]

1. *Fact:* There have been immigrants of Arab descent in Canada for more than a century.
   Implication: Arab Canadians span four to five generations as immigrants and the descendants of immigrants.

2. *Fact:* Since the early days of settlement, there has been a more or less steady stream of Arab immigration to Canada, except for certain periods when the Canadian government applied restrictive measures against the entry of Arab (and other Asian) immigrants.
   Implication: New generations or cohorts of Arab immigrants tend to coexist alongside older groups. The era of entry into Canada has different implications for subsequent second and third generations of Arab Canadians.

3. *Fact:* There was diversity in the post-World War II wave of Arab immigrants by religion, country of origin, and educational and occupational characteristics.
   Implication: The Arab-Canadian community is complex and heterogeneous.

4. *Fact:* Post-World War II Arab immigrants have often come as families, or families joined the head of the household (usually the male) shortly after his arrival.
   Implication: This fact has complicated the integration of Arab-Canadian families in recent years. There are old immigrants and new immigrants. New immigrants are less likely to be in intercultural marriages.

These facts and implications lead us to advance two caveats:

1. *Whatever the parent-youth issues that may confront Arab-Canadian families, they are not uniformly attributable to all families.*

2. *On some issues, the sharpest contrasts are likely to be found between:*
   a. The foreign-born versus the native-born generation
   b. Muslim versus non-Muslim Arab-origin Canadians
   c. People with higher class position versus those with lower class position

Since the early 1990s, there has been a backlash against immigrants and immigration in Canada and the United States, as well as in countries of the European Union, notably Britain, France, Germany, and the Netherlands. The reasons may be different in each case, as are the groups that are targeted for negative treatment.

In Canada and to a large degree in the other aforementioned countries, this backlash is nourished by the general shift to the right in political discourse, even among social democrats (as evidenced by the erosion of social programs, decline in communitarianism, and increased emphasis on the bottom line), and the rise of right-wing and conservative parties such as the Reform Party in Canada. In the Canadian context, the backlash is manifested in many different ways.

1. Calls to curb immigration, particularly from Third World countries that have been the major source of immigration in the last ten or so years
2. Calls to differentiate between genuine refugees (as defined by the United Nations) and bogus refugees
3. Calls to de-emphasize family unification as a goal of immigration policy
4. Calls against the policy of official multiculturalism that was adopted by the Canadian government as far back as 1971
5. The disbanding of public multicultural commissions and consultative bodies
6. Restlessness with court challenges to practices that restrict human rights of ethnic groups, often spearheaded by immigrant or ethnic groups (e.g., use of the turban by Sikhs in the Royal Canadian Mounted Police)
7. Calls against immigrants who do not appear to be behaving like Canadians

In practical and ideological terms, integration is a process that is hampered by discrimination and racism. Consequently, Arab Canadians can face particular challenges in successfully integrating. In Canada, as in the United States, ethnic minorities form a hierarchy of advantage in terms of each other, and at the same time, visible minorities (e.g., blacks, Asians, Caribbeans) are least advantaged compared with the dominant group.[11] Arab Canadians are officially classified as a visible minority in Canada, and despite the presence of very successful and well-placed Arab-origin individuals in Canadian society, the Arab-Canadian community suffers from many disadvantages, not the least of which is stereotyping and discrimination.[12] In crisis situations such as the Gulf War, pressure against Arab Canadians tends to increase, thereby widening the gap between them and the dominant group.[13]

There have been ups and downs in Canada's reception of Arabs and Arab immigrants, ranging from extreme hostility in crisis situations to tolerance. For example, the Gulf War was a crisis situation in which, according to our respondents in the Edmonton survey, the American and Canadian news media took sides with U.S. President George Bush and did not show the Arab side. The entertainment media (e.g., movies, television) frequently portray Arabs as stupid or bad guys, drug smugglers or other criminals, cheaters, or fundamentalist mad people. From time to time, this tension occurs when school teachers are not as sensitive to cultural diversity as they should be or when non-Arab children ridicule or taunt their Arab counterparts.

Historically, attitudes toward Arabs and other Asian immigrants have been negative.[14] For Arabs, the Arab-Israeli conflict has been an added dimension to these negative attitudes.[15] Several research scholars have documented past and present maligning and stereotyping of Arabs in social science textbooks used by junior high and high school students, popular fiction; entertainment media such as cartoons, comic books, radio, television, and films; children's games; and more recently, on the Internet.[16] Even sociological or anthropological analyses of ethnic and minority groups are not entirely free from racism and stereotyping. For example, in a university text on ethnic groups in the United States, Parrillo approvingly quotes anthropologist Edward T. Hall on the purported place of olfaction (i.e., sniffing) in traditional Arab life:

> Not only is it one of the distance-setting mechanisms, but it is a vital part of a complex system of behavior. Arabs consistently breathe on people when they talk. However, this habit is more than a matter of different manners. To the Arab good smells are pleasing and a way of being involved with each other. To smell one's friend is not only nice but also desirable, for to deny him your breath is to act ashamed. Americans, on the other hand, trained as they are not to breathe in people's faces, automatically communicate shame in trying to be polite. . . . Smell is even considered in the choice of mate. When couples are being matched for marriage, the man's go-between will sometimes ask to smell the girl, who may be turned down if she doesn't "smell nice." Arabs recognize that smell and disposition may be linked. In a word, the olfactory boundary performs two roles in Arab life. It enfolds those who want to relate and separates those who don't. The Arab finds it essential to stay inside the olfactory zone as a means of keeping tab on changes in emotion. What is more, he may feel crowded as soon as he smells something unpleasant.[17]

Such totalizing characterizations of "the Arab" and "his" habits are not only wrong but can serve as ammunition for the ignorant. At the behavioral level, anti-Arab hate crimes have been in evidence for many years.[18] In Canada, according to the Bias Crime Unit in Ottawa, bias crime is defined as "a criminal offense committed against a person or property that is motivated by the suspect/offender's hate/bias against a racial, religious, ethnic, sexual orientation or disability group. This can include threatening phone calls, hate mail, physical assaults, vandalism, cross burning, firebombing and the like."[19] Although bias crimes are encountered routinely in Canada and the United States, it should be emphasized that crisis situations, such as the Gulf War, intensify the likelihood of bigotry.

Arab-Canadian Youth, Family, and Integration

In illustrating the culture-specific context for Arab-Canadian families, we consider their characteristic diversities and some preliminary evidence from a study of self-identities of adolescent youth of Arab immigrant descent. This analysis is based on numerous sources of information, including the existing sociological and anthropological literature on Arab Canadians and Americans; earlier empirical studies; participant observation on the part of both authors for more than three decades, with adult representatives of the Arab-Canadian community in the city of Edmonton, Alberta, and elsewhere in Canada; and in-depth interviews of one to two hours, with a sample of 62 Arab-Canadian youth, about 90 percent of whom were in high school. These interviews were conducted in 1992, on the heels of the Gulf War, by a young woman interviewer of

Arab descent. The sample included about equal numbers of males and females. Nearly one-half of the respondents were of Lebanese origin, and the remainder were Palestinian, Iraqi, and Egyptian in origin. Six of ten were born in Canada; about six of ten were Muslim (Sunni, Shi'a, or Druze); and the balance were Christian (Catholic, Antiochian Orthodox, or Coptic). Overall, the sample was fairly representative of the larger Arab-Canadian community in Edmonton.

Although reciprocal kin exchanges are expected in both countries, the prevalence and depth of these expectations tend to be greater in the Arab world. For new Canadians from countries of the Middle East, Canada seems more individualistic and universalistic. Given Canadian norms of universalism, family members are less able to intervene in societal institutions in behalf of kin. Although this may give newcomers a sense of greater freedom from some past family obligations, it can also be seen as a mark of ineffectuality and loss of power for the larger kin group. One consequence is that new immigrants are less embedded in familial institutional supports that might have guided integration and acculturative change.

The new Canadian culture influences the immigrant family through the school system, the peer group, the work group, and the mass media, particularly television. A companion paper in this volume deals with the impact of community and school, or the public sphere, on Arab-Canadian adolescents. Research suggests that the impact of these three agencies of socialization (i.e., school, peer group, and mass media) is noticeable on age and sex differences within the family. As a result, the authority of the older over the younger is more subject to challenge; the authority of males over females is more subject to challenge; and sex-specific child socialization practices are more subject to challenge. In the Arab east, there tends to be a stress on the rights of the collective and hierarchies of power within the family, including less egalitarian marital relationships. In such orientations, the behavior of the young reflects on the family. Obedience tends to be valued over independence. The collective good may take precedence over individual benefit. In a more individualistic culture such as Canada, individual rights tend to be stressed. Acculturation is multidimensional, and parents and children respond to cultural shifts. Children are in school systems that emphasize individualism, egalitarian relationships, and self-reliance. Parents may be between a rock and a hard place, wanting their children and themselves to respond to and successfully navigate the culture but uncertain about how much this will of necessity take away from perhaps valued cultural traditions.

Parent-Youth Tension

Questions concerning the retention of cultural practices from the country of origin are common for new immigrant parents. A sense of ethnic solidarity or identity may increase or attenuate. Canadian society emphasizes official multiculturalism policy by which immigrant groups are not restricted and are sometimes encouraged to emphasize ancestral values. A potential source of parent-youth tension is the ethnic heritage with which the young may not wish to identify, such as ethnic practices that may cause disagreements between the two generations. To test this as a potential source of conflict among Arab Canadians, the respondents in the Edmonton survey were asked the following question: "Are there Arab ethnic customs or practices followed *regularly* by your parents that you disagree with?" Two response categories were provided: "Yes," and "No." Significantly, all but one of the respondents selected the latter response category. The one respondent who was an exception stated that "They [parents] still have an old fashion mind. Girls should not do that; girls should not do that."

A series of questions in the Edmonton survey examined questions of form and degree of ethnic identity. These questions were designed to yield information on how an individual feels about himself or herself, about his or her mixed heritage, about the ancestral heritage, and about Canadian identity. These are all areas that affect relations between the young and the old within the family, as well as relationships between young Arab Canadians and various agents of socialization in the adopted land.

To assess how young Arab Canadians perceive their parents' attitudes toward Canada and their countries of origin and the importance of ethnic self-attitudes in the lives of the young, several questions were asked. "How strongly do your parents feel about being of Arab origin?" "How strongly do your parents feel about being Canadian?" "In general, what do you identify with more—being Canadian or being an Arab?" "How do you feel about being a Canadian?" "How do you feel about being an Arab Canadian?" "As a Canadian, do you feel different in any way from other Canadian citizens (and if yes, in what ways)?"

Parents as Arab

The survey results show that about 86 percent of the respondents perceived their parents to feel "very strongly" about being an Arab and an additional 14 percent thought that their parents felt "somewhat strongly" about their Arab origin. None of the respondents felt that their parents did not have strong feelings about their ethnic origins. These teenagers perceived that their parents had a strong attachment to their ancestral heritage, and they reported that their parents had shown pride in this heritage and admonished them to preserve and stay within the Arab culture. According to the teenagers' responses, parents talked to them about appropriate ways of behavior, about religion, and about family and traditions. They told stories about what it was like in the country of origin and how much they liked it there.

Parents as Canadian

Most parents appeared to present to their children a positive attitude toward being Canadian, while continuing to show a strong attachment to their Arab identity. In response to the question about how strongly their parents felt about being Canadian, a total of 84 percent of the respondents felt that their parents felt "very strongly" (45 percent) or "somewhat strongly" (39 percent) about being Canadian, and only 16 percent checked the category "not strongly at all." In general, the respondents reported that their parents talked favorably about Canada's high standard of living and good educational and job opportunities. They also reported that their parents expressed much pride in being Canadian. On the ambivalent or negative side, however, some of the parents were concerned about being visibly different and often warned their children about undesirable practices among Canadian teenagers such as wild parties, drug abuse, and sexual freedom. Traditional Arab values, with special emphasis on conformity, are invoked by parents as a standard for their children to follow.

The teenagers' perceptions of the identities of their parents do not seem to present a conflictive situation in which Arab and Canadian identities are viewed as being in opposition to each other. On the contrary, the respondents appear to view their parents' Arab identity as having stretched to embrace a Canadian one.

Teenagers' Ethnic Identity

For the respondents' own ethnic identity, the results show that three of four identify more with being Arab than with being Canadian and that one of four identify more with being Canadian than Arab. This result is probably understandable given that about 95 percent of the respondents' fathers and mothers and 40 percent of the respondents themselves were born in an Arab country. But there are interesting gender differences in the results. For example, a larger proportion of females (36 percent) than males (14 percent) identify more with being Canadian than being Arab. Conversely, 86 percent of males, compared with 64 percent of females, identify more with being Arab than Canadian. Further examination of the data indicates that those who identify more with being Canadian than Arab tend to be Christian rather than Muslim youth.

Although the respondents in the Edmonton survey exhibit a clear attachment to their roots, they also feel, perhaps more than their parents, that they are Canadian. In response to an open-ended question about how they felt about being Canadian, most of the respondents were positive about their Canadian identity. They felt good about and proud of this identity, and even respondents who were born outside of Canada felt proud of this newly acquired identity. The respondents' positive feelings about being Canadian are expressed in a wide range of comments, such as "Canada is a nice country"; "Canada is a place where many cultures come together (i.e., multicultural)"; "people are free" and ". . . are equal under the law"; "Canada provides a secure, safe, and democratic environment;" and "Canada provides economic opportunities." Two respondents gave qualified responses about being Canadian for reasons that are extraneous to Arab ethnicity, and only one respondent was negative, saying that he did not like it in Canada.

How do these respondents feel about being *Arab* Canadian? Generally, they feel good about their ethnicity, as evidenced by positive responses such as:

I feel proud, it means respect.

I like it that we are different from whites.

I feel more mature than them [whites] being an Arab Canadian.

It's fine; Canada is the home of multiculturalism.

I am very happy; I am proud that I can bring that part of culture into Canada and share it with my friends.

However, it should be emphasized that one of ten respondents did not feel as positive about being an Arab Canadian. Examples of ambivalent or negative responses: "I am less free, but it feels like I am in a big family"; "I feel like I am held back"; "not strongly"; and "I hate it; it is the most difficult thing for a girl to be."

Nearly four of ten respondents believe that strangers can determine that the respondents are of Arab origin just by looking at them. Ethnicity may be an asset or a liability. When it is perceived to be a liability, it is possible that the individual may wish to hide or camouflage it. The extent to which Arab-Canadian ethnicity is perceived to be a liability is reflected by responses to the following question: "Are there times when you try to hide your Arab-Canadian origin?" The results show that more females (three of ten) than males (one of ten) tried to hide their ethnicity, and within the female group, more Christian (44 percent) than Muslim (13 percent) tried to hide their Arab-Canadian identity.

The survey results show that Arab-Canadian youth, male and female, are symbolically and attitudinally well integrated into Canadian society. For many reasons, they feel unreservedly proud of their Canadian identity. Similarly, they are positive about their Arab heritage and ethnic identity and the many positive things that they say they enjoy as a result of being Arab (e.g., family support, sharing, hospitality, friendliness).

Nevertheless, the results appear to point to a potential tension between parents and youth that may be characterized as mild or random. This generational tension seems to revolve around a wide range of issues that the respondents broadly articulated as follows: overprotectiveness and strictness of parents, inequality of men and women (i.e., male superiority), cultural chauvinism, backwardness, gossiping, and dominance of religion. The tension is neither pervasive nor constant, but it is (potentially always) there. From time to time, this tension surfaces in the relationships between parents and youth and alienates one group from the other.

There is also tension between Arab-Canadian youth and the larger Canadian society that is often triggered by biased or unfair portrayal of Arabs in the print and electronic media. This issue is addressed in the next section.

Media Perceptions

In the Edmonton survey, youth were asked about their own assessments of how Arabs are portrayed in the media, particularly television. Our survey results indicate that these young Arab Canadians are fairly heavy television consumers. For example, almost one of five (18 percent) admit to watching television for sixteen or more hours per week; 47 percent watch seven to fifteen hours per week; and about 35 percent of the respondents report watching six hours or less of television per week. About 37 percent read the newspaper daily, and an equivalent proportion (37 percent) read the newspaper two or three times per week. The balance (26 percent) read the newspaper once each week or less.

The respondents' favorite television programs are by far situation comedies (53 percent), followed by films or detective programs (13 percent), sports (10 percent), and news or documentaries (5 percent). Examples of comedy programs watched include The Simpsons, Evening at the Improv, Married with Children, Beverly Hills, Cheers, Cosby Show, Who's the Boss, and Three's Company.

The newspaper sections most frequently read, in descending order, are sports (36 percent), national news (23 percent), international news (13 percent), city news (6 percent), and comics (6 percent). The remainder of the respondents (16 percent) prefer to read other sections.

To assess how young Arab-Canadians characterize the portrayal of Arabs on television, the following question was asked: Have there been any specific times when you felt that television portrayed Arabs or Arab culture in a *biased or unfair manner*? In response, a total of 63 percent of the respondents felt that television "often" (19 percent) or "sometimes" (44 percent) portrayed Arabs in a biased or unfair manner. The balance (or 37 percent) checked "seldom" (3 percent) or "never" (34 percent). With specific reference to the Canadian media and the Gulf War, the respondents were asked the following question: "Do you feel that media accounts of the Gulf War have in any way affected the attitudes or behaviors of Canadians toward you or toward people of Arab origin?" Three of four respondents checked the category "yes," and the remainder checked the "no" category. Not surprisingly, these results are consistent with the massive evidence that has accumulated over the last thirty to forty years about how the North American media are biased in their portrayal of Arabs or Arab culture. However, about three of ten Arab Canadian youth do not see such a bias. It may be that these youths' selective or limited exposure does not bring them in direct contact with biased portrayals or that they evaluate bias differently from most of their Arab-Canadian peers. In either case, this is an area that merits further investigation.

Young and old Arab Canadians are markedly influenced by the media and what they say about them or about the ancestral heritage. The impact of the media appears to be twofold. On the one hand, negative or biased portrayals of Arabs in the media may cement relations between the young and the old, between the immigrant and the Canadian-born (or raised) generations. This is one form of defense against the excesses of the dominant society. On the other hand, family life presents challenges for most people. Parenting issues can be compounded by the immigrant experience. Are there traditions that can be called on in the process of socializing a child that will empower them in Canadian society? How do children develop positive self-concepts and ethnic identity in a society that is sometimes anti-Arab? What challenges face parents in building positive self concepts in their children? Is there "double" or "triple" jeopardy in diasporic parenting? The literature seems fond of additive characterizations of disadvantage. Can they be multiplicative? Might they, in combination, be deflective or protective in any way?

Contrary to classic accounts of the marginal position that the second generation occupies in American society, the results from the Edmonton survey do not seem to reflect the marginality of Arab-Canadian youth despite the difficult situation that they experience, even though some of them try to cope by hiding their ethnic identity. Nor do these results show intense and insurmountable generational conflict that pits youth against parents, even though parent-youth tension is a reality of immigrant family life. In all probability, this finding results from the relatively high socioeconomic status of the youth covered in the study, which reflects one of the main characteristics of Edmonton's Arab community. Nevertheless, more research is needed to address this specific question.

Preliminary evidence from interviews suggests less intergenerational tension than is often predicted in the literature on immigrant families. There are constants within the

Arab-Canadian family that can lend to distancing between parents and young adult children. Factors in the family development cycle such as differential birth cohorts, period effects, and velocities of change may be constants that are impacted by the inevitability of cultural contrasts and differences. However, the Edmonton study did not find sharp differences between parents and youth. The relative equanimity within this group of relatively advantaged middle-class families may be related to integration or fit with the larger society. Tension may be an accompaniment of asymmetry between parents' adaptation and the child's adaptation. For example, when parent and child embrace change or when both resist change, the potential for conflict is lessened. But when orientation toward change differs between parents and youth, there is ready potential for disagreement, and factors key to the developmental phase in family life may become activated and further exacerbate tensions.

Diasporic parenting may have its built-in pressures and its inherent strains just by virtue of the parenting challenge itself, but factors within the immigrant experience may strengthen or weaken parent-child relationships in adolescence. Parents who are more familiar with the settlement language and the new culture are strengthened in negotiating their and their children's adaptation to a new environment. Although the velocity of change differs, immigrant parents typically are called on to make significantly greater changes than native-born parents. There is need for researchers to examine and trace, in as nonideological a fashion as possible, whether, even under conditions of generational tension, there are distinctive qualities within the immigrant family experience that work to mitigate some of these age-generated cross-currents. For example, to what extent may unique family coalition-building advantages accrue under conditions of discrimination and bigotry? To what extent and in what ways are some immigrant Arab-Canadian families able to provide solace in the adaptation and settlement period. Regardless of built-in, inevitable gaps between parent and mature child, immigrants who are re-inventing their families far away from the traditional supports of home. occasionally under embattled conditions, may have much to teach about parent-youth dynamics in North America.

Conclusions: Strategies for Action and Change

The act of immigrating to a new, unfamiliar setting is a major life stress for families. Parents and children, although part of the same family unit, may react in different ways to the settlement challenge, and the disruptiveness of change may influence their relationships with one another. This may be particularly true for families with adolescent children.

How do family members respond to change and maintain or perhaps strengthen their bonds with one another? Are there ways to fortify families undergoing such change? The strategies we suggest that may aid and facilitate family adaptation are related to factors in the larger community and factors in parent-child relationships. At the community level, Arab-Canadian groups need to be prepared to invest resources and energies to reconcile intergroup differences and raise community status. The Arab-Canadian community could invest in its own development through the use of community organizers, community educators, and professionals in various fields. The experience of youth of Arab descent in Alberta suggests that emphasis on role models from within the community is effective in providing teen support. Perhaps parenting role models could similarly benefit families.

Externally, organizations need to scan the environment for signs that may undermine the respect or collective identity of the Arab-Canadian group. They need to demand and receive the respect that is attainable through the existing legal and political structures. In this regard, there may be much emphasis on the quality of Arab-Canadian leadership that links the community to the external environment. Such leadership needs to be educated and well versed in Canadian culture and social practices. Beyond this, Arab Canadians need to be more fully involved in the political process in the larger society and place more stress on their representation. They need to network more fully and consistently with like-minded groups that also demand respect and equality and that fight prejudice and discrimination. Network building is critical.

Within this strong community, immigrant parents can be brought together to discuss issues relating to settlement and family adjustment. Outside speakers and community-based family counselors who can provide culturally sensitive advice would also be advantageous. New immigrant parents need to be informed about the culture. They need to know English or French in Canada, and they need to be informed accurately about youth culture. Their information and understanding should reflect less bias and stereotype and fewer television-based generalizations about Western youth. Parenting in the diaspora is far from easy, but with active community support, families can prosper, and second-generation youth can be looked on as a rich resource, as a bridge between cultures, and as a pathway for families in their move from the old to the new.

Notes

1. Martin M. Marger, *Race and Ethnic Relations: American and Global Perspectives* (Belmont, CA: Wadsworth, 1997).

2. Citizenship and Immigration Canada. "What Are the Key Elements of a Strategy for Integrating Newcomers into Canadian Society?" In *1994 Immigration Consultations: The Report of Working Group #5* (Ottawa: Ministry of Supply and Services Canada, 1994).

3. As quoted in Muhammad Anwar, "Muslims in Britain." In Syed Z. Abedin and Ziauddin Sardar, eds., *Muslim Minorities in the West* (London: Grey Seal, 1995), pp. 91–92.

4. Compare Marger, *Race and Ethnic Relations,* p. 112.

5. Marziya Yasmin and Baha Abu-Laban, "Ethnicity and Occupational Inequality: A Reconsideration," *Alberta Journal of Educational Research* 38 (1992): 205–18.

6. Betty Carter and Monica McGoldrick, *The Changing Family Life Cycle,* 2nd ed. (Boston: Allyn & Bacon, 1989), p. 18.

7. Sharon McIrvin Abu-Laban, "Family and Religion among Muslim Immigrants and Their Descendants." In Earle Waugh, Sharon McIrvin Abu-Laban, and Regula B. Qureshi, eds., *Muslim Families in North America* (Edmonton: University of Alberta Press, 1991), pp. 6–31; and Nancy Jabbra, "1991 Household and Family among Lebanese Immigrants in Nova Scotia: Continuity, Change, and Adaptation," *Journal of Comparative Family Studies* 22 (1991): 39–56.

8. See Lila Fahlman, "Culture Conflict in the Classroom: An Edmonton Survey." In Earle Waugh, Baha Abu-Laban, and Regula B. Qureshi, eds., *The Muslim Community in North America* (Edmonton: University of Alberta Press, 1983), pp. 202–11.

9. For a classic discussion of parent-youth conflict, see Kingsley Davis, "The Sociology of Parent-Youth Conflict," *American Sociological Review* 5 (1940): 523–35.

10. For a systematic examination of the cohort implications, see Sharon McIrvin Abu-Laban, "The Co-Existence of Cohorts: Identity and Adaptation among Arab-American Muslims," *Arab Studies Quarterly* 2 (1989): 45–63, and her "Family and Religion."

11. Augie Fleras and Joan Leonard Elliott, "Inequality and Stratification." In *Unequal Relations: An Introduction to Race, Ethnic and Aboriginal Dynamics in Canada* (Scarborough, Ontario: Prentice-Hall Canada, 1996), pp. 100–29.

12. See Karim H. Karim, *Images of Arabs and Muslims: A Research Review* (Ottawa, Canada: Policy and Research, Multiculturalism Sector, 1991).

13. Zuhair Kashmiri, *The Gulf Within: Canadian Arabs, Racism and the Gulf War* (Toronto: James Lorimer & Co., 1991).

14. Baha Abu-Laban, *An Olive Branch on the Family Tree: The Arabs in Canada* (Toronto: McClelland & Stewart, 1980); and Farid E. Ohan and Ibrahim Hayani, *The Arabs in Ontario: A Misunderstood Community* (Toronto: Near East Cultural and Educational Foundation, 1993).

15. See Baha Abu-Laban, "Arab Canadians and the Arab-Israeli Conflict," *Arab Studies Quarterly* 10 (1988): 104–26.

16. See Baha Abu-Laban, *Social and Political Attitudes of Arab-Americans: What the 1989 ADC Survey Reveals*. ADC Issue Paper No. 24 (Washington, DC: ADC Research Institute, 1990); Baha Abu-Laban and Sharon McIrvin Abu-Laban, "The Gulf War and Its Impact on Canadians of Arab and Muslim Descent." In Baha Abu-Laban and M. Ibrahim Alladin, eds., *Beyond the Gulf War: Muslims, Arabs and the West* (Edmonton: MRF Publishers, 1991), pp. 119–42; Tamer Anis, *A Profile of Anti-Arab Racism and Discrimination in Canada* (Ottawa: National Council on Canada-Arab Relations, 1996); Edmund Ghareeb, *Split Vision: The Portrayal of Arabs in the American Media* (Washington, DC: American-Arab Affairs Council, 1984); Ohan and Hayani, *Arabs in Ontario*; Suha J. Sabbagh, *Sex, Lies and Stereotypes: The Images of Arabs in American Popular Fiction* (Washington, DC: ADC Research Institute, 1990); Jack G. Shaheen, *The TV Arab* (Bowling Green, OH: Bowling Green State University Popular Press, 1984); and Michael W. Suleiman, *The Arabs in the Mind of America* (Brattleboro, VT: Amana Books, 1988).

17. Edward T. Hall, The Hidden Dimension (Garden City, NY: Doubleday, 1966), as quoted in Vincent A. Parillo, *Strangers to These Shores* (New York: Macmillan, 1990), p. 323.

18. For an account of such crimes, see American-Arab Anti-Discrimination Committee (ADC), *1991 Report on Anti-Arab Hate Crimes* (Washington, DC: ADC Research Institute, 1992).

19. Compare Anis, *Profile of Anti-Arab Racism*.

Part IV

Health and Welfare Issues

Rosina Hassoun

---

10 Arab-American Health and the Process of Coming to America: Lessons from the Metropolitan Detroit Area

In the past 100 years, hundreds of thousands of Arab immigrants came to the United States seeking a new life. Although there are 2½ to 3 million people of Arabic origin now living in the United States,[1] in many ways, the history of Arab immigrants is still in the early stages of being written. As more researchers examine Arab immigration to the United States, a richer understanding of Arab Americans emerges. New questions about the Arab American experience are being asked. As with other immigrants, it is assumed that most Arabs came to the United States with the expectation that economic betterment would bring greater happiness and well-being.[2] Part of the well-being they expected was good health.

Research on Arab-American health has virtually just begun, and there are many questions being asked. What illnesses do Arab Americans suffer from most? How are health patterns changing over time? Are generations of Arab Americans progressively healthier? Is there a health cost associated with immigration? Have Arab Americans achieved the health they expected? Is there a health cost to be paid for the lifestyles changes and sacrifices made by generations of Arab Americans? If there are health costs, how severe are they, and can they be prevented? Do the health problems increase or decrease with each generation in the United States? Are the health costs highest for the first generation of Arab immigrants? What roles do dietary and lifestyle changes play in the overall health patterns of Arab Americans? Is there a tradeoff between health and the search for increased material well-being? The health patterns of Arab immigrants may provide information on changes in illnesses common in Arab populations before and after immigration and provide useful answers for other populations.

One of the first questions that needs to be addressed is whether Arab-American health patterns are similar to those of other ethnic groups and immigrants. For example, studies of health and acculturation in Japanese living in California, Hawaii, and Japan indicate that Japanese Americans who live less traditional Japanese lifestyles in California have the higher rates of cardiovascular disease.[3] This and other studies of people from different cultures suggest that diseases such as cardiovascular disease, hypertension, and diabetes increase during acculturation to a highly industrialized lifestyle. No direct comparative study of Arabs in the United States and the Middle East has been done. However, at least one Arab physician provided anecdotal information when he complained of a rise in cardiovascular disease, hypertension, and obesity in his patients in Bahrain.[4] The physician attributed these conditions to the adoption of more Westernized diets and lifestyles: viewing too much television, lack of exercise, and snacking between meals.[5]

In the absence of comparative data from the Middle East, hypotheses about the interaction of health and acculturation can be tested by examining the disease patterns in recent, first-generation, and second-generation Arab Americans. A brief reexamination of the history of Arab Americans may provide clues about their health patterns. Stronger evidence comes from a community study of health in Arab Americans in Detroit.[6] This seminal study has provided some of the first information on health trends in Arab Americans. The study examined the process of acculturation and health from the viewpoint of biocultural anthropology. This methodology enabled a more detailed survey to be conducted and supplemented with actual participant observation to determine behaviors. This search for answers about Arab-American health was also designed to offer clues about improving Arab-American health. This one study is not a broad-based epidemiological survey that can answer questions about the health of all Arab Americans, but it may point to some important trends.

Reexamining the History of Arabs in America: The Health History of a People

Although the history of Arabs in America is a story that is now being told by many authors,[7] most of the research has focused on the historical, political, and social aspects of Arab-American life. The health and biology of Arab and Chaldean[8] immigrants is an area of growing interest that was virtually ignored in past studies. The collective health history of a people is important to the health of the group, especially in the area of preventive care. Knowing the generalized health patterns of a group and their disease susceptibilities enables physicians to screen for illnesses that may otherwise go undetected and untreated. The health history also adds a deeper dimension to the Arab-American experience.

In the stories of immigrants, Gregory Orfalea[9] found that escaping from political persecution, colonialism, war, epidemics, and famine was a major factor in bringing Arabs to the United States. Regardless of the specific reason for coming to the United States, a better lifestyle and, by default, better health are what Arab immigrants to the United States expect. Many of the early Arab immigrants worked as door-to-door merchants (i.e., peddlers) carrying heavy packs in all sorts of weather.[10] Life was difficult for many of the Arab immigrants at the turn of the century. However, very little first-hand information on the health of that population at that time is available. The chroniclers of the early Arab immigrants describe the experience of that generation of Arabs as a story of assimilation and economic success. Arabs succeeded in America, but at what cost in lives and health?

The biographies of early Arab Americans provide some clues. The biography of Kahlil Gibran[11] provides glimpses of the life of the early Arab immigrants in Boston's Southend. Boston's Southend just after the turn of the century was a teeming, crowded ghetto full of Arab and many other immigrants.[12] These immigrants endured poverty and disease in overcrowded cold-water flats. Most of the early immigrants (Arabs or not) in Boston's Southend suffered the slurs of outsiders who confused the conditions, disease, and poverty with the people themselves. Irish, Italians, and countless other immigrants have suffered the same stigma and worked to raise their standard of living.[13]

In Kahlil Gibran's immediate family, the burden of their way of life is evident. Gibran's 14-year-old sister, Sultana, died in 1902 of "chronic diarrhea and interstitial nephritis."[14] While his mother was hospitalized on one occasion, a smallpox epidemic swept through the hospital.[15] Gibran's mother died of cancer. Gibran's brother, Peter, died of "consumption" (possibly tuberculosis). The famous author and poet suffered heart pains of an unknown nature, eating and sleep disorders, a thyroid problem, and chronic fatigue.[16] The information from a single family is anecdotal, but it points to the kinds of serious health problems that haunted immigrants to the United States at the turn of the century. Tuberculosis, smallpox, cholera, and polio struck immigrant populations.[17] Immigrants, living in crowded neighborhoods without wealth and access to proper sanitation and health care, suffered disproportionately from these and many other illnesses.

Members of the first generation of immigrants were especially determined to see that their children would have a better life. Subsequent waves of immigrants and their children benefited from the advances made in sanitation and medical care in the United States. We can assume that the lives of later immigrants were somewhat easier because of improved work conditions and health care, but there is no accurate accounting of their health conditions.

The second wave of Arab immigrants lived through the Great Depression and World War II, with the bread lines and the food rationing of that era. The influenza epidemics, polio, and tuberculosis probably posed serious health threats for Arab Americans during the period from the beginning of World War I to the end of World War II. Thousands of new Arab-American citizens fought in the trenches during the war.[18] After the war, like many other Americans, Arab Americans began to experience the prosperity of the post-war era, with better health care and sanitation.

From the 1960s to the present, Arab immigrants have worked long hours in small and large businesses, behind counters, and at computers to attempt to better their lives. The impact of the work place exposures to different conditions in the factories and in their businesses has never been studied. The role the long hours and the stressful conditions have played in increasing health risks has yet to be assessed. The combination of lifestyle changes, dietary changes, and stress that are inherent in the acculturation process are part of the concessions immigrants make for survival in a new country or environment. Research into the health of immigrants remains open for further investigation.

Arab Americans: The Health and Environmental History of Metropolitan Detroit

Today, the Detroit area is an example of working class Arab population families that immigrated to work in a large industrial city. The unique role of the automobile industry in shaping the city and the lives of its inhabitants distinguishes this city's population. The role of Arab Americans in the rise of the automobile industry is to a large extent an untold story. Most Americans are unaware of the sacrifices made by Yemeni and Lebanese workers in the factories. The health consequences for Arab immigrants living around and working in the auto factories, with exposure to pollutants and factory conditions, have not been documented. Metropolitan Detroit also has a variety of Arab and Chaldean Americans that are small shop keepers, entrepreneurs, engineers, professionals, and factory line workers.

Metropolitan Detroit hosts the largest population of Arab Americans in North America, with about 250,000 Arabs.[19] There are two major staging areas of Arab and Chaldean immigrants in the Detroit area: one in the Southend and East Dearborn and the other in the Seven Mile and Woodward areas. The Dearborn Arab population is predominantly Muslim (i.e., Lebanese, Yemeni, and Palestinian), and the Seven Mile–Woodward area is a Christian Chaldean enclave. The Detroit area also has sizable pockets of other Arabs scattered throughout the Detroit and tri-county area.

The predominantly Yemeni population of Dearborn's Southend live in working class neighborhoods in the shadow of the huge Ford Rouge Factory and are surrounded by at least a dozen other automobile and parts manufacturing plants in the area. Pollution regulations have lessened the emissions from the plants, but toxic chemicals are still released into the air. Factory workers continue to face health risks, although considerably less than in years past. Unemployment rates are high in this area because of recent factory layoffs.[20] At the same time, there has been a small boom in building, and new Arab-owned businesses in the Southend in recent years.

The Seven Mile–Woodward area lies to the north of Dearborn, away from the large factories but closer to the expressways. It is a Chaldean enclave in the heart of an African-American neighborhood suffering from urban decay and high crime rates. Arab shop owners and home owners in both neighborhoods are trying to revitalize these areas.

There have been four waves of Arab immigrants to Detroit, beginning with the first in 1890. The first wave of Arab immigrants to Detroit arrived just as Detroit was beginning its transformation into an industrial center. Its members were mostly Lebanese men seeking employment. Early Arab immigrants to Detroit found work as door-to-door salesmen and as auto workers in the budding industrial metropolis between 1890 and 1912.[21] The first Arab Muslims settled in Highland Park near the Ford Motor Company's first plant, where many of them worked. The first Palestinians in the Detroit area arrived between 1908 and 1913. Chaldeans first arrived in Detroit between 1910 and 1912.[22]

Yemenis began arriving in the Detroit area as early as the 1900s but did not establish a real permanent presence until 1920 to 1925. It was not until the 1960s that Yemeni families began immigrating permanently to Dearborn's Southend.[23] Yemenis have worked in the Ford factory and in other industrial jobs that required intensive manual labor. Because Yemen did not have widespread modern health care until the 1960s,[24] many of these Yemeni workers from rural villages in their country of origin received comprehensive health care for the first time only after immigrating to the United States.

The second wave of Arab immigrants to the Detroit area began arriving on the eve of the Great Depression. This second wave, which ended in 1960, included increasing numbers of Arab Muslims and Palestinian refugees. Detroit during this period was experiencing a massive influx of African Americans from the south seeking employment in the north. Downtown Detroit experienced the phenomenon of "white flight," and Arabs in the Detroit area were at times welcomed in neighborhoods and at other times experienced "red lining."[25]

Many Arabs settled in the suburbs in Detroit, especially the more affluent second generation. New immigrants still continue to settle in the staging areas (ethnic enclaves) of Dearborn and the Seven Mile and Woodward areas. The residents of Dearborn's Southend have higher exposure to health hazards from the surrounding industry while the inhabitants of the Seven Mile area suffer higher crime rates.

Certain assumptions about some of the trade-offs these different waves of Arab immigrants made are probably accurate. For example, working in the factories probably exposes the men to greater risk of physical harm (accidents) and toxic chemicals. At the same time, the companies and unions provide them with health insurance and access to health care that they might not otherwise have if not employed. Living in the neighborhoods surrounding the plants lessens the cost of transportation to and from work, but it exposes families to more pollution.

Working in neighborhood stores and gas stations in lower-income areas provides some Arab and Chaldean entrepreneurs cheaper real estate and start-up costs for their businesses. It also may place them in conflict with the inhabitants of these areas who view them as outsiders and expose them to more stress and crime. How these trade-offs are balanced influences the health and well-being of the individuals and the group. How immigrants respond and adapt is determined by their behavior (decision-making capabilities) and by their biology (physical endurance).

Health Study of Arabs and Chaldean Americans in Detroit

Compared with other human populations, knowledge about the biology and genetics of Arabic-speaking people and other ethnic groups in the Middle East is limited. This lack of knowledge may prove to be detrimental to the health and treatment of certain conditions in these populations. Lack of knowledge about the more than 200 million Arabic-speaking people in the world hinders the greater understanding of disease and health in the human family. Research may aid in defining the origins and identities of the larger socioeconomic group of Arabic-speaking people in the world—with all of their diversities and similarities.

Popular histories do not provide an adequate biological history of a people. For example, one commonly mentioned fact is the tendency for Arabs and Chaldeans to live and

TABLE 10-1. Age and Physical Measurements

Subgroups and Sample	Mean Height (cm)	Height Std. Dev.	Mean Weight (kg)	Weight Std. Dev.	Mean Body Mass Index	BMI Std. Dev.	Mean Age	Age Std. Dev.
Syrian/Lebanese (n = 89)	164.6	8.0	70.5	11.7	0.037	0.006	36.1	14.5
Iraqis/Chaldeans (n = 79)	165.6	8.7	77	13.2	0.04	0.007	49.2	13.0
Jordanians/Palestinians (n = 46)	164.2	7.6	71.9	13.3	0.038	0.006	41.6	15.4
Yemenis (n = 44)	166.8	5.8	65.1	11.7	0.033	0.005	31.4	13.9

From R. J. Hassoun, "A Bioanthropological Perspective of Hypertension in Arab-Americans in the Metropolitan Detroit Area" (Ph.D. dissertation, University of Florida, 1995).

marry inside village and kinship groups.[26] There has also been a steady stream of foreign invasions, migrations, and emigrations of Arabic-speaking people into and away from the Middle East.[27] This combination of intermarriage and the introduction of new genes means that the variations and similarities in Arabic-speaking populations present scientists with great opportunities and challenges. Studies of the complex relationships of culture, biology, and health are at the frontier of modern science and medicine.

This is one of the first community-based anthropological health studies of Arab Americans and tests hypotheses through the reported health histories of 300 adult Arab and Chaldean Americans living in the metropolitan Detroit area. Reported health histories are supplemented with anthropometric (body) measurements and blood pressure measurements. The reported health histories are compared by time and generation in the United States, age, sex, and subgroup. Adjusting for age, it is possible to compare the changes in reported health and patterns of disease occurrence in the groups studied.

The sampling methods for this project involved a combination of quota and network sampling to ensure a representative sample of the four major Arab and Chaldean subgroups in the Detroit area. The method of network sampling has been successful in many immigrant populations for which legal status, fear of outsiders, and other factors such as mobility make sampling difficult. A quota system of 100 Syrian/Lebanese, 100 Iraqi/Chaldeans, 50 Jordanian/Palestinians, and 50 Yemenis was established. The prerequisites were adults between the ages of 18 and 65 who had both parents from the same Arab or Chaldean subgroup. Field data were collected for this project between September 1991 and March 1994.[28]

One of the first questions researchers face is the meaning of biological and health differences between Arab-American subgroups. This study provides one of the first comparative studies of different groups of Arab and Chaldean Americans. For example, height and weight may have genetic and behavioral (dietary) components. When Arab- and Chaldean-American heights and weights in this sample were compared, patterns of similarities and differences emerged (Table 10-1). The differences in height between the subgroups are not statistically significant.

The popular perception in the Arab community is that the Yemenis are shorter or smaller in stature than other Arabs. In this sample, the observed mean height does not concur with the popular belief. The slighter build (the slightly lower body weights) may be the source of the popular belief. The age and weight differences between the subgroups in this sample are important factors that will be revisited in discussing disease occurrences in this sample.

Because of the variability in the sample, any difference in the mean weights of the four subgroups is not significantly different. However, when the body mass index (which is height-adjusted weight) is used, there are differences in the four subgroups. The Iraqi/Chaldean group had the highest body mass, and the Yemenis had the lowest mean body mass. These differences may correlate with the occurrence of certain diseases, as discussed later. The tables include males and females, and gender is considered in the analysis.

Other physical measurements show differences between the groups in how weight is distributed on the body. It is not just how much overweight a person might be but where on the body the weight accumulates that may predispose a person for certain illnesses. The Syrian/Lebanese group had higher waist, hip and thigh measurements than the other subgroups.[29] Greater similarities exist between Syrian/Lebanese and Palestinian/Jordanians in their height and body mass index than between the other subgroups. Because these subgroups are from the Levant, where they may share more biological, dietary, and cultural factors in common, these similarities in physical measurements are not surprising.

Some changes in weight and body mass index occurred for Arab Americans in this study after immigrating to the United States. When mean body mass and weight for the entire sample of Arabs and Chaldeans is plotted against time in the United States, there is some evidence that body mass and weight are increasing.[30]

Age is another factor in this rise in weight with time in the United States, because many people put on weight as they age and become less active. The low activity levels of Arabs and Chaldeans in this sample may also play a role in this weight gain over time. The causes of the differences between the different Arab and Chaldean groups are still a mystery; this study indicates that differences exist in diet, exercise, and possibly genetics.

Reported Health Histories of Arab and Chaldean Americans

The general health patterns (i.e., disease occurrence) and the change in these patterns with years in the United States and with age provide a complex picture of the health patterns of Arab and Chaldean Americans. The disease occurrence data in this sample come primarily from reported health histories (Table 10-2). These are self-reported data. The possibility exists that some conditions were not disclosed or have not been detected by physicians. When blood pressures were determined, a sizable number of individuals were discovered to have elevated blood pressures. For example, although 40.5 percent of the Chaldean subgroup were reported to be hypertensive (i.e., have high blood pressure), measurement showed that 51.5 percent of those sampled were actually hypertensive.[31] This may mean that reported disease underestimates the amount of disease in a group and some disease goes untreated until the symptoms become critical. When the major diseases of Arab Americans in this study are examined, the danger becomes clear.

TABLE 10-2. Individual Reported Health Histories: Percentages by Total Sample and Subgroups

Condition[a]	Total Sample (%)	Syrian/ Lebanese	Iraqis/ Chaldeans	Jordanians/ Palestinians	Yemenis
Hypertension	16.0	6.7	40.5	20.5	7.0
High cholesterol	15.6	15.4	20.0	18.2	9.3
Diabetes	7.0	4.4	10.0	6.8	9.8
Ulcers	6.0	3.3	10.0	7.0	7.0
Heart disease	3.7	2.2	4.9	4.6	4.7
Blood disorders	3.7	4.4	5.0	2.3	2.3
Cancer	1.4	2.2	0.0	2.5	0.0
Kidney disease	0.9	1.1	0.0	2.3	0.0
Arterial disease	0.9	0.0	0.0	0.0	2.3
Stroke	0.9	0.0	2.5	2.3	0.0
Other conditions	16.0	13.6	16.3	9.1	27.3

[a]Noncompliance and missing data are approximately 18 percent. "Other conditions" are primarily respiratory diseases and asthma.

From R. J. Hassoun, "A Bioanthropological Perspective of Hypertension in Arab-Americans in the Metropolitan Detroit Area" (Ph.D. dissertation, University of Florida, 1995).

The information in Table 10-2 indicates that the three major health conditions found in this sample of Arab and Chaldean Americans are hypertension, high cholesterol, and diabetes. The occurrences of these conditions appear to be as high or higher than the reported prevalence of these conditions in most white populations in Michigan. The occurrence of hypertension in the sample ranges from 9.7 percent in the Syrian/Lebanese group to a high of 51.5 percent in Iraqi/Chaldeans.

When familial rates of hypertension, the individual reported rates, and measured rates of hypertension are considered together, the overall occurrence of hypertension is 21.1 percent. The reported prevalence of hypertension in the white majority population is 22.7 percent.[32]

Because the onset of hypertension often occurs with older age, the older mean age of the Chaldeans and the younger mean age of the Syrian/Lebanese in the sample may mean that hypertension rates will increase with age in the Arab and Chaldean populations. The 51.5 percent occurrence of hypertension in this one sample of Iraqis/Chaldeans is very high. In comparison, 34.9 percent of African Americans report having high blood pressure in Michigan, and that is among the highest percentages of any group in the state.[33] The mean age and sample sizes (and the problem of comparing an occurrence in one sample with general prevalence) should be considered before making assumptions about these figures.

The prevalence of diabetes among Michigan's adult population is 3.6 percent.[34] If this sample is indicative of the general Arab and Chaldean population in Michigan, they may have at least double the prevalence of diabetes of the general Michigan population. Diabetes can cause blindness, loss of limbs, and premature death. The results from this study manifest the possibility that diabetes may occur at very high rates among Arab Americans. Informing more physicians that Arab Americans need to have regular screenings for diabetes may help maintain health and save lives.

What do the differences between the occurrences of disease in the different Arab and Chaldean Americans mean? One of the first things to consider is the difference in the mean age of the different subgroups. The mean age of the Iraqi/Chaldean subgroup may account for many of the differences between groups; the Chaldeans are older. The Yemenis and Syrian/Lebanese are younger subgroups. If mean age alone were considered, one would expect the disease occurrence of age-related conditions to increase in the groups in the following order: Yemeni, Syrian/Lebanese, Jordanian/Palestinian, and Iraqi/Chaldean. For some of these conditions (i.e., hypertension and high cholesterol), this pattern does occur. Ulcers increase and then decrease with age and time in the United States.[35] The Chaldeans, because of their older mean age, may be the model for what happens to Arab Americans as they age. However, as with ulcers, age alone does not explain all the disease patterns.

The high occurrence of other diseases, primarily upper respiratory disease and asthma, in the Yemeni population may be directly related to their environment. Most Yemenis surveyed in this sample live in and around the automobile manufacturing plants and are exposed to higher levels of dust and chemical pollutants. Their exposure to chemicals, unemployment, poverty, and other unhealthy living conditions are suspect in their health problems. Residents in Dearborn's Southend in this sample have twice the overall occurrence of disease that the Seven Mile–Woodward residents have.[36] Although more research is needed to determine the exact cause of the higher rates of disease in the Yemenis in the Southend of Dearborn, their substantially higher occurrence of disease is cause for concern.

The occurrences of many of these conditions (e.g., cancer, stroke, arterial disease) appear to be very low in this sample. This does not mean that they do not present a threat to Arab and Chaldean populations. It may mean that diseases are underreported or undiagnosed because of lack of health screening or access to health care. Of special concern is the need for breast examinations and screening for colon cancer.

Because of the large number of unemployed and those without adequate health insurance and English language skills, the problem of undiagnosed and untreated disease remains highly probable in this population. Unemployment is between 28 and 40 percent in the different subgroups in this sample. Eight percent of those sampled could not speak English (and were interviewed in Arabic or Chaldean), and 7 percent of the 300 adults in the sample have no formal education.[37] For this small segment of the population, access to health care may be hampered by barriers of language and economics.

Differences in reported health conditions exist between males and females in all the subgroups.[38] For most conditions (except stroke, cancer, and blood disorders), women had lower (1 to 10 percent) levels of occurrence of disease. Although cancer occurrence is low, all the cases (2.6 percent) in this sample occurred in women, who had mostly breast and reproductive cancers. Hypertension was 10 percent higher among males than females.[39] What this may mean is that the men have greater susceptibility or exposure to these conditions. It may also mean more of the women's illnesses are going undiagnosed and untreated. The women may not have the same access to health care because of lack of insurance, little or no transportation, fear of the medical system, or lack of awareness of the importance of regular health check-ups. Many of the men may be receiving routine physicals at work. The differences in disease occurrences between the sexes also warrant further research and follow-up.

Lifestyle and Dietary Changes during Acculturation

Explanations for the disease patterns in Arab Americans, other than aging and genetics, may be found in their lifestyle and dietary changes. When questioned about exercise levels, most Arab and Chaldean Americans in this sample reported they did not engage in regular exercise and did not take regular walks.[40] This represents a tremendous change in lifestyle after immigrating to the United States. Even with those who said they did exercise, the amount of exercise is very low. This may indicate that there is a perception of being more active than they really are or an unwillingness to admit, even to themselves, that their lives have become sedentary.

A sampling of Arab and Chaldean foods shows they are generally nutritionally well balanced. The original Arab and Chaldean diet, as quantified by food frequency surveys, 24-hour recalls, and weighed-food records, is moderately high in salt, high in fats, high in vitamin C and phosphorus, and relatively high in calories. This would be an acceptable diet for an active individual who lives in climates such as those found in the Arab world. However, if one takes this basic diet, adds more fats, sweets, red meat, and popular American junk food (i.e., what happens to the Arab-American diet over time) and decreases activity levels, the new diet and exercise habits become very unhealthy.

Other studies have indicated that it is not just an increase in caloric intake or dietary change alone, but the reduction in daily energy expenditures that may contribute to the weight gain associated with acculturation.[41] If so, the combination of dietary changes and decreased activity levels in Arab and Chaldean Americans may explain the weight gain with time in the United States.

Dietary Change and Acculturation in Arab and Chaldean Americans

Further examination of the diets of Arab and Chaldean Americans may offer more clues about their health patterns. An in-depth analysis of the dietary patterns of Arab and Chaldean Americans was conducted as part of this study. This analysis included food frequency surveys, 24-hour recalls, and weighed-food measurement.[42] Recent immigrants were asked to reconstruct their lifestyle and dietary patterns in their villages and towns before coming to the United States. Differences between recent and first- and second-generation Arab and Chaldean Americans with time in the United States were compared.

From these data, the traditional diet in the villages appears to be high in fruits, vegetables, and fiber from grains and cereals. In the traditional diet, meat consumption is lower and reserved for feasts and weekends when family and guests gather. This description of the traditional Arab village diet is corroborated by other writers.[43] The original diet is quite healthy and nutritionally balanced. The lifestyle in the Arab world includes more walking and burns more calories than in the United States.

The diet of Arab and Chaldean Americans is generally nutritionally balanced but does show some consumption patterns of concern for health and weight maintenance. After immigrating to the United States, the diet of Arab and Chaldean Americans becomes high in protein (especially red meat), fats, and sweets.[44] With acculturation, there is an initial rise in the consumption of red meat in the diet (in many cases, two to three times per day) that slowly decreases over time in the United States but still remains high.

Meat is a high-status food in Arab culture and is served for guests and special occasions. Red meat is readily available and relatively inexpensive in the United States. The focus on economic betterment and the availability of lamb and beef in this new country may explain the initial jump in red meat consumption. Red meat, especially lamb, is naturally high in animal fat, cholesterol, and salt. This increase in dietary intake of meat may have detrimental consequences.

Vegetable consumption drops over time in the United States and drops by at least one serving below the recommended daily servings. The whole grains, such as *burghul* (bulgur), are slowly replaced over time in Arab- and Chaldean-American diets by processed white flour. Dairy consumption, especially yogurt consumption, also declines on average by one serving per day after immigrating to the United States.

The core feast foods such as *kibbees* (cracked wheat loafs), roast meats such as *kababs,* and stuffed dishes such as *mahshees* remain in the diet. It is the everyday dishes such as the *yakhnas* (i.e., the village stews of vegetables and some meat served over rice or bread) that are lost in the diets of the first- and second-generation Arab and Chaldean Americans.[45] The number of non-Arabic foods and the number of times one eats in restaurants increases with time in the United States, while the number of Arab traditional meals declines.

Of the four subgroups studied, the Yemenis appear to retain more of their traditional foods and consumption patterns than the other groups. Many of the Yemeni men are single males and tend to eat on the job, but in general their diets remain more traditional than the other groups. Part of this may be their relative isolation in community in the Southend of Dearborn and in other smaller enclaves. Because of economic conditions in the Southend and in Yemen, the Yemenis do not appear to have acquired as high a consumption of red meat as the other groups. Their traditional foods stress wheat, sauces, and vegetables with smaller serving sizes of meat.

However, over time, the junk food and sweet consumption increases in the diet of most Arab and Chaldean Americans sampled. Of particular concern is the food preferences of the younger children. When younger school age children were asked (113 children were questioned, with parental consent, about their eating habits) about their favorite foods, their answers were pizza, candy, and hamburgers. Their reported diets seem lacking in at least one serving of milk and are low in vegetables. Soda pop is popular, with many of the children consuming four or more each day.[46] More worrisome is the fact that some of the Yemeni children in the sample had diets that appeared to be nutritionally inadequate, probably because of their low income levels (food assistance is available for them).

Most of the younger Arab children appear to be following the general patterns seen in most American youth. These eating patterns are not particularly healthy and may place them at risk for the development of diseases and obesity later in life. Older children report a return to and greater preference for the traditional Arab or Chaldean foods, but this may not prevent them from incorporating fast foods and fatty foods into their diets.

Other Health Behaviors—Smoking

In this sample of 300 Arab and Chaldean Americans, 31.4 percent of the respondents smoke.[47] Those that smoke more than a pack per day comprised 17.9 percent of the sample, and most smokers had smoked for ten years or longer. There were few differences in the percent of smokers between Arab and Chaldean subgroups. A higher percent of males (34.7 percent) than females (20.6 percent) tend to smoke. At social gatherings, the air is usually thick with cigarette smoke, and all, including the young children, are exposed to the health risk of smoking. More research is needed to determine the role of smoking in the disease patterns of Arab and Chaldean Americans. Persons suffering from respiratory diseases and asthma may experience more problems when exposed to high amounts of second hand smoke.

Disease and Associated Risk Factors in Arab and Chaldean Americans

From the data presented, the period of acculturation for Arab and Chaldean Americans, as with other immigrant groups, is a period of disequilibrium. It is a period when new behaviors (e.g., eating patterns, activity levels) are acquired. Decisions are made, and there is a trade-off in the consequences of the different behaviors—some positive and some negative in regard to health.

The data show differences in the occurrence of disease among the Arab and Chaldean subgroups and show differences in body mass and shape among the subgroups. This may mean that certain Arab and Chaldean groups, by virtue of their body shape and background, may be more predisposed to certain diseases than other groups. Most Arabs and Chaldeans appear to have an elevated risk of developing diabetes and high cholesterol.

The question these findings raise is whether the increased risk of developing a certain disease condition is caused by belonging to a particular Arab or Chaldean subgroup or whether behavioral or dietary factors appear to play a significant role in the development of the condition. Although this study cannot determine causal agents of disease, comparing behaviors and dietary practices of groups of individuals who have the condition with those that do not may provide useful insights into the association of behaviors and disease. The change in these behaviors with acculturation also provides an association between acculturation and disease.

Hypertensive and Nonhypertensive Arab and Chaldean Americans Sampled

A comparison of the individuals (Arabs and Chaldeans) with hypertension (systolic/diastolic pressures of 140/90 mm Hg or higher) with those without hypertension shows clear differences between the groups. The mean age (55 years) of those with hypertension is higher than the mean age (36 years) of those without.[48] Hypertension in Arabs and

Chaldeans in this sample appears to increase with age and time in the United States, but neither age nor time an immigrant has lived in the United States explains why certain individuals develop hypertension and others do not.

Behaviors and dietary intakes differentiate the hypertensives from the nonhypertensives. Meat consumption of at least one additional serving each of lamb and beef per week is much higher for hypertensives. The fats consumed by the two groups show startling differences. The reported intake per week of margarine, butter, *samnee* (ghee or clarified butter), olive oil, and all other oils is significantly higher in the hypertensive group.[49] The reported frequency of consumption of olive oil at 5.1 times per week by the hypertensives is almost double that reported (2.6 times per week) of the nonhypertensives.

The hypertensives have a higher reported overall food intake. The differences in other food intakes is also interesting. Those with hypertension report eating, on the average, one more serving of bread and cheese per week than those without hypertension. The group without hypertension reports consuming one more serving of sugar than the hypertensives. Carbohydrate intake (i.e., rice and bread consumption) and salad and fruit intakes are somewhat higher for the hypertensives.

Differences also exist in the physical (anthropometric) measurements. The mean height of those with and without reported hypertension is not significantly different. However, the mean group weight is different and corresponds to the greater intake of calories, fats, and meats by the hypertensives. The mean weight of the hypertensives (78.4 kg) is 8 kg more than the mean of the nonhypertensives.[50] Weight is not the only difference between hypertensives and nonhypertensives. Arm, waist, and hip circumferences have larger means in the hypertensive group. The fact that the hypertensives are eating more fats and meat may account for their heavier weights and larger body measurements.

In other behaviors, the hypertensive group had a lower number of smokers (16 percent) compared with the 27.6 percent of nonhypertensives.[51] Quitting smoking may be one of the first recommendations prescribed by doctors for patients with hypertension. The lower smoking rates among those with hypertension may be because their doctors have warned them to stop smoking.

Results for stress and exercise are interesting. The nonhypertensive group had many more persons (37 percent) who report that they are moderately active than the hypertensive group (14 percent).[52] Because exercise is thought to be beneficial in lowering blood pressure, these results are expected. It may mean that increasing the amount of exercise may help prevent high blood pressure. In the case of perceived or reported stress, the nonhypertensives reported feeling more stressed. This inverse relationship between reported stress and high blood pressure has been previously researched and is referred to as the Winkerby-Ragland-Syme hypothesis.[53] The inability to perceive stress or to admit to being stressed may be the cause for the higher blood pressure. For Arab and Chaldean Americans, it may be culturally difficult to admit (except perhaps to very close relatives) that they are experiencing stress or personal problems.

Cholesterol Levels in Arabs and Chaldeans Sampled

The profile of those who report high cholesterol levels is similar to the profile of the hypertensive group. The group with the high cholesterol levels has a higher mean body weight and higher hip, thigh, waist, and arm circumferences. There is a higher percent of heavy smokers in the group reporting high blood pressure. The difference in the mean age (49 ± 13.6 years) between those with high cholesterol and the age (36.2 ± 14.5 years) of those without is not as great for hypertension or diabetes.[54] This finding indicates that there is an earlier onset of elevated cholesterol levels. The group with high cholesterol concentrations reportedly consumed more meat and more fats and oils in their diet than did those without high cholesterol. This means they are consuming more cholesterol despite the fact that the individuals know they have high cholesterol levels. More of those with high cholesterol levels reported feeling moderate amounts of stress than did those with normal cholesterol levels. This pattern in reported stress is different from that of hypertension and diabetes. However, the group without high cholesterol levels had lower mean blood pressures.

Diabetes Among Arab and Chaldean Americans Sampled

The diabetics in this sample had an older mean age (54.5 ± 9.2 years) compared with the mean age (36.8 ± 15 years) of the nondiabetics.[55] This finding indicates that the Arabs and Chaldeans sampled suffer from late onset (type II) diabetes. There was no difference in mean heights between the nondiabetics and the diabetics. The mean weight (76 ± 11.1 kg) of the diabetics was higher than the mean of the nondiabetic group (70.5 ± 13.5 kg), but there is substantial variation in the samples.[56] The physical measurements did not follow the same pattern as seen with hypertension.

The average mean blood pressures (systolic of 133 ± 10.3 mm Hg and diastolic of 80 ± 7.2 mm Hg) in the diabetics is higher than the mean pressures measured in the nondiabetics (123.5 ± 16.0 mm Hg and 76 ± 9.2 mm Hg). A correlation between diabetes and hypertension has been established in this and other studies.[57] People with these health conditions may be in double jeopardy from both illnesses.

The consumption patterns of the diabetics indicate that they are attempting to follow the prescribed diabetic diet and that some are not succeeding. The diabetics still report consuming some sugar and sweets in their diets (some recent diabetic diets allow some sweets). The overall consumption of meats by the diabetic group is lower than that of the nondiabetics, but lamb consumption is the same. Lamb is very high in fat and may still be contributing to overweight. Fish or chicken may be healthier choices, but the diabetics also report eating one less serving of fish a week on average than the nondiabetics.

Sweets and red meat may not be the only problem for this group of Arab and Chaldean diabetics. The diabetics report eating more carbohydrates (e.g., rice, pasta, Arabic bread) than the nondiabetics. Control of diabetes rests in controlling the sugar and the carbohydrate intake because the body breaks carbohydrates into sugars. The diabetic group appears to be overconsuming carbohydrates. The kind of carbohydrates consumed by the diabetics are more refined; they report eating lower amounts of whole grains such as burghul than the nondiabetics. The body easily converts refined carbohydrates into sugars, defeating the purpose of lowering sugar intake.

Fewer diabetics report smoking than nondiabetics. The diabetics, however, have fewer percents (26.7 percent) reporting they are moderately active compared with the 39 percent of nondiabetics who perceive themselves to be moderately active. More nondiabetics reported that they felt high and moderate amounts of stress than the nondiabetics (perhaps similar to the Winkerby-Ragland-Syme effect seen in the hypertensives).

Conclusions

After examining the findings from this study of Arabs and Chaldeans in the Detroit area, some answers about Arab and Chaldean health patterns are beginning to emerge. Arab and Chaldean Americans may suffer disproportionately from diabetes, high cholesterol levels, and hypertension. These three conditions increase with age and appear to be increasing with time in the United States in Arabs and Chaldean Americans. However, it is not aging alone that may be causing an increase in the occurrence of these and other illnesses in the Arabs and Chaldeans sampled.

It appears that specific behaviors, dietary patterns, and environmental factors are associated with the occurrence of certain diseases in Arab and Chaldean Americans. The behaviors and dietary patterns may therefore be more significant indicators of disease risk than just belonging to a particular Arab or Chaldean subgroup. The one exception may be the Chaldeans, for whom an additional biological or genetic predisposition for hypertension cannot be excluded.

From this study, some general behaviors and dietary patterns appear to be associated with the most common diseases (i.e., hypertension, diabetes, and high cholesterol levels) in all Arab and Chaldean groups. The behaviors and practices associated with the common diseases are high red meat consumption, high fat consumption, lack of exercise, and perhaps an inability to express or perceive stress. Higher weight and body mass also appears to be associated with these diseases and may result from the lack of exercise and high fat diet. The Iraqi/Chaldean group, with their higher body mass and consumption of more red meat, may be placing themselves at even higher risk for hypertension and related diseases such as stroke than the other groups.

This study also shows that Arab and Chaldean dietary patterns change over time and that diets are becoming higher in salt, fat, and sweets. This pattern of dietary acculturation is expected to lead to higher disease occurrence (and preliminary findings indicate this is happening) in subsequent Arab and Chaldean generations.

There appears to be a tendency among the Arab and Chaldean Americans interviewed to ignore or cover up health issues. For example, some of the Lebanese interviewed were reluctant to discuss or admit that conditions such as diabetes or thalassemia run in their families. Beta-thalassemia, found in Arab and other populations in the world, is a genetic blood disorder.[58] It is similar to sickle cell anemia in that it reduces the blood's ability to take up oxygen. People with double inheritance of this trait can face life-threatening crises. Some families do not want to admit that tha-lassemia, diabetes, or other conditions run in their families for fear that it will affect the marriageability of their daughters and sons. In generations past, when many of these conditions were untreatable, this may have been true, but modern treatment and bet-ter health screening can provide nearly normal lives and are helping to remove this stigma.

Knowledge about a condition and how to manage it empowers people. The interac-tions between diet and behaviors can help or hurt people with these conditions. For example, fava beans (*foule*) contain a chemical that can cause persons with thalassemia to enter into a crisis. Knowing that you have the condition means avoiding fava beans and other foods that could cause trouble. Covering up or denying stress or illness may contribute to the ill effects of a condition such as hypertension. People can take meas-ures, such as avoiding sugary foods and too many carbohydrates with diabetes, to live longer, healthier, and more normal lives.

Changing habits is difficult. Physicians interviewed for this study complained that Arab and Chaldean patients are not very compliant with diet and medications. In one case, a woman who was being interviewed said she was diabetic and never ate sugar. She then poured herself a cup of tea, added two spoonfuls of sugar, and drank the cup—regardless of any protestations that this could be harmful. This is an otherwise rational and delightful woman. Because diabetes, high cholesterol levels, and high blood pres-sure can be silent killers or have delayed effects, people may not take their doctor's warn-ings seriously. If they do not immediately feel bad, there is a tendency to think that noth-ing is wrong. Results from this study show that many of the Arabs and Chaldeans interviewed are not conforming to the prescribed diets and exercise regimens.

The most powerful conclusion of this study is that, although body shape and family histories of disease (which may be inherited) may predispose Arab and Chaldean Amer-icans to a particular disease or condition, it is the behavioral differences that are sig-nificant. Although it is not possible to change the genetic predisposition, behaviors and lifestyles can be consciously changed with awareness and education.

This study also indicates that lifestyles and diets are changing in the Arab-American communities—many times for the worse. Some of these changes are occurring without conscious awareness of their impact of daily lifestyle and dietary choices. For example, the longer their stay in the United States, the more Arab women are using prepackaged and canned foods in their cooking.[59] Canned chick peas (hummus) have much higher measurable amounts of salt than the dried beans traditionally used in Arab cuisine. The sugar and other taste enhancers in the prepared and canned foods mask the higher salt content, and subsequently, cooks add even more salt to the food. A person with a pre-disposition for hypertension who may be salt sensitive may experience a rise in blood pressure resulting from the higher salt intake. In this way, subtle changes in the com-position of foods may affect the pathogenesis of diseases.

Arab food is calorically dense and moderately high in salt. Although olive oil is low in cholesterol, it is still a fat. Using excessive amounts of olive oil in salads or consuming foods fried in olive oil adds many fat calories to the diet. One tablespoon of olive oil contains approximately 124 calories. Add chips and American junk foods to the tra-ditional Arabic diet, and the overall dietary intake of salt, fats, and sugars becomes very unhealthy. The positive benefits of the traditional Arabic diet can easily be lost with the addition of a little junk food.

In this study, because there were few individuals who performed regular healthy exercise, it is not possible to calculate the positive impact of regular exercise. If the lack of exercise is a major factor in the weight gain associated with acculturation,[60] this problem should be addressed in preventive care programs for Arab and Chaldean populations.

The patterns of disease occurrence, lifestyles, and dietary changes in this study may not represent all Arab Americans. They do indicate the possibility of certain health trends in Arab and Chaldean populations. The results of this study are hypotheses for future studies. The findings also underscore the need to develop culturally sensitive and appropriate health education and interventions aimed specifically at Arab and Chaldean Americans.

If higher waist, hip, or thigh measurements; excess body weight; and low activity levels are strong factors in the development of hypertension, diabetes, and other conditions in Arab and Chaldean Americans, appropriate interventions can be created. Asking *sitti* or *jiddo* (grandmother or grandfather) to eat a cottage cheese and cracker diet while "sweating to the oldies" with Richard Simmons is not going to entice them to change their diets and lifestyles. These may work for other Americans, but there is a real need to develop a lower fat and lower salt diet that maintains the taste, texture, and vitamin content of the traditional Arabic foods. The popularity of the Mediterranean diet could also enhance the popularity of Arabic foods to health-conscious Americans.

Small behavioral changes, such as reducing the number of servings of red meat consumed per week or adding less olive oil and butter to foods, can be accomplished. Behavioral change is not easy; it can be accomplished with education and awareness. The dietary preferences of Arab-American children for a high-fat, high-salt, high-sweets diet may place them at increased risk for illness later in life. Initiating change in this younger generation may be easier than trying to change behaviors established over a lifetime. The higher incidence of these illnesses in the older population calls for the development of special programs for elderly Arab Americans. While conducting research in the Arab and Chaldean communities, the lack of social programs and healthy activities for seniors in these communities was apparent.

The bad news of this study may be that Arab and Chaldean Americans, like other ethnic minorities in the United States, suffer disproportionately from hypertension, high cholesterol levels, diabetes, and other conditions. The good news is that there are identifiable changes that can be made in the lifestyles and dietary patterns to avoid the conditions. The irony is that the changes required for good health could mean going back to a more traditional Arabic diet and lifestyle. By consuming less meat, more fresh fruits and vegetables, more beans, and less fat and refined sugars and by approximating the activity levels experienced before immigrating to the United States, Arab Americans may live healthier lives.

This study also demonstrates the need for more health research on Arabs and Arab Americans. Although funding and institutions dedicated to studying these diseases and the health of other ethnic groups exist, very few of these resources are available for work on Arabs and Arab Americans. Individuals identified in this study have life-threatening conditions and are in need of appropriate education and intervention programs designed to meet their needs—and none are available. Research on Arabs and Arab Americans is needed so that appropriate interventions can be designed. Studies of Arab Americans, as an understudied group in the United States, may also provide valuable insights in combating and preventing disease. There is a critical need for Arab Americans and the research community to take up the challenge of actively developing and funding research, education, and intervention programs to follow up on this and other related research.

The investigation of the health costs and benefits associated with acculturation in immigrants such as Arab and Chaldean Americans is only just beginning. When the United States was founded and when massive numbers of people immigrated here at the turn of the century, few researchers were chronicling the health impacts of their acculturation or assimilation experiences. Results of this study indicate there are health costs associated with acculturation. For Arab Americans, there is still an opportunity to understand the acculturation process, and there is time to intervene where needed.

Notes

1. Precise numbers of Arab Americans are not available. The 3 million figure is provided by S. El Badry, "The Arab Americans," *American Demographics* (January 1994).

2. The following references provide insights into the early Arab-American experience: Alixa Naff, *Becoming American; The Early Arab Immigrant Experience* (Carbondale and Edwardsville: Southern Illinois University Press, 1985); and Barbara Aswad, ed., *Arabic Speaking Communities in American Cities* (New York Center for Migration Studies, 1974).

3. The research conducted by M. G. Marmot is a classic example of comparative studies. See M. G. Marmot, S. L. Syme, A. Kagan, H. Kato, J. B. Cohen, and J. Belsey, "Epidemiological Studies of Coronary Heart Disease and Stroke in Japanese Men Living in Japan, Hawaii, and California: Prevalence of Coronary and Hypertensive Heart Disease and Associated Risk Factors," *American Journal of Epidemiology* 102 (1975): 514–525; and M. G. Marmot, "Culture and Illness: Epidemiological Evidence." In M. J. Christie and P. G. Mellet, eds., *Foundations of Psychosomatics* (Chichester: Wiley, 1981), pp. 323–40.

4. A. O. Musaiger, "The Newly Industrializing Countries—Nutritional Education in the Face of Rapid Change: Experiences in Bahrain" (Presented at the Proceedings of the XIII International Congress, London 1985), pp. 917–20.

5. Musaiger, "The Newly Industrializing Countries."

6. R. J. Hassoun, "A Bioanthropological Perspective of Hypertension in Arab-Americans in the Metropolitan Detroit Area" (Ph.D. dissertation, University of Florida, 1995).

7. Some helpful books on Arab Americans include B. T. Mehdi, ed., *The Arabs in America, 1492–1977: A Chronology and Fact Book* (Dobbs Ferry, NY: Oceana Publications, 1978); and B. Abu-Laban and M .W. Suleiman, eds., *Arab Americans: Continuity and Change* (Belmont, MA: AAUG Press, 1989). Recommended introductory articles to the Detroit Southend communities are S. Y. Abraham, N. Abraham, and B. Aswad, "The Southend: An Arab Muslim Working-Class Community." In S. Abraham and N. Abraham, eds., *Arabs in the New World: Studies on Arab-American Communities* (Detroit: Center for Urban Studies, Wayne State University, 1983), pp. 164–84; N. Abraham, "The Yemeni Immigrant Community of Detroit: Background, Emigration,

and Community Life." In S. Abraham and N. Abraham, eds. *Arabs in the New World: Studies on Arab-American Communities* (Detroit: Center for Urban Studies, Wayne State University, 1983), pp. 109–34.

8. Chaldeans are Christian immigrants from Iraq, one of the Arabic-speaking countries of the Middle East.

9. See G. Orfalea, *Before the Flames: A Quest for the History of Arab Americans* (Austin: University of Texas Press, 1988), pp. 52–53.

10. Naff, *Becoming American,* focuses on the "peddling" experience.

11. Kahlil Gibran's namesake and cousin, together with his wife, provide one of the better biographies of Kahlil Gibran in J. Gibran and K. Gibran, *Kahlil Gibran: His Life and World* (New York: Avenel Books, 1981).

12. Gibran and Gibran, *Kahlil Gibran,* p. 26.

13. Many of the chronicles of immigration and ethnicity in America omit Arab Americans. A historical overview of American immigration can be gained from R. Daniels, *Coming to America: A History of Immigration and Ethnicity in American Life* (New York: HarperPerennial, 1990).

14. Gibran and Gibran, *Kahlil Gibran,* pp. 92–93.

15. Gibran and Gibran, *Kahlil Gibran,* pp. 116–17.

16. Gibran and Gibran, *Kahlil Gibran,* pp. 358–59.

17. Daniels, *Coming to America,* pp. 168–69.

18. G. Orfalea, *Before the Flames.*

19. P. Gaurilovich, "Detroit-Area Arab Community is North America's Largest," *Detroit Free Press* (18 October 1990): 2E.

20. Hassoun, "Bioanthropological Perspective," p. 118.

21. S. Abraham, "Detroit's Arab-American Community: A Survey of Diversity and Commonality." In S. Abraham and N. Abraham, eds. *Arabs in the New World: Studies on Arab-American Communities* (Detroit: Center for Urban Studies, Wayne State University, 1983), pp. 84–86.

22. M. C. Sengstock, *Chaldean Americans: Changing Conceptions of Identity* (Staten Island, NY: Center for Migration Studies, 1982), p. 29.

23. N. Abraham, "The Yemeni Immigrant Community in Detroit." In S. Abraham and N. Abraham, eds. *Arabs in the New World: Studies on Arab-American Communities* (Detroit: Center for Urban Studies, Wayne State University, 1983), p. 122.

24. S. Lambeth, "Health Care in Yemen Arab Republic," *Journal of Nursing Studies* 25 (1988): 171–77.

25. J. T. Darden, R. C. Hill, and J. Thomas, *Detroit: Race and Uneven Development* (Philadelphia: Temple University Press, 1987).

26. A. H. Bittles, "Perspectives in Human Biology," *When Cousins Marry: A Review of Consanguinity in the Middle East* 1 (1995): 71–83.

27. A. Hourani, *A History of the Arab Peoples* (Cambridge: The Belknap Press of Harvard University Press, 1991).

28. Hassoun, "Bioanthropological Perspective." Chapter 4 (pp. 85–104) discusses methodology; Chapter 5 (pp. 105–146) refers to the demographic and sociocultural data; and Chapter 6 reports on health and anthropometric data.

29. Hassoun, "Bioanthropological Perspective."

30. Hassoun, "Bioanthropological Perspective."

31. Hassoun, "Bioanthropological Perspective."

32. The Michigan Department of Public Health, *Minority Health in Michigan* (Lansing: Michigan Department of Public Health, 1988), p. 18.

33. Michigan Department of Public Health, *Minority Health in Michigan.*

34. Michigan Department of Public Health, *Minority Health in Michigan.*

35. Hassoun, "Bioanthropological Perspective."

36. Hassoun, "Bioanthropological Perspective."

37. Hassoun, "Bioanthropological Perspective."

38. Hassoun, "Bioanthropological Perspective."

39. Hassoun, "Bioanthropological Perspective."

40. Hassoun, "Bioanthropological Perspective."

41. P. T. Baker and J. Hanna, "Perspectives on the Health and Behavior of Samoans." In P. T. Baker, J. M. Hanna, and T. S. Baker, eds., *The Changing Samoans: Behavior and Health in Transition* (New York: Oxford University Press, 1986).

42. Hassoun, "Bioanthropological Perspective," pp. 179–283.

43. H. Salloum and J. Peters *From the Land of Figs and Olives* (New York: Interlink Books, 1995).

44. All data on food consumption patterns can be found in Chapter 7 of my dissertation. See Hassoun, "Bioanthropological Perspective," pp. 179–233.

45. Hassoun, "Bioanthropological Perspective."

46. Hassoun, "Bioanthropological Perspective."

47. Hassoun, "Bioanthropological Perspective."

48. Hassoun, "Bioanthropological Perspective."

49. Hassoun, "Bioanthropological Perspective."

50. Hassoun, "Bioanthropological Perspective."

51. Hassoun, "Bioanthropological Perspective."

52. Hassoun, "Bioanthropological Perspective."

53. M. Winkerby, D. Ragland, and L. Syme, "Self-Reported Stressors and Hypertension: Evidence of an Inverse Relationship," *American Journal of Epidemiology* 127 (1988): 124–34.

54. Hassoun, "Bioanthropological Perspective."

55. Hassoun, "Bioanthropological Perspective."

56. Hassoun, "Bioanthropological Perspective."

57. Hassoun, "Bioanthropological Perspective."

58. A. P. Polednak, *Racial and Ethnic Differences in Disease* (New York: Oxford University Press, 1989).

59. Hassoun, "Bioanthropological Perspective," pp. 214–15.

60. Baker and Hanna, "Perspective on Health and Behavior."

Barbara C. Aswad

11 Attitudes of Arab Immigrants Toward Welfare

Lena is divorced with four children and far from her relatives in Yemen. She feels more secure on welfare, and without it, she says would "probably go back to my husband and be miserable again." Another says, "Men will get lazy because they will just wait for the check." A Lebanese woman states, "I would like to go to work and get off welfare, but I have no education and my husband doesn't want me to work."[1]

Welfare and the Arab Family

The statements reflect some of the views and issues of welfare and the Arab family. The effects of welfare assistance and dependency on family structure in the United States has been discussed extensively in regard to different ethnic groups, particularly African Americans, Hispanics, and Anglo-Americans.[2] What is its effect on Arab-American families? In most countries of the Middle East, extended family relations rather than welfare has been the traditional means of support, and in previous years in the Dearborn immigrant working-class Arab community, welfare was not common or accepted. Many who were eligible in those days did not have access to it because of language and transportation problems, or they felt shame for their family if they accepted it. However, this pattern is changing, with more persons accepting it in this community.

The purpose of my study was to find if and how attitudes have changed and if outside income, given often to women, has affected gender roles, as it has in other American ethnic groups. A major consideration in this regard is that most families in the United States are of a bilateral kinship model. Does the patrilineal nature of the Arab family present different adaptations?

Most studies of poor urban African Americans, for whom welfare has interacted with racism, show that discrimination of a direct and indirect form, such as the exit of jobs from the inner cities and poor education, helped to displace husbands from needy families, or at least the husbands were not there when case workers came around. Wilson finds that only one-fourth of blacks in inner-city neighborhoods are husband-wife families, a figure that may drop to 15 percent in the lowest income areas. This rate compares with one-half of Puerto Rican and white families. However, three-fourths of Mexican families have two parents, even though many are very poor.[3]

The context affecting urban African-American families also includes the fact that many men are jailed, murdered, or handicapped, and some use drug peddling as an economic alternative. These developments among poor urban African Americans developed primarily in the last 40 years, before which 75 percent of the black male population had full-time jobs, whereas it is now 48 percent. Among other economic factors, outsourcing and downsizing by corporations has contributed to unemployment or part time employment for urban and nonurban persons.

However, just because they are not the nuclear family of husband-wife-kids does not imply that many black welfare families do not have extended kin networks of some design. Stack has vividly portrayed the strong kin and nonkin networks of reciprocity, especially by women, that evolved in black families on welfare.[4] In another important study, Browner and Lewin found a role shift among Mexican-American families, in which the women began to depend on their children and shift their future hopes to them rather than their husbands.[5]

There are different reactions to welfare among ethnic groups because of family structure, norms, and values in racial and economic contexts in this country and in their home countries. It is an interactive process. What are the tendencies in the patrilineally based families of poor Arabs?

This study looked at 57 Arab immigrant women and men on welfare in 1993 to examine the following issues: their demographics and characteristics; why they are on welfare; attitudes toward being on welfare (i.e., shame or acceptance) and whether religion affects these attitudes[6] ; attitudes toward marital relations in the home in relation to welfare (i.e., relative power of women and men); and their job history, attitudes toward child care outside the home, and their future hopes. The study examined significant differences between men and women and between the two major communities in the area, the Lebanese and Yemeni.

Immigrants may receive their work permits after entering and receiving their green cards, but cannot receive welfare, except for medicaid, for 3 years after entering the country. Their sponsor is required to support them, but this regulation has not been strongly enforced. Persons can work up to 100 hours each month and still be eligible. In 1996, Michigan lifted this limit and instituted a program called "work first" in 1996, which stated that recipients work or attend classes 20 hours each week, and more recently required 30 hours.[7] It also mandates that persons must get a job after 2 years of benefits and that a family receives no more than a total of 5 years of benefits.

On the other hand, those who entered on refugee status were entitled to receive welfare benefits immediately on entry before 1996. The new laws place restrictions, such as a single person can receive only 8 months of benefits. States have been given some leeway on deciding some issues and may give up to 20 percent waivers for some conditions.[8] It is fair to say that there is much confusion regarding the effects of the reform provisions. This study was done before the 1996 bill was passed, and attitudes reflect earlier regulations.

The new restrictions on welfare reflect feelings of a shrinking job market and feelings by employed persons that welfare has generated a perpetual welfare class, many of whom are cheating and many of whom are foreigners. But there is also evidence that many persons go on and off welfare between jobs,[9] and Julian Simon, an economist at the University of Maryland, found that each foreign-born worker contributes $2,500 per year more in taxes than he uses in services.[10]

Norms and Values of the Arab Patrilineal Family

What does patrilineal descent involve? How is it different from bilateral descent? In patrilineal and matrilineal descent groups, one is born into a preexisting group defined by gender. It is not something one chooses; the structure exists. Members have certain obligations to particular people because of the group into which they are born. In a patrilineal system, this group is traced through males but includes females; in a matrilineal system, it is traced through females but includes males. Patrilineality does not mean that you do not have obligations to your mother's family, but it does indicate that the father's family is primary, and vice versa for a matrilineal system. In the Detroit area, these patrilineal kin groups often operate as corporate groups to monopolize chains of small shops, known locally as party stores.

Most North American families originating from Europe trace descent in a bilateral fashion through mother and father indefinitely. It is more individually centered because there is no preexisting defined group. It is a flexible model, and extended kin are defined more by choice than assignment. It usually varies and is changeable, depending on who you live near, who you like or do not like, or who has money or does not, and you have the option of not relating to them at all in the American industrial capitalist system.

Patrilineality and patriarchy are distinct, with the latter designating male power or control, not descent or kinship, and one can have patriarchy or male control in bilateral families in the United States. However, control of property in the patriline and patrilocality, in which males of the patriline live near each other, acts to concentrate male members of Arab families economically or politically, often bringing added male power to the family. If women are separated from their patriline, they risk losing power. Women share the power of a strong patriline and bring that power to their marriage. This is a point seldom understood by Westerners regarding the role of women.

In addition to descent factoring, the extended rather than the nuclear family model is seen among Arabs culturally, whereas among many in the capitalist industrial U.S. system, extensive kin relations have sometimes broken down. In migration situations, males and females are sometimes separated from their families, but it is usually temporary. Strong attempts are made at reconstruction of villages such as Bint Jbail and Tibnine.

Cultural attitudes that accompany patrilineality and relate to employment include a strong mandate in Arab and Islamic cultures for husbands to be responsible for support of the family. It is commonly given as a reason for sons getting twice the inheritance of daughters among Muslims and for supporting a son's education over a daughter's. Among a wife's guarantees in Islam is one that she should not be forced to work outside the home. The influence of Islam has risen in the community, evidenced by the proliferation of mosques from two major ones to a one-half dozen new ones in the past ten years. Islamic dress by women is also evident to a much greater degree than previously, primarily because of the immigration of southern Lebanese Shi'a and their imams.

Economic class is also important in the consideration of welfare and women's employment. I previously examined what I called the "rich peasant" attitude of men who feel that, when they get enough money, their wives should not "have to work"; it shames men's honor. I witnessed this in villages in the Middle East and in Dearborn.[11] This attitude is not limited to Muslims or Arabs but is shared with many around the world.[12]

There are cultural, economic, and political barriers to Arab women gaining power through employment. On the other hand, education is seen as a good thing, and families often support education for daughters, in some cases mainly to increase their chances for an educated husband. Whatever the motive, education can be used by women to gain entrance to more economic control in the family.

The Dearborn Community

The Dearborn area has been an entry point for Muslims from the Arab world for the last one-half century.[13] It has recently expanded, and its population of 18,000 represents approximately 20 percent of the population of Dearborn compared with 6 percent twenty years ago. In a previous article,[14] I observed that welfare had increased in the community and was caused by three primary factors. First, a depression in the auto industry in the early 1980s forced many layoffs and was followed by increased automation and out-sourcing, thereby reducing the need for unskilled laborers. We see a plurality of the jobs (35 percent) reported by men in this sample who work at gas stations, while only 23 percent worked for the big three auto companies. The largest portion wanted to work in the auto factories.

The second reason was the simultaneous infusion into the area of persons especially from Lebanon, but also from Yemen and Palestine, because of the conflicts in their homelands. The Lebanese civil war, which lasted for sixteen years from the mid-1970s to the early 1990s, and the war with Israel in the 1980s, which resulted in occupation of part of south Lebanon, greatly affected the southern Lebanese Shi'a. Some of their villages such as Bint Jbail are in occupied territory today. Immigration rules give first priority to nuclear family relatives, and there is an existing large ethnic community in Dearborn full of relatives to join.

A third reason is the existence of a social service center, the Arab Community Center for Economic and Social Services (ACCESS), located in the heart of the community and staffed by bilingual persons. Before the 1970s, assistance was of a limited nature for Arab immigrants because of lack of Arabic-speaking social workers and the distances necessary to travel to social agencies. ACCESS celebrated its 27th anniversary in 1998, and during that time, it has developed from a storefront staffed mainly by volunteers with a $20,000 budget to the current organization with 120 full-time staff members who operate in six buildings, and it has a $4.2 million budget.[15]

As with others on welfare, there is some dishonesty in this community, such as putting a wife on welfare while the husband continues to work above the low income requirement or, less frequently, getting or reporting a separation or divorce for the sake of welfare and using two addresses while living together.[16] Because of these irregularities and misuses, nonwelfare persons in the community often looked down on all welfare persons. This is particularly true of those of earlier generations among the Arab community who felt they had worked and not taken welfare.

The low income of most of the Center's clients (75 percent of the clients are among those receiving $5,000 to $10,000 annually[17]) indicates that most are struggling economically. Welfare is merely another strategy of survival in an unstable employment market for persons who often have limited skills and have suffered upheavals in their countries of origin. A manager of welfare assistance at ACCESS said that about one-half of the welfare claims listed women as the head of the household in 1996.

The study included more women than men, and members were not of the same families.[18] It was a snowball sample, one in which interviewees suggested other persons or were known by the interviewers to be on welfare. The sensitive nature of this topic made a random sample impractical. The participants were not asked in whose name the welfare came for the same reason. The study included Lebanese (64 percent) and Yemeni (35 percent), in approximate relation to their number in the community.[19]

Demographics and Reasons for Being on Welfare

In contrast to previous studies, I found very few of the Lebanese in this sample came from a rural peasant background (13 percent of the women and 14 percent of the men). This is probably because their roots are in south Lebanon, but they or their parents were forced to flee the area to larger cities such as Beirut during the wars and Israeli bombings of the last 20 years. Among Yemenis, 43 percent of the women and 60 percent of the men still list their father's occupation as a peasant and their origins as rural.

Length of Time in the United States

All but one of the participants were born abroad, and most of those interviewed had been in the United States ten to fifteen years (38 percent). Men had been here on average longer than women. Forty-seven percent of women were in their twenties, and 77 percent of men were in their thirties. Significantly, only one person had a parent on welfare. They do not fall into the generational welfare patterns so often discussed publicly.

Education and Job Skills

The educational skills and work experiences of the women and men in this sample were low, with approximately one-third never having been to school and one-third receiving only up to six years of education. A very high percentage of each group said that they spoke, read, and wrote English, but this does not necessarily attest to their level of fluency. The Yemeni women had scores higher than the Lebanese men or women and higher than Yemeni men, apparently reflecting the fact that four times as many Yemeni women reported taking English classes at ACCESS than Lebanese women (64 versus 15 percent).

All said they spoke Arabic, and one-half of each category said they could read or write it. Two-thirds of the women had never ever been employed, and one-third of the men had not. It appears that there are limitations in their backgrounds for finding a job easily. One benefit of learning English is to get a driver's license, which for women gives them a new-found independence, according to workers at ACCESS.

Marital State

Two-thirds of the women are married, 16 percent divorced, 5 percent separated, and 9 percent widowed.[20] All the men interviewed were married. Divorce does not carry the stigma for Yemeni that it does for Levantine women, and there were more divorced Yemeni than Lebanese. I would caution against seeing divorce as a sign of women's freedom, because the divorce may be influenced more by their fathers or their husbands than by the women themselves.

The average number of children they had was 3.5 (72 percent said they had between one and four, and 38 percent said they had between five and ten). This is higher than the national average, and as with other low income minorities, children are seen as a safety net for the future. The provisions of welfare that assist those with more children do not slow this trend. Seventy-seven percent of the women and 92 percent of the men said their children lived with them. Children who did not live with them lived in Lebanon or Yemen.

Reasons for Migrating to the United States

Seventy percent of the women said they came to the United States to accompany their husbands or parents, whereas the major reasons for men's migration were the war (38 percent) and employment possibilities (23 percent).

Many reasons were given for being on welfare. Sixty-seven percent of women and 81 percent of men were on Aid to Families with Dependent Children (AFDC), with about 20 percent on General Assistance. (General Assistance was eliminated in Michigan after this study.) Women reported that their husbands had lost their jobs (34 percent) or just did not have enough income. About one-fourth mentioned health reasons, including medical insurance (14 percent) and illnesses (12 percent). The high price of medical care was seen as a justifiable reason, and they often mentioned their children in this regard. Fourteen percent reported divorce, 10 percent reported being separated, 5 percent said the reason was migration, and 5 percent mentioned that their sponsor withdrew. A 14-percent divorce rate is low for those dealing with American welfare clients nationally, but Zogby reported 4.5 percent for all U.S. Arabs.[21] Sixty-four percent of the men indicated they received welfare because they lost their jobs or had no income, and about 30 percent attributed it to a need for health insurance (23 percent) or to illness (8 percent).

Overall, most men and women stated that they obtained welfare because of the lack of jobs or low incomes; fewer claimed reasons of health care. Most are married, one-fourth of the women indicated divorce or separation, and very few related it to migration or sponsors. Men and women have low levels of education, and few of the women have been employed or know English well. Most were not recent immigrants. The women are in their twenties and so far have an average of 3.5 children. Large families are an asset in terms of AFDC, and this trend will probably continue. The men came because of war or the lack of work. They are older by a decade on average, and few are divorced.

Attitudes Toward Welfare

Attitudes toward welfare and how people felt others thought about it were important issues in assessing a change from the previous attitudes of shame and dependency on the family. Seventy-two percent feel welfare has beneficially affected their lives, and most importantly, 90 percent said their immediate family members did not object. This seemed to be an important sign of change in the community and an acceptance of an alternative to family help in times of need. The number of men and women who indicated they relied primarily on welfare was twice that of those who said they relied primarily on their families. This indicates welfare is becoming an alternative to the wider family networks or may be contributing to their network in a positive way.

When asked if they felt embarrassed by it, 58 percent of women said "no," but 62 percent of men said "yes." More women than men said they gained a feeling of independence when they were on welfare. Similarly, many more women felt happier with it than without it (54 versus 16 percent). Men were more divided (32 percent happier versus 41 percent less happy) but were definitely less happy than the women.

The positive experiences of other people on welfare within women's networks also affected them. Three-fourths of the women felt that their friends had also had a positive experience with it, and 53 percent of the men did too. The stigma seems to be lifting for women but is still there for some men.

When asked how many of their friends received assistance, one-third mentioned six to thirty persons, with the remainder indicating fewer. The Lebanese women reported having a higher number of acquaintances on welfare than Yemeni women, and more felt they had a good experience with it than the Yemeni. However, Yemeni women reported feeling more independence on welfare than Lebanese women. It probably is a question of relativity.

I think it is important that, among welfare recipients, women reported wider networks of support outside their nuclear family than the men. Women had twice as many relatives living close by as men (50 versus 23 percent), and the men on welfare seemed more isolated overall. This lack of extended kin for men would be an important reason for them to need and seek governmental assistance. Very few men or women reported feeling lonely; however, three-fourths of the men listed their spouse as their best friend, while less than one-half (44 percent) of the women did, who frequently listed their mothers and sisters instead. For financial help, women go to their husbands and brothers, but men seek out brothers or persons outside the family.

Women also visit with others more often everyday or twice each week, while men visit once or twice each week. Men travel outside the area more frequently than women, every day or once each week, but about one-half of the women said once per week and one-half said "almost never." The desire to get a license and drive is a major factor in their independence.

In the area of religion and attitudes, about one-half of males and females belonged to mosques and reported that they attend regularly, but the women said their spouses attended much less than they did. We wanted to know what the religious leaders were saying about welfare. The highest proportion of men and women (about 70 percent) mentioned that the leaders say nothing or they do not know. Approximately 20 percent of each group said that the imams felt it was a good thing. None reported that the imams spoke against it. There were periods in which some religious leaders felt ACCESS was in competition with them for caring for the community; however, these tensions have eased.

When we analyze feelings toward welfare, women are happier and less ashamed than men on welfare, and they have more friends on it. This is particularly true of Lebanese women. Women also have more family members living in the community than men. Men on welfare seem more isolated from their families, depend more on their wives, and feel more embarrassment. However, both genders felt their families did not object. Although religious attitudes have increased in the community and approximately one-half attend the mosques, those on welfare felt there were no major objections from the religious leaders. In their view, there is no feeling of public shame, but the men did express that they were embarrassed that they are not providing enough. The networks women have and the ease of obtaining assistance may also be attributable to the fact that most of the intake workers at ACCESS are women. The negative effect of applying to a female worker by a woman is less than for a man applying to that worker.

Power Relations in the Home

Was there a shift in husband-wife relations, as we have seen in other ethnic groups where men are sometimes alienated or wives put more faith in their children? When asked who has the most power in the household, one-half the women said it was their husband, but one-third reported that they did. Because 25 percent reported they were divorced or separated from their husbands, this is not a strong difference, if in fact they were separated. All the men reported that they thought they had the most power. There may be a slight shift in perception, but overall, it is not great. The husband is seen as head of the house by most women and by all the men.

However, when asked who controls the money in the family, I think there is a shift, especially for Lebanese women, 71 percent of whom said they controlled the family budget, compared with 29 percent of Yemeni women. The men also felt that they did, with 71 percent of the Lebanese men and 100 percent of the Yemeni men claiming control. Even with the number of reported divorces and separations among the women

(14 percent of Lebanese, 21 percent of Yemeni), this is a significant finding of perceptions among Lebanese women. I think it represents an increase in women's control from an earlier study of women not on welfare, in which women reported buying items for their children and in which all the women, Lebanese and Yemeni, said their husbands handled the budget, and the women were given spending money.[22] This trend was confirmed by ACCESS social workers, who felt women getting the checks empowered them in paying for household items. They mentioned that this was especially true as they increased their ability to drive by learning English to get a license and thereby increased their mobility and access to stores outside the community.

The question of women relying more on children than on their husbands in later life, which was crucial in the Mexican-American case,[23] was viewed differently by gender. One-half of the women said "yes," but men thought that wives should rely on them rather than on their children.

Overall, men retain their position at the head of the household as perceived by men and women, unless there is divorce or separation. Each gender feels they control the household money more, and we find that there is increasing power going to women in the control of the budget and household money. At least one-half the women indicate that, in later life, a mother should depend on her children more than on her husband, a pattern similar to the Mexican-American case.

Cases of Divorced and Separated Women

Let us examine several cases of divorced women who felt welfare was a necessity.[24] In regard to divorce and separation, we asked if they felt women should gain custody of children, to which 93 percent of the men and women answered in the affirmative.

Maha from Yemen is 48 years old. She is divorced with seven children between the ages of eighteen and thirty-one who live in California, Yemen, Chicago, and Dearborn. She says she depends on her son in Dearborn for help. She does not have enough money, and she would like to get a job, but she has only 2 years of schooling and some ESL (English as a Second Language) classes. She feels welfare helps women but does not weaken men at all. She likes life here and is not lonely at all but misses her family and the country of Yemen and wants to go back to live with her children.

Lena from Yemen is thirty-seven years old with four children. She reported that she was separated from her husband who lives in New York. Her parents were deceased, and she was far from her relatives, who were in Yemen, and she must depend on herself. She reports she is happy and does not feel lonely. She definitely feels more secure on welfare and without it would "probably go back to my husband and be miserable again." Her children are young, and she feels she cannot get a job because she never went to school and does not know English. She thinks men resent women on welfare and that it may be risky for men, but that it does not create the family problems. She definitely feels welfare strengthens women's roles, is not sure if it weakens men's roles, but likes the freedom in the United States. In contrast to Lena's situation, most of the husbands of the women who are separated or divorced live in and around Dearborn, not abroad.

Another divorcee from Lebanon who was thirty-four years old and had two children likes it better here, but most of her relatives are in Lebanon. She goes to ACCESS for help or to one aunt who lives close by. She has few people to help with her children, is unhappy and depressed about the war, but is not lonely here. She has many friends on welfare and some aunts here. She has had three years of education, her children are young, she knows no English, and consequently she feels she cannot get a job.

Leila is a Lebanese woman who is separated and wants a divorce. She has seven children and no education. She came because of the war and strongly feels men do resent welfare. She also depends on her brother and son. She is not happy and said she and her kids would starve without welfare. She thinks her husband is ashamed of her being on welfare.

One of the few who felt lonely is a forty-five-year-old Yemeni widow who misses her husband. She has five children between five and fifteen years of age. She depends on her father and sisters who live nearby. She definitely would like to work, and her sisters would help with her children, but she worries about the fact that she has only two years of education.

In these cases of women who are divorced and separated, we find they do need the money and feel it helps them to be independent of their husbands. Most were not educated and felt at a disadvantage in working, especially those with young children.

Gender Differences in Perceptions of How Spouses Feel About Welfare

What is their perception of their spouses' attitudes toward welfare? Most women felt their husbands did not resent them being on welfare. A Lebanese woman said, "No, because they don't like to go themselves to the welfare offices, and they push their wives into it." As if to confirm this, 85 percent of the men say they do not resent their wives being on welfare. However, 69 percent of Yemeni women said they felt the men resented it, much more than the 19 percent of Lebanese women who thought their men resented it.

Men feel their wives are relieved with welfare. Women do not usually think men are, but women do not resent their husbands being on welfare.

Significantly, 85 percent of the women and 61 percent of the men feel welfare strengthens the women's role, and when asked if it weakens men's roles, all said "yes," except Yemeni men, and 80 percent of them said it did not. One Lebanese man said forcefully, "Welfare will fulfill her needs rather than her husband. She will think she is financially independent without me. It will weaken or destroy my role."

More Lebanese women (56 percent) think welfare is threatening for a husband's role than Yemeni women do (14 percent). One said, "He will start to be lazy, because he just waits for the check." Another said, "It weakens his personality; he should be responsible for the family."

Yemeni women show a more traditional approach, feeling that their men are ashamed but that their husbands are not threatened with it and that the relations will remain as they are. This difference is also shown when asked who would control the money if a couple is separated, with 96 percent of the Lebanese women saying for sure the wife would while 75 percent of Yemeni women think the husband would. When we asked if they think it leads to divorce or separation, most men and women said "no," but more men than women (38 versus 12 percent) think it leads to family problems.

Overall, men and women concur that welfare strengthens women's roles, and all except the Yemeni men feel it weakens the man's role. Yemeni women concur with their husbands, feeling it does not change their husband's power and does not weaken them. These Yemeni women also think that their husbands resent women being on welfare more than Lebanese women do.

Relation to Work Experiences and Raising Children

When asked if they would like to go off of welfare, all the men said they would. Most of the women said they would, but 40 percent said they would not. When asked if they would like to work, all the men said "yes" if they got more money, and three-fourths of the women said they would also. They were positive about it. One said "I'd rather work; I feel tied up." Very few (9 percent) said "no" and that was because they were too old or had young children.

Selwa, who was 30 years old and had two young children, said she felt "like a slave to welfare," that it was not enough money to live on, and that she would rather work: "I can't put money in the bank, can't buy a house, can't save money for the kids' future." She was trained as a beautician and eventually wants to open up a beauty shop. Her husband works in a bakery but does not want her to work. She comments that "her husband thinks welfare spoils her, that she doesn't have to care for her husband anymore; welfare replaces him."

Most men and women said they did not have sufficient funds. In terms of inheritance from their families, 65 percent of women said that they did not control their inheritance but that their family did, and 35 percent said their husbands did. Most men did control their inheritance, with only one-third saying their fathers did.

What kind of work could or would clients attempt? The answer is especially important in view of the new mandate for employment. In order of preference, women listed caring for children, secretarial work, cleaning houses, sewing, working in a store, and working in a factory. For the men, the most preferred choice was work in a factory. Auto factory wages in the Detroit area are very high, about $40,000 to $60,000 for line workers, but there have been many layoffs, and many are now turning to jobs in gas stations, often owned by relatives.

Workers at ACCESS who process welfare claims mentioned forthrightly that they did not think women would clean other persons' homes, because many had had their own maids in Lebanon. In the Middle East, maids are often a sign of status, and some have been abused in various ways, especially financially. However, the possibility of cleaning stores, schools, and other buildings was considered to be acceptable. For the women dressed Islamically, ACCESS workers felt there is a chance of discrimination in hiring. They indicated the Islamic scarf alone probably did not represent a hindrance in being hired, but the long dark Islamic gowns or the brightly colored peasant dresses worn by many women were seen as hindrances.

Day care can be a particular problem for women who want to work. In close ethnic neighborhoods, family members often help. When asked who would care for the children if they worked, 24 percent said their mothers, but 31 percent of the women said they had no care at all. All the men said their wives would.

Personal attitudes toward day care vary, and when asked if they approved of using day care centers, the women were about evenly split, but 77 percent of the men said "no." Both genders felt that women with small children should not work, but men were stronger (100 versus 73 percent). In relation to problems with children, very few (8 percent) said they had any. This contrasts with the results of studies of other welfare parents and reflects the continuing strength of the Arab family with its generational respect, two parents, and extended character.

Caring for children of other employed women of the community in their homes may become a major avenue for work, but for most, some training will be required. Because the second generation and many of the educated immigrant women are working, there does seem to be a growing market. Other initiatives may include cleaning or sewing enterprises.

Women were asked about their husbands' attitudes toward wives being employed. Two-thirds said "no," their husbands did not want them to work, while only 11 percent said yes, and 17 percent said maybe. In many ways it was felt that women contributed to the home economy and raised their power through welfare. This was preferable to working outside, because of their husbands' restrictions and the other constraints mentioned previously.

Long-Range Plans

When asked about their long-range plans, the women gave varied answers, but in order of preference, they included going to school, getting a job, going to Lebanon, living better, raising children, and divorce. For men, it was to get a job (70 percent), to live better, and raise kids.

Women and men liked it better in the United States than in Lebanon or Yemen, but women did so by a much higher degree (78 percent) than men (53 percent). The women's primary reason (60 percent) was that there was no war. Although life style was a weaker answer (18 percent), Lebanese women complained that the war had separated them from their families. The men felt the negative effects of the war financially and so found life better in the United States. One man, who was 30 years old and had two children, who came here as a visitor and got stuck because of the war, commented, "In Lebanon I was stronger financially. I had a business with my brother, whereas here I am employed by someone." He prefers Lebanon. Others said they preferred the social life in Lebanon more. Hassan Jaber, Deputy Director of ACCESS, mentioned that many had returned with high hopes to Lebanon and found it changed with few chances for jobs. They then came back to the United States with the decision that this will be their home.[25]

Conclusions

Arab Americans on welfare sampled in Dearborn do not all think alike; they have different situations and adaptations. However, over time, there has been a shift in the attitudes toward welfare, with a more accepting attitude toward it. We also found that most think it strengthens a wife's role, particularly in the control of the household budget, and all but Yemeni men think it weakens a husband's role. There is a shift to strengthen women as in other cultures.

Within the patrilineal Arab families, however, the shift is made with less alienation of the male than has been observed among some other ethnic groups. Women are given power within the family structure as a substitute for working outside. This has been especially attractive among women who have limited skills, education, or employment history and whose husbands do not want them to work. The attitudes against women's work outside the home persist, but welfare allows a woman greater participation and raises her self-esteem in relation to her husband and other family members. Those with the traditionally positive view of large families, which is found among many poor from the Middle East, find justification for the welfare programs.

Religion does not affect their attitude toward welfare negatively, because among the one-half who attended mosques, most thought the imams supported it or were neutral. Welfare assists in making separation and divorce a possibility for abused or dissatisfied wives and can serve as an added threat against a husband's misbehavior.

The changes resemble those in the Mexican-American family to some degree, which indicates that the strength of the family in the home culture and the lack of skills and education in the host culture are crucial variables. The patrilineal ideology and defined gender roles of Arab families add to the strength of the role of the husband. The shift to dependence on children rather than the husband in the future of welfare women is not as strong as it appears to be among Mexican Americans, but this attitude is expressed by one-half of the women and is viewed as a stronger option for Arab women than Arab men think it is.

There are short- and long-term consequences of welfare assistance. For many, it is a short-term solution, but real empowerment to break dependency will require more education and economic opportunities and a change in attitudes toward women's employment outside the family and about large families. Most women indicate they want to work. However, the 1996 regulations mandating employment will eventually force some off welfare (without the benefit of employment) because of constraints of limited skills, discrimination in hiring, or unchanged attitudes against work outside the home. This may be difficult for those who genuinely need it to escape a bad marriage, and they will turn again to their families for support. As this happens, it will reduce the community's wealth overall.

Day care is a problem for women with many children. One possibility for work in the home by some may be in caring for the children of others who go out to work. Training for day care employment would be important in such cases.

The men on welfare, who have fewer kin and networks in the United States, will undoubtedly turn more to working cheaply for friends, or they may be forced to migrate back to Lebanon or Yemen. The recently arrived Iraqis and other legal immigrants without skills or extended families in the United States are in a precarious position since the immigration bill has cut many benefits. Some of these benefits have been secured from the state of Michigan.

ACCESS is being greatly challenged to increase educational and employment programs for men and women. It must continue its success in maintaining its political networks with the state, because it may need to request employment exemptions for some of the poor, and it will need to make alliances with other social service groups or compete with them to gain assistance.

Notes

1. Research for this chapter was conducted in 1993. There have been changes in welfare policy since then, and the attitudes discussed here reflect the earlier period of research. There has been a recent major influx of up to 6,000 southern Iraqis, who had been in camps in Saudi Arabia since the Gulf War of 1991. They came with refugee status, and many have traveled to Dearborn to be with an Arabic-speaking Muslim community, having come from other states where they were originally located by the U.S. Immigration Service. Most have low-level employment and English skills. Their status under the new laws on legal immigrants is precarious, and exemption or special help is being sought for them. Their claims that Immigration and Naturalization Service authorities misrepresented benefit expectations before they came adds to disorientation and mistrust in the community.

2. M. Tienda, "Familism and Structural Assimilation of Mexican Immigrants in the United States," *International Migration Review* 14 (1980): 383–405; Ronald Angel and Marta Tienda, "Determinants of Extended Household Structure: Cultural Pattern or Economic Need?" *American Journal of Sociology* 87 (1982): 1360–83; and Carole Browner and Ellen Lewin, "Female Altruism Reconsidered: The Virgin Mary as Economic Woman," *American Ethnologist* 9, no. 1 (1982): 61–75.

3. William J. Wilson, *When Work Disappears* (New York: Knopf, 1996); *Newsweek* (9 September 1996): 48ff.

4. Carole Stack, *All Our Kin* (New York: Banton, 1974).

5. Browner and Lewin, "Female Altruism Reconsidered."

6. A preliminary analysis of this section was mentioned in Barbara C. Aswad, "Attitudes of Immigrant Women and Men in the Dearborn Area Toward Women's Employment and Welfare." In Yvonne Y. Haddad and Jane I. Smith, eds., *Muslim Communities in North America* (Albany: State University of New York Press, 1994), pp. 501–19.

7. See *Family Independence Agency Digest* 7, no. 4 (May 1996).

8. In 1991, Michigan eliminated General Assistance for "able-bodied" persons, with the result of 30 percent getting employment, although often not permanently, and many went on disability or AFDC.

9. In a sensitively written book, Elliott Liebow has described how many homeless women use welfare in this way in seeking jobs, and for several reasons, many have problems holding them. See his *Tell Them Who I Am* (New York: Penguin, 1995).

10. Editorial, *Detroit News* (8 September 1996): B2.

11. Barbara C. Aswad, "Family Size and Access to Resources: A Case Study from the Middle East." In K. Michaelson, ed., *And the Poor Get Children* (New York: Monthly Review Press, 1981); and B. C. Aswad, "Attitudes of Immigrant Women and Men in the Dearborn Area Toward Women's Employment and Welfare."

12. I witnessed this attitude among the Italian families of peasant background with whom I grew up in the Philadelphia area. I have also witnessed it among those in the upper classes in the suburbs in this half of this century, especially before the 1970s.

13. See Barbara C. Aswad, ed., *Arabic Speaking Communities in American Cities* (New York: Center for Migration Studies, 1974); Barbara C. Aswad, "Family Size and Access to Resources;" and Barbara C. Aswad, "The Lebanese Muslim Community in Dearborn Michigan." In Albert Hourani and Nadim Shehadi, eds., *The Lebanese in the World: A Century of Emigration* (London: I.B. Tauris, 1992), pp. 167–87; and Sameer Abraham and Nabeel Abraham, eds., *Arabs in the New World* (Detroit, MI: Wayne State University, Center for Urban Studies, 1983).

14. B. C. Aswad, "Attitudes of Immigrant Women."

15. Interview with Hasan Jaber, Deputy Director of ACCESS, July 1998.

16. The state of Michigan estimates that 20 percent in the state are engaged in fraud (interview with Hasan Jaber, Deputy Director of ACCESS, September 1996).

17. ACCESS statistics for 1995/1996, given by Hasan Jaber (September 1996), who reports that 1,400 households, or 35 percent of their clients, are on public assistance.

18. The original intent was to examine women's attitudes. It was soon realized that men's attitudes were also important, but because time permitted interviewing fewer men, more women were represented than men (77 versus 23 percent). The study was conducted in 1993. I interviewed one-third, and three trained assistants conducted the other interviews. Chi-square analysis was used at a 0.05 level of significance.

19. There are also a smaller number of Palestinians in the community who were not sampled.

20. I am fairly confident this represents their actual state. However, we cannot be sure this is how they are represented on applications.

21. John Zogby, *Arab America Today: A Demographic Profile of Arab Americans* (Washington, DC: Arab American Institute, 1990).

22. Barbara C. Aswad, "Yemeni and Lebanese Muslim Immigrant Women in Southeast Dearborn." In E. H. Waugh, S. M. Abu-Laban, and R. B. Qureshi, eds., *Muslim Families in North America* (Edmonton, Canada: University of Alberta Press, 1991), pp. 256–81.

23. Browner and Lewin, "Female Altruism Reconsidered."

24. Names are not the actual names of individuals discussed.

25. Personal communication, September 1996.

12   The Deteriorating Ethnic Safety Net Among Arab Immigrants in Chicago

Estimating the number of Arab Americans and Arab immigrants in the Chicago metropolitan area is extremely difficult. Census data are so grossly off the mark that they can only be used to locate areas of high Arab concentration in the city. Based on knowledge of the patterns of Arab migration to and settlement in Chicago and the Arab participation in community organizations and religious institutions, informed sources estimate that there are about 150,000 persons, excluding Assyrians, of Arab ethnicity in Chicago, 57 percent of whom are Palestinian. This makes Chicago one of the largest cities of Arab and Palestinian settlement in the United States today.

Originating largely from the Levant (i.e., Lebanon, Syria, Jordan, and Palestine), Arabs started immigrating to Chicago before the turn of the twentieth century. The largest number settled on the south side of the city, but smaller groups, mostly Palestinian Christians and Assyrians from a number of Middle Eastern countries, settled on the north side. The south side of Chicago and its southwestern suburbs still contain the largest number of Arabs in Chicago.

Aware of recent social and economic changes within the Arab-American and Arab immigrant community in Chicago, some of which were cause for alarm and community action, the Arab-American Action Network (AAAN) proposed to undertake a needs assessment of the Arab community in greater Chicago. With initial funding from the Chicago Community Trust, the Needs Assessment Project began in the Fall of 1996, focusing on the Arab community residing on the southwest side of the city, the area of the largest concentration of Arabs in Chicago and a major reception area for new Arab immigrants. The Needs Assessment Project is planned to be completed in stages based on geographic area. Phase 1 was completed in 1997. Phase 2 will focus on the southwest suburbs, Phase 3 on the north side, and Phase 4 on the remaining suburban areas. Goals of the Needs Assessment Project include obtaining better estimates of the size and place of origin of the Arab community in greater Chicago, understanding migration patterns within its various subcommunities, creating a profile of the economic and employment status of Arabs in greater Chicago, and ascertaining community needs and resources, especially as these relate to the social and economic health of the community.

This chapter summarizes the socioeconomic conditions within the Arab community on the southwest side of Chicago. It is based on current and historical research conducted as part of the Needs Assessment Project, Phase 1.[1] Evidence from the Needs Assessment Project and a review of the daily operations of the AAAN and Arab-American Community Center, the home base of the AAAN, indicate that the Arab community on the southwest side is facing a critical shortage of social and economic resources. In the 100-year history of the Arab community in Chicago, this situation appears unprecedented. Our research indicates that current problems within the community exist partly because of a deteriorating "ethnic safety net," which is defined as internal Arab community networks that provide for the cohesion, safety, security, and prosperity of Arab families through interaction, assistance, and intervention. That such a safety net existed in the past and as recently as the mid-1980s is documented by prior research on the community.[2] As the following discussion reveals, the deterioration of this safety net did not occur on its own or as part of some organic loss of tradition within the Arab community. It is intimately related to larger economic changes occurring in the city of Chicago, the United States, and in immigrants' homelands. With the decline of ethnic resources to enable the cohesion, safety, security, and prosperity of Arab families in Chicago, a void emerged. As members of the Arab community looked outside their community for resources to fill the void, they found barriers in place. These barriers are cultural, linguistic, economic, and political. An objective of the Needs Assessment Project is to begin removing these barriers to Arab community access to resources lying outside the community.

Historical Perspective of the Arab Community on the Southwest Side of Chicago

The first large migration of Arabs to the United States occurred at the same time as the large migration of southern and eastern Europeans—between 1880 and 1921. Most Arab immigrants came from the area known to the West as the Levant (i.e., Syria, Lebanon, Jordan, and Palestine or Israel). Although a handful of Levantine Arabs migrated to the United States every year between 1820 and 1886, their migration increased markedly after 1887. In the peak years, between 1899 and 1921, 3,000 to 8,000 Levantine Arabs migrated to the United States annually. An interesting feature of this migration is that during World War I (1916 to 1919), more than 90 percent of the Arabs came not directly from the Middle East but from other countries in the Americas. National quota limits on immigration legislated by the U.S. Congress in 1921 put an end to this era of booming Arab migration, as they did for other non-Northern European groups not previously restricted.[3] The 1910 U.S. Census recorded 55,102 foreign-born Syrians (including Lebanese) and Palestinians in the United States, a number roughly parallel to the number of foreign-born Croatians or Slovaks in the United States at the time. Arab-American scholar Philip Hitti estimated that there were about 200,000 "Syrians" in the United States in 1924, including immigrants and their American-born children.[4]

These Arabs were known officially and popularly in the United States as "Syrians," referring to the Turkish (Ottoman) designation of this geographic area and the Bureau of Immigration's racial classification of the people originating there. "Syrians" were officially considered "white" until eligibility for naturalization based on race became a heated national issue after the turn of the twentieth century. Geographically, the Levantine Arab countries were in Asia, and Asians were barred from becoming naturalized U.S. citizens. The issue of racial origins was a matter of utmost importance to the U.S. government, which denied rights to people based on race. It was also important to white Americans seeking to protect their financial interests, white Americans facing job competition from nonwhites and new immigrants, and to persons considered nonwhite, who were routinely excluded by all of them.

After numerous cases of denial of naturalization rights, the issue of whether "Syrians" were white or not was officially resolved in 1915 in *Dow v. The United States*. The appellate court judges ruled in the case that "Syrians" were of the Semitic branch of the Caucasian race; they were therefore eligible for U.S. citizenship.[5]

These debates in American society played themselves out on the streets (and continue to do so under new terms). Whether one was considered white or not, a real American or not, and Christian or not affected the responses immigrants and their children received from others and, in turn, their responses to the strong push for assimilation into white, Christian American culture that existed at the time. In Chicago, different patterns emerged within the Arab immigrant community. These patterns leave their imprint in numerous ways on the Arab community of the 1990s. They also affect our ability to find and count persons of Arab ethnicity.

In Chicago, the size of the Arab immigrant community by 1920 was large enough to form two notable residential clusters on the south side. Syrian and Lebanese Christians established a community of families between 12th and 15th Streets and California and Kedzie and a smaller community near 63rd and Kedzie. Palestinian immigrants were more likely to be male and Muslim, and they lived in boarding houses near 18th Street and Michigan. The history of this era is not well recorded, but it appears that the Syrians and Lebanese were engaged in wholesale and retail trade, including urban and rural peddling, supplied from the market network center they developed in Chicago. The Palestinians were largely urban peddlers, probably initially trained and supplied by local Syrians and Lebanese or New York Palestinian wholesalers. Their primary trade routes were among the newly emerging black communities on Chicago's south side.[6]

According to Al-Tahir, the Syrian-Lebanese sought assimilation into American society. As Christians and as persons at least officially regarded as white, they were able to do so, although not without facing the prejudices and obstacles other white ethnics faced at the time. As part of their assimilation, according to Al-Tahir, they adopted the anti-black, segregationist attitudes of the dominant white culture and refused to engage in business in the black community. The Palestinians, on the other hand, were mostly Muslim and males without family in the United States who planned to return to Palestine. As sojourners and as Muslims, they did not see themselves as Americans nor seek to engage in domestic American racial conflicts. They therefore had the proper orientation toward American society to work effectively as a "middleman minority."[7]

These divergent responses to American society between the two groups left Palestinians, among Arabs, to dominate the Arab trading niche in the black community.

Palestinians expanded this niche as the "black belt" of Chicago expanded because of increased migration of southern blacks. They maintained peddling routes, and they opened food and dry goods stores. Because they preferred to live close to their stores or peddling routes, they became a residentially scattered community, spread out from 18th to 45th Streets and from Lake Michigan to Cottage Grove. Often they lived behind their stores in very modest conditions.

The Syrian-Lebanese community, through cultural assimilation, abandonment of the occupation of trading and shopkeeping by American-born generations, upward economic mobility, and intermarriage, became widely dispersed. There are almost none to be found currently living on the south side of Chicago, and it remains for future research to determine where in greater Chicago they live.

In the post–World War II era, Palestinian Muslim women began immigrating to Chicago, largely as the wives of men already here, and starting families. Many Palestinians had become American citizens. Those who served in World War II could bring their wives to the United States under the War Brides Act, and the post-1948 creation of the State of Israel on Palestinian land fostered an increased migration of family members and the admission of some Palestinian refugees to the United States. The change from single males to families required new thinking about household dwellings. Boarding houses and stores were not fit for family residences. Palestinian families moved into homes and apartments just west of the black belt. It was also at this time that Palestinian Christians began migrating to the United States in larger numbers along with Assyrians, Iraqis, and Jordanians. These latter groups tended to settle on Chicago's north side. Despite their addition to the ethnic map of Chicago, the Palestinian community on the south side of Chicago remained the largest Arab presence in the city, a phenomenon that continues to this day.

Since the post-World War II era, Chicago has been characterized by rapidly expanding, segregated black neighborhoods and parallel "white flight." Palestinians were in the middle of this movement. They moved south and west into the transitional neighborhoods being abandoned by whites as the black belt expanded nearby. As a consequence of racism and discrimination against black Americans, black belt neighborhoods were poor and suffered from high unemployment, physical deterioration, and other urban problems that accompany poverty and exclusion. Palestinians worked in these neighborhoods but did not want to live in them. Unlike many black Americans, they could afford not to live in them, and unlike all black Americans, they were not blocked from access to housing in white ethnic neighborhoods. The Palestinians served as a convenient barrier population between black and white, a role Mexicans moving southward from the inner city also served in Chicago. Arabs and Mexicans still occupy this position in the residential demography of Chicago's south side.

By the 1970s, the Palestinian community had reached the Gage Park and Chicago Lawn areas of Chicago's southwest side, areas characterized by white ethnic residents violently opposed to black home ownership or residence. Targeted by civil rights activists for open housing campaigns in the late 1960s and the 1970s, these neighborhoods were the site of the violent 1966 attack on Dr. Martin Luther King, Jr., in Marquette Park. (Dr. King observed that Chicago was one of the most segregated places in the United States.) Race riots broke out in these neighborhoods in 1972, when Gage Park High School was integrated, and again during the open housing campaigns of the late 1970s.

The Ku Klux Klan and American Nazi Party were active in the area, inciting residents against housing integration, and the latter organization maintained an office in the neighborhood. Black residents moving into the eastern section of these neighborhoods were subject to violent attacks on their homes in the form of bricks and rocks thrown through windows, molotov cocktails, arson, and personal attacks.[8]

White flight began, and Arabs and Mexicans moved in. In the 1980s, both neighborhoods became racially integrated as African Americans moved west of Western Avenue, although they were still steered to housing at the eastern border. As so often happens parallel to white flight, the social and economic climate of these neighborhoods deteriorated during the transition process. In the late 1980s and early 1990s, many of the middle-class Palestinians who lived in these neighborhoods, concerned about safety and housing values, moved to the suburbs, following the lead of white ethnics. They were replaced by new Arab immigrants, Polish immigrants, upwardly mobile Mexican immigrants, and on the eastern side, by African Americans. These two neighborhoods still contain the largest concentration of Arabs in Chicago. They are home to a continuously increasing number of new Arab immigrants—largely Palestinians—and the Arab families who cannot afford to move out.

In Chicago in the 1960s, as in other northern U.S. cities, riots broke out in black neighborhoods as a result of decades of racial discrimination and oppression and the absence of progress in civil rights. In the process of rioting, local properties (largely not black owned) were damaged and looted. Afterward, corporate chain stores and many small Jewish and Italian merchants pulled their investments out of these neighborhoods. Palestinians and a growing community of south side Jordanians moved in, purchasing newly available grocery and liquor businesses. With years of experience in trading and shopkeeping in the black community, Arab entrepreneurs knew how to survive in small businesses where costs were high, inventory small, and personal safety risky. They also had an advantage over local African Americans—access to capital through family and savings. Institutional lenders were largely unwilling to provide loans for businesses in these areas, ruling out working class African-American investment, and middle class African Americans expressed little interest in "ghetto shopkeeping."

Another important part of the Arab business strategy was using co-ethnic or family labor. Family members or new Arab immigrants could be counted on to work ten- to twelve-hour days for little compensation. Family members did it as part of a collective family enterprise. New immigrants did it to earn a living while learning job skills in a context that did not require much English. The goal was to learn the ropes of small business ownership and save money for the purchase of one's own business.

By the early 1970s, Arabs owned nearly 20 percent of all small grocery and liquor stores in Chicago, most in black neighborhoods.[9] Not all southwest side Arabs worked as shopowners or shop clerks. Others worked as laborers in local factories, such as Nabisco and Sweetheart Cup. These were unionized jobs with benefits in a work environment characterized by a substantial number of Arabs. Preexisting job and English skills were not necessary for many entry-level jobs. More important was the recommendation of a worker to his or her supervisor, many of whom were also Arabs. After years of factory work, some of these laborers invested in a small business with their savings.

The successes of Arab immigrants in small business and in securing factory work and the growth in the size of the Arab community through immigration and childbirth led to the development of an expanding ethnic business market on the southwest side in the 1970s and 1980s. Grocery stores, bakeries, restaurants, insurance agents, realtors, barbers, beauticians, doctors, dentists, and lawyers catering to Arab clients emerged. (Another Arab ethnic business district developed on the north side of the city.) Most of the service establishments were owned by well-educated or well-established members of the community, not new immigrants. On the southwest side, businesses clustered on 63rd Street and on Pulaski Avenue.

Throughout the 1970s and much of the 1980s, the Arab community on the south side of Chicago was able to support itself internally through job, social, family, political, and community networks. New immigrants were assisted socially and economically within the community and did not seek outside help for their adjustment needs. Family and community social problems were dealt with within this internal system.

In the 1970s, Arabs in Chicago began feeling a significant increase in ethnic discrimination.[10] Negative portrayals of Arabs had appeared with regularity in the American media since 1967, fueling anti-Arab sentiment among Americans. Arabs were dehumanized and subjected to negative stereotyping, not because of anything they did in America, but because Arabs were the adversaries of Israel, America's strategic ally. Israel commenced its military occupation of more Palestinian land in 1967, forcing a new wave of Palestinian refugees, and the American government and popular media supported these actions. When Arab Americans began exercising their right to free speech, they discovered that their voices were locked out. Their viewpoint was ignored by the media and political figures, and the FBI began a campaign of hounding Arab-American political activists. As a result of these experiences, the Arab ethnic community in Chicago became more insular. As they were cut off from participation in mainstream institutions, they also withdrew from aspiring to be part of them.

With insularity grew community strength and resilience. After nearly 70 years in Chicago, the Palestinian community became more Palestinian, not more American. This process was fed by the continuing stream of new immigrants and university students, fresh from the homeland, who were living carriers of Palestinian culture and news of increasing human rights abuses back home. Palestinian political organizations emerged in Chicago in the 1970s, providing another layer of support to the family and community networks. Support and problem resolution not managed at lower levels were managed by these organizations and their community institutions. New student migrants, coming without family to study in the United States and largely from areas of Palestine not part of the family networks, were acclimated to America through the social networks of political organizations. In the 1970s, approximately equal numbers of Palestinian and Jordanian students were admitted to the United States as immigrants. In the 1980s, their numbers far exceeded immigrants.

Until the late 1980s, although locked out, stereotyped, and subjected to government harassment, the Palestinian community in Chicago appeared to be holding its own. The isolation from mainstream American society felt by most Arab immigrants (except some professionals with distant attachments to the community and their children) encouraged continued employment in the shopkeeping niche, where contact with white American institutions and prejudice was limited. Rare were stories of Arab poverty, criminality, broken families, or substance abuse. Pride in Arab culture and Palestinian nationalism was strong, and these ideas were developed in the American born children of immigrants.[11]

Community-wide Palestinian organizations met their demise after the 1990–1991 Gulf War, from which the Palestinians and the Palestinian Liberation Organizaiton (PLO) emerged weak. Most Palestinian community centers in Chicago closed, and the community-wide cohesiveness that provided newcomers and youth with pride, strength, and resilience in the face of discrimination and political disappointments started shattering.

In 1997, on the southwest side of Chicago, we find a different Arab community profile, economically and socially. Economic vulnerability characterizes 60 percent of southwest side Arab families, because of unemployment (30 percent) or low-paid employment (30 percent), usually as a clerk in an Arab-owned store. Sixty-six percent of households in the Needs Assessment survey reported receiving some type of public support. Although poor families are more likely to be headed by recent immigrants who are not U.S. citizens, there is also a substantial amount of poverty among southwest side immigrants who came to the United States more than fifteen years ago. Because about 50 percent of Arabs on the southwest side are children younger than 14 years of age,[12] most Arabs living at or below the poverty level are American-born children.

Seventy percent of our survey respondents disliked their neighborhood. They cited problems with crime, drugs, gangs, and shootings as the main reasons they felt unsafe. Of these, 70 percent say they cannot move for economic reasons, because of unemployment or underemployment. Sixty percent of respondents from these and neighboring areas reported having domestic problems they need help with. Alcoholism, drug abuse, and domestic violence are readily apparent in the community. Broken families are no longer unusual, nor are Arab youth held at the police station or in juvenile court, as measured by calls for intervention received at the Arab-American Action Network. Arab street gangs are part of the local scene, and Arab theft ring members, who largely victimize other Arabs, have instilled fear and distrust among community members. Many Arab parents feel they have lost control of their children and, as immigrants, do not know how to handle parenting in urban America. There is no longer a strong, insular Arab community to provide them with help. They want programs for their children to keep them off the streets, but few are available.

Seventy percent of respondents felt their English language skills were inadequate to access the services they need, to get better jobs, and to work with their children's teachers and school counselors. As parents reach out to the larger society's institutions to improve their conditions and the conditions of their children, they find a large language barrier and no Arab-oriented English language program to help remove this barrier. Community support is lacking, and help from city-wide institutions almost nonexistent. The AAAN is working to fill the vacuum created by the lack of informal community help networks and a similar absence of institutional support. To do this, it must assess the problems that exist and their causes. The following discussion addresses some of the causes of this change in the Arab community on the south side of Chicago.

Immigration

Every year since 1965, when the U.S. government removed country quotas and opened up immigration from non-European countries, the number of Palestinians and Jordanians immigrating to the United States has increased. Since the 1967 Israeli occupation of East Jerusalem, the West Bank, and Gaza, reasons to emigrate have grown. Chief among these are Israeli confiscations of Palestinian land, largest in the areas most Palestinian immigrants to the United States have traditionally been from, and human rights abuses by the Israeli military. An initial Palestinian policy of steadfastness, staying on the land no matter what the costs, required families to send some members abroad so they could live on remittance incomes. When opportunities for lucrative work in the Arab Gulf States lessened in the mid-1980s and ended altogether after the 1990–1991 Gulf War, the United States became one of the few available destinations for Palestinians seeking to support their families. Since the 1993 Oslo Peace Accords, from which the Palestinians have derived few benefits, unemployment among Palestinians in the West Bank and Gaza has doubled, according to a joint World Bank–Palestinian study, largely because of their being cut off from the Israeli labor market.

Changes in U.S. immigration law opened the doors for Palestinian movement from east to west. Because the new immigration law established family reunification as its priority in awarding immigrant visas, new Palestinian immigrants were largely relatives of persons already here. Some of these were the families of Palestinians studying in the United States in preparation for work in the Gulf, work that was no longer available after 1985; most were relatives of the earliest Palestinian immigrants. Palestinian immigrants, like all immigrants, tend to settle in larger numbers in places where co-ethnics already have a significant presence. Chicago is one such place. Probably 10 to 15 percent, possibly more, of all new Palestinian immigrants to the United States have settled in Chicago since 1965. A large percentage of them settle on the southwest side of the city. This increased level of immigration greatly expanded the number of Palestinians and Jordanians in Chicago.

The profile of Palestinian immigrants in Chicago is a diverse one. Few have been from among the wealthiest or most educated families in Palestine. The earliest immigrants were largely unskilled peasants from villages in the Jerusalem, Ramallah, and Bethlehem areas of Palestine. Because most of these migrants sent remittances to the family back home, relatives who followed them to Chicago were a bit more skilled and educated than their predecessors. As the economics of life in America have changed with rises in the cost of living and more Palestinian and Jordanian immigrants are supporting their own families here, remittances sent back have decreased. Fewer relatives back home are being supported on a smaller amount of dollars. This affects their socioeconomic condition back home and the type of human and capital resources new immigrants arrive with and the amount of help they can expect from relatives once here. According to 1990 Census data, Arab immigrants living on the southwest side who entered the United States between 1987 and 1990 (49 percent) were more likely to have less than eight years of formal education than those who entered between 1980 and 1986 (5 percent) or between 1965 and 1979 (32 percent). These data suggest an increase in hardship, nonselective emigration among Palestinians; those who once stayed behind to hold onto the family land are increasingly pressured to leave. Nowadays, when Palestinian immigrants come, they come as entire families. This presents more difficult economic circumstances than those faced by earlier immigrants, because an entry-level job in the Arab business niche can support a new immigrant, but it cannot support an entire family.

Job Opportunities

In the United States, most immigrants, especially nonprofessionals, find jobs through ethnic networks. Unless highly educated and fluent in English, a new immigrant cannot find a job working in the company of native-born, skilled Americans. Immigrants are instead routed into jobs in which their co-ethnics have established a niche.[13] In Chicago, new Palestinian and Jordanian immigrants have been traditionally routed into two types of work: as peddlers or clerks in Arab-owned businesses or as unskilled laborers in local factories. Both of these arenas have faced negative changes in the past ten years.

The city of Chicago lost 60 percent of its manufacturing base between 1967 and 1987.[14] This translated to the loss of hundreds of thousands of positions for unskilled laborers, the type of work new immigrants usually started with. Immigrants do not obtain work in any factory; they find work in factories where co-ethnics already work. A number of the main employers of Arab immigrants on the south side of Chicago closed their factories and moved out of the country (e.g., Rheem) or downsized (e.g., Nabisco, Sweetheart Cup) in the late 1980s. Fewer industrial jobs are available for everyone in Chicago, and employers not already dependent on Arab labor have no incentive to accept new Arab employees. They prefer to use their own internal co-ethnic recruitment system.

This leaves the shopkeeping sector—the entrepreneurial niche—as the main source of employment for Arab immigrants. Arabs in Chicago are disproportionately engaged in retail trade, and their entrepreneurial successes have made them, historically at least, an upwardly mobile ethnic community. Fifty-eight percent of southwest side, 42 percent of southwest suburban, and 46 percent of north side employed Arabs work in retail trade.[15] The proportions of owners compared with workers varies by area. Although 76 percent of southwest suburban Arabs working in retail trade own their business, only 35 percent of southwest side Arabs are owners; the rest are retail workers. This niche is not capable of absorbing the large numbers of Palestinian and Jordanian immigrants that it must to keep Arab unemployment down, nor is it providing sufficient wages to keep a working family out of poverty. There are a number of reasons for this.

First, it is not expanding enough horizontally or vertically to accommodate the volume of new immigrants. The two other main entrepreneurial ethnic groups in the United States today are the Koreans and the Cubans. The ability of these communities to absorb new immigrants has been fostered by their expansion into wholesaling and production.[16] The Cubans in Miami are characterized by an "institutionally complete" economy, including production, retail, and wholesale markets. Although initial adaptation was difficult with new immigrant waves, the Cuban economy expanded to meet the needs of new immigrants and at the same time expanded job openings. The Korean entrepreneurs in Chicago share many of the characteristics of Arab entrepreneurs that lead to success in small business, but they have an additional resource the Palestinians will never have (without independence) and the Jordanians do not have—an export-oriented homeland economy. Ahne notes,

> the export-oriented economic policy of the South Korean government . . . may be a larger
> factor than is generally presumed in understanding the Korean concentration in small

business in America. The same export-oriented economy that pulled rural labor into Korean cities to manufacture garments, wigs, toys, shoes, and electronic goods had to find large overseas markets for these goods.[17]

Korean manufacturers benefited from government subsidies, Chicago-based wholesalers received incentives, and retailers selling inexpensive commodities expanded all over Chicago. Arabs in Chicago work largely in retail liquor and grocery and purchase from Jewish wholesaling companies. There is only one small-scale Arab wholesaler and almost no production activity among Arabs. Successful Arab shopowners who seek to expand invest their capital in another shop or a larger shop, an investment that provides few additional job openings.

A second factor influencing underemployment is that owners experience lessened gross receipts and smaller profit margins as the incomes of their clientele plummet and as local pressure has forced Arab merchants to hire African-American clerks. Most of the neighborhoods on the south side of Chicago where Arabs own businesses have witnessed increases in the percent of population living in poverty between 1980 and 1990.[18] When residents have less money to spend, shopkeepers make less money. These problems, poverty and reduced sales, will undoubtedly increase with welfare reform and the extensive reduction of food stamp eligibility and benefits, and gross receipts will shrink even smaller. Local communities have also exerted pressure on Arab shopkeepers to hire African-American personnel, who have largely responded to this demand. African-American clerks do not work 12- to 15-hour days, as immigrant Arab clerks are forced to. Two non-Arab employees are to be hired to replace one Arab. This lowers the profit margin for owners and the number of job openings for Arab immigrants.

A third reason for underemployment is that, as owners' profit margins drop, the salaries they are willing to pay their workers do not rise commensurate with changes in the cost of living. Average pay ten years ago for working as a clerk in an Arab store was about $800 per month. Today, it is $1200 per month. This places store clerks just below the U.S. poverty level for a family of four ($14,800 in 1994). Because Arab families tend to have more than two children, they are actually living further below the poverty level. No benefits are offered in addition to these wages, workers are expected to be on duty at least 60 hours per work, and work can sometimes be life-threatening. Working at an Arab store in a poor neighborhood therefore becomes a high-risk, exhausting, and underpaid proposition offering little possibility for savings and no benefits for family members.

Many men[19] in the community have lost motivation because of this economic situation. For some, public aid appears to offer a better option. With public aid, the family at least has health care benefits. Some have lost hope in the American experience and have resorted to alcohol, drugs, and gambling for relief. This economic situation has secondary effects. People who cannot save money cannot think of buying a store and pulling out of their situation, as the older immigrants could. They are stuck where they are. The number of newly opened stores will decrease in proportion to the population, as will the number of job openings. People who cannot save cannot send money back home. This hurts relatives back home, who, if they seek to immigrate to the United States, will have less help of any kind when they arrive. A cycle of unemployment and poverty will grow if job opportunities and the rewards for working do not improve for

Arabs in Chicago. Employed and unemployed men interviewed for the Needs Assessment stress the need for job-training programs and access to city jobs to turn this situation around.

Neighborhood Change

Arab male and female survey respondents living in the neighborhoods of Gage Park and Chicago Lawn said their neighborhoods had some positive characteristics, such as proximity to other Arabs, Arab stores, and a mosque, but 70 percent of those interviewed said overall neighborhood conditions were bad. They complained of gang, crime, and drug problems; lack of police protection and even police harassment; and a general lack of safety and security. Although they would like to move, the finances required for such mobility are not there. This neighborhood context for the Arab community represents a significant change from the past. Earlier Arab immigrants and their families in Chicago were one step ahead of neighborhood deterioration; now they are in the middle of it. Gage Park and Chicago Lawn are now considered transitional neighborhoods. Several community organizations are actively working to stabilize these communities, but in the meantime, they are facing the usual problems of transitional areas in Chicago—deteriorating housing, poverty, crime, and gangs.

This neighborhood context affects Arab-American children growing up in these areas. They are exposed to criminality, drugs, and gang membership at a young age, and some have proven susceptible to these influences. In either case, they are required to be tough to survive. Arab-American female teenagers interviewed for our study reported "staying alive" as the number one goal they had when they woke up each day. Arab parents report feeling "out of control" with regard to their children. The Arab family is facing stresses that are new to it in Chicago. The perceived danger of the neighborhood has also encouraged parents to be more vigilant with their daughters, resulting in losses of freedom for young females. A common solution to this predicament has become family-arranged teenage marriages. Young girls, without completing high school, are forced into a parenting role before they reach adulthood and a spousal role before they are old enough to know themselves and their personal strengths.

Departure of the Middle Class

The Arab community on the south side of Chicago also suffered a resource drain when its more established and economically successful members began leaving the city in the late 1980s. Co-ethnic support and community cohesion were shattered by this loss as the poor and newcomers were left to care for themselves. Along with their departure, these members of the community lessened their support for Arab community organizations operating in the city.

The first generation of American-born Palestinian children reached adulthood in the 1970s and 1980s. As young adults, some of them gave much volunteer time to community activities and community centers, But because they were fairly well educated (male and female alike), when they began careers as entrepreneurs, skilled technicians, white collar workers, and professionals, they also moved to the suburbs. When they physically moved out, their level of commitment to new immigrants and less successful immigrants, as well as Arab institutions still existing in the city, lessened. This departure of middle class immigrants and their children left Arab immigrants and Arab Americans living in the "old neighborhood" to fend for themselves in a context characterized by a service and support vacuum.

Gap in Community Organizing and Loss of Strong Ethos

The movement of the middle class to the suburbs happened around the same time as the collapse of Palestinian political organizations that followed the 1990–1991 Gulf War. A global phenomenon, the lack of external support for Palestinian political organizations in Chicago, struck another blow to the community, because these organizations were the primary vehicles for community programs, organizing, empowerment, recruiting volunteers, and developing ethnic pride. With this loss, another support structure in the safety net was gone.

After the 1993 peace treaty between the PLO and Israel, Palestinians in Chicago lost hope of ever returning home. Palestinians in exile were not part of the treaty, nor did it allow for positive development in Palestine. Loss of hope and loss of mechanisms to build community pride hurt the morale of community members, especially those facing dire economic circumstances. The drive to educate all their children, boys and girls alike, was lost. The unity of the community was shattered into smaller clan and family groups, and the middle class separated from the poor.

To a certain degree, Islam has provided a new source of strength and pride among Muslim Arabs in Chicago, especially among the poor. Islamic religious institutions have stepped in to fill some of the service gap, primarily in the field of education. However, as religiosity increases, the level of discrimination Muslims face from the society around them increases, while the service capacity of external social service providers decreases.

Service Vacuum

With all of these features of the ethnic safety net gone, Arab immigrants and their families faced a service and support vacuum. When they looked outside their community for assistance, they found overwhelming language and cultural barriers, if not outright hostility. Until recently, no locally based, non-Arab institutions or agencies had Arabic-speaking staff or culturally sensitive programs. Families facing disintegration were left without resources, youth had no place to go where they could feel welcomed as Arabs, and parental interactions with teachers, police, and juvenile authorities were mired in miscommunication. Arab youth who had become Illinois Department of Children and Family Service cases were assigned to case workers who knew nothing about Arab culture and who could not converse with the youths' parents. Family crises were left to spin out of control, and victims of domestic violence had no recourse but to stay in that situation.

Concerned Arab Americans began meeting in 1995 to strategize about how to begin to meet these community needs. They knew that they had to seek support from the city government and local foundations for their own community-based programs. Having been pushed away by so many institutions and organizations in Chicago for being Arab, community organizers had historically built their strength on internal community solidarity and homeland ties. Now they had no choice but to look outside. Local activists, mostly Arab women, formed the AAAN and began developing programs and seeking external support for them. Their initial reception was not positive, even though the needs of the community were great.

This situation is now beginning to change. Foundations, the city government, and local service providers are beginning to respond to program support requests from AAAN. With Community Development Block Grant money from the mayor's office, AAAN established a youth after-school program, and through another city program, it established a summer youth employment training program. Support from various foundations enabled AAAN to offer family counseling, parenting classes, crisis intervention, and liaison and mediation services. In recognition of its accomplishments and ambitions, United Way awarded AAAN a Venture Grant in 1997, which supports new organizations working with underserved communities. Also in 1997, AAAN was awarded the Marshalls Domestic Peace Prize from the Family Violence Prevention Fund for its domestic violence intervention program, one of only seven organizations nationwide to receive this award. In 1998, AAAN added English as a Second Language classes and Citizenship classes, and its Board of Directors was awarded a capacity building grant. However, these programs touch only the surface of the problems that exist within the community.

Recognizing that without firm, scientific documentation of the size of the Arab community and the extent of its needs further external support would not be forthcoming, AAAN determined that commissioning a needs assessment was crucial to its growth and to enhancing the responsiveness of local institutions. In 1996, AAAN approached the Chicago Community Trust to support a needs assessment of its community and was awarded a modest grant to begin the process. Phase 1, a study of the Arab community on the southwest side of Chicago, was launched. To make it useful for a community facing substantial discrimination, the research process focused on community needs and investigated the community's positive contributions to the society in which it lives. Published in May 1998 and released to the press in June, the needs assessment proved to be a tremendous boost to AAAN's work and to public recognition of the Arab community in Chicago. Every major newspaper and radio station featured the story of the Arab-American community; they were now on the map.[20]

Conclusions and Solutions

The needs assessment was not only a piece of research, it was a political step forward for Arab Americans in Chicago. In addition to pointing out service needs in the community, it called for recognition of the long history of Arab-American contributions to Chicago's small business economy. It called for an end to stereotyping and the political and social exclusion of Arab Americans. It called for Arab-American participation on decision-making bodies, planning committees, and boards. It called for schools to be more aware of the stereotyping of Arabs in their educational materials. It suggested that external service providers working in areas of Arab residential concentration hire Arabic-speaking staff and train non-Arab staff in Arab culture and values. It also called for Arabs to develop leadership in their own community and to take steps to assist less fortunate community members. One method of assistance suggested was the establishment of an internal small business loan system, as is done in other successful immigrant merchant communities, to assist newer immigrants in getting started in business.

Overall, the Needs Assessment Project pointed out that new immigrants and their children, especially those who are poor, need access to resources that will help them stabilize their lives in the United States and develop their talents. These largely revolve around job and language training, access to employment opportunities outside the ethnic network, access to civil service jobs, and services for youth and families. The primary concern of parents was that their children have access to healthy activities that build positive Arab identity. The fear of losing their children to American "street culture" was severe. Most Arab women in this sector of the community choose not to work outside the home when their children are young, but among those who had attempted to locate jobs in local chain stores and supermarkets, many felt they were denied employment because they wore a head scarf. This problem indicates that the social, the political, and the economic are intertwined, and efforts at change must engage many levels. Detailed findings of the needs assessment study are available in the report, *Meeting Community Needs, Building on Community Strengths,* available from the AAAN in Chicago.

Actions to address problems that exist within the Arab community in Chicago must be multilayered. Some require global solutions. If Palestinians had independence and a vigorous economy in their homeland, they would not be forced to flee to circumstances that appear to be little improvement over what they left. Most of our survey respondents felt life in the United States had not met their expectations, and most women wanted to go back. Public support for struggling families has proven crucial to their survival. So far, the State of Illinois has not cut off immigrant noncitizens from public benefits.

Other actions must be generated from within the Arab community, especially from its middle-class, more-resourced members. Foundations, decision-makers, school boards, and elected officials must make efforts to engage Arab Americans and to overcome their historic exclusion. Local institutions and service providers must improve their capacity to service Arab clients. The local community ("the neighborhood") must now replace some of the functions of the larger ethnic group. Feelings of safety, strength, and pride must be recreated at this level. The safety net will be stronger if it involves collaborative efforts on the part of all members of the geographic community, if it is a multi-ethnic, multi-racial safety net that builds on the strengths of each resident subcommunity.

With sufficient funding for identified program needs, AAAN can, along with these other actors, begin to weave a new safety net for Arab Americans. Phase 2 of the needs assessment process will be launched in the Fall of 1999. Funding for this phase has been rather easy to secure as a result of the great success of Phase 1, which has been called a "model for all communities" by the head of Chicago's Human Relations Commission.

Notes

1. For more information, a map and eighteen charts of census data on Arabs in Chicago and the United States can be found in the Addendum to *Meeting Community Needs, Building on Community Strengths* (Chicago: Arab American Action Network), 1998.

2. Abdul Jalil Al-Tahir, "The Arab Community in the Chicago Area: A Comparative Study of the Christian-Syrians and the Muslim Palestinians" (Ph.D. dissertaion, University of Chicago, 1952); and Louise Cainkar, "Coping with Tradition, Change and Alienation: The Life Experiences of Palestinian Women in the United States" (Ph.D. dissertation, Northwestern University, 1988); publication of a work based on the dissertation is forthcoming from Temple University Press.

3. See Cainkar, "Coping with Tradition, Change and Alienation," for detailed information on Arab immigration to the United States.

4. Philip K. Hitti, *The Syrians in America* (New York: George H. Doran, 1924).

5. Alixa Naff, *Becoming American: The Early Arab Immigrant Experience* (Carbondale, IL: Southern Illinois University Press, 1985). In the 1990s, nearly 100 years later, although blatant racially based legislation would be considered unconstitutional, legislative efforts that effectively target some American ethnic groups more than others are on the increase. For Arab Americans, the Anti-Terrorism Law is one such effort. On a social level, Arab Americans increasingly report being treated as a people different from the white American core group.

6. Al-Tahir, "Arab Community in the Chicago Area."

7. A middleman minority is a group inserted between the dominant and subordinate who can deal with both and is part of neither. See Edna Bonacich, "A Theory of Middleman Minorities," *American Sociological Review* 38 (October 1973): 583–94.

8. Chicago Urban League, *Marquette Park* (Chicago: The Urban League, 1977).

9. Kevin Blackistone, "Arab Entrepreneurs Take over Inner City Grocery Stores," *Chicago Reporter* 10, no. 5 (May 1981).

10. Cainkar, "Coping with Tradition, Change and Alienation."

11. Cainkar, "Coping with Tradition, Change and Alienation."

12. Unpublished data from the 1990 U.S. Census.

13. Roger Waldinger, "The Making of an Immigrant Niche," *International Migration Review* 28, no. 1 (1994): 3–30.

14. Walda Katz-Fishman and Jerome Scott, "Diversity and Equality: Race and Class in America," *Sociological Forum* 9, no. 4 (1994): 569–81.

15. 1990 U.S. Census.

16. Ivan Light, "Immigrant and Ethnic Enterprise in North America," *Ethnic and Racial Studies* 7, no. 2 (1984): 195–216; and Ivan Light and Parminder Bhachu, eds., *Immigration and Entrepreneurship: Culture, Capital, and Ethnic Networks* (New Brunswick, NJ: Transaction, 1993).

17. Joseph Ahne, "Koreans of Chicago: The New Entrepreneurial Immigrants." In Melvin Holli and Peter d'A. Jones, eds., *Ethnic Chicago* (Grand Rapids, MI: Eerdmans Publishing Co., 1995), p. 485.

18. The Chicago Fact Book Consortium, eds., *Local Community Fact Book* (Chicago: University of Illinois, Sociology Department, 1990).

19. Work as clerks in Arab stores is largely done by males because of the perceived danger of the neighborhood.

20. Copies of press articles are available from the Arab-American Action Network (http://www.aaan.org).

Part V

Political Activism

Helen Hatab Samhan

13   Not Quite White: Race Classification and the Arab-American Experience

Issues of race and identity are dominant factors in American social history. The dual legacies of slavery and massive immigration—and how they have intersected over time—deeply conditioned the ways in which the citizenry relates to race and how the government intercedes to classify the population. Throughout the more than 100 years that Arabs have immigrated to the United States, there has been the need to clarify, accommodate, and reexamine their relationship to this peculiar American fixation on race. In each historical period, Arabs in America have confronted race-based challenges to their identity. Today, the constituency known as Arab American is situated at interesting social crossroads, where issues of minority and majority affiliation demand more attention—and reflection.

This chapter examines race classification policy as it has impacted the Arab-American experience. Rather than approach the question of identity development from within the ethnic boundaries (which continues to be ably and amply studied), this view principally examines the externally imposed systems of classification in the American context: how and why they have developed, how they have changed over time, and how they have related historically to Arab immigrants and ethnics.

The first major question to be addressed is what were the social and political motivations of racial classification. How did these change during the past century and take on different roles in identity issues? Reviewing the two principal arenas where classification occurs in the public sector—immigration policy and the U.S. Census—this chapter traces the policies that drove each of these government tools. I also look at the sociopolitical impact of racial categories on society and on the subgroups themselves.

Once put in historical perspective, the second issue covered is the direct impact racial classification in this American context had on Arab immigrants. An important feature of this discussion is the recurring theme of "not quite white," which appears to impose itself, albeit in different intensities depending on the era. The ways in which official U.S. policy on race and classification confounded the Arab population is examined in two periods that epitomize the country's classification policies in the twentieth century: turn of the century nativism and the civil rights era. An important postscript under consideration is the post-civil rights "millennial period" to cover current trends and attitudes toward race-based policies in particular and multiculturalism in general.

This historical survey of U.S. policy serves as a resource for further study of Arab-American responses to racial classification and remedies that have emerged to rationalize the somewhat confusing and often awkward fit of relating to race. As Arab ethnic initiatives force a diversity-conscious society to recognize its existence and interact with nongovernmental entities and governmental bodies structured for "official" minority representation, an interesting debate is prompted on how ethnic action can promote and demand inclusion. This overview seeks to inform that debate and to place in perspective the yet unsettled issue of where Arabs fit on the ever-changing prism of race in America.

Immigration Policy and Race: The Gatekeeper's Dilemma

A cursory review of immigration policy since the mid-nineteenth century reveals that classification by race has dominated official attitudes toward new Americans. With the possible exception of the period immediately after World War II, when cold war political motives were of prime importance, the United States has continually struggled with reconciling its northern European settler identity with new groups whose culture, language, or religion have not conformed to their Anglo-centric concepts of American identity. Although the second half of the nineteenth century was replete with examples of prejudice and intolerance toward immigrants, even within the northern European context (i.e., German and Irish immigrants), official policy in this period was preoccupied with the pace and pattern of immigration from the Far East.

Excluding Asians and limiting their rights to citizenship and property dominated the attention of federal statutes from the 1870s through the 1920s. Precipitated by the immigration of large numbers of Chinese that coincided with economic depression, anti-Chinese attitudes motivated a series of anti-Asian laws. Chinese immigration was made illegal in 1882, and by the first decade of the new century, steps were taken to limit the impact of Japanese immigrants as well.[1] The significance of these anti-Asian restrictions to the early Arab immigrants are explored in the next section.

If late nineteenth century U.S. immigration policy fixated on excluding Asians as "undesirable" Americans, the first two decades of the twentieth century ushered in a new era of exclusion—policies that focused on the millions of new arrivals from southern and eastern Europe and the Mediterranean. The turn of the century period was characterized by competing forces of an industrial economy that demanded foreign-born labor and nervous sectors of the U.S.-born population that feared these new groups for their strangeness; cultural, linguistic, and religious practices; and political ideologies. Encouraged by business interests, immigration policy in this period allowed admission of the largest numbers of immigrants in U.S. history (peak immigration occurred between 1905 and 1907, when more than a million newcomers arrived each year).[2]

Dominant national groups in this immigration wave included Italians, Poles, Russians (mostly Jews), Slavs, and Greeks. This is also the period that witnessed the first sustained influx of immigrants from the Arab world.

These massive numbers of newcomers prompted competing social and civic ideologies on how America should deal with such change. It was common to refer to the "race" of the new groups, despite their common European origin. Concerns about diluting the American race emerged aside fears that the highly urbanized, often poor immigrants would undermine cherished American values by retaining the political, social, and cultural loyalties of their foreign heritage. Some writers continued to allude to the benefits of new blood, assuring the nation that from the proverbial melting pot would emerge a cultural amalgam that was uniquely American. In the same vein, Americanization programs abounded to make sure the foreign born would learn the language, civic values, and cultural ways of their new homeland. This, however, occurred within a pervasive public ideology that viewed the new immigrants as racially, culturally, and intellectually inferior.[3]

These Americanization programs, implemented in the public and private sectors, received new impetus on the eve of the First World War. July 4, 1915, was the first official "National Americanization Day," with the motto "Many Peoples, But One Nation."[4] This slogan soon was replaced by "America First," and the seeds of nativism took strong root throughout the war years, culminating in the law of 1924, which dramatically altered the face of immigration for four decades. Nurtured by restrictionist movements that emerged as early as the 1890s,[5] the authors of immigration reform in the early 1920s sought by force of law to reestablish the balance of "European stock" to its pre-1890 characteristics. The 1924 National Origins Act put an overall ceiling on European immigration (150,000), prohibited immigration from Japan, and set quotas based on a percentage of each national origin group already present in the United States. Originally proposed at 3 percent of the population enumerated in the 1910 census, it was revised to even further affect the less desirable groups to be no more than 2 percent of each group's foreign-born population in the 1890 census.[6] Like the Italians, Greeks, Poles, and Slavs of the era, the number of Syrian immigrants permitted by the new law was drastically diminished: the prewar peak of over 9,000 per year was reduced to a few hundred.

The anti-Asian laws of the 1880s and the 1924 attempt to cut back the number of newcomers and give preferential quotas to the original settler groups from northern Europe represent the most drastic interventions to control the classification and complexion of new Americans. Two subsequent periods witnessed government initiatives that affected how immigrants would be classified. With the exception of President Roosevelt's wartime request to Congress to relax temporarily the quotas on nationals of China and India (both U.S. allies), no major change in immigration policy occurred until the postwar period. As Dolce observed, it was the Cold War period that symbolized the shift of immigration policy from the domestic domain of congress to become a "focus of the executive branch as a tool of foreign policy."[7]

Beginning in 1948 with Truman's push for the "Displaced Persons Act" to deal with German, Baltic, and East European war victims, postwar laws began to adjust to the diplomatic priorities of the state, although not yet abrogating the intent of the 1924 reforms. The McCarran-Walter Act of 1952, notorious in Arab-American circles for its contemporary role in justifying the case against the "L.A. 8,"[8] represented the first complete codification of immigration and naturalization laws in the modern period. The 1952 Act took five years of congressional study and retained the national origin quota system but based it on the 1920 census, allocating two-thirds of the total to northern Europe.[9] Although the 1952 Act reduced the total volume of immigration, it established "first preference" quotas that targeted persons with useful education and training, thereby injecting a "quality" variable into the classification of immigrants that affected the composition of postwar arrivals.[10]

The persistence of the quota system and its control over the race or ethnicity of new arrivals remained until the immigration Act of 1965 removed the 1924 formulas from the books. The reform bill established an overall annual quota of 170,000, for the first time fixed immigration from the Western Hemisphere at 120,000 per year, and set a per-country annual cap of 20,000. The act has been said to reflect the evolution of public policy toward the foreign born in general and President Kennedy's view in particular of immigrants as a source of national strength.[11] The central innovation of the 1965 law was to replace the quota system with a more egalitarian policy of "first come, first served." Its provisions stressed preferences for family unification, outstanding skilled workers, and refugees. These reforms that lifted the quotas and opened up the criteria for new immigrants contributed to the expansion and diversification of Arab immigration to America. By the late 1960s, annual immigration from the Arab world reached an average of 14,000 to 15,000; Egypt, Jordan/Palestine, and Iraq joined and often surpassed Lebanon and Syria as major sources of new Americans. By the late 1970s, annual Arab immigration increased by several thousand, in part as a result of the Lebanese civil war and sustained high numbers of new arrivals from other countries.[12]

Reforms to American immigration policy during the 1980s had less direct impact on the Arab community but reflected a need to deal with a significant shift in immigration trends, mostly from Asia and the Western Hemisphere. The Refugee Act of 1980 came in response to the huge influx of refugees from Southeast Asia, a move that standardized refugee definitions and created the first right of asylum. Six years later, attention focused on the rise of illegal penetration, especially from Mexico and Central America.[13]

By 1995, Congress again turned its attention to the increasingly daunting problems of illegal immigrants, this time taking a swipe at the annual quota of legal arrivals as well. In an effort to reduce the ripple effect of family unification provisions, the reformists sought to tighten the circle of family members a citizen could bring in and to begin phasing back the total number of newcomers admitted annually. A neo-nativist attitude, although not as overtly racist as in the 1920s, seemed to surface during the course of this most recent congressional debate, bolstered by the statistics that Europe has been replaced—perhaps definitively—by Central America, South America, and Asia as the source of new Americans. This debate continued throughout the 104th session of congress, creating concern among immigrant communities and their advocates that the reforms of the 1960s might not be permanent. The social and economic impact of illegal and new immigration has become a prominent feature of the debate that will be factored into future policies. Particular provisions about immigration and counter-terrorism are projected to have a narrowly focused but visible impact on certain Arab immigrants with political affiliations identified by the U.S. government as "terrorist." Such political exclusions, while targeting a narrow class of immigrants, introduce highly controversial and visible aspects to the Arab immigrant experience that promise to reverberate beyond its original intent.[14]

Census Categories: Serving the Oppressor and the Oppressed

If post-1850 immigration classification mirrors the nation's fixation on the race of the foreign born, census measures of the population's racial composition reflect historical fixations on its black population. From the first census of 1790 through the civil war, the decennial census served to differentiate white citizens from free blacks and slaves, because the latter group was counted proportionally (three-fifths) for purposes of political representation. Throughout the 1800s, beyond the civil war and well into the twentieth century, census classifications were rooted in racist intent, whether to create as many slaves as possible or to reflect the society's obsession with miscegenation. Slaves were specified by color (e.g., B for black, M for mulatto), and in 1890, the census further broke down black ancestry to quadroon (i.e., black grandparents) and octoroon (i.e., black great-grandparents).[15] In twentieth century Jim Crow America, the "one-drop rule" took over these intricate formulas with the segregationist premise that a person with any black ancestry would be classified as black.

How the census dealt with other issues of race is less distinctive but also reflected the needs to identify nonwhite populations. The impact of the post–civil war surge in immigration on census categories could be seen in two main areas: new questions on the foreign born and new race categories for Asians. The 1870 census, for example, included the first question on citizenship and birthplace of parent. By 1880, questions on the ability to read, write, or speak English reflected the demographic realities of the times.[16] In 1890, foreign-born persons were asked their year of immigration (a question discontinued from 1940 through 1960), and in 1910, the language of parent was asked.[17]

As for new "racial" categories, the forms used by census takers early in the twentieth century included broader color and race check-offs, adding to White, Negro, and Indian the largest Asian subgroups, notably Chinese and Japanese. Given the civic and sociological thinking at the turn of the century, it is not surprising that "race" definitions could include subgroups of immigrants who were in some way distinguishable from the native-born majority. Mexicans, Jews, Hindus, and even Syrians were among the national and religious origin peoples referred to as racial groups. In some cases, racial classification changed over time. From 1920 to 1940, Asian Indians were classified as Hindu by "race," but from 1950 to 1970, they were coded with Whites. Through the standards set in 1978 by federal Directive 15 (discussed later), the people from the Indian subcontinent became classified as Asian.

After the Second World War, there was some speculation that the race question would be phased out altogether in the United States, as it was in Canada, in favor of a simple question on national origin. Concern about the racist origins of the categories prompted the American Civil Liberties Union to petition to drop the race question from the 1960 survey. Although this did not transpire, it was the enactment of civil rights laws during that decade that changed dramatically the motives and uses of race data collection in the United States. When the Voting Rights Act was passed in 1965, the government found itself in need of highly detailed information about minority participation. Federal data collection, most notably the decennial census, had to supply legislators and the courts with accurate data on which to enforce civil rights protection for blacks. Meanwhile, advocates for other groups displaying large disparity with the white population as a whole (most notably Mexican and other Spanish-speaking Americans) were mobilizing for protection offered by the new civil rights legislation.

The various federal agencies charged with implementing civil rights policies soon found the need for common definitions of the racial and ethnic groups being monitored. In 1974, the Federal Interagency Committee on Education (FICE) was asked by the Secretary of Health, Education, and Welfare to recommend standard racial and ethnic definitions for use by government agencies. The interagency ad hoc committee released a report in 1975 proposing five categories that would serve as the basis for the policy promulgated three years later by the Office of Management and Budget (OMB).[18] The committee set its focus on "disparities between black, Latino, American Indian and Asian American population in comparison to the white population based on existing census data . . . in large part due to earlier policies of limited or total exclusion in various areas—such as citizenship, property rights and immigration—directed at these groups."[19] This focus served as the rationale for the subsequent scope and definition of "minority" programs and policies.

The categories promulgated in 1978 by the OMB did draw distinctions but, unlike earlier policies, not on the basis of skin color. Known as "Directive 15," the standards identify four race categories:

American Indian/Alaska Native: This category includes indigenous north American groups, and despite genetic similarity, remains distinct from indigenous persons from Central and South America because of certain land and treaty obligations.

Asian or Pacific Islander: This category originally covered persons with origins in countries East of the Indian subcontinent but was adjusted after the Association of Indians in America lobbied the OMB to move their group out of the white race category.

Black: This category of persons with origins in the black racial groups of Africa purposely does not encompass continental Africa to distinguish North African regions and European settler populations.

White: This category included persons originating in Europe, the Middle East, and North Africa.

The most problematic of all the groups was the Hispanic population, for which the FICE decided to designate an "ethnic" category that referred to Spanish culture or origin regardless of race or region.[20]

The 1978 classification scheme served as the legal framework for the race/Hispanic origin categories that appear in government surveys and reporting requirements, including the census as of 1980. These categories also permeated most record-keeping and application procedures in the public sector and private sector activity subject to federal state or local statutes to monitor civil rights. Forms used by schools, health professionals, social service agencies, and most businesses eventually conformed to the federal standards. The new impetus for racial classification as a civil rights check transformed dramatically the role of the census, which acquired a political importance that it never had in the past.[21] Equally transformed were assumptions about the subjectivity of race and ethnicity in particular and the concept of self-enumeration as a census policy. Before 1960, when the shift to a mailed census occurred, surveys were administered by an enumerator who processed observed responses to the census questions, including race and ethnicity, following a set of instructions.

This shift in policy and procedure toward the validity of self-identification prompted the census to introduce in 1980 a question on "ancestry," regardless of racial classification. For the first time, the census transcended the objective identifiers of ethnicity (e.g., mother tongue, nativity, parental birthplace, Spanish surname) for a subjective, open-ended question on ethnic origin. Despite considerable debate among researchers on the validity and reliability of ancestry data and the lack of any common definition of ethnicity, the Census Bureau initiated a question in the 1980 sample survey that identified ethnic origin for the entire population, rather than the immigrant generation and their children as had been the case since 1850.[22]

In some ways, the introduction of the ancestry question responded to the gaps in the federal standards of racial classification. Data on large ethnic groups of European origin and on smaller groups such as Arabs whose classification was white were previously unavailable beyond the first and second generations. The benefits of identifying the country's full ethnic makeup for demographic analysis and research or outreach programs for discrete population groups and encouragement from ethnic organizations and scholars convinced the census to repeat the question in 1990.

Stepping beyond the specific confines of the U.S. census and its evolving role as the national yardstick, it is apparent that the impact of the 1978 federal guidelines was felt well beyond the arena of demographics into the civic, political, and economic life of the country. Although this is a discussion that demands more attention than can be offered in this chapter, it is important to touch on the general repercussions of race categories to better understand the Arab-American response.

Racial categories in the civil rights era could be evaluated as having positive and negative ramifications for the society at large and for the subgroups themselves. Taken broadly, the societal benefits of classifying the population by race include the ability to monitor the health and welfare needs of a diverse population, protect civil rights, and attempt to narrow the socioeconomic gaps among the citizenry. These same categories carry a negative residue: the citizens are pitted against each other on an immutable rather than needs basis. Similarly for the subgroup, a separate classification can serve to reinforce and legitimize group cohesion, pride, and perhaps political clout, as well as tangible and intangible benefits to the group (e.g., affirmative action). The unwelcome results of separate categories include becoming targets for stereotyping, resentment, and dealing with issues of government dependency.

An equally compelling subtext of the current debate that is reevaluating racial categories is the addition of immigrant groups (i.e., Asians and Hispanics) to the class of disadvantaged persons deserving of certain legal protection and social interventions. Immigration historian Leonard Fuchs argues against including immigrants as the beneficiaries of affirmative action by asserting that, although all "people of color" have been historically victims of discrimination, no group, despite their experience of poverty or prejudice, were victims of the pervasive, systemic legal discrimination inflicted on blacks in America.[23] The importance of considering these costs and benefits of minority status is a central issue for future discussion of the direction of Arab identity and classification in America.

Arab Immigrant and Ethnic Encounters with Race Classification

When compared with other non-European groups, the effect of racial classification on the lives of Arab Americans has been relatively minor, with the exception of two distinct periods in their immigrant history. In both periods, issues of race became important because of larger social policies that were shaping views on minority groups. In each period, the interjection of race issues circled around the proposition that Arabs are not quite white.

The Arabs' first and most dramatic encounter with classification in America centered on the question of citizenship in the period before World War I. According to nineteenth century immigration categories, the first wave of immigrants from the Ottoman provinces of Syria, Mount Lebanon, and Palestine were classified along with other Ottoman subjects as originating from "Turkey in Asia." By the turn of the century, reforms of immigration regulations that began in 1893 resulted a in new classification for the Arabic-speaking immigrants as "Syrians" after 1899, an adjustment that Naff speculates might have been introduced to deal with the need to differentiate the increasingly diverse national groups still arriving with Turkish passports.[24] Nevertheless, this new immigration category did not spare the Syrians their scuffle with naturalization procedures that reverted precisely to their Asiatic birthplace.

Although the early Syrians were by no means singled out by the focus of turn-of-the-century nativism and xenophobia—larger groups (e.g., Asians, southern and eastern Europeans) were far more concentrated and conspicuous, and by 1909, they did confront a particular challenge to their right to citizenship. Following directives by the Bureau of Immigration and Naturalization to crack down on the eligibility of certain immigrants for naturalization (which had previously been virtually automatic), the courts began to question whether the Syrians' birthplace and racial appearance qualified them as white or as Asian and therefore ineligible for citizenship. In several states, petitions of Syrian-born immigrants were challenged on the grounds that having been born in the dominions of Turkey (i.e., Asia Minor) and therefore of questionable racial stock, the Syrian was not a white person or a person of African descent or birth, as the 1870 statute required.

After the first case appeared in Georgia in 1909, leaders of the Syrian community protested the ruling by organizing the "Association for Syrian Unity" and sending a delegation to Washington, D.C., to appeal. The immigrant leadership, which included historian Philip Hitti, presented historical and genealogical evidence of the Syrians' Caucasian origins. Similar cases brought before the circuit courts in Cincinnati and

St. Louis attracted enough attention for *The New York Times*' editorial page of September 30, 1909, to comment "Is the Turk a White Man?" In a reply, Lebanese-born journalist Salloum Mokarzel pointed to the central dilemma of his countrymen: "The main point at issue in this question . . . is not the practicability of considering the Turk a white man, but the possibility of considering every Turkish subject a Turk, eliminating in this general classification all distinction of race, language and religion."[25]

Mokarzel's comments underscore another prevalent notion of the era that treated the concept of race in its anthropological dimension (i.e., Mongoloid, Caucasoid, and Negroid) and in the common usage to connote national origin. In both cases, he argues, Syrians are not Asiatic: "Is it not a fact that the peoples conquered by the Turks of old retain an indisputable claim to their racial descent? In other words, how could the Caucasian blood of the Greek, the Slav, the Armenian, the Arab and the Syrian be contested, since they were the aborigines of the lands where they now live?"[26]

The 1909 case was overturned on appeal, but the Syrians found themselves caught in the midst of policies that were being redefined and laws being reinterpreted to deal with the naturalization of groups who were considered racially borderline. Although the immigration categories as of 1899 classified Syrians and Palestinians as white by race, the courts still were interpreting the 1870 law's applicability to Arabs, Armenians, and other western Asian immigrants. By 1910, their eligibility was further complicated by the U.S. Census Bureau's classification of these groups as "Asiatic" by nativity and by a new directive ordering the courts to reject citizenship applications from aliens who were neither white nor of African descent, a policy in part intended to control illegal naturalization of immigrants for voting purposes.[27]

Similar cases occurred in subsequent years, each resulting in the ultimate granting of the Syrian petition, until 1914, when a judge in South Carolina reopened the wound of ineligibility. In this case, the judge ruled that, although Syrians might be free white persons, they were not "that particular free white person to whom act of Congress [1790] had donated the privilege of citizenship,"[28] a privilege he ruled was intended for persons of European descent. Again the nascent Syrian institutions, notably the Arabic press, rallied around the case and provided lengthy historical and cultural arguments, each of which was refuted by the judge who clung to contemporary nativist tenets that any "mixture of blood" disqualified one from the white race. The case was appealed in 1915, at which time the court accepted the findings of the Dillingham Report of the Immigration Commission that "physically the modern Syrians are of mixed Syrian, Arabian, and even Jewish blood. They belong to the Semitic branch of the Caucasian race, thus widely differing from their rulers, the Turks, who are in origin Mongolian."[29]

Despite this victory, this issue was not finally put to rest until 1923. In that year, the same District judge from South Carolina attempted to deny a Syrian petition for naturalization on the grounds that Syria fell under the 1917 Restrictive Immigration Act, which barred immigration and naturalization for natives of most countries east of the Persian Gulf. At a rehearing, it was shown that Syria did not fall within those wartime restrictions.

As Naff astutely observes, this "yellow race crisis," while the most intensely discriminatory experience of the early Arab immigrants, did not have a very penetrating effect on their identity nor on their civic assimilation. On the contrary, it reinforced the

Arab immigrants' conviction that their heritage was not the true target of these policies—they were simply being confused with others (e.g., Turks, Asians). The external
classification issues imposed in America did not alienate or even deter their civic loyalty to their new homeland. The outcome of the yellow race crisis no doubt strengthened the immigrants' resolve to value and cherish their exonerated racial status as
white.

In the decades that followed World War I, there is evidence of continued run-ins with
racial classification, particularly during the ascendancy of the Ku Klux Klan, when the
Arabs were often considered "colored" and their country of origin was less important
than skin tone and appearance. Particularly in voting rights, it was not uncommon for
recent immigrants to confront disenfranchisement in the segregated South. A candidate
for local office in Birmingham in the 1920s passed out handbills that read, "They have
disqualified the Negro, an American citizen, from voting in the white primary. The Greek
and the Syrian should also be disqualified. I DON'T WANT THEIR VOTES. If I can't
be elected by white men, I don't want the office."[30]

Despite these and other encounters with racial prejudice, which though less frequent
did occur throughout the three decades that followed the immigration restrictions of
the 1920s, it was not until later in the civil rights era that Arabs in America would seriously revisit issues of racial classification, ethnic identity, and the dilemma of being not
quite white.

Arab Americans in the Civil Rights Era

The same twin policies of the 1960s that ushered in civil rights laws and dropped immigration restrictions laid the groundwork for changes in Arab attitudes and experiences
with race in America. In the past thirty years, not only did new Arab immigration
diversify and expand the Arab American community, it also brought political, cultural,
and religious identities that contrasted with the assimilated identity of the U.S.-born
co-ethnics. Where offspring of the first (mostly Christian) immigrants had faced the
intensive civic assimilation of that largely European wave, the post–World War II immigrants arrived in a wave predominantly from the Third World, a factor that would also
characterize their identity and attitudes toward assimilation in general and classification in particular.

Government programs and other structural interventions that developed in the 1970s
and 1980s around racial integration and affirmative action contributed to corresponding awareness and societal attitudes of tolerance of diversity in America. An important convergence occurred that affected ethnic identity, including that of Arab Americans: a developing national awareness driven by federal guidelines and the
institutionalization of equal opportunity, with a cultural awakening in which black and
other Third World heritages were studied, celebrated, and politicized. Into this external arena of expanded ethnic attention and opportunity, the Arab community's internal generational transformation, diversification, and politicization found enough common ground to grow a new branch of Arab ethnicity in America. Contrasting with the
highly assimilated, European-dominated experience of the American-born generations,

this era of multiculturalism and minority rights forged a new paradigm that situated Arab (and later Muslim) culture and politics more squarely outside the white "majority" context.

The current classification system, which places Arabs and other persons with origins in the Middle East and North Africa in the same white category that identifies the European majority, has been a source of confusion and a challenge. The pervasive influence of the four race/one ethnic categories promulgated in 1978 has affected Arab Americans to different degrees. Because racial categories permeate nearly every bureaucracy, public and private alike, for Arabs who contest, resent, or misunderstand their white classification, the reminders of this identity disconnect are constant. In school and medical forms, job and loan applications, political caucuses, polls, and even market surveys, the race consciousness of American demographics is such that some Arabs have become accustomed to perennial "other" status or to straddling their technical white identity with their practical affinity to "people of color"—meaning every other non-European national origin group.

The confusion created by federal classification as it relates to Arabs is not limited to subjective identification and ethnic preference. School administrators are frequently unclear about where to place immigrant students from the Middle East, because most foreign-born children fall in nonwhite categories that assist in reporting and outreach efforts. In a 1988 national longitudinal study of eighth graders, for example, it was reported that the Asian/Pacific Islander category incorrectly included 15 percent students actually from countries in the Middle East.[31]

The need to comply with federal guidelines in most cases defines the way in which nonfederal entities and even nongovernmental ones relate and attend to ethnicity. For the most part, diversity programs in organizational and public culture are framed principally by official minority categories (including women), which tend to overlook subgroups now classified as white. Exceptions to the federal standards are found in civic, educational, and social science structures, in which space is made for religious minorities (mostly Jews but also Muslims) and women. Not unlike Jewish Americans—and in part because of them—Arab Americans have been able to circumvent the official classification structure to create patterns of inclusion. Individuals and institutions alike have for more than two decades needed to stretch the diversity yardstick to achieve representation in fields of research, education, employment, and civic and political life, regardless of racial classification. In a few instances, these efforts formally intersected with the federal system; in most cases, accommodations have been made by local institutions to incorporate Arab-American constituencies and recognize their participation.

Although the debate over the benefit to Arab Americans of formal government recognition as a disadvantaged minority continues to evoke spirited opinion among proponents and opponents in the Arab-American community, the issue of discrimination has underscored the initiatives to date that have challenged the official classification of Arabs as part of the white majority. In the case of a Small Business Administration (SBA) special designation awarded to a Palestinian-American federal contractor, the agency based its decision on the evidence of that Palestinian American's particular professional experience and the fact that he could document specific economic disadvantage based on his national origin.[32] Unlike federal minority designations, this SBA status did not transfer to the entire class of co-ethnics. In an even more ground-breaking decision, the Supreme Court in 1987[33] expanded the definition of protected classes in civil suits based on discrimination to include national origin or religious groups, in this case Arabs and Jews. In both examples, Arab Americans demonstrated sufficient evidence of discriminatory behavior to stretch the existing definition of protected class.

The structures that have more frequently accommodated Arab-American inclusion have been outside the federal arena, and the motivation has centered on demographic reality or the cultural and academic imperative of recognizing Arab-American presence. Examples of when demographic reality is the momentum for change are most common in states such as Michigan, where the concentration, growth, and sheer visibility of the population demands attention. Statewide agencies, including the offices of Minority Health and Bilingual Education, classify the Arab/Chaldean populations for purposes of service delivery and statistical research.[34] Similarly, state universities responded to pressure from their student bodies to include the Arab population in their minority achievement programs; curriculum development has been more problematic when federal funding is required to be more strictly allocated by official minority designations. In a more recent initiative, the business community in San Francisco asked the city to expand its human rights ordinance that defines groups qualifying for minority contracts. After public hearings and a disparity study to review evidence of under-representation of the Arab business population in city contracts, the city agreed to recommend adding Arabs to the groups protected by the city ordinance.

In other aspects of educational life, Arab students and scholars alike have been among the most consistent advocates for including Arab, Muslim, and Middle East issues in the ever-expanding framework of multiculturalism in schools and on campus. In public education, the demographic reality often dictates the adaptive strategies school systems follow. The influx of new immigrant families, for example, has required local officials to respond through bilingual programs, PTA outreach, curricula review, and cultural activities. In areas such as southeast Michigan, northern Virginia, San Francisco, Chicago, and Cleveland, Arab and Muslim parents and experts are recruited to serve on local boards and commissions to advise educators and raise concerns.

In higher education the dual visibility of Middle East studies departments and organized Arab student groups has provided its own opportunity for inclusion in multicultural structures. In the United States Student Association, for example, the National Student Coalition of People of Color includes an Arab and Muslim caucus that generates active and vocal leadership. In the broader arena of humanities and social science research, Arab Americans are slowly breaking into the race or ethnic paradigm, frequently finding an already crowded field of diversity-conscious professionals who are willing to make room. When obstacles prevent an open-door approach to Arab-American inclusion, they usually have been connected with ideological and political struggles of the Arab-Israeli conflict, especially during the 1970s and 1980s, when an Arab presence was obstructed by objections from some pro-Israel counterpart.[35] This phenomenon transcended academe into broader political, civic, cultural, and employment circles.

Despite such tactics and diversions, the resiliency of American multiculturalism and the natural solidarity offered by other people of color have allowed Arab Americans increasing opportunity for a place at the table. The "ripple effect of affirmative action," as George Bisharat aptly notes, has rendered public institutions, civic coalitions, and private businesses sensitive to inclusion of Arab Americans, regardless of official classification.[36] One arena in which the ripple effect of a diversity-conscious establishment is encouraging for Arab Americans is civic and political life. Attention to inclusion has been driven by the demographic reality of a local Arab population and even more so by the visibility of Arab Americans in local politics and elections. In the past fifteen years, there has developed a causal relationship between electoral activity and public service recognition that is usually reserved for designated minorities. After the elections of 1988, for example, when many community activists mobilized around the presidential campaigns, especially that of Rev. Jesse Jackson, the new visibility of Arab Americans in both parties was rewarded by appointments to state, county, and municipal boards and commissions. In San Francisco and Fairfax County, Virginia, Arab Americans were offered almost a dozen posts, including EEOC, planning, aging, education, human rights, and economic development commissions. Because in most communities such boards have unofficially designated slots for minority representation, Arab Americans were able to insert themselves into such informal public service "quotas," establishing a new reality for future politicians to sustain.

In national politics and government, similar systems prone to minority representation have slowly begun to make adjustments for the emerging Arab-American presence. In constituency-conscious places such as the national party committees or the White House Office of Public Liaison, the inadequacy of traditional "desks" dealing with racial minorities, women, labor, and related issues was particularly evident in trying to fit Arab Americans in and resulted in beefing up the underused "ethnic outreach" assignments, in which Arab Americans are factored into the mix when White House conferences, appointments, and such take constituencies into consideration. In preparing for the 1996 conventions, the Democratic delegate-tracking system for the first time accounted for Arab Americans. Similarly in 1995, a national voter list broker added the first Arab surname file to its inventory of ethnic registered voter lists.[37] Even in the Census Bureau, where the federal government is obliged to match its outreach efforts to existing race and ethnic minority populations, the Department of Commerce in 1995 designated a seat on the 2000 Census Advisory Committee for Arab Americans, the only nonminority population group to merit representation. It was this awareness that racial categories may be too rigid that led the government to review its statistical procedures, a debate in which Arab-American issues featured prominently.

Federal Review of Race and Ethnic Classification: Preparing for the New Millennium

In the nearly two decades since the standardization of race and ethnic measurement, policy makers, researchers, and statisticians have been seeking ways to refine and reexamine the rationale of the current system. Government initiatives since 1990 have focused the attention of data providers and users alike on the challenge of keeping measurement standards in step with the changing face of the population. In a 1992 international conference on the subject, the U.S. Census Bureau as co-sponsor sought to address the official challenges of measuring an ethnic world within the context of science, politics, and social reality.[38] Among the conclusions reached by the conferees were these:

Ethnicity is multidimensional, continuous, and dynamic; surveys need to use consistent
   definitions but allow for flux in ethnic identification.
Constitutional and legislative needs must be given a priority in collection of data on
   ethnicity; more research is needed on the impact of data collection on stereotypes and
   divisiveness; participants noted that race and ethnic data are not neutral and can be
   used for many purposes, some of which may not be benign.[39]

The issues debated by data providers and data users at this forum underscore the critical connection between the social, political, and legal reasons for collecting data on
race and ethnicity. At stake are some of the assumptions that precipitated the federal
guidelines in the mid 1970s, the need to evaluate the changing social attitudes toward
race, and the controversy inherent in that evaluation.

The following year, at the initiation of the congressional subcommittee that oversaw
census operations, the government opened a multi-year review of federal Directive 15
in preparation for the next major national survey, the 2000 census. Representative Tom
Sawyer (D-OH) kicked off the process by holding public hearings in 1993 to receive
comment on the existing race and ethnic categories. Testimonies were solicited from
government agencies, scholars, constituency groups, and other stakeholders on evalu-
ating the current standards and proposing changes.

It was in this context that the Arab American Institute (AAI), as part of its continuing focus on census and demographic issues, submitted testimony pointing to the growing disconnect between ethnic identification among the Arab-American population and
the undifferentiated white race category stipulated by Directive 15. Because the guidelines were promulgated as *minimal* standards that did not prohibit further specificity,
the AAI proposal suggested disaggregating the non-European population groups (i.e.,
those with origins in the Middle East and North Africa). Such a regional category could
identify Arabs and other ethnic subgroups as distinct from other whites who make up
the country's European-based majority—not as an additional minority class but to deal
with the unique data needs of these populations.[40]

The effect of racial classification on Arab Americans became one of the topics that
continued to be debated throughout the three-year review process. Under the heading
of "emerging categories," the AAI proposal was presented at the next major phase of
the review process, a workshop sponsored by the National Research Council in February 1994 to discuss further the federal standards and make recommendations to the
OMB.[41] The other principal emerging category issue proposed was the addition to the
race choices of a multi-racial check-off for individuals of mixed parentage who in the
current framework are obliged to select one identifying race. Although other refinements
to the federal guidelines were entertained, such as reclassifying Hawaiians as Native
Americans and merging Hispanics into the race categories, the mixed-race question was
clearly the most controversial recommendation, one that generated the most organized
public pressure and one that virtually every stakeholder requiring data on race, including the minority communities, opposed on the grounds that it skews continuity of race
data and, in effect, serves to undermine policies that implement affirmative action.

Although overshadowed by the mixed-race issue, the Arab-American proposal continued to be raised in the final phase of the federal review: a series of public hearings
sponsored by the OMB around the country during the summer of 1994. By then, a

similar proposal for a specific "Arab American" category—as a linguistically based identifier—was introduced by the American-Arab Anti-Discrimination Committee (ADC). Testimony for the regional category (i.e., Middle East/North African) with ethnic subgroups (e.g., Arab, Iranian, Turk, Cypriot, Assyrian) was presented alongside support for a distinctly Arab-American classifier—a mixed signal cited in the OMB report as a lack of consensus over the definition of the population in question. This was one of several findings cited by the OMB as not justifying further research in this area at this time; another factor was the relatively small size of the population.[42] By September 1997, the review process was complete, and the OMB decided against the Arab-American proposals, leaving open the possibility of study at some future date.

Although those responsible for racial and ethnic statistics for the Census Bureau remained sympathetic to the concerns over Arab-American measurement, other, more political factors were at play, not the least of which was a public mood with strong support in the new congress that increasingly viewed racial or ethnic categories as a symptom of the disuniting of America, rather than a useful tool with redeeming social worth. Even media attention to the OMB hearings and the 2000 census, as limited as it has been, was mostly negative. The conservative press took several swipes at the review process itself, deriding the very utility of race categories, not to mention entertaining new ones.[43]

Current Classification of Arab Americans:
The Ancestry Question

Even in the midst of the OMB review, it became evident that adding a new ethnic category was not among the priority issues that would be earmarked for research and testing in time for 2000. By 1995, rumors started to surface in census circles that the only remaining source of demographic data on Arab Americans—the question on ancestry— was in jeopardy of being dropped in 2000. The question, distinct from the race and Hispanic origin questions, had provided intergenerational data since 1980 on ethnicity regardless of race, using an open-ended question based on self-identification of up to two ancestral origins. Ancestry data on Arabs have received mixed reviews: the undercount (i.e., in 1990, the aggregated Arab-origin populations did not exceed 900,000) drew concern, as did the obvious drawback that the question only appeared on the long-form survey that is sent to a 17 percent sample of the nation's households. Nevertheless, census ancestry data on Arabs remain the only official, reliable source of information on this ethnic community. The chance that even this imperfect measure might be eliminated, with nothing to replace it, was cause for concern among researchers and advocates alike. Attention quickly shifted away from the dream of creating a new and more responsive category for ethnic measurement to the reality of needing to safeguard the only governmental tool available to study the mobility, acculturation, and participation of the Arab-American constituency.

In mid-1996, a coalition of ethnic organizations was organized by AAI to develop a strategy to keep the ethnic question on the 2000 census. By early 1997, a full-scale campaign was in place, and the "Working Group on Ancestry in the U.S. Census" encompassed about 80 organizations, scholars, and advocates. Although the network initially focused on the white ethnic groups for whom ancestry data were uniquely important, it grew to include minority organizations as well. This broad umbrella avoided the appearance of one race group working at the expense of another. The immediate target of the group was to convince Congress by their spring 1997 deadline that the ancestry question should be included in the topics for the 2000 census. The campaign grew to include organizing "Ancestry Day" on Capitol Hill in March 1997, the introduction of a concurrent resolution to support the ancestry question, and offering testimony at several congressional hearings on the census. By the spring of 1998, having succeeded in securing the question on the topics proposed by the Census Bureau, the ancestry coalition worked with Representative Connie Morella (R-MD) on a new resolution reiterating the importance of census data collection to a Congress that had begun its own war on the census on the more controversial issue of methodology for census 2000. The long-term goal of the working group remains to ensure that all ethnic constituencies, regardless of race, are engaged in and supportive of census outreach efforts to assure a full count in the year 2000.[44]

What happens in the area of race and ethnic measurement—and Arab-American classification specifically—will depend on a number of factors, all of which require the careful consideration of advocates, scholars, and policy makers. Among the influential issues are several interrelated themes of identity and classification, each of which demands further analysis. Foremost among these is to look at Arab-American approaches to minority status. From initiatives that began in the early 1980s to new proposals currently being implemented in California, it is important to research the compelling reasons for supporting an official minority designation and the drawbacks for the constituency, for other minorities, and for the society.

More discussion is needed about inclusion of Arab ethnics into structures set up to promote diversity. Do we anticipate convergence or divergence between those who relate more comfortably with white ethnics and those who see themselves as people of color? What demographic factors influence each affinity, and how dominant is religious affiliation in these trends? These queries are only part of the complexity that surrounds questions of race and identity in America. A constituency at a rather dramatic crossroads, Arab Americans are weighing the critical options of their changing demographics. Differences of class, education, occupation, religious affiliation, geographic location, and length of time in America are just some of the variables that complicate previously simple solutions. Balancing objective classification procedures with issues of such subjective importance is a daunting task for any bureaucracy, particularly when society as a whole is less satisfied with the formulas of the past but equally unsure of the path to follow into the new millennium.

Notes

1. See Frank Ching, "The Asian Experience in the U.S." In Frank J. Coppa and Thomas Curran, eds., *The Immigrant Experience in America* (Boston: Twayne Publishers, 1976), pp. 192–214. By 1884, Chinese made up 50 percent of farm labor in California.

2. Lawrence H. Fuchs, *The American Kaleidoscope: Race and Ethnicity and the Civic Culture* (Hanover, NH: Wesleyan University Press, 1990), p. 58.

3. For details about the programs of the prewar period, see Fuchs, *The American Kaleidoscope,* and Roger Daniels, *Coming to America: A History of Immigration and Ethnicity in American Life* (New York: HarperPerennial, 1990).

4. Fuchs, *American Kaleidoscope,* p. 61.

5. The Immigration Restriction League was founded in 1894 to defend "Americanism" and protect the country and American civic life from contamination.

6. Fuchs, *American Kaleidoscope,* p. 60.

7. See Philip Dolce, "The McCarran-Walter Act and the Conflict over Immigration Policy during the Truman Administration." In Frank J. Coppa and Thomas Curran, eds., *The Immigrant Experience in America* (Boston: Twayne Publishers, 1976), pp. 215–31.

8. In the "L.A. 8" case, U.S. Immigration officials arrested and sought to deport seven Arabs and the Kenyan wife of one of them, alleging that they were involved in illegal activities, specifically that they belonged to the Popular Front for the Liberation of Palestine (PFLP). The Immigration and Naturalization Service argued that aliens did not have the same rights of free speech as citizens. Arab-American organizations felt that their community was intentionally targeted in an attempt to silence its members from speaking about Middle East issues. For more information on the "L.A. 8" case, see the chapter by Kathleen Moore in this book.

9. See Philip Dolce, "The McCarran-Walter Act," pp. 227–28, for details of President Truman's veto of the 1952 Act over objections that the 1924 quota system was a "slur on the patriotism, the capacity and the decency of a large part of our citizenry." His veto was overridden.

10. By 1953 the Refugee Relief Act authorized 209,000 refugee immigrants above the quotas. It was reported that, of the 2,000 slots allotted to the Middle East, 50 Palestinian refugees were the first to be admitted under the new law. See *The Lebanese American Journal,* "Who's Getting into U.S. Now: 2000 Arab Refugees to Start New Life Here" (undated, c. mid-1954).

11. Daniels, *Coming to America,* p. 338.

12. Immigration and Naturalization data as cited in Gregory Orfalea, *Beyond the Flames: A Quest for the History of Arab Americans* (Austin: University of Texas Press, 1988), pp. 316–17.

13. Daniels, *Coming to America,* p. 393.

14. The provision dealing with exclusion based on "terrorist" affiliation is in 8USC S212 (a)(3)(d)(i)(V).

15. See Lawrence Wright, "One Drop of Blood," *The New Yorker* (25 July 1994): 46–55.

16. Only in two censuses before 1980, those of 1880 and 1950, was a question asked on the ability to speak a foreign language.

17. See Dan Halacy, *Census: 190 Years of Counting America* (New York: Elsevier/Nelson Books, 1980).

18. See Juanita Tamayo Lott, "The Continuing Significance of Race and Ethnicity: A Reassessment of Statistical Policy Directive 15," testimony presented to the House Subcommittee on Census, Statistics and Postal Personnel (March 31, 1993).

19. Lott, "The Continuing Significance of Race and Ethnicity," p. 2.

20. In the 1960 census, the Latin American ancestry groups had been counted as white. The Federal Interagency Committee on Education recognized that race was not a useful identifier for Hispanics and therefore created the only designated "ethnic" category. When Congress passed PL 94-3-1, which required selected agencies to publish data on Hispanics, it gave the Office of Management and Budget the legal impetus to keep Hispanic as a category distinct from race.

21. Wright, "One Drop of Blood," p. 50.

22. See Nampeo McKenney and Arthur Cresce, "The Identification of Ethnicity in the U.S.: The Census Bureau Experience," presented at the Population Association of America conference, Toronto (1990).

23. Fuchs, *American Kaleidoscope,* p. 453.

24. See Alixa Naff, *Becoming American: The Early Arab Immigrant Experience* (Carbondale: Southern Illinois University Press, 1985), p. 108.

25. Salloum A. Mokarzel, Letters to the Editor, *The New York Times* (1 October 1909).

26. Mokarzel, Letters to the Editor.

27. Naff, *Becoming American,* pp. 252–253.

28. Hon. Henry A. M. Smith, *In Re Dow,* 213, F. Rep. 355 (D SC 1914), as cited in *The Syrian World,* 1 (Feb. 1928), p. 7.

29. Naff, *Becoming American,* p. 257, quoting Reed Ueda's "Naturalization and Citizenship", *Harvard Encyclopedia of American Ethnic Groups,* p. 741.

30. Alan Dehmer, "Birmingham, Alabama: The Politics of Survival." In James Zogby, ed., *Taking Root, Bearing Fruit* (Washington, DC: American-Arab Anti-Discrimination Committee, 1984), pp. 38–39.

31. Lott, "Continuing Significance of Race and Ethnicity," p. 7.

32. For a summary of this case, see Omar Kader, "Arab Americans Would Benefit from Minority Status," in N.B., Arab American Institute (December 1993), p. 5.

33. See *St Francis v Al-Khazraji* 481 US 604 (1987) and *Shaare Tefila Congregation v Cobb* 481 US 615 (1987).

34. Details are available from the Arab Community Center for Economic and Social Services (ACCESS) in Dearborn, Michigan. Such initiatives do not contradict the federal guidelines, which were promulgated only as the minimum standards required by law.

35. See Helen Hatab Samhan, "Politics and Exclusion: The Arab American Experience," *Journal of Palestine Studies,* 16, no. 2 (Winter 1987), pp. 11–28.

36. George Bisharat, "Arab Americans and Affirmative Action." Paper presented at the 29th Annual Conference of the Association of Arab-American University Graduates (AAUG), 20 October 1996, p. 8.

37. The Arab American Institute (Washington, D.C.) assisted in the development of this database and acquired it for its own use in 1996.

38. "Challenges of Measuring an Ethnic World: Science, Politics and Reality," proceedings of the Joint Canada-U.S. Conference on Measurement of Ethnicity, 1–3 April, 1992 (issued September 1993), p. 3.

39. "Challenges of Measuring an Ethnic World," pp. 5–6.

40. See Helen Hatab Samhan, testimony presented to House Subcommittee on Census, Statistics and Personnel (Washington, DC: Arab American Institute, 3 June 1993).

41. See Helen Hatab Samhan, presentation on "Emerging Ethnic Categories" at the Workshop on Race and Ethnic Classification: An Assessment of the Federal Standard for Race and Ethnicity Classification (Washington, DC: Arab American Institute, 17 February 1994).

42. Office of Management and Budget, "Standards for the Classification of Federal Data on Race and Ethnicity Notice," *Federal Register,* 60, no. 166 (28 August 1995), p. 44681.

43. See Lawrence Wright, "One Drop of Blood," pp. 46–55; Deroy Murdock, "New Pigeonholes Would Create More Barriers to Unity," *Tampa Tribune* (7 July 1994); Dinesh D'Souza, "My Color 'Tis of Thee," *The Weekly Standard* (16 December 1996): 17–19; and John McCaslin, "Inside the Beltway," *The Washington Times* (30 January 1997).

44. For more information on the Working Group on Ancestry, contact the Arab American Institute (www.aaiusa.org), 918 16th St. N.W., Washington, D.C. 20006, telephone (202) 429-9210.

Lawrence Davidson

14   Debating Palestine: Arab-American Challenges to Zionism 1917–1932

Arab Americans Before 1917

In the years after World War I the Arab-American community was a small and scattered one. Numbering perhaps 200,000 people, they had arrived mostly from "Greater Syria" (i.e., Lebanon, Syria, and Palestine) and worked initially as laborers, peddlers, mechanics, and merchants. Concentrated in the eastern third of the United States, their "mother colony" was Little Syria, which was centered on Washington Street in New York City.[1] Most were Christians of the Maronite sect or Greek Orthodox. A minority were Muslims.[2] The inflow of Arab immigrants into the country slowed down considerably during the 1920s because of post-war immigration restrictions. In that decade, only a little less than 8,000 from the "Greater Syria" region were allowed into the country.[3]

The behavior of the Arab Americans was not unlike that of other immigrant groups. They initially gravitated into ethnic ghettos like that of Little Syria in New York City. They concentrated their energies on improving their economic lot. Professor Philip Hitti, in his groundbreaking work on *The Syrians in America,* rather unkindly characterized this as a "rush for material betterment" that produced a "mercenary spirit."[4] However, it is hard to see how this was much different from the attitude of other first- and second-generation immigrant groups. Puritan mythology aside, most who have and continue to come to the United States do so for economic reasons. The "rush for material betterment" was and is one of the hallmarks of the New World.

As the Arab Americans congregated in ethnic communities, they organized themselves in ways that reflected their origins. What was most important in terms of self-identity back in the Middle East was religion. Maronites, Greek Orthodox, Muslims, and other smaller denominations, now finding themselves in the United States, segregated into subgroups that often had minimal contact with each other. Within these subgroups, there might be further divisions along lines of geographic or regional origins. Rather than one unified Arab-American immigrant community, there were many religiously and geographically exclusive subgroups. The societies, clubs, and other organizations put together by Arab Americans most often reflected these divisions: the Maronite League, the Beirut Society, the Ramallah Society, and others. Noting this proliferation of religiously and geographically based organizations, Hitti quotes a "young physician" (most probably Fuad Shatara) as describing the Arab Americans as suffering from "societitis."[5]

This "societitis" often was benign and even helpful in the lives of people not yet integrated into the life of their adopted country, but it also accented the fractionalized and insular nature of the Arab-American community. Before World War I, their organizations were largely social and apparently had little to do with relations to the outside world. They did not function to explain Arab Americans and their ways to the rest of American society or influence that society's attitude toward them. Except in rare cases, they took no cognizance of what the U.S. government was doing domestically or in its policy toward the Middle East.[6]

This fractionalization also influenced how Arab Americans related to Greater Syria. They maintained an interest in their place of origin, because their culture and family ties drew them to it. There was frequent travel back and forth. However, it was to their old villages and towns that most of them related and not to national entities.

World War I changed much of this pattern. The war cut off the Arab-American communities from their Old World roots and swept them up in wartime American patriotic fervor that was in good part hostile to the Ottoman Empire. They increasingly saw themselves as permanent residents in the United States, and this led them to become more politically active and assertive. They grew particularly interested in the post-war fate of Greater Syria.[7] It is within this context that representative Arab Americans entered into the evolving debate over the one Middle East–related issue of the 1920s that engaged the American imagination: the fate of the Holy Land or Palestine.

Arab Americans Contest the Balfour Declaration

After World War I, the Middle East, including Greater Syria, was carved into mandates that served as administrative vehicles for imperialist control of the region by Britain and France. However, the notion of future statehood for Middle East territories (as a hypothetical end product of the mandate process) was also raised. The Arab-American community was too divided to react initially to this prospect in a united fashion. Hitti described the situation, which as a contemporary he knew first hand, "The Syrians here . . . are by no means of one accord as to things political. There are those among them, mainly Muhammadans and Druze . . . who aspire to virtual union with al-Hijaz [western Arabia] and Mesopotamia in a pan-Arab empire. Others, chiefly Christian, stand for an independent Syria, with an independent Lebanon under French Mandate."[8] He goes on to explain that "while the soul of every Syrian is deeply stirred with a desire for the welfare of Syria, yet the lines of cleavage among the people [of the Arab-American community] are too deeply marked to admit the possibility of any united effort for a united cause."[9]

With one significant exception, later authors have used this theme of disunity to discount any Arab-American interest in Palestine or Zionist activities. For instance,

Jacqueline and Tareq Ismael asserted that "Arab-American communities remained essentially non-assertive in character."[10] In the debate over the fate of Palestine after World War I, Arab Americans came up short. "Within the American political arena," they tell us, "there was no fundamental challenge representing Arab interests to the Zionist proposition that the United States support the transformation of Palestine into a Jewish homeland."[11] Richard Cottam, following a position first put forth by the historian Frank Manuel, goes even further when he suggests that "throughout the interwar period, and indeed up through 1948, so little was heard from this group [Arab Americans] that [one] is in fact justified in ignoring them."[12]

This interpretation, however, has been challenged by Michael Suleiman, who tells us that "in the political arena there were ... numerous efforts to get the United States to support foreign policy positions advocated by the Arab community, most particularly in regard to Palestine."[13] For the period between 1917 and 1932 (and, I suspect, for the rest of the years running up to 1948), there can be no doubt that Professor Suleiman's position is the correct one. Despite the underlying divisions among Arab Americans, a determined lobbying and educational effort on behalf of the Palestinians arose. The group that undertook this effort came together immediately after the issuance of the Balfour Declaration and sought to organize around, persuade about, and debate the issue of Palestine within the Arab-American community and American society at large. This group included Arab Americans such as Doctor Fuad Shatara and the writer Ameen Rihani.[14]

Fuad Shatara was a Christian Arab American of Palestinian descent. He came from the town of Jaffa. A surgeon practicing in the New York City area and instructor in the Department of Anatomy and Surgery of the School of Medicine of Long Island College Hospital, he was also a prolific writer and talented organizer. He contributed numerous pieces to Arab-American publications such as the *Syrian World* and academic journals such as *The Annals of the American Academy of Political and Social Science*. He was one of the founding members and long-time leaders of a series of Arab-American organizations. An articulate and patient man, he was called on to testify before the House Committee on Foreign Affairs when, in 1922, it debated a resolution endorsing the Balfour Declaration.

Ameen Rihani was a renowned poet and essayist who wrote in English and Arabic. He traveled widely and contributed articles to popular magazines of the day such as *Asia* and *The Nation*. Lebanese by birth but resident in New York for much of the 1920s, he described himself as "an independent thinker and an impartial observer" and then added in reference to Palestine, "as impartial as it is humanly possible under the circumstances."[15] He was a man who adhered to his principles even in the face of overwhelming odds.

Shatara and Rihani were fully and consistently engaged in the American debate over Palestine. They were recognized as spokesmen for the Arab point of view and were sought out by government officials and publicists to express it. Along side them were many others such as Habib Katibah, N. A. Katibah, Peter S. George, Elias Joseph, George Sadak, Frank Sakran, Jacob Handal, Andria Mansour, and the Reverend Abraham Rihbany, a unitarian minister from Brookline Massachusetts whose general writings, according to Hitti, had "been a potent factor in acquainting the American public with the Syrian mode of thought and living."[16] In 1919, Rihbany was among those sent by the Arab-American organizations interested in the fate of the Middle East to represent their views at the Paris Peace Conference.

What was the organization put together by these men to debate the Zionists? Founded in 1917, it was initially called the Palestine Antizionism Society. It would change its name in the early 1920s. The Society's first president was N. A. Katibah, and Fuad Shatara was its corresponding secretary. Unfortunately, we know very little of the Society's organizational details. We do not know its size, meeting schedules, financial arrangements, or the nature of its internal debates. We do know, however, that its leaders on occasion acted as spokesmen for the Arab-American community and that the Society was capable of allying itself with other Arab-American groups to mount demonstrations.

For instance, the Palestine Antizionism Society, along with a local New York City-based group called the Ramallah Young Men's Society, staged a demonstration in Brooklyn, New York, on 8 November 1917. The Balfour Declaration had been issued one week before, on 2 November. According to the *New York Times,* the demonstration was held at the Hotel Bossert and drew "500 Syrians." N. A. Katibah, Fuad Shatara, and Philip Hitti were present. A resolution was passed stating,

> Resolved that we protest against the formation of any Government or body politic based on religious principles, by a minority, contrary to the principles of the majority. We further protest against the usurpation of the homes and property of a people weakened and impoverished by centuries of misery, by a race rendered more powerful and wealthy through contact with the western civilization thus applying might against right. We further protest against any scheme of artificial importation of Zionists flooding the country against its natural capacities and thus forcing an emigration of the rightful inhabitants.[17]

This first shot, in what would prove to be a long-term effort, put forth the basic ideas these Arab Americans sought to convey to the public:

1. In Palestine, Zionism represented an infusion into the country of an alien people associated with the West who were therefore in terms of finance and technique, much more powerful than the indigenous population.
2. This represented "might against right" and was a flagrant violation of the principle of majority rule and self-determination.
3. In the end, the Zionists planned to displace the native people in one fashion or another.

This message, although self-evident to men like Shatara and Rihani, did not ring true to most Americans. American awareness of Arab civilization, the Arab people, and Arab Americans was, as Hitti had written, characterized by "colossal ignorance and prejudice."[18] With the standard picture of Arabs being that of "uncivilized" and "backward" desert dwellers, Hitti complained that "one would expect at least a Sunday school acquaintance with this people of the Holy Land, yet this is not always the case."[19] Hitti had correctly named the most common source of awareness about Palestine but had assigned its benefits to the wrong people. It was not so much the Arabs who captured that "Sunday school acquaintance" with the Holy Land in the minds of the American public, but rather their opponents in the brewing debate over Palestine. It was the Jews, now represented by the Zionists "flooding the country against its natural capacities," who had long ago captured the image of descendants (and rightful heirs) of the ancient biblical occupants of Palestine.[20]

It is unclear whether the Arab Americans of the Palestine Antizionism Society fully understood this situation or recognized how difficult it would make it to get their message across. Aware or not of the psychological barriers, they persisted. Having begun with a rally large enough to catch the eye of the *New York Times,* they then sought to address the Federal government.

On 23 November 1918 and again on 15 February 1919, Fuad Shatara, writing for the Palestine Antizionism Society, communicated with Robert Lansing, Secretary of State under Woodrow Wilson. In his 1918 letter, he told Lansing that on the question of Palestine, "we had faith in European and American governments' sense of justice, and we still believe that, finally, however plausible the Zionists' plan may sound, the Powers [the victorious powers of World War I] will not abet a scheme that has for its ultimate aim the usurpation of every right a nation, however small, has." He continued, "we understand that the Powers, thus far, have had only one side of the question presented to them. We have been taken unawares. May we therefore be allowed to present, at this late hour, our side to the President of the United States [Woodrow Wilson] so that, with him, our cause may not be left unchampioned at the forthcoming peace conference."[21]

Shatara went on to suggest that support for Zionism was a violation of Wilson's own principle of self-determination—one of the Fourteen Points that had constituted U.S. war aims. He systematically repudiated Zionist claims based on religious heritage or ancient occupation and argued that the Zionist takeover of Palestine would not solve the problems Jews faced in other lands. He concluded, "Palestine is our home" and "in laying our case before the U.S. government we feel we can fully rely upon the American sense of justice and fair play."[22]

It was a heartfelt plea but one that was badly misplaced. Although Lansing had serious misgivings about Zionism, Wilson, who had the last word in terms of government policy on this issue, did not. The President was a fundamentalist Christian who fully backed the Balfour Declaration.[23] The Zionist leader Rabbi Stephen Wise once asked him how he responded to those who argued against Zionism. Wilson "pointed to a large wastepaper basket at his desk. 'Is not that basket capacious enough for all their protests.'"[24] The President paid no attention to the arguments of Shatara and his organization.

In the meantime, the Society had sent off representatives, including Reverend Rihbany, mentioned earlier, to the Paris Peace Conference. They carried with them a set of formal resolutions asking for self-determination for Greater Syria and that Zionist activities in Palestine be allowed only in so far as they were undertaken by those willing to become "Syrian citizens" and act in accord with Syrian laws. Shatara sent a copy of these resolutions to Lansing on 15 February 1919. It was accompanied by a cover letter pleading that the Secretary of State use his influence at the Peace Conference to "champion our just cause. We do not claim what does not belong to us. We merely demand the right to our homeland. We beseach [sic] you to come to our defense as a champion of right and justice."[25]

Neither the U.S. government nor the Paris Peace Conference paid much attention to the wishes of Arab Americans or, for that matter, to the Arab population of Greater Syria. Some help might have been expected from the findings of the King-Crane Commission. It had gone to the Greater Syria region in 1919 to determine the popular will of the population as to their political future. The Commission's findings had actually corroborated the Palestine Antizionism Society's claims that most Arabs of the region sought a unified Greater Syrian state that would include Palestine and that most also opposed Zionism. However, the Commission's report was subsequently suppressed and only made public by *The New York Times* in August 1922.[26] In an editorial at the time, the paper speculated that if the report had been made public in 1919, immediately on the conclusion of the Commission's investigatory tour of the region, "it might have helped prevent ... a Zionistic program in Palestine."[27] As it was, however, American Zionists such as Louis Lipsky, Louis Brandeis, Felix Frankfurter, and Stephen Wise were able to launch a campaign for government endorsement of the Balfour Declaration without any embarrassing reports on Palestinian popular opinion.

Sometime between 1919 and 1921, the name of the Palestine Antizionism Society was changed to The Palestine National League. This was no doubt done to accentuate what the group stood for rather than what it stood against. Debating the question of Zionism was, however, still its main focus. In 1921, the League sponsored the publication of a book entitled *The Case Against Zionism,* edited by Habib Katibah.[28] The book drew on the writings of Arab Americans and American Jewish leaders and scholars who had taken a stand against Zionism. It ended with a section entitled "Our Demands," which reflected the importance the group placed on the basic notion of self-determination. Unable to reference the King-Crane Commission report, the work concluded that

> the question of a mandate for Palestine [should] be postponed until the will of the people ... has been declared in a free manner. That a national government responsible to a parliament elected by those Palestinians who lived in the country before the war—Moslems, Christians and Jews—be constituted. That the principle of the creation of a national home for the Jews in Palestine be abolished. That Palestine not be separated from her Arab neighboring sister states.[29]

In 1922, Shatara debated the leaders of the American Zionist Organization in front of the House Committee on Foreign Affairs. In that year, Henry Cabot Lodge in the Senate and Hamilton Fish in the House of Representatives had introduced bills in support of the Balfour Declaration. They had done this at the urging of American Zionist leaders. Only the House held hearings on the issue, and Shatara, representing the Palestine National League, was called to testify. This was in the month of April or four months before the August publication of the King-Crane Commission report. In a long interview before the Committee, during which he and Louis Lipsky, representing the American Zionist Organization, often exchanged views, Shatara presented basically the same arguments found in the 1918 and 1919 letters sent to Lansing and Wilson as well as those elaborated in the Katibah book. He then called for an investigation of the situation in Palestine by a "neutral commission" and asked that Congress suspend judgment on the matter until it saw the report of such a commission. Essentially, Shatara was asking for an updated repeat of the suppressed King-Crane Commission. "We are willing to abide by the report of a neutral commission into the affairs of Palestine prior to settling this question," he told the Committee.[30]

It was to no avail. Representative Hamilton Fish, who had initiated and structured the House bill and the hearings, was clearly a Zionist. His tone toward Shatara was sometimes that of a prosecuting attorney. Others on the Committee viewed the matter through a number of distorting stereotypes. Representative W. Bourke Cockran of New York likened Jewish immigration into Palestine to the white man's arrival in the New World,[31] and Representative Henry Allen Cooper of Wisconsin refused to believe Shatara's accurate assertion that there was a significant socialist element among the Zionists in Palestine because, he insisted, the Jew is "proverbially a believer in private property."[32] The attitude of these men reflected the prejudicial view held by the Congress as a whole. Cindy Lydon, in an article entitled "American Images of the Arabs," tells us that "a survey of Congressional opinion reveals that virtually no favorable characterizations of Arabs found their way into debates on Middle Eastern issues during the lengthy period from 1919–1931." Most of these debates had to do with Palestine, and in them "the Arab was depicted as backward, poor and ignorant," while Zionist colonialization held out the promise of turning "a ravaged and spoiled land" once more into a "land of milk and honey." Congress considered that aiding the Zionist movement was "in line with the principles of self-determination," that is self-determination for the "Jewish nation," and not for the unfit "backward" Arabs.[33] Under the circumstances, the House and the Senate readily passed a joint resolution supporting the Balfour Declaration.

It must have been a shock to Shatara and his colleagues. There is every reason to believe that, at least initially, they were sincerely convinced that the United States stood for majority rule, self-determination, and representative government. These sentiments should have led the United States, by reason and empathy, to support the rights of the Arabs in Palestine and the rest of Greater Syria. What Shatara and his fellows seemed not to have realized was the depth of prejudice and the distorted picture of Palestine and the Arabs held by Congress. For these Arab-American leaders, the passage of the joint resolution must have demonstrated a glaring American double standard. Independence and democracy were seemingly reserved for Europeans (including European Jews) but not for Arabs. This revelation seems to have paralyzed the group for a time.

Attitudes Through 1932

For most of the middle years of the 1920s, there is little to document the activities of the Palestine National League. In March 1924, the League, along with another organization called the National Independence Party of Syria, sponsored a dinner at the Hotel Astor for Dr. Abdul-Rehman S. Shahbender. He was one of the nationalist Syrian figures leading resistance to French occupation. At the dinner, Shahbender reportedly attacked the French as oppressors and the Zionists as "a small minority seeking to impose their will on an Arab population which vastly outnumbers Jews in Palestine."[34] In November of 1925, Fuad Shatara reappeared at a forum held at the New York City

Civic Club on West 12th Street. During the discussion moderated by Philip Hitti, Shatara laid out a detailed "solution to the Syrian crisis." He called for the withdrawal of French troops from occupied Syria and the founding of a "national provisional government" and "a constitution along democratic and liberal lines as far as possible."[35]

From 1925 to 1928, no activities of the Palestine National League can be traced. The League must have still been in operation, but no record of its deeds have been discovered. In 1929, the League reappeared in the news in an assertive way. In August of 1929, major disturbances broke out in Palestine, initially triggered by the Jewish-Muslim dispute over the status of the Wailing Wall religious site in Jerusalem. Soon, a full scale Arab rebellion was under way, giving violent expression to all the Palestinian fear and resentment created by the imposition of imperialist control since the end of the war. Many Jewish and Arab lives were lost in this rebellion. Back in the United States, Zionists labeled the Palestinians "barbarians" and asserted that attacks on Jews were motivated by anti-Semitism. There was considerable pressure put on the American government to intervene on the side of the Zionists or, at the very least, to pressure the British to harshly suppress Arab resistance.[36]

It was in response to the Zionist assertions and pressure that Fuad Shatara, with the active help of the Arab-American writer Ameen Rihani, again became an active public spokesman. Representing the Palestine National League, both men sought to put the Arab rebellion of 1929 in context and explain to the American people that the bloodshed, as unfortunate as it was, was a response to British-Zionist policies over the past decade. In this effort the League, with Shatara as President, allied itself with two other Arab-American groups: The New Syria party headed by Abbas Abushakra and the Young Men's Moslem Association led by Abd M. Kateeb.

This effort first drew the attention of the press on August 29, 1929 when *The New York Times* reported that "a group of Arabian citizens and sympathizers living in or near New York met yesterday afternoon [August 28th] to protest against the unfairness [of press reports] dealing with the present Palestine rioting." The trouble was "political and economic" Mr. Abushakra told the *Times*' reporter. The Zionists had been "given a permanent home at the expense of the majority." The meeting forwarded explanatory cables to "several clerical and secular leaders denying the allegation that the attacks of the Arabs on the Jews were motivated by religion." One of these, sent to the Permanent Mandate Commission of the League of Nations at Geneva, explained that "present deplorable events in Palestine are the outcome of the Balfour Declaration. The Wailing Wall is merely an incident" flowing from conditions created by Zionist settlement. To President Hoover, Secretary of State Stimson, and Senator Borah, they cabled, "We regret present situation in Palestine. Zionism is responsible for these conditions. Application of Balfour Declaration under British mandate deprives Arabs of all their rights. Abrogation of declaration is only means to ensure permanent peace. Arabs the world over look to American sense of freedom and justice to uphold Arabs in their struggle for national independence." Other telegrams were sent to Pope Pius XI, Prime Minister MacDonald in England, King Feisal of Iraq, and other Arab leaders.[37]

On 9 September 1929, representatives of the three groups met in Washington, D.C., with Secretary of State Stimson and the British Ambassador, Sir Esme Howard. Led by Ameen Rihani, the group also consisted of Peter S. George, Elias Joseph, George Sadak,

Frank Sakran, and Ally Joudy. They told Stimson that, although they "deplore the acts of violence" and "mourn the dead of both Arabs and Jews," events had to be understood within context.

> For ten years the Arabs of Palestine have in vain protested and petitioned both to the British Government and the League of Nations. . . . Their demands for a national representative government . . . have all met with a deaf ear. . . . For ten years the Arabs have struggled and they have persisted and they have been patient. And all this time a small Jewish minority from Central and Eastern Europe, supported by funds from America and by the fiat of British power, have been making encroachments upon the rights of the overwhelming Arab majority. . . . Here is the fundamental cause of the present uprising. Religion has nothing to do with it. Racial feeling has nothing to do with it. It is a conflict between the Arab nationalism of the native majority and the Zionism of a small minority of foreign Jews.[38]

They then presented to the Secretary of State the same demands for self-determination that the Palestine National League had been putting forth for a decade.

Stimson's reply to the group was remarkable for its simple-minded nature. He was receiving pressure from American Zionists to condemn the Arabs and perhaps his political instincts dictated that he not address the substance of the Arab-American argument. In any case, Stimson told Rihani and his colleagues that "the cause of civilization, the cause of better understanding among peoples of different races and religions is never served by violence and recrimination." What the United States wanted to see in Palestine was "peace and cooperation." He then concluded this way, "if your delegation can play a part in emphasizing the qualities of moderation and thoughtfulness which are so needed in any approach to the present problem of Palestine, you will have served an eminently useful and eminently American purpose."[39]

As much as Stimson's reply avoided the issues and stuck to righteous pronouncements, it was at least more polite than that received from the British Ambassador. Esme Howard simply read to the group a statement from the British Prime Minister MacDonald labeling the Arab uprising in Palestine an "ordinary crime" and the work of "lawless mobs."[40]

The next month, MacDonald was visiting the United States, and Ameen Rihani, representing the Arab-American community, was able to get an appointment "to inquire about the recent Arab-Jewish disturbances in Palestine." He saw the Prime Minister on Saturday, October 12th (an American Jewish delegation had seen him the day before). All MacDonald would tell him was what he had told the American Jewish group, that "Great Britain would fulfill all of its obligations toward Palestine."[41] Rihani, who had a clear sense of the contradiction between British "obligations" to the Zionists and those to the Palestinian Arabs, must have found the session greatly frustrating.

Nonetheless, for the next several years, Rihani and Fuad Shatara engaged in an ongoing debate with American Zionists. In the newspapers, popular magazines, and academic journals, they put forth an energetic effort to get the Arab perspective on Palestine across to the American people. In the 2 October 1929 issue of *The Nation*, Rihani debated the American Zionist leader Bernard Flexner on the question of Palestine. Briefly analyzing Zionist religious and historical claims to the Holy Land, Rihani concluded that ultimately the Zionist position rested on force. "Zionism . . . cannot feel secure and cannot prosper—cannot even exist—without an army strong enough to defend it." The maintenance of oppressive force in Palestine destabilized more than that one little country. "The peace of the world depends in large measure on the peace in the heart of the world, in the Near East. And peace in the Near East depends in a greater measure on the settlement of the question that caused in the past ten years three uprisings in Palestine." He went on to predict "a Moslem uprising against the British in India, against the French in Syria, even in Morocco against the Spanish in the Rif, against the Italians in Tripoli. And Zionism in Palestine will be the cause of it all." Playing to the isolationist mood in the United States, Rihani then suggested that "Americans too should consider the consequences" of suppressed national aspirations in Palestine. "With American interests increasing in the Holy Land ... and with American Jews agitating for Zionism there and bringing pressure to bear upon the Government here, might not the United States be also drawn into the conflict?"[42]

The next month, Rihani repeated this exercise in the November 1929 issue of the journal *Current History,* in which he took on the Zionist leader Meyer Weisgal. Rihani traced the evolution of the Arab nationalist movement, observing that "never have they relinquished their claims to independence." He described the British agreement of 1916 with Sherif Hussein, which laid the basis for a post-war independent Arab state with boundaries that, "clearly" included "Palestine as well as Syria." He pointed out that, in contrast, the post-war summit conference at St. Remo awarded mandates to the victors "discounting altogether the free choice of the native population." Instead of getting "enfranchisement, complete and final" as the British had promised, "the northern provinces [Palestine, Syria/Lebanon, Iraq] have been placed under a peculiar form of modern subjugation."[43]

Rihani went on to ask what will happen if "Zionism, with the British mandate as a shield and money as a weapon" finally succeeds. He prophetically predicted that a Jewish Palestine would, by virtue of inevitable population pressures, become expansionist. "The territory is there, Syria and Trans-Jordan. . . . the Jews of Zion, who have come into the country during the past ten years ... are the vanguard of a dream of conquest, a dream of empire which the Arabs resist, must resist and will resist to the end." There was only one way out of the dilemma according to Rihani and that was by having the British create a real representative government in Palestine that would accord the Jews presently there equal civil, religious, and political rights but restrict further immigration. "I cannot see how else the problem can be solved to the satisfaction of all three parties."[44]

Rihani continued speaking out into the early 1930s. He debated Jacob De Haas (a protégé of Louis Brandeis) before the Foreign Policy Association in New York City on 18 January 1930, and he again called for the revocation of the Balfour Declaration.[45] At a conference "on the cause and cure of war" in Washington, D.C., in January 1931, Rihani attacked imperialism, in this case particularly French control of Syria.[46] In 1932, he and Fuad Shatara contributed essays to a special issue on Palestine put out by *The Annals of the American Academy of Political and Social Science.* Rihani wrote on "Palestine and the Proposed Arab Federation," and Shatara wrote on the prospects, such as they were, for eventual "Arab-Jewish Unity in Palestine."[47] In Shatara's piece, he put forth a "proposed solution" to the problem in Palestine based once more on

representative government and immigration control that would maintain an Arab majority in the face of what was by now an apparently irreversible Zionist presence. Shatara
proposed to allow an increase in the Jewish population to 750,000. "That number,"
he suggested, "should furnish enough material for reviving Hebrew culture and traditions."[48] Painfully, the emphasis was shifting from unbending resistance to a position
of compromise that would save some semblance of the rights of the majority. What the
Palestinian Liberation Organization (PLO) went through in the 1970s and 1980s, the
leaders of the Palestine National League experienced in the 1920s.

Conclusions

The efforts of these men to bring the Arab perspective before the American people did
not meet with success.[49] The Zionist point of view became the dominant one in the
United States. However, this fact does not in any way warrant the conclusion, as rendered by Jacqueline and Tareq Ismael, that "within the American political arena, there
was no fundamental challenge [to Zionism] representing Arab interests." Nor does it
justify Richard Cottam's conclusion that "so little was heard from this group [the Arab
Americans] that [one] is justified in ignoring them."

   The problems faced by the Palestine Antizionism Society and its successor organization, The Palestine National League, were formidable. Philip Hitti observed that the
Arab-American community was a divided one when it came to Syria and Palestine.
Mostly Christian, some of them actually welcomed imperialist intervention in the Middle East. Those Maronite Christians who supported French control of Lebanon were
not likely to join with men like Shatara and Rihani in vigorously opposing the British
and Zionists in Palestine. However, the American Jewish community of the day was
also divided. Reform Jews in particular were inclined to be anti-Zionist, although not
out of any sympathy for the Palestinians. They instead feared an erosion of the citizenship rights held by Jews in America and Europe if a Zionist state were realized in
Palestine. However, no alliance ever developed between anti-Zionist American Jews and
Arab Americans.

   Over time, the Zionists were successful in winning over most of their American Jewish skeptics and unifying the Jewish community behind their cause. This allowed them
to ever more effectively use a network of connections that American Jewry had built
up over decades—one that reached into the highest levels of political and economic
power in the United States. The Palestine Antizionism Society and the National League,
faced with a religiously fractionalized ethnic constituency, could never match that unity
and influence. At best they could attempt to publicly debate the issues and try to build
a counter-network in the face of continuous Zionist opposition. It is an effort that goes
on to this day.

   The American Zionists had, however, another advantage of even greater significance. This was the long-standing and deep-seated religiocultural identification between
Jews and the Holy Land within the American psyche.[50] Bred of Bible reading and Sunday School education from the time of the Puritans onward, this identification created
a pre-existing and fertile psychological context for popular American acceptance of

the Zionist message. When combined with the equally common stereotype of the Arabs as desert-dwelling, uncivilized people, the advantage held by the American Zionists was formidable.

In the face of it all, these were Arab Americans who stepped forward and began a debate that has not ended. Their efforts produced a body of material reflecting cogent analysis that still has relevance today. In other words, their activities are part of the on-going history of the Arab-American community and the Palestinian-Israeli conflict and must be acknowledged and studied as such. These men were individuals of great integrity and courage whose lives are a source of inspiration to the Arab-American community.

Notes

1. Philip K. Hitti, *The Syrians in America* (New York: George Doran, 1924), pp. 65–77.

2. See Yvonne Haddad, "Muslims in the United States." In *Islam: The Religious and Political Life of a World Community,* edited by M. Kelly (New York: Praeger, 1984), pp. 259–60.

3. Adele L. Younis, "The Coming of the Arabic-Speaking People to the United States" (Ph.D. dissertation, Boston University, 1961), p. 320.

4. Hitti, *Syrians in America,* p. 91.

5. Hitti, *Syrians in America,* p. 91.

6. The only time in the 1920s the Arab-American community seems to have forgotten its religious and regional differences and reacted more or less in unison was in the Spring of 1929. It was then that Senator David Reed of Pennsylvania, speaking in the midst of an on-going debate on immigration quotas, referred to Arab immigrants as "Mediterranean trash." In response, "leaders and writers among the various [Arab-American] communities urged organizational unity to combat 'irresponsible statements' hurled against them." Younis, "Coming of Arabic-Speaking People," p. 291. See also the *Syrian World* 3, no. 11 (May 1929): 39.

7. See Michael W. Suleiman: "Arab-Americans and the Political Process." In Ernest McCarus, ed., *The Development of Arab-American Identity* (Ann Arbor, MI: University of Michigan Press, 1994), pp. 37–60; Suleiman, "The Arab-American Community in the United States: A Comparison of Lebanese and Non-Lebanese." In Albert Hourani and Nadim Shehadi, eds., *The Lebanese in the World: A Century of Emigration* (London: I.B. Tauris, 1992), pp. 189–207; and "The Arab-American Left." In Paul Buhle and Dan Georgakas, eds., *The Immigrant Left in the United States* (Albany, NY: SUNY Press, 1996), pp. 233–55.

8. Hitti, *Syrians in America,* pp. 59–60.

9. Hitti, *Syrians in America,* p. 95.

10. Jacqueline Ismael and Tareq Ismael, "The Arab Americans and the Middle East," *Middle East Journal* 30, no. 3 (1976): 393.

11. Ismael and Ismael, "The Arab Americans and the Middle East," p. 398.

12. Richard Cottam, "The United States and Palestine." In Ibrahim Abu-Lughod, ed., *The Transformation of Palestine* (Evanston, IL: Northwestern University Press, 1971), p. 389.

13. Suleiman, "Arab-Americans and the Political Process," p. 45.

14. The Arab-American community in these years had a number of newspapers most of which were printed in Arabic. As Shatara, Rihani, and others took a pro-Palestinian perspective to the American public, the issue was likewise debated in this ethnic press. Most Arab-American papers agreed with Shatara *et al.* One exception was *Al-Hoda,* a Maronite Christian–owned paper that

supported the mandate system and, on occasion, defended Zionist activity in Palestine. See excerpts from the Arab-American press published in the *Syrian World* 4, no. 2 (October 1929): 46–47; and *Syrian World* 1, no. 12 (June 1927): 48.

15. Ameen Rihani, *The Fate of Palestine* (Beirut: Rihani Printing and Publishing House, 1967), p. 106.

16. Hitti, *Syrians in America,* p. 89.

17. *New York Times* (9 November 1917): 4.

18. Hitti, *Syrians in America,* p. 89. In June of 1917, Shatara had had to write a letter to *The New York Times* explaining that "Syrians are not Turks." This was a significant distinction given the emotions aroused by World War I. *New York Times* (1 June 1917): 8.

19. Hitti, *Syrians in America,* p. 88. For American views of Arabs see Cindy A. Lydon, "American Images of the Arabs," *Mid East* (May/June 1969): 3–14; and Helen McCready Kearney, "American Images of the Middle East, 1824–1924" (Ph.D. dissertation, University of Rochester, 1975).

20. See Lawrence Davidson, "Historical Ignorance and Popular Perception: The Case of U.S. Perceptions of Palestine, 1917," *Middle East Policy* 3, no. 2 (1994): 125–47.

21. *Records of the Department of State Relating to the Internal Affairs of Turkey, 1910–1929,* Record Group 59, 867n Palestine, 867n 01/37.

22. *Records of the Department of State,* 867n 01/37.

23. See Davidson, "Historical Ignorance." For Lansing's point of view see his correspondence with Wilson in A. Link, ed., *The Papers of Woodrow Wilson* (Princeton, NJ: Princeton University Press, 1983), vol. 45, p. 286.

24. Cited in Stephen Wise, *Challenging Years* (NY: Putnam's Sons, 1949), p. 191.

25. *Records of the Department of State,* 867n.01/54.

26. *New York Times* (20 August 1922): VII-4ff.

27. *New York Times* (20 August 1922): II-4.

28. Habib Katibah, ed., *The Case Against Zionism* (New York: Syrian-American Press, 1921); a copy of this volume can be found in the New York Public Library.

29. Katibah, ed., *The Case Against Zionism,* p. 46.

30. *Hearings Before the House Committee on Foreign Affairs* (House Congressional Resolution 52), April 18–21, 1922, p. 161. In a letter to *The New York Times* dated 8 November 1922 but not printed until the 16th, Shatara noted that, during the Foreign Relations Committee hearings the previous April, the Committee had refused to consider the King-Crane Commission report. In the Senate, where the resolution was sponsored by Henry Cabot Lodge, there were no hearings at all. Shatara concluded that "the manner in which the Lodge resolution was passed has been described by Zionists as princely. In my humble opinion it was very un-American." *New York Times* (16 December 1922): 14.

31. *New York Times* (16 December 1922): 14.

32. *New York Times* (16 December 1922): 156.

33. Lydon, "American Images of Arabs," pp. 8–9.

34. *New York Times* (28 March 1924): 16. Just seven months before Shahbender's speech, another group, The Syrian-Lebanon Committee, made up of New York area Maronite Christians, had entertained the French General Gouraud. Gouraud had been France's first High Commissioner in Syria. In recognition for his service, the Committee gave him "a gold loving cup, twelve inches high and valued at $1,000." *New York Times* (22 August 1923): 15. Clearly there were those in the Arab-American community who supported imperialist intervention in the Middle East.

35. *New York Times* (15 November 1925): 15.

36. *Records of the Department of State,* 867 n404.

37. *New York Times* (29 August 1929): 2. The *Syrian World* described the same meeting as a "national convention" of the "three organized bodies." *Syrian World* 4, no. 1 (September 1929): 51–52.

38. *New York Times* (7 September 1929): 3.

39. *New York Times* (7 September 1929): 3.

40. *New York Times* (7 September 1929): 3; see also *New York Times* (8 September 1929): 22.

41. *New York Times* (13 October 1929): 2.

42. Ameen Rihani, "Zionism and the Peace of the World," *The Nation* 129 (2 October 1929): 346–47.

43. Ameen Rihani, "Palestine Arabs Claim to be Fighting for National Existence," *Current History* 31, no. 2: 272–78. See also *New York Times* (27 October 1929): 11-3.

44. Rihani, "Palestine Arabs Claim," p. 278.

45. *New York Times* (19 January 1930): 11-6. The debate was broadcast over WEAF radio in New York City.

46. *New York Times* (22 January 1931): 48.

47. *Annals of the Academy of Political and Social Science* 164 (November 1932).

48. *Annals of the Academy of Political and Social Science* 164 (November 1932): 182.

49. In the case of Fuad Shatara, this eventually led to personal tragedy. Dr. Shatara's work as a physician was apparently affected by his efforts on behalf of the Palestinians. Those who remember him believe that, in the 1940s, he may have lost his position at the New York hospital at which he practiced because of Zionist hostility. This led to a decline in his health and his death shortly thereafter.

50. See Davidson, "Historical Ignorance," and John De Novo, *American Interests and Policies in the Middle East 1900–1939* (Minneapolis: University of Minnesota Press, 1963), p. 6.

Janice J. Terry

15 Community and Political Activism Among Arab Americans in Detroit

Since the late 1960s, increasing numbers of Arab Americans have become politically active in local and national organizations. What motivated these individuals to donate money, often from rather meager resources, and more importantly, to devote considerable amounts of time in addition to the demands of school, work, and family to community and political organizations? Do these individuals share any common characteristics or life experiences? The Arab population in the Detroit area has been estimated to be as high as 250,000, making it the largest Arab population in North America. As home to a large and diverse Arab population, Detroit is therefore an appropriate place to look for answers to these questions. Because the Arab community in Detroit continues to grow annually by at least 3,000 new immigrants, pinpointing factors that motivate Arab Americans to mobilize and energize the community is all the more crucial.[1]

Detroit has been the center for many successful Arab-American organizations. These successes are all the more remarkable because many in the community number among the "working poor," lacking the wealth and leisure time enjoyed by more advantaged immigrant groups in the United States. However, without substantial financial resources or the benefits of higher education and socioeconomic status, many within the community have established, funded, and maintained a remarkable variety of viable organizations.

The events described in this chapter are an outgrowth of an ongoing oral history project conducted among activist Arab Americans in the Detroit tri-county area.[2] The study attempts to delineate the political and social motivations of leading Arab-American activists in Detroit and to provide a historical overview of the Arab-American organizations that originated or have been active in Detroit during the past three decades.

The first Arab immigrants to the Detroit area in the 1800s followed the general patterns described by Alixa Naff and others.[3] From Lebanon and Syria in the old Ottoman Empire, they were predominantly Christian, with a smattering of Sunni Muslims. Many were peddlers and small shopkeepers. Like other immigrants, they believed the United

States was a land of endless opportunity, and they eagerly sought to assimilate within the larger American society. They tended to downplay their ethnic identities and, if Muslims, sometimes even denied or ignored their religious affiliation.

These upwardly mobile immigrants placed enormous emphasis on education and hard work. A family anecdote recounted by Lila Howard, a secondary school teacher of Palestinian origin, is illustrative of the work ethic within the larger community. As a teenager, Lila's brother asked his parents for permission to join the high school football team. They were furious, not because the sport was dangerous, but as his mother said, "We did not come to this country to do such frivolous things."[4] School yes; football, no.

As they prospered, Arabs in Detroit followed the pattern of countless other immigrants and moved out of the downtown core, gravitating to the more affluent northern areas or eastern suburbs of the Grosse Pointes. After both World Wars and the 1967 and 1982 Arab-Israeli wars, the stream of Arab immigrants grew. Many of the newcomers were refugees who had lost their homes and jobs as a result of upheavals in the Middle East. Immigrants fleeing ongoing wars and crises in the Middle East continued to move into the area until the present. They include Palestinians, Lebanese (particularly Shi'a from the south of Lebanon), Yemenis, and Chaldeans from Iraq. From the outset, the course of Arab immigration has been determined by the vagaries of world history.

Many new immigrants settled in urban areas, particularly in the western suburb of Dearborn, home to the Ford Motor company. From the 1940s through the early 1970s, many of the new immigrants quickly found jobs, often at the lowest possible pay levels in the burgeoning automotive industry. The "South End" or Dix area of Dearborn became home to a growing number of Yemenis who, lacking education and English language skills, tended to be the poorest of the Arab immigrants.[5]

The Yemenis also differed from other Arab immigrants in that they were almost entirely men who engaged in a pattern of serial migration, returning to Yemen often for several years at a time before traveling back to the United States. Only over the past ten to fifteen years have Yemenis migrated with or brought their families to the United States, where their children are now gradually acculturating with general American mores. As a result of continued close ties with the homeland, Yemeni associations tended to reflect the political divisions between the North and South (Aden).[6] However, the Yemenis have been strong supporters of local organizations that provide services to the community.

The more affluent—in relative terms—Palestinian and Lebanese immigrants settled several miles further north along the Warren Avenue area of Dearborn. The Chaldeans, many of whom opened small grocery or party stores purchased from owners moving out of the increasingly African-American urban core to largely white suburbs, settled in Highland Park, an urban enclave and former home to the Chrysler Corporation, and the Nine Mile area of Detroit. As they prospered and diversified into other businesses, the Chaldeans moved into the richer northern suburbs.

The Chaldeans, who are frequently characterized, even by themselves, as "clannish,"[7] have maintained close affiliations with the local Chaldean churches and social clubs, particularly the large, rather lavish Southfield Manor, a major venue for weddings and parties. Before World War II, the Chaldeans socialized extensively with the large and more established Lebanese Maronite community. They attended St. Maron, the

Maronite church and even held wedding ceremonies there, but after the establishment of a separate Chaldean church, Mother of God, the ties between the two communities gradually disappeared.

The Chaldean American Ladies Charity, established at the behest of a local Chaldean priest in 1961, provides services and economic assistance to new immigrants. Since its inception, the Charity has been led by four to five stalwarts with twenty to thirty active workers and several hundred dues-paying members. Recognizing the different pressures and mores of the United States, the women have also raised moneys to establish a senior citizen center. Under the auspices of the Church, construction for the senior center was begun in 1997.[8]

New immigrants—including the Chaldeans—differ from earlier arrivals who tended to avoid political or community organizations that operated outside the close confines of specific ethnic, religious, or village-based memberships. For most early Arab immigrants, churches, mosques, and clubs based on village or ethnic affiliations were the focus of social life outside the immediate extended family. For many second-generation Arab Americans, mosques and churches were important venues for broadening their circles of friends; some even met their future spouses through church- or mosque-sponsored events or youth organizations. Clubs such as the Ramallah and Chaldean associations were—and for the older generations of male immigrants still are—important centers for social and political exchanges. However, later generations have often eschewed or downplayed affiliations with village- or ethnic-based clubs, seeking membership in organizations with broader-based Arab-American memberships.

The newer generations who became active after the 1967 war are the focus of this chapter. These newer immigrants reflect the national, socioeconomic, religious, and political diversity of the Arab world. The Detroit Arab-American community is not monolithic; it is a mosaic of many "mini" communities, including Lebanese, Palestinian, Iraqi, Egyptian, Muslim (Sunni and Shi'a), and Christian (with many different rites represented).

The socioeconomic status of the communities runs the gamut from prosperous businessmen and professionals to working class and unemployed or underemployed immigrants. Not surprisingly, many activist leaders tend to have higher educational levels, with a disproportionate number of college graduates compared with the national average. On the other hand, a number of the most committed community leaders, particularly among the Yemenis, do not have university degrees. It is not unusual for activists to have families, hold full-time jobs, attend university to earn higher degrees, and still volunteer in community organizations. The occupations of community activists are exceedingly diverse; they include, among others, lawyers, professors, medical doctors, business people, engineers, teachers, fire fighters, law enforcement officers, factory workers, and homemakers.

Although specific priests, imams, and teachers motivated some to become active in the community, most support secular organizations. In keeping with the era of secular nationalism popular during the 1960s and 1970s, none based his or her political involvement in religion or religious movements. Although some now hold full-time paid jobs in Arab-American organizations, all the community leaders originally volunteered their time and resources, and most remain volunteers.

As in the Arab world, politics is a major interest for most Arab-American leaders. In the words of one activist, "Politics is mother's milk to all Palestinians."[9] Many Yemenis emphasize that, during the 1960s and 1970s, they believed themselves to be the freest of all Arabs to discuss and criticize events and leaders in the Middle East.[10]

Although politics were discussed in their homes, activists do not generally come from families who were politically active on the national or local level. The parents of most were far too busy making it economically to have spare time for outside activities. Several leaders raised in the United States feel that their parents discouraged political activism, fearing that it would be dangerous, harmful, or economically detrimental. These attitudes are still held among many older Chaldeans. Nor is there a discernible pattern of support for specific leaders or political parties. Political sympathies are as diverse as the Arab world is diverse.

Reflecting the conclusions of studies on childhood and adolescent development by Adelson, Gallatin, and others, the activists all became politically aware around the age of nine or ten, becoming active in their early teens.[11] Early political memories vary from relatively benign to extremely traumatic. For example, activist Abdeen Jabara, who grew up in a small town in Northern Michigan, remembers his father listening to broadcasts of Radio Cairo over a shortwave radio.[12] After Gamel Abdel-Nasser nationalized the Suez Canal Company in 1956, Jabara sent him a congratulatory telegram. When the telegram was read over Radio Cairo, Jabara's entire family was absolutely thrilled. Radio broadcasts and publications from Egypt were important factors in the politicization of many Arab Americans. During the 1960s, many Arabs and Arab Americans viewed Nasser as a hero and supported him, even when he made major mistakes. Younger generations tend to be much more skeptical. Terry Ahwal, who grew up in occupied Palestine, saw her father beaten by Israeli soldiers in 1969. From that moment on, Terry vowed to do something to prevent such injustices.[13] For younger Palestinians, the Palestinian people are the heroes, not a single leader. They distrust one-man leadership and hard-line political parties and are keenly aware of the failures of past and present Arab leaders. Except for specific causes, the youth are more cautious and careful about pledging their allegiance.

As a major industrial center, with a large, unionized labor force and a racially and ethnically diverse population, Detroit was the center for many of the movements that changed the political and social landscape of the United States during the 1960s and 1970s. The civil rights and anti-Vietnam War movements had a lasting impact on all Americans, and Arab Americans were no exception. Given their own history of dispossession and displacement, it is not surprising that many young Palestinians were deeply affected by these struggles for social and racial justice. In 1967, long unresolved political, social, and economic problems led to violent confrontations in the Arab world and Detroit.

The stunning loss of the rest of historic Palestine in the 1967 Arab-Israeli war was a traumatic blow to the Palestinians and to Arab nationalists as well. The war, described as a "humiliation" and a "wake-up call," was a major turning point in the political development of many Arab Americans.[14] The war and the 1967 urban rebellion in Detroit engendered a wave of new activism.

During the 1970s and 1980s, the South End became a center for political activity, much of which had a decidedly leftist bent. Many saw the struggle for Palestinian self-determination as part and parcel of the Third World revolutionary movement. The plethora of publications distributed by the various Palestinian parties radicalized many students. Arab youth, men and women, became directly or indirectly involved with specific factions within the Palestinian movement, particularly Fatah, the Popular Front for the Liberation of Palestine (PFLP), and the Popular Democratic Front for the Liberation of Palestine (PDFLP). On the Wayne State University campus and other area universities and colleges, Arab and Arab-American students held raucous debates and fiercely contested access to public platforms from which to publicize their particular political ideologies.[15]

The focus for most of these young student activists was Palestine, not the local community. The old village-based clubs, such as the Ramallah Club, were viewed with some disdain and were approached only to host events or political rallies for particular factions. However, the 1967 war also led older organizations to widen their horizons; many Palestinians, who previously had identified with their villages or clans, began to emphasize their Palestinian roots. For example, the American Federation of Ramallah added Palestine to its name.[16]

Various Palestinian factions competed with one another to secure the support of local clubs for their projects in the Occupied Territories, Lebanon, and elsewhere. Activists vied with one another to secure donations of money, clothing, other goods, and time from the various local clubs and well-known Arab-American community leaders. With the benefit of hindsight—always 20/20—activists involved in these activities conclude, with some dismay, that a great deal of energy and time had been expended, often "for very little return."[17] Independent of one another, they emphasize the error of not having worked harder to coordinate and cooperate with older Arab-American leaders. In retrospect, they also regret not having devoted more time and effort toward the establishment of local organizations.[18]

Local coffee shops, such as Kamel's on Dix in the South End, were popular venues for political debates that often dragged on late into the night. Demonstrations and marches for the Palestinians and Lebanese and against Israel became commonplace. The entire community—men, women, and children—participated in large protests against the Israeli invasions of Lebanon in 1978 and 1982.

In Detroit, many Arab Americans, particularly the Yemenis, supported local unionizing efforts and participated in strikes and walkouts at local automotive plants. In 1973, one of the two lines in the huge Dodge main automotive plant was forced to shut down (an unheard of stoppage) because Yemeni workers failed to show up for work.[19] Rather than working their shift, the Yemenis instead participated in a very public and noisy demonstration against Leonard Woodcock, the United Auto Workers' (UAW) leader. Woodcock's support for Israel was well known, and on this occasion, he was to receive a B'nai B'rith award at an event in Cobo Hall, the cavernous Detroit convention center in the center of the city. The demonstration outside Cobo Hall attracted widespread media coverage, but the union forced the Yemenis to pay for their absenteeism; although leftist Palestinian groups helped compensate them, some Yemenis still remain bitter about what they perceive to have been the failure of other Arab Americans and unions to rally behind their cause.

Yemeni involvement with union disputes and support for African-American workers highlight the issue of race and class. Many Arab Americans, particularly the earlier immigrants, had sought to distance themselves from working class struggles. Arab

Americans had also generally defined themselves as "white." The question of racial identity and relations with people of color, particularly African Americans, remains a sensitive one within the Detroit community and with Arab Americans across the country. Through their actions, the Yemenis placed themselves squarely within the working class and in alliance with African Americans. Unfortunately, as a result of unresolved issues within the African-American and Arab-American communities, the alliance between them has failed to flourish.

At the same time, a few, mostly university-educated professionals in the area decided to meet together. Many of these professionals had come to the United States as students and had stayed because repressive regimes in the Arab world and their political affiliations made it dangerous for them to return home or because as Palestinians they had nowhere else to go. Some were also drawn by the social and economic opportunities in the United States. These professionals, mostly academics, felt the need for a national organization to present the Arab point of view to the general American audience. On the occasion of the International Congress of Orientalists, about a dozen people met in Ann Arbor in August 1967 in the basement of the home of Dr. Rashid Bashshur, a sociologist and public health expert from Syria who is a professor at the University of Michigan. The attendees had a wide variety of political affiliations, including the Arab Nationalists Party (Nasserists), and the Syrian Social National Party (PPS). All had secular rather than religious orientations. At the first meeting, "there was an incredible amount of angst and extremely sober tones among the people; there was no humor or frivolity."[20] After some discussion, the participants decided to start an organization to present Arab viewpoints. The participants set up an organizing committee with Abdeen Jabara, a new lawyer who in his own words had "plenty of time on my hands," as coordinator. The organization was to become the Association of Arab-American University Graduates (AAUG).

In Detroit and elsewhere, the inclusion of "University Graduates" in the name of a new organization engendered considerable debate. Some argued that limiting membership to university graduates was elitist and exclusionary. The argument over the organization's name reflected the fundamental differences between those who wanted a grassroots, mass-based organization and those who favored a narrower, more focused membership base. This fundamental difference of approach is still periodically debated among Arab Americans and within the AAUG.

Under Dr. Muhsin Mahdi, then at the University of Chicago, a second meeting was held during the conference of the Middle East Studies Association (MESA), itself a relatively new organization. About 43 people attended the second meeting, and each pledged $50 to $100 to underwrite the work of the new organization. The first executive committee was established with Dr. Fawzi Najjar, a professor at Michigan State University, as the first president and Abdeen Jabara as the executive secretary. From the outset, AAUG had a democratically elected board, from which a slate of officers was drawn.

In 1968, Dr. Ibrahim Abu-Lughod, at Northwestern University, agreed to put together a program for the first AAUG convention held during a terrible snow storm in Washington, DC. About one hundred people attended the first convention. Until the organization moved to Massachusetts and ultimately to its own building in the late 1970s, the AAUG was headquartered in Detroit. As it evolved, the AAUG came to stress the Palestinian struggle. This was natural, because the Palestinians tended to be the most politically aware and active; from the outset, AAUG had a national rather than a community focus.

In Detroit, Abdeen Jabara was also particularly active in establishing the local AAUG chapter that many activists joined. But as local AAUG chapters lost support from the national office and the original founders moved on to other activities, the local Detroit chapter floundered and ultimately disbanded. A number of activists credit Jabara for his energy and creativity in getting local and national organizations off the ground. Jabara is often mentioned as having served as a mentor or role model for many Detroit activists.

During the 1970s and 1980s, other national Arab-American organizations emerged. Some, such as the National Association of Arab Americans (NAAA), were primarily lobbyists for the Arab cause in Washington. Although NAAA had local members, especially among second- and third-generation Lebanese and Syrians, it was not locally based. On several occasions, the organization also took positions (e.g., support for the Camp David Accords) that were extremely unpopular in the Middle East and among politically conscious Arab Americans, particularly in the Detroit area. Rather than influence decisions, NAAA became an instrument for support of American policy rather than for change. Some Arabs in Detroit also supported James (Jim) Zogby's attempts to involve Arab Americans in electoral politics through the Arab American Institute.

Other organizations, such as the Holy Land Fund, Palestine Human Rights Campaign (PHRC), and Palestine Aid Society (PAS), focused their efforts on the Palestinian cause. An outgrowth of AAUG, the PHRC brought a new style of activity to Arab Americans. Taking the civil rights movement as a model and coordinating with other American organizations, the PHRC mounted public campaigns and protests involving massive numbers of people. Although the PHRC had a grassroots membership, it tended, like many other Arab-American organizations, to have a rather narrow leadership base. All of the aforementioned organizations had numerous members in the Detroit area, and some, particularly PAS, remain active in the region.

In the early 1980s, in reaction to widespread stereotyping, anti-Arab racism, and scandals such as ABSCAM, James Abourezk, a former Senator from South Dakota, to his "everlasting credit," took on what was arguably the most unpopular cause in the United States at the time: the rights and image of Arabs and Muslims. Abourezk called together approximately sixty to seventy Arab-American leaders from around the country to a meeting in Washington, DC. The American-Arab Anti-Discrimination Committee (ADC) was established in 1980 as a result of this meeting. ADC mobilized Arab Americans, many for the first time, from all backgrounds across the nation. ADC was a grassroots organization but had a personality-based leadership. It undoubtedly raised the collective consciousness of Arab Americans about themselves, American society, and the U.S. government.

The ADC chapter in Detroit had a particularly important impact within the Arab-American community and throughout Detroit and Michigan.[21] Jim Zobby recruited Nabeel Abraham, a local activist who had also been Executive-Director of AAUG (1978 through 1979), to head up the local ADC office. Abraham brought Jessica Daher, of Lebanese and American heritage, on board. They then recruited Harold Samhat, Razook Samaan, Terry Ahwal, and many others. Terry Ahwal was originally brought in to help with the memorial service for Alex Odeh, an ADC official assassinated by a bomb attack—a crime that remains unsolved. Ahwal eventually became the ADC director in Detroit before leaving to work in county and city politics.

During the Israeli invasion of Lebanon in 1982, the Detroit ADC chapter had a major impact in Detroit. It contacted the press, brought wounded Lebanese and Palestinians to Detroit for much needed medical care, and made the general American public aware of the injustices perpetrated on largely defenseless Palestinians and Lebanese. In Detroit, ADC made it hard on pro-Israeli activists, cost them "propaganda points," and changed the focus of discourse. This was a brief, short-lived moment in which an organization that already existed on the ground was able to take advantage of the confluence of events to launch proactive, rather than reactive, programs. As a result, the Arab-American community saw itself depicted in positive terms by the establishment media and thereby gained increased confidence and awareness. ADC succeeded in putting the Arab-American community on the map and contributed to making it a player in local and state politics.

From the beginning, there tended to be much overlap in the membership of various Arab-American organizations. Many Arab Americans were active in local and national associations. However, as the fortunes of national organizations waxed and waned, many turned almost exclusively to involvement in local organizations. However, Arab-American activists view their community involvement as an integral part of their political struggles.

The 1967 war also provided the incentive for the creation of several Arab-American social service centers. Arab Americans, particularly in the South End, had long talked about the need for an institution that would provide much needed social services to the growing community. The Yemenis had already established the Yemeni Benevolent Society, which provided English language lessons and some social service.[22]

By the mid-1970s, the International Center in downtown Detroit was providing minimal social services to new Arab immigrants. In 1978 and 1979, Wayne County Community College obtained a grant to underwrite an outreach program to the community and an advisory board composed of a cross-section of the Arab community, including Chaldeans, was established. Subsequently, the Arab Chaldean Social Service (now the Arab-American and Chaldean Council [ACC]), led by Haifa Fakhoury, was created. With Fakhoury's dedication and dynamism and with the support of the Chaldean community, the ACC grew to provide a wide range of programs for new immigrants and for the general Arab-American community.

The Arab Community Center for Economic and Social Services (ACCESS) is arguably one of the longest lived and most successful of the local Arab-American organizations. After 1967, in a coordinated effort that persists until the present, Arab immigrants and Arab Americans, many of them of Lebanese or Palestinian origins, organized what was originally called the Arab Community Center for Employment. The name was ultimately changed to Arab Community Center for Economic and Social Services, as it is still called. ACCESS was created in 1971 with a board of directors of ten people and a constitution and by-laws.

Although the Yemenis already had their own social service association, they supported the creation of a center that would serve the entire Arab community. From the onset, the founders of ACCESS came from a wide variety of Arab countries and were a representative cross-section that reflected the religious and political complexity of the community. Although this diversity has occasionally caused strains within the internal management of ACCESS, it has also proved to be a major strength in its continued viability within the Arab and mainstream American communities.

To secure the necessary funds to initiate the project, several activists, including a number of Arab Americans who had also been instrumental in blocking the city of Dearborn's plans for the "urban renewal," or destruction of the residential, working-class South End neighborhood, approached AAUG for money.[23] A longtime community volunteer, Katherine Nagher, was especially instrumental in convincing the AAUG to provide $1,000 for the new effort.

Based in a shop front on West Vernor, a working-class neighborhood, ACCESS served slightly more than 100 people in its first year. George Saad, a local businessman, provided the rent money for the first year. Volunteers George Khoury and Don Unis sold huge trays of qataif and falafel to local shopkeepers to pay the telephone and electric bills. An engineer, Khoury also held classes for Arab workers so they could learn the English names for the tools they used. ACCESS provided some immigration and legal advice, as well as English language instruction.

From West Vernor, ACCESS moved to the Hashemite Hall, also on the west side, where it remained for slightly over a year, after which it moved to the newly purchased Yemeni Benevolent Society building that the Yemenis generously provided free of charge. Ultimately, ACCESS was able to raise enough money to pay for the space.

During this time, Aliya Ogdie Hasan agreed to serve as the unpaid director.[24] Of Sunni Lebanese parentage, Aliya Hasan had returned to Detroit after working in New York City for many years. She remained director of ACCESS for ten years, and the growth of programs owed much to her considerable abilities.

For ACCESS supporters, the roughest time financially and psychologically came after the first fire in 1979 and the arson fire in 1983, when the building housing ACCESS burned to the ground. In addition to these setbacks, ACCESS faced considerable hostility from the Dearborn political machine headed by long-term mayor, Orville Hubbard. Known ACCESS supporters and volunteers, such as Don Unis, received hate mail, and their cars and houses were vandalized. As late as the mid-1990s, Unis was still receiving "love notes" from racist citizens in Dearborn.

The community rallied to rebuild ACCESS, which ultimately moved into its current main building on Saulino Court in the South End. It also maintains several other offices in Dearborn. Although more radical community groups, such as the White Panthers, had urged ACCESS not to accept or seek financial aid from government agencies, the leaders of ACCESS concluded that, to extend the agency's programs and services, they would have to secure outside funding. Littlefield Presbyterian church, led by Dr. William Gepford, supported ACCESS efforts to secure a grant of about $50,000. That grant gave ACCESS early credibility, and the center subsequently obtained a block grant of about $10,000 from the city.

During the 1980s, changes in the Dearborn administration after the death of Mayor Hubbard made the position of ACCESS in the community more secure. The Democratic administration under Governor Jim Blanchard also provided additional support to the center. Local telethons brought in much needed money, with the 1986 telethon raising $60,000 to $80,000. Even when the new Republican administration under Governor Engler cut off funding in the 1980s, ACCESS was able to mobilize enough community and political support to have the funds reinstated—the only community organization able to do so.

Initially, ACCESS and ACC, the two main Arab-American social service centers, openly competed for state funds. Each viewed the acquisition of grants and public funding as a zero-sum game, in which a gain for one was a loss for the other. There was also considerable rivalry over programs and status within the community. In the mid-1980s, after the state government made it clear that it would not support one Arab-American agency to the exclusion of the other, ACCESS and ACC saw the advantage of cooperating with one another—at least publicly. The two now coordinate their efforts to secure annual state funding.

With increased revenue and considerable success in receiving grants from a wide variety of public agencies, ACCESS has grown into a major provider of social services to the community. Services include English language classes, family and mental health counseling, athletic and musical programs for children, and programs for women. In 1993 and 1994, ACCESS served 62,415 people through forty-five to fifty different programs with fifty to eighty paid personnel, including longtime volunteers and professionals.[25] More than 1,000 people, including Senator Carl Levin and many representatives from non-Arab organizations, attended the twenty-fifth anniversary celebration for ACCESS in 1996.

In addition to its social service programs, ACCESS is probably the biggest provider of Arab arts in the country, sponsoring events such as the Fann wa Tarab cultural arts program held in the Detroit Institute of Arts. ACCESS has also become the largest organizer of multicultural events in the city. It also has an active educational outreach program. With the financial support provided by a wide variety of government and foundation grants, ACCESS regularly sponsors workshops to educate teachers, journalists, law enforcement officers, and other Detroit area professionals about the Arab world and Arab Americans. Acknowledging the importance of religious institutions within the community, ACCESS regularly invites local imams and priests to lecture at these events. Workshops also usually include tours of the community and a visit to the Dix mosque located down the street from the main ACCESS building.

In the 1990s, ACCESS sought to establish links with other community groups, particularly with African American, Hispanic, and Asian communities. During 1996, leaders from these communities held regular seminars to learn about the history, politics, and culture of each ethnic group. ACCESS remains actively committed to fostering better relations among Detroit's diverse ethnic populations and, importantly for the future, to forging alliances with other communities who also struggle against prejudice and economic hardships.

Ish Ahmed, Director of ACCESS for more than fifteen years, emphasizes that ACCESS has become "a city-wide player," with members on the executive committee and boards of a number of Detroit area institutions. In Ahmed's words, ACCESS has "a network that is pretty awesome, given who we are and how small we are." ACCESS has also made a conscious effort to hire and work with young Arab Americans. During the mid-1990s, it restructured its governing board to ensure the replacement by newer, younger members within five years. Older board members were appointed to an executive board in advisory capacities. Ahmed views the success of ACCESS, locally and nationally, as a tribute to the Arab-American community.

As a result of the successful organizing efforts of large numbers of Arab Americans in Detroit, the community is recognized as a potential economic and political force. The print and electronic media regularly cover activities in the community, run feature articles on it, and interview Arab Americans regarding events in the Middle East. Encouraged by these successes, increasing numbers of young Arab Americans have become involved in politics. Although a few Arab Americans had previously been elected to judgeships and other offices, until the 1980s, they tended to downplay or remain silent as to their ethnic identities. The current generation of political hopefuls—Democrats and Republicans—openly seeks support from the community. For example, Detroit Mayor Dennis Archer has a Chaldean on his staff, and one of Michigan's Senators, Spencer Abraham, is an Arab American of Lebanese descent.

Although ACC, ACCESS, and other Arab-American organizations have undoubtedly made major contributions to the community and toward improving the image and status of Arabs in the greater Detroit metropolitan area, their survival is still an uphill battle. All Arab-American organizations constantly struggle against the anti-Arab, anti-Muslim climate of opinion that permeates American society at all levels. Because of its size and visibility, the Arab-American community in the Detroit area is especially vulnerable to hostility, scrutiny and surveillance by government agencies, and occasional violent attacks by civilian citizens. By organizing and educating themselves, Arab Americans in Detroit are engaged in an ongoing process to develop the wherewithal to respond to such threats through the media and appropriate political and legal channels.

Several other major problems also plague local Arab-American organizations; two are largely cultural in nature, and the others are systemic and endemic in other ethnic and community organizations. The persistence of patriarchal and sexist leaderships remains an impediment to the growth and development of Arab-American organizations. Many younger Arab Americans, particularly second and third generations, have criticized the reluctance of traditional, patriarchal leaders to step down or to pass on leadership roles to the next generation. One local activist has jested that "Arab leaders—here and there—are often legends in their own minds." Continued sexism, particularly in the organizational structure of some Arab-American associations, is a closely related issue. For organizations to remain strong and vibrant, women must be included as equal partners. The structural changes in the governing board of ACCESS represents a serious attempt to address these problems.

The influx of new immigrants with highly traditional mores poses another set of challenges. On one hand, they add energy and vigor to the community, but on the other hand, new arrivals are often suspicious and fearful of organizations with members from outside their own narrow religious, clan, or village affiliations. They also cling to deeply ingrained traditional behaviors, particularly with regard to patriarchal authority and gender relations.

The economic well-being of Arab-American organizations is particularly worrisome to community leaders. Lacking endowments or secure, long-term commitments from large donors or foundations, all Arab-American associations are constantly in a state of imminent financial collapse. As a result, community leaders spend enormous amounts of time and energy obtaining donations, grants from foundations, and allocations from government agencies. With a large portion of their budgets coming from government allocations or grants, ACCESS and ACC are vulnerable to shifting political sentiments and annual cutbacks. Their financial vulnerability makes planning and commitment to long-range programs difficult, if not impossible.

Arab Americans often fail to understand these problems. Most still lack sufficient education and motivation to recognize the importance of giving money to keep Arab-American groups alive. Activists commonly express the sentiment that, "We need more political philanthropy." However, the problem of economic viability plagues many community agencies, not just Arab-American organizations.

Convincing more Arab Americans to join community organizations is another major difficulty. Community activists consistently bemoan the failure of others to get involved, arguing that if more people were to join in the work, more could be done and, presumably, more funds could be raised. Most activists in Detroit are also eager to motivate young Arab Americans to volunteer their services. Those with grown children are justifiably proud that most of them are continuing the family tradition of community service. Second- or third-generation Arab-American youths are not impeded by language barriers or cultural differences. Although they fit easily into American society, most have retained an active pride in their Arab heritage and are therefore well-placed to make qualitative and quantitative differences in the community.

Those with young children are also cautiously optimistic—perhaps an inherent characteristic of community activists—regarding the future involvement and contributions of Arab-American youth. Attracting additional workers for community activities is essential to the success of individual foundations and to community influence on local and national levels. In talking with Arab Americans, Abdeen Jabara persistently emphasizes that 5,000 to 10,000 organized and committed people can have a major impact on American domestic and political life. There are many times that number of Arab Americans in the Detroit area. Those who have already committed their time, energy, and financial support have begun to make a difference, but they recognize that a great deal more can, and given the numbers of Arab Americans, should be done.

Notes

1. Estimates place the Arab population in the Detroit tri-county area at 40,000 to 50,000 Iraqi Chaldeans, 12,000 Yemenis, and 30,000 Palestinians; the rest are predominantly Lebanese or Syrians, with some Egyptians and a smattering of immigrants from other Arab countries. In the absence of any hard census data, these are approximations, with census figures representing an undercounting and figures provided by community organizations being inflated. In the past, Christians were estimated to make up one-half of the total; however, over the last decade, the largest number of new immigrants have been Shi'a Lebanese from South Lebanon; the population is now probably predominantly Muslim.

2. For advice and explanations about conducting oral history projects, see Donald A. Ritchie, *Doing Oral History* (New York, Twayne Publishers, 1994), and *Living Memories: How to Do an Oral History* (Washington, DC: The ADC Research Institute, 1985).

3. Alixa Naff, *Becoming American: The Early Arab Immigrant Experience* (Carbondale, IL: Southern Illinois University Press, 1993).

4. Interview with Lila Howard, 6 June 1994. Born in the United States, Lila Howard's parents are Christians from Ramallah in Palestine. She is married to a third-generation Arab American of Lebanese descent and has children.

5. For further details on the Arab community in southeast Dearborn, see Barbara C. Aswad. "The Southeast Dearborn Arab Community Struggles for Survival Against Urban 'Renewal.'" In Barbara C. Aswad, ed., *Arabic Speaking Communities in American Cities* (New York: Center for Migration Studies and Association of Arab-American University Graduates, 1989), pp. 53–83.

6. For a detailed analysis of the political divisions in local Yemeni associations, see Nabeel Abraham, "National and Local Politics: A Study of Political Conflict in the Yemeni Immigrant Community of Detroit, Michigan" (Ph.D. dissertation, University of Michigan, 1978). See also Nabeel Abraham, "The Yemeni Immigrant Community of Detroit: Background, Emigration, and Community Life." In Sameer Y. Abraham and Nabeel Abraham, eds., *Arabs in the New World: Studies on Arab-American Communities* (Detroit: Wayne State University Center for Urban Studies, 1983), pp. 109–34.

7. Interview with Margarett Sarafa, 29 June 1996. Margarett Sarafa and her husband, Haithem Sarafa, have been active in the Chaldean community for more than thirty years. Born in the United States to Chaldean parents, Mrs. Sarafa is a homemaker with children; her husband, a successful businessman, was born in Iraq.

8. For more extensive documentation on the Chaldean community, see the work of Mary C. Sengstock, particularly *Chaldean-Americans* (Staten Island, NY: Center for Migration Studies, 1982).

9. Interview with George Khoury, 31 July 1994. Born into a Christian family in Palestine, Khoury came to the United States as a student. He is an engineer and independent businessman. Khoury is married to an American and has children.

10. Interview with Yahia Mawari, 28 July 1994; Interview with Saleh Muslah, 28 July 1994. Mawari is a businessman and Muslah is a medical doctor; born in Yemen, they are both Sunni Muslims, married to Yemeni women, and have children.

11. Judith Gallatin, *Democracy's Children: The Development of Political Thinking in Adolescents* (Ann Arbor: Quod Publishing Co., 1985).

12. Interview with Abdeen Jabara, 20 July 1994. A lawyer, Jabara was instrumental in the creation of numerous community organizations; his parents, Sunni Muslims, were from Lebanon.

13. Interview with Terry Ahwal, 15 July 1994. Ahwal, executive assistant to the Wayne County executive, is from a Christian Palestinian family and came to the United States as a teenager.

14. Interview with Hasan Nawash, 7 August 1996. Nawash, a Sunni Muslim from Palestine, is an engineer and writer. He is married and has children.

15. Interviews with Nabeel Abraham, 26 August 1996, and with Ismail (Ish) Ahmed, 12 June 1996. Abraham was born in the United States to Palestinian, Sunni Muslim parents. He is married to an Arab American of Canadian and Egyptian ethnicity. Ahmed is Director of the Arab Community Center for Economic and Social Services (ACCESS). He was born in the United States to an Egyptian father and an Arab-American mother of Lebanese parentage. He is a Sunni Muslim, is married to a French Canadian, and has children. George Khoury and Hasan Nawash also spoke extensively about the political fervor during those heady days of political activism.

16. Detroit hosted the first Ramallah convention in 1959, an event sponsored by *Hathihi Ramallah* (This Is Ramallah) magazine, begun in 1952 and still published bimonthly. There are now about 23 Ramallah clubs around the country.

17. Nabeel Abraham interview.

18. Interviews with George Khoury, Hasan Nawash, and Ish Ahmed.

19. See Nabeel Abraham, "Yemeni Immigrant Community of Detroit," for a fuller description of this little known and largely misunderstood event. The involvement of Arab Americans, particularly Yemenis in the labor movement in Detroit and the Seaman's Union merits a full scholarly exposition.

20. Much of the following narrative is based on Abdeen Jabara's account.

21. Much of the following account is based on the narratives of Nabeel Abraham and Terry Ahwal.

22. Interview with Ali Baleed, 20 August 1996. The Yemeni Benevolent Association continues to operate. Along with social and athletic programs, it offers four classes in Arabic for about 100 students, with five teachers paid for by the Association. The Arab American Yemen Association provides similar social services. Past attempts to unify the two organizations have failed, but efforts to at least coordinate efforts are continually in process.

23. For a fulsome account of the Arab community's struggle to survive concerted attempts by Dearborn city government to raze homes in the South End under the guise of urban renewal, see Aswad, "The Southeast Dearborn Arab Community Struggles for Survival Against Urban 'Renewal.'" The following narrative is based on the accounts of Don Unis (interviewed 29 July 1996), George Khoury, Hasan Nawash, and Ish Ahmed. Early supporters of ACCESS included Helen Atwell, the Amen family, Hasan Jaber, Barbara Aswad, Yusuf (Joe) Barakat, and Mohsin Jabary.

24. Aliya Ogdie Hasan was born in South Dakota in 1910 and moved to live with cousins in Detroit in 1925. She had a career in law enforcement in New York City. Active in Muslim organizations, she helped to arrange Malcolm X's pilgrimage to Mecca. She died in Detroit in 1990.

25. Barbara C. Aswad and Nancy Adadow Gray, "Challenges to the Arab-American Family and ACCESS." In Barbara C. Aswad and Barbara Bilge, eds., *Family and Gender among American Muslims: Issues Facing Middle Eastern Immigrants and Their Descendants* (Philadelphia: Temple University Press, 1996).

Part VI

Arab-American Identity Negotiations

Suad Joseph

---

16   Against the Grain of the Nation—The Arab-

To Be Free to Be a Citizen

In 1914, an immigrant by the name of George Dow was denied U.S. citizenship. The denial was justified on the basis of the statute approved on March 26, 1790 defining citizens as "free white persons." Based on his ancestry as a "Syrian of Asiatic birth," George Dow (most likely what today would be a Lebanese Christian) was judged as not a "free white person." The decision was reversed on appeal. The decision notes, "The appellant, George Dow, a Syrian, was denied naturalization on the sole ground that a Syrian of Asiatic birth is not a free white person within the meaning of the naturalization statute. After the first decision of the matter a rehearing was granted at the instance of other Syrians interested. In his two opinions the District Judge reached the conclusion, which he supported with remarkable force and learning, that the 'free white persons' made eligible to naturalization by the statute included aliens of European nativity or descent, and no others."[1]

The 1790 statute was reviewed and repealed and reinstated numerous times in the 19th century. As late as 1875, Congress reinserted the words "free white persons" in the naturalization law. Later the term "free" was dropped, but "white" was retained. The George Dow appeal was granted solely on the basis of the argument that Syrians were of mixed Syrian, Arabian, and even Jewish blood, belonging to the Semitic branch of the Caucasian race and were to be considered white persons.[2] Immigrants of what we now call Arab origin were again allowed citizenship as they had been since the 19th century, based on their whiteness.

Although the George Dow case is indicative of the exclusionary practices toward non-European immigrants of that period, the story also captures a recurrent dilemma of immigrants of Arab origin. Immigrants of Arab origin are eligible for citizenship, gain citizenship, and yet often are experienced as against the grain of the nation. There is an enduring representation of "Arab-" as not quite American—not quite free, not quite white, not quite male, not quite persons in the civil body of the nation. Arabs- therefore are seen as not quite citizens, despite their possession of formal papers and passports. The hyphen after Arab- is not firmly attached to American, not yet embedded in the body politic of this nation.

In this chapter, I explore the delimiting marker of "free" as a criterion for citizenship and the representations of the "not free" Arab- as a basis for exclusion from discourses and, at times, practices of citizenship in the United States. I argue that, through a variety of discourses, the Arab- is represented as essentially different from the Western, the American. Although difference is often constructed and understood in racial or color terms, I argue a more subtle and in some ways damning designation of difference is also affixed to the Arab- as a not-independent, not-autonomous, not-individual, not-free person. Such representations are woven into many scholarly and popular discourses on Arab religion, politics, and social order.

Citizenship and the Yearning for National Identity

If, as Sami Zubaida argues, the nation-state has become compulsory, then the idea of citizenship, the essential foundation for nationhood or statehood, must be interrogated for the conditions to membership in the national community.[3] What criteria must a person fulfill to be fully a citizen? What kind of person does one have to be to be a citizen of this nation-state, the United States of America?

Gauri Viswanathan argues that "the yearning for a condition of hybridity—the happy merging of discrete identities" into a unity is "a precondition of national identity."[4] She adds, "the idea of syncretism as existing in nature—innate to peoples everywhere, anterior to regulated definitions of selfhood, and recoverable by a will to see sameness in place of difference—is a purposeful fiction constitutive of the will to nationhood."[5] The state, she contends, is the "instrument for such incorporations: disinterestedness is the stance that invites the service of individuals, the merging of differences in one overarching social unity."[6]

Full citizenship entails a sameness. Differences may be tolerated, but become irrelevant to the nation and national identity.[7] If the condition for full citizenship is that one is shaped to conform with a social unity, as Viswanathan implies, the persistent representation of Arabs as essentially different and not comprehensible to the Western mind is designed and has the effect of precluding the full citizenship for Arabs as Americans.

To be a citizen of the United States of America, there has been an enduring explicit assumption that one is free and there are enduring implicit assumptions of whiteness and masculinity. To be free has been understood as having free will, independence of mind, autonomy of action—to be an "individual." I take "individual" to be an historically specific construct of personhood that emerged concomitantly with and embedded in liberal, bourgeois, capitalist Western societies. C. B. MacPhearson argued that liberal capitalism produced "possessive individualism."[8] The possessive individual is an exclusive property owner, with the property exclusively owned being the self. The assumption underpinning such liberal thought was that obligation not to the self, other than the most basic socially required for order, would compromise the free-willed action of the self. The self was to be unattached, unrestrained by obligation to be free. This construct of citizen as a free individualist self, I argue, is represented in much scholarly and popular literature as contrary to the Arab- self.

Carole Pateman and other feminist political theorists have contended that this "individual," embedded in liberal political thought, is a masculine contractual self.[9] Pateman argues that the contract, in liberal political theory, is seen as the paradigm of free agreement. She contends that the "individual" conceptualized in contemporary contractarian theory is seen as "naturally complete in himself. The boundaries that separate one individual from another are so tightly drawn that an individual is pictured as existing without any relationships with others. . . . The contractarian individual necessarily is the proprietor of his person and his attributes. . . . The individual owns his body and his capacities as pieces of property, just as he owns material property."[10] For early contract theorists, such as Locke, Hobbes, Pufendor, and Rousseau, "Women are excluded from the status of 'individual' in the natural condition."[11]

Jennifer Nedelsky argued that there is a close linkage between notions of property and rights in American constitutionalism.[12] Property must have boundaries to be owned and alienable. Boundedness, as a fundamental descriptor of property, became a foundational principle for conceptualizing rights in American constitutionalism, Nedelsky contended. Property, understood as having the capacity to be bounded and separable, became a symbol of the rights of citizens to limit the authority of government. Nedelsky suggests that the notion of rights as limits to government was built on the notion of "rights as boundaries," metaphorized on the basis of rights as bounded property. Nedelsky suggests an alternative notion of rights based on relationships. Property rights are "not primarily about things, but about people's relation to each other as they affect and are affected by things," and in practice, our laws regularly enact rights as relationship.[13]

Pateman's and Nedelsky's works conjoined help us understand the construction of the free person as not only white, but also as an historically specific construct of self, the contractual, masculine, individualized self. The undoing of these tenets of citizenship in the United States has been the work of the women's movement from the nineteenth, twentieth, and no doubt the twenty-first centuries.

To be white has been understood historically to mean being of European extraction. The United States census, however, categorizes Arabs- as white. Phenotypically, Arabs range from black to blond and blue eyed. However, as Nadine Naber has pointedly argued, Arabs are represented in the media as not quite white and not quite colored.[14] Naber contends, the popular representation of Arabs "taints" but does not color them enough to be considered a racial minority. The tainting of Arabs, she argues, is accomplished through a racialization of Islam.

Mary Ramadan offered a further insight that helps explain the ease with which Islam has been racialized in the United States.[15] Ramadan argues that in the discourses of United States citizenship, white has meant Christian. Although most pre-1960s Arab- immigrants were Christian, the Arab world is overwhelmingly Muslim. Arabs- are associated with Islam, and Islam is identified as a religion of color, Naber argues. This presents a dilemma for many young Arabs- who feel compelled to choose between being white and being colored when they are not fully recognized by either set of communities. The net outcome of this ambivalent racial identification is exclusion, Naber argues:

Arabs- are white, but not quite. To Naber's argument I add, being not quite white, Arabs- are not quite citizens.

The citizen, by implication, has been assumed to be an "individual" in the historically specific meaning outlined previously—an autonomous, free-willed, white male. I argue that there is enduring representation of Arabs- as not free, not individuals in this sense, not white, and not male—and not quite citizens. Because Edward Said has convincingly documented the processes by which Arabs were feminized in Orientalist scholarship[16] and Nadine Naber has forcefully demonstrated the processes by which Arabs- have been racialized,[17] I focus on the arenas in which Arabs- have been represented as not free, not individuals. I read the story of George Dow as emblematic of the disqualification of Arabs- for full citizenship. Focusing on the not-free standard as a criterion for disqualification from full citizenship, I analyze scholarly and popular representations of Islam, of politics, and of social order as sites in the construction of the not-free Arab-. In the last section of this chapter of Arab- political activism in the past 30 years, I evaluate the efforts made by Arabs- to claim full citizenship.

Conflation: Difference Erasing for Difference Making

I argue there are multiple conflations that underpin these representations: a conflation of Arabs, Middle Easterners, Muslims on the one hand and a conflation of those representations with Arabs- in America. Arabs are highly diverse. When I teach courses on the Middle East, I start by arguing that it is impossible to find agreement on a definition of Arabs. There are Lebanese, Syrians, Palestinians, Iraqis, Kuwaitis, Yemenis, Saudi Arabians, Bahreinis, Qataris, Dubais, Egyptians, Libyans, Tunisians, Moroccans, Algerians, Sudanese, Eritreans, and Mauritanians; there are Maronites, Catholics, Protestants, Greek Orthodox, Jews, Sunnis, Shi'a, Druze, Sufis, Alawites, Nestorians, Assyrians, Copts, Chaldeans, and Bahais; there are Berbers, Kurds, Armenians, bedu, gypsies, and many others with different languages, religions, ethnic, and national identifications and cultures who are all congealed as Arab in popular representation whether or not those people may identify as Arab.

In the second step of this conflation, the Middle East is represented as all Arab, erasing the linguistic, cultural, racial, and historical differences between Arabs and Turks and Iranians and the differences among and between Iranians and Turks. In the third step in this conflation, Arabs and Middle Easterners are conflated with Islam, belying the reality that most Muslims are neither Arab nor Middle Eastern but are Indonesian, Malaysian, Filipino, Indian, and Chinese. These sets of conflations are glossed on to Arabs in America, again covering the historical fact that almost all Arabs in America were, until very recently, Christians and that Christian Arabs- still constitute the majority of Arabs in America. This erasure of difference among Arabs and Arabs in America serves the creation of another difference: the difference between the free, white, male American citizen and this constructed Arab-. This difference making is accomplished through representations of Islam, politics, and social order in the Arab, Middle Eastern, and Muslim world.

Representations of Islam

Some political analysts have argued that Islam is the West's new evil empire. Islam is frequently represented as a militaristic religion bent on jihad (holy war), inherently and historically hostile to the democratic, capitalist, Christian West.[18] Islam's tenets often are represented as inscrutable. Adherents of Islam are frequently viewed as mindless, fanatic followers of mad clerics. Such representations of Muslims help to underwrite the notion of the not-free Arab-.

This representation of Islam is achieved by misrepresenting and then essentializing and homogenizing a highly complex and diverse religion that has many different sects, legal systems, beliefs, and practices. As Trinh Minh-ha acutely observes, such homogenization of the "other" is a classic colonialist strategy.[19] In American media, rarely is a distinction made between contemporary political Islamic movements and historical Islam. The media present contemporary Islam as being the same in all countries in which it is practiced and as a historically unbroken continuous set of beliefs and practices at odds with modernity. The collapse of history and diversity solidifies Islam as a monolithic, homogeneous, rigid, unchanging religion. The subtexts of such representations is that adherents of such an obdurate, unyielding, fixed religion could not be free.

Further consolidating the notion that the Muslim is not a free person is the misreading of the Arabic word *Islam*. The Hans Wehr standard Dictionary of Modern Arabic translates Islam as "submission, resignation, reconciliation (to the will of God)."[20] Islam comes from the root word *salima,* which means, according to Hans Wehr, "to be safe and sound, unharmed, unimpaired, intact, safe, secure; to be unobjectionable, blameless, faultless; to be certain, established, clearly proven; to be free."[21] Islam comes from the same root as the word for peace (*salam*) and the most commonly used word for welcoming and parting, *salamat* and *ma' issalami* (peace on to you and go in peace). In Islam, peace is the free-willed reconciliation of self to God.

The centrality of free will to Islam has been argued and documented by numerous scholars of religion.[22] The idea of free will is central to Arab culture. Leila Abu-Lughod, in her popular study of Bedouins in Egypt, argued that the Awlad Ali Bedouins (who think of themselves as the true Arabs) believed that honor could be achieved only by the free-willed action.[23] The centrality of the idea of free will to Islam is part of the explanation of why, some scholars argue, classical Islam, unlike classical Christianity, did not produce a religious hierarchy or a clerical bureaucracy and resisted intermediaries between the believer and God.

In Orientalist scholarship, however, Islam was taken to mean blind obedience. The Muslim, by submitting, was seen to have relinquished free will. Without free will, the Muslim could not be an "individual" in the Western understanding of that autonomous, bounded, contractual, possessive self. Stripped of individuality, the Muslim has been portrayed almost always in the collective. Rarely is a Muslim portrayed in American media in the solitude of private prayer or with head upright and eyes looking forward to God. Prayer is usually represented in crowds and in mosques, and almost invariably Muslims are represented in that moment of prayer with their heads bent touching the ground and shoeless. (This is a common prayerful posture of Mediterranean Christians but is rarely associated with Christianity in the popular media.) Popular representations of the holy pilgrimage, the *Hajj*, similarly focus on the hordes, the hundreds of thousands of people who seem to be mindlessly circling a black stone structure (the *Ka'aba*) in "primitive rituals." Muslims are seen as blind followers, willing to risk life for the word of their clerics—characteristics understood to be incompatible with a free person.

The rhetoric of clerics or politicians in political Islamic movements who invoke the idea of *jihad* (holy war) on behalf of their political causes is in the American media seen as a manifestation of the essence of Islam as a religion, rather than the contemporary use of Islam for contemporary political aims. Political struggles of the Arab world are readily glossed as religious wars, conflicts over doctrinal belief. Revolutionary, nationalistic, resistance movements and the politically aggressive acts they may inspire are more likely to be called terrorist if they are in any way linked with Islam.

These and other representations of Islam add up to its being seen as alien to Western rational thought and practice. One Op-Ed piece in *The New York Times* during the Gulf War (1991) stated that, even if a Western person were fluent in Arabic, they still would find the Muslim world inscrutable, incomprehensible. Associations of Islam with submission, obedience, relinquishing of free will, lack of individuality, subordination to the collective, blind following of irrational clerics all feed into the representation of the Arab- as not free.

Representation of Politics

Political processes in the Arab world are almost uniformly described in American media and academia as undemocratic. Political rulers mostly are seen as dictators or, at best, benign autocrats. Although most political regimes in this region (as in much of the Third World) are relatively undemocratic, American political analysts often make the illogical jump from the political regimes to the culture. The common argument is that Arab, Middle Eastern, Muslim culture is incapable of producing democratic regimes. As the neo-Orientalist Daniel Pipes put it, "Muslim countries have the most terrorists and the fewest democracies in the world."[24]

A 1950s–1960s version of this Orientalist view of Arab societies came in Daniel Lerner's *The Passing of Traditional Society*, a standard textbook when I received my graduate training.[25] He observed, "A complication of Middle Eastern modernization is its own ethnocentrism—expressed politically in extreme nationalism, psychologically in passionate xenophobia. The hatred sown by anticolonialism is harvested in the rejection of every appearance of foreign tutelage. Wanted [meaning they want] are modern institutions but not modern ideologies, modern power but not modern purposes, modern wealth but not modern wisdom."[26]

Yehya Sadowski has argued that, since the 1980s, a new generation of Orientalist scholars began linking the absence of democracy with the absence of civil society in their critiques of Arab, Middle Eastern, Muslim societies.[27] Civil society is generally taken to mean those "autonomous social organizations that resist arbitrary exercises of state power."[28] Civil society theorists have often argued that democracy is not possible without the creation of unions, political parties, citizen action groups, professional associations, and the like that intervene to protect citizens from the excesses of arbitrary state power. Orientalists, Sadowski argues, assert there are cultural prohibitions to democracy in the Middle East. Not only are there few democracies there, but they inherently cannot create or support democratic processes.

Classical Orientalists argued that Arab states were too strong and groups were too weak for civil society to emerge. The strong state led to Oriental despotism. Classical Orientalists reasoned that Islam was inherently a religion of obedience, both religious and political. Islam, unlike Christianity and Judaism, they argued, was not only a religious doctrine but a social order, a way of life, a culture, and a psychology. Overly strong states, despotism, totalitarianism, political quietism, fatalism, and obedience were Islam's outcomes.[29]

Since 1980, neo-Orientalists, among whom Sadowski includes Patricia Crone, Daniel Pipes, John Hall, and Michael Mann, have been arguing that democracy is not possible in the Arab, Middle Eastern, Muslim world, because society is too strong and the state is too weak. The main reason, however, has been Islam. These younger Orientalists claim that Islam is the only major world religion that embeds political ideals as part of its religious code. This, they argue, leads the faithful to distrust any form of political government. Political scientist John Hall argues that Islam is "monotheism with a tribal face,"[30] producing a social order that cannot support political authority. As a result, Muslim societies produce weak states, weak civil society, and no democracy, the neo-Orientalists contend.

The Western political discourse on the Arab world represents politics in terms of the predominance of despotism, dictatorships, authoritarian regimes, the lack of civil society, democracy, citizens' political participation. The emergence of political Islam, most prominently in Iran but also in Algeria, Egypt, and Turkey, has served to further consolidate the view of politics in that area of the world as undemocratic and Islam as the primary obstacle to democracy. In popular representations, the image is that the area produces terrorists, suicide bombers, hijackers, and fanatics. Such societies, one is supposed to conclude, could not produce free persons.

Representations of Social Order

Arab societies are frequently represented as resistant to modernity—blindly traditional, hierarchical, and oppressive to women. Central to this critique of Arab societies is the argument that Arab societies repress individuality, that they do not and cannot produce individualized citizens—that is, Western-styled individuals. I have elsewhere argued that there are multiple constructs of selfhood present in Arab societies as in any society. Western-styled individualism is very much in evidence, but other constructs are present and institutionally supported as well. One construct, which I have called connective selfhood, is a more porous, fluid, and relationally oriented notion of selfhood. Connectivity is highly adaptive in societies with strong family systems and in which kinship units are critical in the economic, political, social, and religious systems. Against those steeped in Western individualist tenets, I argue connectivity is highly functional in such societies.[31] Contractarian, possessive selfhood does exist, but connectivity thrives.

Not only is connectivity taken in many Arab societies as a sign of health and maturity, but such relationality is vital to the enactment of citizenship, as I have argued for Lebanon.[32] People transport with them into all areas of social action the reciprocal obligations and duties implied in connective relationships. Connective relationality often underpins patron-client relationships, because patrons are expected to respond to the needs of their clients and intervene on their behalf in multiple spheres of social life, and clients are reciprocally expected to offer loyalty to their patrons in diverse arenas. Connective relationality lubricates the workings of the *wasta* (brokerage) system that is the engine for exchanges of many goods and services politically, economically, and socially in Lebanon and many countries of the Middle East. Although I argue that these and similar modes of operation are found quite widely in the contractarian or individualist West, their displacement or dysfunctionalization in discourses of selfhood permits a rhetoric of citizenship disallowing the Arab- from access to the criteria for citizenship qualification.

The dysfunctionalization of other constructions of selfhood is the founding premise for Western Orientalists' and neo-Orientalists' singling out of family and gender systems of the Arab world in their unveiling of the repressiveness of Arab societies. In much of the Orientalist and neo-Orientalist scholarship on the Arab world, family and gender systems have been depicted as rigidly patriarchal, subordinating, and silencing women and young people. It is a place for male domination and male sexual fantasy.

Sociologist Juliette Minces' *The House of Obedience* is an extreme depiction of this classic take on family and gender systems in the Arab world. The book jacket summarizes, "The House of Obedience is about women in the Arab world who are still largely subject to a traditional set of beliefs and customs employed to justify a multiplicity of practices against them. The veil, physical mutilation, forced marriage, incarceration in the home, repudiation and polygamy are manifestations of this commitment to a traditional lifestyle, with the Islamic concept of the family as its keystone." Minces goes on to assert sociological statements such as Arab men despise women outside their family[33] and can see them only as sexual prey,[34] and "they think about it [sex] all the time, obsessionally."[35] She asserts there is widespread male homosexuality in the Arab world and "a taste for young boys is seen as the epitome of refinement throughout the Islamic world—a supplement rather than a substitute for the harem."[36] "The incarceration of women, leaving the men with no outlet except masturbation or homosexuality, has produced societies which fall sick the moment the traditional system is weakened."[37]

As for the women, Minces claims, "Hypocrisy, deceit and duplicity are, in the end, the only weapons available and many women do not hesitate to use them. Amongst the rich who do not work, one might add arrogance, laziness and vanity."[38] She concludes that "the position of most immigrant Arab women in Europe [and by extension immigrant Arab women elsewhere] is much the same as in the Arab countries."[39] Even immigration and contact with Western culture do not improve this despicable family and gender system. This account is not nineteenth century travel journalism. It was published as sociology in 1982 by the reputable and relatively progressive Zed Press.

Although Minces is an extremist among those who dysfunctionalize Arab societies through caricatures of systems of family, gender, and personhood, continuities with her logic are evidenced in the works of many reputable scholars of the region.[40] Fouad

Moughrabi argued early on that the use of social-psychological tools of analysis for such negative stereotyping of the Arab world represented a continued reliance on national character studies, long after such studies had been debunked for other regions of the world.[41]

The veil, polygyny, clitoridectomy, and honor crimes are all represented as evidence of the backwardness of Arab society and the ill prospects that those societies could produce free individuals, particularly free women. These practices are frequently construed as Islamic, giving further evidence of the incompatibility of Islam and democracy. The veil is a pre-Islamic practice. Historically, wearing the veil was practiced by a very small percentage of women, mainly elite. In parts of the Arab world, men historically wore veils as well.[42] The modern usage of the veil still accounts for a minority of women in the Arab world and is very much linked with the rise of a political Islam—a historically new phenomenon. Similarly, polygyny is pre-Islamic, widespread throughout the world and practiced by a very small percentage of Arab males. Clitoridectomy, primarily an African sub-Saharan ritual, is not Islamic and is practiced in very few Arab countries. Honor crimes also are not uniquely Islamic or Arab. They are features of a Mediterranean culture that is shared with all the southern European countries—Spain, Portugal, southern France, Italy, Greece, and their New World derivatives in South and North America.

The net message of such representations of social order in the Arab world focusing on family and gender systems, however, is that Arab societies do not and cannot produce free individuals. Details of this picture are filled in with depictions of tribalism, religious and ethnic "primordial" ties, and Arab society as hordes, always seen in the collective. Such representations help draw the image of the not-free Arab-.

Arab- Political Activism

How have Arabs- responded to these depictions of their societies of origin and the glossing of these depictions onto them?[43] Earlier generations of Arab immigrants generally did not identify as Arab. From the nineteenth to the mid-twentieth century, most Arabs in America were Christians from Lebanon or Syria. The U.S. census of that time tended to label them as Ottomans, Turks, Asians, or Syrians. Given the smallness of their numbers and their tendency to scatter across small towns and rural areas, rather than consolidate in numbers in urban areas, most assimilated into mainstream culture in their local areas, joining mainstream businesses and the religious and social institutions and identifying mainly in terms of their families and religious sects.

The 1967 Arab-Israeli war was a turning point. The often indiscriminate attacks on and public displays of hatred for Arabs and Arabs- during and after the war galvanized Arabs- to organize in America to fend off discriminatory representations of themselves and their homelands. The Association of Arab-American University Graduates (AAUG), founded in 1967, was the first Arab- organization with political-scholarly goals.[44] The National Association of Arab Americans (NAAA) was founded in 1972. Its goal was to act as a political lobby in Washington on behalf of Arab issues.[45] The first organization to systematically focus on discrimination against Arabs in America was the

American-Arab Anti-Discrimination Committee (ADC), founded in 1980 by former Senator James Abourezk. For nineteen years, ADC has compiled and disseminated data on discrimination, taken legal actions, and met with American media representatives (especially the notoriously anti-Arab Disney Productions) to educate and pressure them to change their representation of Arabs in the media. ADC made sources, materials, and speakers available to the school systems, worked against the blacklisting of Arab- intellectuals and political activists. ADC has been a milestone in political activism on behalf of creating a space for Arabs- as American citizens.

Perhaps the most interesting organization in terms of the argument of this study is the Arab American Institute (AAI), founded in 1985 by James Zogby, an experienced activist leader in ADC. The goal of AAI has been to increase the political participation of Arabs- in the American political process. AAI has worked to create Arab Republican and Arab Democratic clubs, to support Arabs- of both major parties running for office, and to elect Arabs- to the national conventions and local offices of both parties.

When AAI was founded, I was taken aback. AAUG and ADC had made sense to me, and I joined both when they were formed. As a progressive, it was difficult for me to accept that people whom I knew and accepted as progressives were willing to work for conservative candidates as AAI was willing to do. In retrospect and in the context of the argument I propose in this study, I now see their moves as claims for full citizenship for Arabs- in America. The outline of this program for active citizenship is laid out by Helen Hatab Samhan in her analysis of the 1988 elections, in which she argues that Arab Americans were a constituency come of age.[46]

Arabs- had not been politically effective, Samhan argues, because they were unable to identify as a single community or because candidates, particularly Democratic party candidates, refused to be associated with them. George McGovern in 1972 rejected the endorsement of a group of Arab-American academics. In 1976, Jimmy Carter accepted a Lebanese American Committee rather than an Arab- committee. In 1980, an Arab-support group for Jimmy Carter was dissolved. Ronald Reagan in 1980 also did not accept Arab- support committees but accepted Lebanese American and Syrian American support committees. In 1984, Walter Mondale returned the checks of a group of Arab-American businessmen who had met with him and supported his campaign with checks of $1,000 each. He later apologized and appointed Mary Rose Oakar (D-OH), Nick Rahall (D-WV), and George Mitchell (D-ME) to serve as liaisons to the Arab-American community.

The first time in the political history of Arab-American citizenship in this country that specifically defined Arab-American support committees were accepted by any presidential candidates—Jesse Jackson and Ronald Reagan—was in 1984.[47] Other firsts in 1984 were the appointments of Arab Americans in prominent roles in presidential campaigns. George Salem was chief of the Ethnic Voters Division of the Reagan campaign, and James Zogby served as vice-chair and liaison to the Arab-American community for Jackson's campaign. In that campaign, Arab Americans became the largest single constituent group organized by the Ethnic Voters Division of the Reagan-Bush campaign.[48] For the first time, an identified Arab-American activist, James Zogby, took the podium of the Democratic Party's national convention to offer a nominating speech for a presidential candidate—Jesse Jackson. For those of us aware of the struggle to get there, it was an overwhelming moment.

For the 1988 elections, AAI made a national effort to organize Arab Americans as a coherent force in the elections. Eleven thousand people and fifteen national institutions signed its election planks, eleven states participated in focused local organizing work, town meetings were held to discuss the 1988 Issues Agenda for Arab Americans, and intense work was invested in educating Arab Americans on how to get elected as delegates to national conventions. In California, thirty-nine Arab-American Democrats ran for national delegate positions, and in Texas, more than 125 ran.[49] James Zogby served as national co-chair of the Jesse Jackson campaign. Arab Americans were co-chairs of several state level Jackson campaigns committees—Virginia, California, and Washington, D.C. Samhan reports that the largest constituency support for the Jesse Jackson campaign, after blacks, came from Arab Americans.[50] John Sununu, governor of New Hampshire and later in the Bush administration, served as National Co-Chair of the Bush campaign and Oregon's former governor, Victor Attiyeh, served as honorary national chair. Mounzer Chaarani served as national co-chair for Senator Robert Dole's election efforts.

The 1988 election was a watershed in the efforts of Arab Americans to put issues of Middle Eastern policy, particularly Palestine, into the national debates, a watershed with many low points and achievements. The New York primaries saw intense baiting of Jesse Jackson by New York City Mayor Ed Koch. Jackson backtracked, averring on *Face the Nation* that he would not talk to the Palestinian Liberation Organization (PLO) or Yasir Arafat, although he supported Palestinian national rights. James Zogby and Edward Said spoke directly with Jackson after these remarks to assure the community that Jackson had not betrayed them. Arab-American Democrats worked with Jesse Jackson to put a resolution in the national platform supporting Palestinian statehood. The negotiations, defeats, and achievements of this experience were another watershed of experience as politically active full American citizens for Arab Americans. As a spokesman for the Israeli embassy put it, "The significance of this is not in the adoption or non-adoption of the Jackson Mideast plank, but in the issue being debated as a major issue by one of the great parties."[51]

Perhaps even more interesting was the statement by Larry Cohler and Walter Ruby in the *Washington Jewish Week*,[52] in an article entitled "The New Arab American Activists." Cohler and Ruby observed that "the style of the Arab Americans is distinctly American and acts as a powerful tonic against the stereotype many Americans have come to hold of this ethnic group."[53] The implication of this article is that Arabs- were operating according to the rules of the strategizing, contractarian, possessive individualist, rational actors recognizable as free persons, as citizens. Samhan takes these actions and statements as evidence that Arab Americans had come of age as citizens in the body politic of this nation.

I am less sanguine in interpreting these events, as the Gulf War only a short three years after the 1988 elections painfully demonstrated. The shameful demonizing of Arabs during that war terrorized those of us with any sense of identity with the Arab-community. General Norman Schwartzkopf, head of our military operations in the Gulf, in a nationally televised news briefing, asserted that the Iraqis "are not part of the same human race we are. I have to pray that it is true."[54] *Time* magazine printed an advertisement depicting the pictures of Ayatollahs Khomeini and Khameini of Iran, President Saddam Hussein of Iraq, and President Muammar Qaddhafi of Libya, all looking dark and furtive. The caption underneath their menacing portraits read, "If you're uneasy about nuclear electricity, consider the alternatives."[55] *The New York Times* ran a cartoon by noted cartoonist David Levine depicting "The Descent of Man" in which Clark Gable, looking his most dapper free white male self, is depicted on the extreme left. To the right of him is an ape, then a monkey, then a snake, and to the extreme right, President Saddam Hussein of Iraq.[56] The expression "sandnigger" mobilized free white male citizens to kill Iraqis, and "mother of" became a debasing commentary in common American English.

The *Sacramento Bee* carried a story, reproduced in little of the national press, reporting that U.S. Representative Norman Mineta "pointed to a 1987 contingency plan the FBI and the Immigration and Naturalization Service drew up to detain Arab Americans at a camp in Oakdale, La., in the event of war with certain Arab states. Mineta said that plan could still be initiated to 'round up' Arab-Americans."[57] Around the country, Islamic mosques were broken into or bombed, shots were fired into the homes of known Arabs-, a taxi driver in Fort Worth, Texas, was attacked and killed, some Muslim schools and Islamic societies were vandalized, and hate calls were received by Arabs- throughout that period.

In more recent years, the response to the bombing of the World Trade Center in New York City added to the furor against Arabs, Muslims, and Middle Easterners. The immediate assumption by the major national media, fed by comments by Attorney General Janet Reno, after the bombing of the federal building in Oklahoma City in 1995, was that this was an act of Muslim, Arab, Middle Eastern terrorists. For days after the arrests of free, white, male, Anglo, right-wing militia members as suspects in the bombing, the media persisted in making the association of bombings with Muslims, Arabs, and Middle Easterners. A number of legal and political theorists have argued that the Anti-Terrorism Act of 1996 is specifically targeting Arab, Muslim, Middle Eastern peoples in the United States.[58]

The Hyphen That Never Ends

What are the prospects of full citizenship for Arabs-, what are the prospects for closure of the hyphen? The prospects are better now than they were before 1967, but as President Clinton's silence or reticence to act on Israel's invasion of Lebanon in April of 1996 or the October 1996 uprising in Palestine and his propensity to bomb and kill Iraqis; and as the news blackout on the presidential candidacy of Ralph Nader all indicate, the hyphen is still open.

Arabs- are portrayed as submissive to Islam, to religious fanaticism, to tribalism, to patriarchs and familism, to autocrats and dictatorships, to reliving history again and again—and therefore not free: not quite free, not quite white, not quite male, not quite individual persons, not quite citizens. I argue that this is a constructed notion of the Arab- that has little to do with Arabs, with the Middle East, with Muslims, or with

Arabs in America. As Gauri Viswanathan argued, I suggest that this idea of the not-free Arab- serves the United States nation. It is constitutive of the national identity, the will to nationhood. The nostalgia for an originary community, the urge for an overarching social unity is constructed by positing an internal sameness that systematically differs from the constructed sameness of the other, and the other for the post-communist bipolar world, I fear, may be emerging as the Arab, Middle Eastern, Muslim.

Notes

Acknowledgments: I would like to express my appreciation to Smadar Lavie, Ghada Masri, and Nadine Naber for challenging discussions related to this paper and to Michael Suleiman and Baha Abu-Laban, whose article provoked my thinking on the idea of the not-free construct. Michael W. Suleiman and Baha Abu-Laban, "Introduction." In Baha Abu-Laban and Michael W. Suleiman, eds., *Arab-Americans: Continuity and Change* (Belmont, MA: AAUG Press, 1989), pp. 1–13.

1. *Dow v. United States et al.*, No. 1345 (4th Cir. 1915).
2. *Dow v. United States et al.*
3. Sami Zubaida, *Islam, The People and the State. Essays on Political Ideas and Movements in the Middle East* (London: Routledge, 1989), p. 121.
4. Gauri Viswanathan, "Beyond Orientalism: Syncretism and the Politics of Knowledge," *Stanford Humanities Review* 5, no. 1 (1995): 24.
5. Viswanathan, "Beyond Orientalism," p. 31.
6. Viswanathan, "Beyond Orientalism," p. 24.
7. Viswanathan, "Beyond Orientalism," p. 22.
8. C. B. MacPhearson, *The Political Theory of Possessive Individualism* (London: Oxford University, 1962), p. 22.
9. Carole Pateman, *The Sexual Contract* (Stanford: Stanford University Press, 1988).
10. Pateman, *The Sexual Contract,* p. 55.
11. Pateman, *The Sexual Contract,* p. 52.
12. Jennifer Nedelsky, "Law, Boundaries, and the Bounded Self," *Representations* 30 (1990): 162–89.
13. Jennifer Nedelsky, "Reconceiving Rights as Relationship," *Review of Constitutional Studies* 1, no. 1 (1993): 13.
14. Nadine Naber, "Race, Religion, and Kitchen Resistance: Examining the Paradoxical Gendered Existence of Arab-American Women." Forthcoming in Lenora Forestell, ed., *Women in the Media* (submitted).
15. Mary Ramadan, "Anti-Arab Racism and Arab-American Response." Paper presented at Association of Arab-American University Graduates Convention (Anaheim, CA, October 1996).
16. Edward Said, *Orientalism* (New York: Pantheon Books, 1978). Orientalist scholarship and popular representations also masculinize the Arab, but a negative masculinity. These masculinized representations range from the sexually insatiable or perverted to the physically violent and warlike (terrorist).
17. Naber, "Race, Religion, and Kitchen Resistance," submitted.
18. Barber, Benjamin, *Jihad vs McWorld* (New York: Times Books, 1996).
19. Minh-ha Trinh, *Woman, Native, Other: Writing Postcoloniality and Feminism* (Bloomington: Indiana University Press, 1989).

20. J. Milton Cowan, ed., *Hans Wehr: A Dictionary of Modern Written Arabic* (Ithaca: Cornell University, 1966), p. 426.

21. Cowan, ed., *Hans Wehr,* p. 424.

22. John Esposito, *Islam: The Straight Path* (New York: Oxford University Press, 1988).

23. Leila Abu-Lughod, *Veiled Sentiments: Honor and Poetry in a Bedouin Society* (Berkeley: University of California Press, 1986).

24. Yehya Sadowski, "The New Orientalism and the Democracy Debate," *Middle East Reports* no. 183 (1993): 14.

25. Daniel Lerner, *The Passing of Traditional Society: Modernizing the Middle East* (New York: The Free Press, 1958).

26. Lerner, *The Passing of Traditional Society,* p. ix.

27. Sadowski, "New Orientalism," p. 14.

28. Sadowski, "New Orientalism," p. 15.

29. Sadowski, "New Orientalism," p. 16.

30. Sadowski, "New Orientalism," p. 19.

31. Suad Joseph, "Connectivity and Patriarchy Among Urban Working Class Arab Families in Lebanon," *Ethos* 4 (1993): 465–86.

32. Suad Joseph, "Problematizing Gender and Relational Rights: Experiences from Lebanon," *Social Politics* 1, no. 3 (1994): 271–85.

33. Juliette Minces, *The House of Obedience: Women in Arab Society* (London: Zed Press, 1982), p. 33.

34. Minces, *The House of Obedience,* p. 36.

35. Minces, *The House of Obedience,* p. 36.

36. Minces, *The House of Obedience,* p. 37.

37. Minces, *The House of Obedience,* p. 39.

38. Minces, *The House of Obedience,* p. 44.

39. Minces, *The House of Obedience,* p. 45.

40. For examples and critiques of such approaches, see L. Carl Brown and Norman Itzkowitz, eds., *Psychological Dimensions of Near Eastern Studies* (Princeton, NJ: Darwin Press, 1977); Raphael Patai, *The Arab Mind* (New York: Charles Scribner's Sons, 1973); Fouad Moughrabi, "The Arab Basic Personality: A Critical Survey of the Literature," *International Journal of Middle East Studies* 9 (1978): 99–112; Ernest Gellner, *Muslim Society* (Cambridge: Cambridge University Press, 1981); Hisham Sharabi, *Neopatriarchy: A Theory of Distorted Change in Arab Society* (New York: Oxford University Press, 1988); Dale Eickelman, *The Middle East: An Anthropological Approach* (Englewood Cliffs, NJ: Prentice-Hall, 1989).

41. Fouad Moughrabi, "A Political Technology of the Soul," *Arab Studies Quarterly* 3, no. 1 (1981): 68–89.

42. Robert Murphy, "Social Distance and the Veil," *American Anthropologist* 66 (1964): 1257–74.

43. For fuller accounts of Arab- activism and responses, see Abu-Laban and Suleiman, 1989; Janice Terry, "Political Activism on a Local Level—Detroit, MI," presented at Association of Arab-American University Graduates Convention (Anaheim, CA, October 1996); Kathleen Moore, "The Selective Enforcement of Law: *American-Arab Anti-Discrimination Committee vs. Reno* and the Future of U.S. Immigration," presented at Association of Arab-American University Graduates Convention (Anaheim, CA, October 1996)—both of these papers are included in this volume (chapters 5 and 15); Ernest McCarus, ed., *The Development of Arab-American Identity* (Ann Arbor: The University of Michigan Press, 1994); Sameer Abraham and Nabeel Abraham, eds., *Arabs in the New World: Studies on Arab-American Communities* (Detroit: Wayne State

University Center for Urban Studies, 1983): Barbara Aswad and Barbara Bilge, eds., *Family and Gender Among American Muslims* (Philadelphia: Temple University Press, 1996).

44. Abu-Laban and Suleiman, *Arab Americans,* p. 6.

45. Abu-Laban and Suleiman, *Arab Americans,* p. 6.

46. Helen Hatab Samhan, "Arab Americans and the Elections of 1988: A Constituency Come of Age." In Abu-Laban and Suleiman, eds., *Arab Americans,* pp. 227–50.

47. Samhan, "Arab Americans and the Elections of 1988," p. 229.

48. Samhan, "Arab Americans and the Elections of 1988," p. 229.

49. Samhan, "Arab Americans and the Elections of 1988," p. 233.

50. Samhan, "Arab Americans and the Elections of 1988," p. 233.

51. Samhan, "Arab Americans and the Elections of 1988," p. 245.

52. Cohler, Larry and Walter Ruby, "The New Arab American Activists," *Washington Jewish Week* (28 July 1988).

53. Samhan, "Arab Americans and the Elections of 1988," p. 245.

54. News briefing, NBC, Feb. 27, 1991.

55. *Time* (29 April 1991), p. 5.

56. *The New York Times* (1 February 1991): A15.

57. *The Sacramento Bee* (24 January 1991): A9.

58. Moore, "Selective Enforcement of Law"; Abdeen Jabara, "Arabs and Arab-Americans under Threat: The Anti-Terrorism Law." Paper presented at the Association of Arab-American University Graduates Convention (Anaheim, CA, October 1996); Simon Mikhael, "U.S. Immigration Laws and Arab Americans." Paper presented at the Association of Arab-American University Graduates Convention (Anaheim, CA, October 1996).

Lori Anne Salem

17   Far-Off and Fascinating Things: Wadeeha Atiyeh and Images of Arabs in the American Popular Theater, 1930–1950

Wadeeha Atiyeh was an Arab-American singer, dancer, and storyteller who performed in the United States in the 1930s, 1940s, and 1950s. Atiyeh's career offers an interesting glimpse into the complexities of Arab images in American entertainment, although even at the height of her career, she was never more than a minor celebrity. Most of her performances were given in the humblest of venues, and she would probably be entirely unknown today if her extensive scrapbooks, files, and stories had not been donated to the public archives at the Balch Institute for Ethnic Studies in Philadelphia.[1] However, Atiyeh's career provides us an opportunity to study the sorts of images of Arabs that appeared in the American popular theater and to describe how her performances fit in that history.

My analysis draws on the theories associated with cultural studies and on recent cultural studies research in American theater history. The central premise of this work is that the meaning of a theatrical act is not inherent in the act itself but is constructed by the performers, audiences, critics, and publicists according to the beliefs and desires that spring from their social identities—their race, class, and gender—as well as from idiosyncratic personal experiences. I have tried to uncover the choices that Atiyeh made as a performer and the concerns of her audiences. This socially situated analysis offers insights about Atiyeh and her audiences, and it challenges our way of thinking about images of Arabs in American entertainment.[2]

For some time, Arab-American scholars have argued that American entertainment in its various forms stereotypes Arabs by casting them into narrowly defined and usually "negative" images. The argument that this scholarship ultimately develops is that these negative images insinuate themselves into the American consciousness and that this process inevitably has political consequences. As an antidote to stereotyping, some writers assert that Arabs should have a say in how Arabs are depicted.[3] However, Atiyeh's career, particularly when it is considered against the history of Arab acts in the American theater, challenges each of these points. Does American entertainment cast Arabs in negative roles? Do American audiences read these images in the same way that Arab-American scholars suppose they do? What effects do these images have on broader political questions? Are Arab images different when Arabs create them?

Arab Acts in the American Theater Before 1930

From the early 19th century, Americans surrounded themselves with images of Arabs and Arab culture. These images appeared in commercial art, songs, literature, and the popular theater. Although theater acts were the most transitory of these, they also had a unique meaning because they were embodied; the presentation of an Arab body in the same physical space as the viewer gave theater acts a sort of implied "in the flesh" authenticity. More than art, songs, and literature, the theater acts were read as true depictions of Arabs, because the viewer does not doubt what is right before his eyes. In many cases, this authenticity was an illusion, because most of the Arab acts that appeared in the United States were performed by Americans costumed as Arabs, and most had only the most tenuous connections to Arab theater or culture.

Among the more well-known depictions of Arabs on the American stage were performances of Arab-themed plays and operas, such as Cleopatra, Ali Baba and the Forty Thieves, Salome, and Aladdin, which appeared in full-production theaters. Arabs also appeared in "educational" performances that were supposed to be scientifically accurate portrayals of Arab culture. The best known of these were the elaborate "living village" exhibits at the 1893 Chicago World's Fair, but there were many similar exhibits on a smaller scale. The most common performances were by the Arabian acrobats, tumblers, dervishes, "contortion" dancers, giants, and sword swallowers who appeared in curiosity shows, dime museums, circuses, variety theaters, and other venues for popular entertainment.[4]

How did American audiences make sense of these performances? In "The Grotesque Body and Its Sources," Mikhail Bakhtin argues that bodies in public forums, as in the theater, are infused with elaborate and usually inexplicit somatic metaphors that derive from cultural values.[5] For example, he found that the Western ideology of individualism translated to a valorization of bodies with discrete boundaries, bodies whose surfaces are smooth and unbroken and whose orifices are closed or masked. He suggests that what we find disgusting and shameful about images of pregnancy, eating, vomiting, obesity, and sexual intercourse is that they show a body whose boundaries are permeable. Bakhtin's central claim is that because bodies bear this metaphorical meaning they are like voices that "speak" about their bearers' social position and identity. Just as having a public voice is a matter of power and position, the question of how and whether a body appears in public space is profoundly political.

Because Arab acts were created by and for Americans, the bodies were not speaking about Arab concerns but rather about what Americans believed or wanted to be true of Arabs. The question is what the American theater was "saying" somatically about Arabs in these performances. One of the defining characteristics of these Arab acts was their physical difference. Consider, for example, the Arabian giants whose performance was nothing more or less than the display of their abnormally shaped bodies. Performances by Arabian sword swallowers, tumblers, and contortion dancers also offered the specter of distortion: bodies bent out of shape, curled, swollen, and twisted into moving masses that denied the normal human form. In short, they created a physical metaphor for racial difference. Moreover, because difference and distortion are essentially comparative terms, these acts not only constructed Arabs as abnormal other, but also the American audience as normal. They positioned the American audience as the subject and "self" and Arabs as the objectified "other."

That Americans read these metaphors into Arab performances is evidenced by their reaction to "educational" performances, such as the one described in an 1880 review of O. W. Pond's Troupe of Arabs. According to the review, the troupe performed scenes that depicted the manners and customs of Arabs, including Arabs' way of greeting, bargaining, eating, marrying, praying, dancing, and punishing crime. Each of these scenes transformed everyday activities into subtly painful distortions. The greeting scene, for example, showed two men repeatedly knocking their foreheads together, and the eating scene showed the Arabs rolling dough into huge wads that they stuffed forcefully into each others' mouths. In the end, even the humor of the scenes did not, for the audience, undermine their essential veracity; the reviewer wrote ". . . that they are really genuine Arabs and that they portray truthfully the remarkable customs of their country, there seems no reason to doubt."[6]

Even more than physical distortion, the Arab acts that appeared on American stages were marked by overt expressions of excessive and deviant sexuality. This is evident, for example, in the darkly sensuous depictions of Cleopatra, in the cooch dance performances at the Chicago World's Fair, and even in the pliability of the Arab women tumblers and contortion dancers. Because sexual self-control was one of the hallmarks of American Victorianism, these lascivious Arab bodies in performance were another way of setting the American self apart from and above the Arab Other.

That Arabs were different and inferior, however, was only part of what these sexualized performances had to say. Consider, for example, the phenomenal popularity of performances by so-called Circassian Slaves. In the American theater, Circassian Slaves were supposed to be white women who had been captured and sold into sexual slavery in Arab harems. Originally, their theatrical acts consisted of telling elaborately detailed stories about the sexual depravities they had witnessed in the harem, but they later began appearing as "waiter girls" in turn-of-the-century concert saloons. In the saloons, the scantily clad Circassian waitresses circulated among the customers, serving drinks and flirting. According to entertainment reviews, patrons were more attentive to these waitresses than they were to the stage show.[7]

The fact that the concert saloons had names such as The Sultan's Divan and The Egyptian Gardens provides the most telling clue to the meaning that these Circassian performances had for American audiences. As these names suggest, the saloons were posing as harems where American men could find themselves surrounded by sensual pleasure. For the time he was in the saloon, an American man was the harem master: beautiful, accommodating "slaves" pleased him with drinks and conversation, and their availability to his gaze was symbolic of the harem concubines' sexual availability.

At the Sultan's Divan, surrounded by Circassian Slaves, American men could play the part of the sensuous Arab man, experiencing the exotic and forbidden Arab sexuality. For a moment, he could become the Other.[8]

This desire to transgress racial boundaries is, according to Peter Stallybrass and Allon White, an inevitable result of self-other dichotomies. What is forbidden and reviled, they argue, is appealing, and this appeal creates a will to be near the Other or even to experience being the Other. This was the central, contradictory message of Arab images in American entertainment. Although they used distortion and excessive sexuality to depict Arabs as Other, they also revealed that this Other was intensely appealing. They gave Americans the opportunity to try on forbidden roles and behaviors, and because these racial transgressions were theatrical, they were temporary and safe. The man who "became" an Arab sultan in the concert saloon could shift back to his privileged American identity simply by leaving the theater.[9]

Beyond their hidden appeal, the excessive sexuality of these theater acts also conferred on Arabs a subtle symbolic power. In *The History of Sexuality,* Foucault observes that sexuality is always a site of physical pleasure (and punishment) and the means of growing and reproducing populations.[10] He argues that, when the Victorian middle classes distanced themselves from sexual pleasure and relegated it to racial Others, such as Arabs, they also unwittingly ceded the power of reproduction. In other words, even as the excessive sexuality of the Arab theater acts set Arabs apart as the repulsive-fascinating Other, it also constructed Arabs as a threateningly potent force. With an insatiable sexual appetite, the acts seem to say that the Arab population would inevitably swell and expand into an uncontrollable mass power.

The fact that these Arab performances were enmeshed in ideas about sexuality and power meant that American women and men responded differently to them. Victorian beliefs imposed a sexual double standard on American men and women. Women, positioned as the guardians of purity, were required to uphold a strict moral code, but men were permitted greater sexual license. This double standard was mirrored in separate theatrical codes: entertainment intended for mixed audiences minimized sexual display, but entertainment for men might be quite risqué. It is no accident, for example, that the Circassian Slave performances appeared in concert saloons, which catered to exclusively male audiences. Nor is it surprising that the most vocal critics of Arab acts in the American theater were women.

Concert saloons were favorite targets of women's reform groups, as were the lascivious cooch dancing performances at the World's Fair and performances of Salome's "Dance of the Seven Veils." Women saw the presence of such illicit sexuality—even when it was attributed to the racial Other—as a threat to American morality. Theatrical reformer Marie Cahill captured the central argument of these women's reformers—that immorality is contagious—in this essay arguing for a ban on Salome performances: "Is it not, therefore, the duty of the true citizen to protect the young from the contamination of such theatrical offerings as clothe pernicious subjects of the Salome kind in a boasted artistic atmosphere, but which are really an excuse for the most vulgar exhibition this country has ever been called on to tolerate?"[11]

In the years before Wadeeha Atiyeh began performing, images of Arabs in the American theater offered a complex message for American audiences. They presented physically distorted and sexualized representations of Arabs that spoke of racial difference and inferiority. At the same time, these images offered audiences the opportunity to witness or even experience an exotic sexuality that was forbidden to them.

Atiyeh's Early Career

When Wadeeha Atiyeh began performing as a classical singer in the 1930s, her act had little in common with the earlier Arab performances. Her debut performances took place in small but reputable recital halls, and her repertoire was composed almost entirely of American and European concert songs. Her presentation completely conformed with the simple, unembellished format of the classical vocal recital; she included no narratives, scenes, or props that might have distracted from her vocal technique. In this way, she marked her act not as an "ethnic" or "folk" performance, which had a relatively low status, but as "art." Critics typically commented more on the richness and virtuosity of her mezzo-soprano and her confident stage presence than on her Arab heritage. If they mentioned her ethnicity at all, it was often to indicate that being an Arab did not interfere with her English diction, which they described as "faultless."[12]

Atiyeh did, however, draw attention to her ethnicity in several ways. Although she married an American man, she continued to perform under her Arabic patronym. She also included in her repertoire five "Old Arabic Songs," including a love song, a death chant, a wedding song, a dance song, and the Call to Prayer. These were presented as a set and given at the end of the program. A short intermission before the set allowed Atiyeh to change into a "traditional" Arab costume, which was usually an elegant, modest, red and gold draped gown.

Moreover, Atiyeh's publicity made occasional appeals to an Orientalist sensibility. She titled her recital "The Spirit of the Mysterious East," and her brochures and program notes offered a smattering of the same somatic metaphors, such as "pliancy," that had infused earlier Orientalist entertainment: "In her voice lies all of the mystery of the ageless East. . . . Her dusky eyes . . . her hands . . . her pliant figure . . . all know the Arab's subtle art of song and storytelling. The haunting beauty of her singing is like the odor of lemon trees in Mount Lebanon, or the desert at the hour of sunset."[13]

In her early incarnation as a performer, Atiyeh courted an American audience by presenting herself as an artist. Her publicity and performance occasionally deployed Orientalist images, and she even made subtle gestures toward the sexualized body that had characterized earlier Arab theater acts; however, she avoided overt distortions and sexual displays and instead encased herself in the refined, highbrow style of the vocal recital. The Arab elements in Atiyeh's performances probably read as nothing more than the singer's attempt to distinguish herself from the swath of other aspiring concert singers. It was not unusual for musicians to append their repertoire with one or two unusual songs that showed dramatic and technical range. Although these recitals never propelled her to stardom, Atiyeh did earn a few positive reviews in major periodicals such as the *Chicago Herald Examiner* and the *Los Angeles Times*.[14]

The Modern Scheherazade

After World War II, during which her career, like those of many other performing artists, was largely suspended, Atiyeh steered her performances in a dramatically different direction. She abandoned the vocal recital, and she replaced it with a series of dramatic scenes of Arab life. Her new work combined singing, dancing, storytelling, and pantomime, and she invested it with elaborate costumes and props. At the same time, she left her previous manager and signed on with Columbia Concerts Lecture Bureau, a theatrical management firm that represented a more diverse array of performing artists. Columbia promoted her as an "entertainer," rather than as a "singer" or "actress," and dubbed her "The Modern Scheherazade."[15]

Atiyeh's new program opened with an elaborately acted and costumed version of the Call to Prayer, with Atiyeh playing the role of the muezzin. This was followed by a suite of four stories from the Tales of Arabian Nights, with Atiyeh acting the role of Scheherazade and then a number of secondary characters. The rest of the program consisted of character studies. "The Blind Woman," for example, told the story of a bitter old beggar-woman who found hope and love when a small boy (possibly Jesus) wept for her. A piece titled "The Silk Peddler" depicted a "characteristic" Arab merchant as a "philosopher, fool, rogue, and saint," who was filled with laughter and song. "The Baker's Wife" told the story of a baker who ogled his beautiful customers but decided to remain true to his (equally faithful) wife. Atiyeh also included two stories from her childhood experiences in Lebanon. One told of a time when a kindly neighbor chided her for stealing grapes. The other depicted an Arab proverb that says "A young man in love is like a donkey; he knows not which way to turn until he is prodded."[16]

This program was organized around a subtle metanarrative that positioned Atiyeh in a liminal space between the Arab world and her American audience. The Call to Prayer functioned as a symbolic point of entry, inviting the audience into a mosque or, metaphorically, into the private and intimate space of Arab life. By next enacting the frame story of the Tales of Arabian Nights, Atiyeh established her role in relation to the audience as well as to the Arab world. Like Scheherazade, she was the entertainer, but she was also the mediator and translator. She was, as she called herself, a "bridge between the two civilizations," and through her, American audiences could experience the Arab world. Ruth St. Denis, a prominent figure in the American theater, wrote an endorsement of Atiyeh's performance that perfectly captured Atiyeh's "in-between" stance: "As a true ambassador comes this vivid personality, Wadeeha Atiyeh, who combines within her the haunting native richness and deep elemental folkways of the true Orient, with the modern understanding and presentations of the West. Her programs bring to every audience a breath of far-off and fascinating things."[17]

In the rest of the program, the stories Atiyeh chose to tell and the characters she chose to portray coalesce around a few interconnected themes. Each of her narratives proffered a comforting, uplifting message about the triumph of goodness. Scheherazade saves the kingdom, the husband survives temptation, the blind woman sees the light; in each case, the goodness inside the protagonists is revealed unambiguously and rewarded richly. In her publicity, Atiyeh implied that Arabs were good in this way because they were of the Holy Land. As for herself, Atiyeh made frequent mention of the fact that her name, translated, meant "Lamb of Heaven."[18]

When Atiyeh's characters did commit transgressions, as with the young girl who stole grapes and the husband whose eyes strayed, they were redeemed by the intercession and guidance of neighbors, family, and friends. The second characteristic of Atiyeh's Arab world was a foregrounding of tightly woven social relationships based on caring and helpfulness. The blind woman, for example, was the only one of Atiyeh's protagonists not integrated into a family, and her bitter unhappiness about her isolation was the central conflict of the story. The story resolved when she recognized that a stranger cared about her, suggesting that even those who think they are abandoned are actually loved, if they could only "see" it.

One of the best stories that Atiyeh told about the cohesiveness of the Arab community was about her own journey to the United States. According to the story, Atiyeh was seven when she traveled from Lebanon to the United States, where her father was already living. For the journey, she was entrusted to the care of a Greek couple, who promised to bring her safely to New York. However, when Atiyeh and her guardians got as far as Marseilles, the evil Greek couple tricked her and abandoned her in a hotel room. Luckily, the hotel proprietor was a good and moral man, and he took Atiyeh in. He made great efforts to find her family, but all in vain until, in desperation, he wrote a letter and mailed it to "Any Syrian in New York." The letter made it to the Arab-American community, whereupon it was immediately delivered to Atiyeh's father. When poor Atiyeh finally arrived in New York, she was welcomed by a throng of Arabs who were moved by the story of her rescue.[19]

Atiyeh's narratives recreated the Orientalist image of the Arab world as old and unchanging. Atiyeh's press releases and brochures repeatedly announced that her ancestors, a "warrior tribe," had been living on Mount Lebanon and practicing their "old folkways" since A.D. 500. Her press release continued, "Born into a country where change is slow, where the spirit of ancient days still hovers, [Atiyeh] has absorbed the rich heritage of an ancient and powerful race . . . the Arab. Sensitive, with a mind and heart attuned to the old philosophies, the old ways and thoughts, she searched and found the deep inner truths that have guided and strengthened her people for so long."[20]

One of the "old ways" that Atiyeh inherited, according to this account, was storytelling. In her publicity, Atiyeh implicitly credits storytelling with the cohesiveness of the Arab community. Stories are not written but are instead passed along from person to person and from generation to generation; they are Arabs' links to each other and to a shared past. Arabs, according to Atiyeh, are inherently emotional, and storytelling and poetry are natural forms of communication for them, especially because the Arabic language is so rich. She wrote, "[For an Arab] it is impossible to tell some news or describe even the smallest detail without putting one's heart and soul into it—almost a blending of speech, song and pantomime. . . . old people, young people, camel drivers, mountaineers all sing their thoughts, their feelings, their everyday life, making up the poetry as they go along."[21]

Atiyeh's performances, in form and content, constructed the Arab world as a sort of pre-modern fantasy village. The people in her world were emotional and creative, and they were connected by strong social ties and a common moral order. Implicit in this was a romantic critique of modern American society, whose modernization and technology dissolved social cohesion. She wrote, "Today, the world is so modernized and mechanized that it is too vast, too complex, too impersonal. Speed! Progress! Change! Hurry! have become the watchwords." Through her performances and especially through her publicity writings, Atiyeh situated herself in the role of savior. The ancient arts, such as storytelling, were in danger of being forgotten. To revive them, Atiyeh suggested, would be to restore modern America to the fantasy Arab village, which was its "true" past self. "Today more than ever," she concluded, "people are reaching out to recapture the beauty and peace that has always had a special place in the hearts of men. So ... I hope above all things that in their humble way, these stories will spread good will and understanding between the East and the West."[22]

Far-Off and Fascinating Things

Atiyeh performed this new program before a variety of American audiences, who responded warmly to it. However, the most enthusiastic supporters turned out to be middle-class American women. In their reviews and letters, women described the stories as "enchanting" and the performer as "lovely," "touching," and "sincere." By the late 1940s, Atiyeh was filling her schedule with performances at luncheons, benefits, and fashion shows organized by women's groups such as Junior Leagues, garden clubs, and homemaker's associations.

It is ironic, given that middle-class American women of an earlier generation were the most vocal critics of Arab theater acts, that women should turn out to be Atiyeh's core audience. However, their response makes a certain sense when it is considered against the redefinition of women's roles in post-World War II America. After the war, women were pressured out of the manufacturing jobs that they had taken to help the war effort. At the same time, the GI Bills were making possible the development of suburban housing tracts, and middle-class adult women found themselves out of the work force and in the home, where they were expected to conform to an ideology that glorified the "domestic arts" such as cooking and cleaning. Social clubs afforded women a much needed public space to meet others and to enact a social identity. However, because these groups were typically organized around "women's activities" such as cooking, gardening, and fashion, they more often solidified rather than challenged domesticity.

The glue that held this domestic role together, according to historian Brett Harvey, was insecurity. Although women navigated a barrage of powerful media messages about what it meant to be a woman—how clean and lovely her house was, how nurturing she must be—they also internalized unspoken messages about the penalty for noncompliance, which was to be alone and left out. A woman who was not sufficiently domestic could look forward to becoming a spinster, a lonely misfit among married friends and family. However, many middle-class women, even those happily married, were alone much of the time. While their husbands worked and their children immersed themselves in a burgeoning youth culture, adult women found themselves contained in their suburban houses, separated from friends and extended family, keeping company with the telephone, the household appliances, and eventually, the television. As Harvey points out, for this generation of women, having experienced first the depression and then the war, the move to suburban domesticity was only one in a series of dramatic changes in their lives. It was little wonder that the fear of being alone and being left behind had such potent force.[23]

For these women, Atiyeh's stories were about remaking American society in a more emotional, creative, and nurturing mold—about feminizing it. At one level, American women heard Atiyeh's performance as a validation of their gendered role. At another level, audiences found in Atiyeh's performance an acknowledgment of their isolation. When Atiyeh worried aloud that the ancient art of storytelling was in danger of being lost, she voiced women's fear that close connections to family and friends were growing more difficult to sustain. When Atiyeh positioned herself as the savior of ancient arts, women had the comfort of knowing that the problem was being handled. When Atiyeh sang and told stories, women were "transported" to that fantasy Arab world, escaping momentarily from isolation of modern American domesticity.

Nothing But a Dry Desert

For all its romanticism, Atiyeh's presentation of the Arab world as old and unchanging should have been problematic for Arabs. It was a cornerstone of the Orientalist philosophy that had facilitated European colonialism. Nevertheless, Arab Americans applauded Atiyeh's performances. She earned favorable reviews in Arab-American newspapers, and she was publicly endorsed by Philip Hitti and Habib Katibah, both respected Arab-American scholars. Katibah called her a "true reviver of her people's folk-art"; Hitti vouched for the authenticity of her interpretations and said that gave audiences "rare glimpses of the romantic Arab East." The Reverend Antony Bashir, leader of a Syrian diocese, said, "Without artists like Miss Atiyeh, the world would be nothing but a dry desert." Bashir's expression is hackneyed, but it was suggestive of a broader issue in Arab Americans' reading of Atiyeh's work.[24]

There are several reasons why Arab Americans may have embraced Atiyeh's performances, in spite of their appeals to Orientalism. It may be that they saw Atiyeh's popularity with American women as evidence that she was defeating Arab Otherness and that after a century of Circassian Slaves, sword swallowers, and cooch dancers, she was taking a step in the right direction. It may be that the implicit social conservatism of Atiyeh's message was congruent with their beliefs, or Arab Americans might have embraced the performances simply because Americans did and they were proud to have one of their own deemed successful by the dominant culture.

The reason that Arab Americans were attracted to Atiyeh's performances might have been that, like middle-class American women, they were attracted to the fantasy that she was presenting. One of the biggest concerns that Arab-American communities faced at mid-century was that their assimilation was too successful. Alixa Naff suggests that even those immigrants who lived in established Arab-American communities worried about the rapid encroachment of modern American values and the dissolution of Arab cultural practices. Atiyeh's Arabia served as a nostalgic reminder of all that was best about life in the Arab world, even for those who recognized its sugary unrealism. Philip Hitti, for example, wrote about Syrian village life in far less starry-eyed terms, but he spoke of the authenticity of Atiyeh's vision.[25]

Clinging to an unrealistically rosy image of the Arab world might have been something of a defense against the pressure of carving out a new life in the United States, where failure meant living in a sort of "dry desert" in a harsh, unforgiving environment among strangers. This fate, it turns out, was not so far-fetched, for it overtook Atiyeh herself. In two short autobiographical stories, Atiyeh tells how after a successful, twenty-year performing career, she found herself utterly alone. Her husband, an American singer with whom she had collaborated in her performances, died, and she was left to find a place to live on her own. She landed in a small, ugly apartment in a dangerous section of New York City, where her interactions with her neighbors seemed to be confined to smelling their dinner cooking and occasionally waving from the fire escape.[26]

This was a bitterly ironic turn for the woman who built her career on the fantasy of an idyllic tightly woven society, but it was also indicative of a simple truth: immigrants had no guarantee of finding a place in American society. For Arab Americans, it must have seemed better to romanticize the Arab world and even to capitulate in part to Orientalist notions of Arab backwardness than to live without at least a fantasy of a safe and stable life elsewhere.

Conclusions

Although they seem quite different, Atiyeh's performances and the earlier Arab theater acts were similar in function. Both sets of images served as a loose fabric into which audiences wove multiple and sometimes contradictory meanings. Both served as a ground for defining and managing contradictions and tensions in audiences' social positions. The earlier Arabs and Atiyeh's performances symbolically situated Arabs and Americans in a complicated relationship, in which the boundary between self and other was alternately blurred and reasserted. Given this persistent complexity, the notion of stereotyping—of stamping out flat, identical pictures—does not seem quite apt. It is true that themes and types, such as lusty Arab men, emerge repeatedly in these performances, but this in itself does not explain the role that these images had. What gave them their power and importance was the meaning that audiences invested in them.

Did Atiyeh, as an Arab American, create images that were somehow better than those produced by Americans? Her performances were more overtly sympathetic toward Arabs than the earlier Arab theater acts; they bathe the Arab world in the cozy warm glow of hearth and home. However, in the process, they wind up reifying the Orientalist notion that Arabs are backward. More importantly, in their urge to present an appealing picture of the Arab world, Atiyeh's performances denied its historical reality. At the height of Atiyeh's career in 1948, the Arab world was being shattered in what would become the defining conflict of the region.

This last point raises the difficult question about the relationship between popular entertainment and politics, or between symbolic power and material power. The research on Arab stereotypes in American entertainment assumes some sort of causal relationship between these images of Arabs and American foreign or public policy. For example, some assume that negative images of Arabs cause or facilitate political domination or that negative images of Arabs are caused by or reflect American racism. However, the history of Arab images in the American theater does not bear out the assumption. During the nineteenth and early twentieth centuries, when images of Arabs were at their most titillating and threatening, Americans had little political or material presence in the Arab world, nor were there sufficient numbers of Arab immigrants to warrant a full-scale propaganda campaign (as were launched against Irish and Chinese immigrants). By mid-century, when the United States did become a political player in the Middle East, the Circassians, sword swallowers, giants, and cooch dancers were a distant memory, and American women were embracing Atiyeh's romantic vision of Arab village life. There is no clear correspondence between image and policy. This is not to say that these political events and entertainment images were completely unrelated, only that the relationship between the two is slippery and complicated.

More to the point, the nature of entertainment imagery militates against any simple correspondence between entertainment and politics. Arab images, especially the embodied images of the theater, are not simply marked for race, but also for gender and class, and these registers, when refracted off the race, gender, and class of the audience, produce multiple and often contradictory meanings. Because Americans themselves are also situated in their own struggles for power and place and because they read these struggles into theatrical imagery, the meaning of Arab acts becomes flexible and situated. In short, we cannot say that Americans have a stereotypical notion of the Arab Other, because it is not always clear who is the empowered self at any moment.

Notes

1. All of Wadeeha Atiyeh's stories, programs, and clippings cited in this chapter are housed at the Balch Institute for Ethnic Studies in Philadelphia.

2. Three good examples of this literature are Eric Lott, *Love and Theft: Blackface Minstrelsy and the American Working Class* (New York: Oxford, 1993); Robert C. Allen, *Horrible Prettiness: Burlesque and American Culture* (Chapel Hill: University of North Carolina Press, 1991); and Karen Halttunen, *Confidence Men and Painted Women* (New Haven, CT: Yale University Press, 1982).

3. Jack Shaheen, *The T.V. Arab* (Ohio: Bowling Green State University Press, 1984); "The Arab Image in American Film and Television," a supplement appearing in *Cineaste* 17, no. 1 (1989); see also Sari J. Nasir, "The Image of the Arab in American Popular Culture" (Ph.D. dissertation, University of Illinois, 1962).

4. Lori Anne Salem, "The Most Indecent Thing Imaginable: The Image of Arabs in American Entertainment, 1885–1990" (Ed.D. dissertation, Temple University, 1995).

5. Mikhail Bakhtin, "The Grotesque Image of the Body and Its Sources," In *Rabelais and His World*. Translated by Helene Iswolsky (Bloomington: University of Indiana Press, 1984), pp. 303–67.

6. "Odd Sights in Brooklyn," *New York Times* (11 December 1880): 7.

7. Salem, "Most Indecent Thing Imaginable," pp. 93–99.

8. Salem, "Most Indecent Thing Imaginable," pp. 93–99.

9. Peter Stallybrass and Allon White, *The Politics and Poetics of Transgression* (Ithaca: Cornell University Press, 1986), p. 193.

10. Michel Foucault, *The History of Sexuality*, vol. 1: An Introduction. Translated by Robert Hurley (New York: Vintage Books, 1980), p. 145. Edward Said makes essentially the same point in *Orientalism* (NY: Random House, 1979), pp. 311–12.

11. "The Salome Dance Gets into Politics," *New York Times* (24 August 1908): 2.

12. "Wadeeha Atiyeh's Recital: Press Comments," publicity brochure, The Balch Collection.

13. "Spirit of the East," *Chicago Daily News* 30 (October 1932), n.p.; "Wadeeha Atiyeh," concert program, The Balch Collection.

14. "Wadeeha Atiyeh's Recital: Press Comments."

15. "Wadeeha Atiyeh: The Modern Scheherazade," concert program, n.d.

16. "Wadeeha Atiyeh: The Modern Scheherazade," and "Wadeeha Atiyeh," Columbia Concerts concert program, n.d.

17. "Wadeeha Atiyeh: The Modern Scheherazade."

18. "Wadeeha Atiyeh," unpublished notes for publicity brochures and introductory speeches.

19. "Wadeeha Atiyeh," press release, n.d.

20. "Wadeeha Atiyeh," Columbia Concerts concert program; "Wadeeha Atiyeh," unpublished notes for publicity brochures and introductory speeches.

21. "Wadeeha Atiyeh," press release, n.d.

22. "Wadeeha Atiyeh," press release, n.d., and "Wadeeha Atiyeh, Striking Arabian Dramatic Soprano."

23. Brett Harvey, "Introduction," in *The Fifties: A Women's Oral History* (New York: Harper Collins, 1993), pp. xi–xxi.

24. "Wadeeha Atiyeh: Singer-Dramatist," concert program, n.d.

25. Alixa Naff, *Becoming American: The Early Arab Immigrant Experience* (Carbondale: Southern Illinois University Press, 1985), pp. 267–93; Philip Hitti, *The Syrians in America* (New York: George Doran, 1924), pp. 19–61.

26. Wadeeha Atiyeh, "A Peach Tree in Times Square," unpublished manuscript, n.d.; Wadeeha Atiyeh, "I Live in Hell's Kitchen," unpublished manuscript, n.d.

Ibrahim Hayani

---

18 Arabs in Canada: Assimilation or Integration?

The Arab community in Canada is one of the least studied ethnic groups, despite the fact that over the past three decades Arabs have been immigrating to Canada in ever greater numbers. For the 1960s, 1970s, and 1980s, respectively, 27,042, 36,506, and 61,893 immigrants from different countries in the Arab world came to Canada. In the first eight years of the 1990s alone, the number of these immigrants almost exceeded the total for the whole previous two decades. There are now about 375,000 Canadians of Arab origin, accounting for 1.3 percent of Canada's total population.

With the exception of the work of Baha Abu-Laban,[1] hardly any research has been done on Arab Canadians. This omission may be explained in part by the relatively small size of this population in Canada. There is also the distinct possibility that Arabs have been ignored because they are perceived to be "too different," "too problematic," or just plain "alien." Canadians tend to associate Arabs with images they derive from the media, and these have been largely negative. In the minds of many, "Arab" and "Muslim" have become associated with violence, brutality, terrorism, and fanaticism.[2] Where these images have prevailed—in schools, government services, the media, the work place, and the political sphere—Arab Canadians have paid dearly.[3]

This chapter attempts to fill some of the gaps in knowledge about Arab Canadians. It looks at group processes associated with Arab immigration to Canada and at individual factors surrounding assimilation and integration into Canadian society.

Part 1: Arab Immigration to Canada

Arab immigration to Canada began in 1882, with the arrival to Montreal of reportedly the first Arab, Abraham Bounadere, a native of Zahleh in present-day Lebanon.[4] At that time, only the very adventurous few, mostly Lebanese and Syrian Christians, left home and kin to seek their fortune in distant lands. Most went to the United States, but a few made it to Canada. At the turn of the twentieth century, the number of Arab immigrants in Canada had reached 2,000. By 1951, Arab Canadians numbered slightly more than 12,000.

The immigration patterns of these early years illustrate the factors that determine the rate at which immigrants, Arabs and others, came to Canada. In the nineteenth and early twentieth centuries, the salient view among most English Canadians was that the values and way of life of the white race were superior to all others, especially as these manifested themselves in British institutions. Preference was therefore given to British and American immigrants, followed by immigrants from western and northern Europe and then by those from the rest of Europe. Asians and blacks were the least preferred of all immigrants and were allowed in only when there was a demonstrated need for their labor.[5]

Concerns about "ethnic purity" and the need to protect Canadians from the "grave consequences" of having more Orientals come to Canada had a serious effect on immigration from the Arab world. In 1919, the Reverend James S. Woodworth stated that "The Oriental [Chinese, Japanese, and East Indians (Hindus)] cannot be assimilated."[6] He also asserted that the "Levantine Races [Syrians, Lebanese, Armenians, Greeks, Turks, and Persians—probably Assyrian Christians] . . . constitute one of the least desirable classes of our immigrants."[7]

During the first half of the twentieth century, restrictive immigration legislative measures, the economic depression of the 1930s, and the two world wars took their toll on immigration from the Arab world. An inspection of Table 18-1 shows that 5,597 Arab immigrants (largely Syrian and Lebanese) entered Canada in the first decade of the twentieth century, but throughout all the next forty years, no more than 3,085 Arab immigrants came to Canada. The growth of the Arabic-speaking population in Canada between 1914 and the end of World War II was for the most part because of natural growth, not immigration.

It was only in the second half of the twentieth century that discriminatory restrictions on immigration began to ease. World War II and Canada's entry into the United Nations in 1945 forced Canadians to reexamine their view of immigrants. After that, it was only a matter of time before artificial barriers to immigration came down— although old attitudes and beliefs persisted and have occasionally resurfaced since then.

Canada's Immigration Act of 1953 repealed many of the previous discriminatory measures. Prospective immigrants from certain Middle Eastern countries came to be classed with Europeans rather than Asians and were subject to more liberal rules of sponsorship by relatives who were Canadian residents. It also became possible for visitors to Canada to apply for landed immigrant status.

In 1967, the Immigration Act was further amended to abolish all discrimination based on national origin. This act established three categories of applicants:

1. Sponsored applicants who were essentially dependents or close relatives of Canadian residents
2. Independent applicants who were to be assessed on a point system based on such objective criteria as language skills (English and/or French), education, training, and age
3. Refugees who are admitted on the basis of humanitarian grounds, usually to facilitate escape from political persecution or violence.

TABLE 18-1. Arab Immigration to Canada, 1882–1997

Period	Number
1882–1889	2,000
1900–1909	5,597
1910–1919	919
1920–1929	1,041
1930–1939	933
1940–1949	192
1950–1959	3,374
1960–1969	36,569
1970–1979	64,147
1980–1989	75,899
1990–1997	133,489
Total	324,160

From Statistics Canada, The Census, and from Citizenship and Immigration Canada, Citizenship and Immigration Studies.

Except for some minor changes, Canada's Immigration Act has maintained the same fundamental objectives: to reunite families, protect refugees, and promote Canadian economic development.

The Post–World War II Period

With each change in the immigration laws and regulations, it became easier for Arabs to immigrate to Canada. The post-World War II period witnessed a dramatic increase in the number of Arab immigrants (Table 18-2). A period of social tranquility and economic prosperity in Canada, coupled with unfavorable conditions in their home countries, made Canada a choice destination for many Arab immigrants.

Canadian Egyptians are an example of how "push factors" determine the origin, religion, and socioeconomic profile of Arabs who immigrate to Canada. Starting in the mid-1950s, there was a significant upsurge in the number of Arab immigrants from Egypt. Until 1954, their numbers in Canada were relatively insignificant, but within a period of less than twenty years (1956 to 1974), more than 17,000 Arab immigrants who came to Canada gave Egypt as their country of origin. Today, Egyptians are second only to the Lebanese in making up the Arab-Canadian population.

The Egyptian immigrants of the late 1950s and the 1960s were largely Copts and middle-class Muslims who were disaffected with the socialist transformation of their country under President Gamal Abdel-Nasser. Concerned about religious and economic freedom, they left their country in search of better living conditions elsewhere. The same was true for immigrants from other Arab countries. The precarious balance that had kept in check volatile and explosive religious forces in Lebanon came apart with horrendous consequences for the Lebanese people in the mid-1970s. Tens of thousands of Lebanese came to Canada, where most already had relatives who could sponsor or nominate them. Some came under the new immigration category of business

TABLE 18-2. Arab Immigration to Canada by Country of
Origin, 1946–1997

Country	Number	Percent of Total Arab Immigration
Lebanon	97,027	30.9
Egypt	46,200	14.7
Morocco	21,786	6.9
Somalia	20,002	6.4
Iraq	19,464	6.2
Saudi Arabia	18,853	6.0
Syria	17,371	5.5
Kuwait	13,045	4.1
United Arab Emirates	11,256	3.6
Algeria	9,914	3.2
Jordan	9,415	3.0
Tunisia	3,895	1.2
Other	26,120	8.3
Total	314,348	100.0

From Citizenship and Immigration Canada, Citizenship and Immigration Statistics.

investors, and others came as refugees. Many of the latter were probably of Palestinian origin.

The civil war and related famine and loss of life in Somalia precipitated a massive wave of Somali immigration to Canada. Within a period of ten years commencing in the early 1980s, an estimated 30,000 Somalis entered Canada, most of whom were refugees fleeing the civil war.

Canada has also become home to many Palestinians. These people have been direct victims of the creation of the state of Israel in 1948, subsequent Israeli expansionist policies in the West Bank and the Gaza Strip, and various Arab conflicts. Later, more than 350,000 Palestinians were expelled from Kuwait, allegedly because their political leadership sided with Saddam Hussein in his misguided attempt to occupy Kuwait. No doubt some of those expelled from Kuwait found their way to Canada.[8]

Until 1980, immigration from Arab Gulf countries was a rare phenomenon. Since then, almost 18,000 immigrants came to Canada from Gulf countries: Saudi Arabia (6,394), Kuwait (5,975), and the United Arab Emirates (5,595). Most of these immigrants probably are Arabs from other countries who may have lived and worked in the Gulf for some period. Most are Palestinian, although they include Lebanese and Egyptians as well. Natural citizens of these wealthy Gulf countries are well provided for and enjoy a high standard of living and therefore have few economic or political incentives to emigrate.

Immigration patterns from North Africa have changed, although not in a uniform manner. Tunisia still accounts for 1.3 percent of the total Arab immigrants to Canada. Algeria more than quadrupled its share of Arab immigrants during the period between 1992 and 1997 compared with the period of 1946 to 1980. Meanwhile, Morocco's share declined considerably, falling from 11.6 percent over the 1946–80 period to 4.3 percent during that of 1992–97.[9]

TABLE 18-3. Arab Immigration by Country of Origin as a
Percentage of the Total Arab Immigrants to Canada

Country	1946–1980	1981–1991	1992–1997
Lebanon	44.0	41.0	12.7
Egypt	29.0	10.0	10.2
Morocco	11.6	6.6	4.3
Syria	6.2	6.3	4.2
Somalia	<1.0	6.4	9.8
Saudi Arabia	<1.0	5.3	9.9
Iraq	1.4	4.7	10.2
United Arab Emirates	<1.0	4.7	4.5
Algeria	1.0	2.5	5.0
Jordan	1.9	2.9	4.5
Tunisia	1.3	1.3	1.1
Sudan	<1.0	1.3	2.3

From Citizenship and Immigration Canada, Citizenship and Immigration Statistics.

Immigration patterns from Syria have remained relatively constant, accounting for slightly more than 6 percent of Arab immigrants to Canada. Jordan has recently been sending more immigrants to Canada. Given the size of the Palestinian population in Jordan (1.7 million) and that most residents of the West Bank still hold Jordanian citizenship, a significant portion of these immigrants are likely to be Palestinian.

It is difficult to estimate the number of Arab immigrants from Israel because they enter Canada as Israeli citizens. Community leaders estimate that the number of such immigrants over the last fifteen years has been in the thousands.

The previous remarks suggest that immigration from the various Arab countries varied in response to many factors in the Arab homeland and in the host country (i.e., Canada). Table 18-3 demonstrates the changes that have been occurring in the national mix of immigration from the Arab world, especially among those who have arrived since 1981.

Part 2: The Acculturation Process: Assimilation or Integration?

Broadly defined, acculturation refers to the changes that occur when "groups of individuals having different cultures come into continuous first-hand contact, with subsequent changes in the original cultural patterns of either or both groups."[10]

How an immigrant reacts to his or her new situation in Canada depends on a variety of factors. Some of these will be determined by *pre-contact characteristics* and may include the following: age, education, occupation, gender, marital status, prior knowledge of language, intercultural experience, degree of modernization, and motives for immigration. It is generally accepted, for example, that the higher the level of education or occupational status, the easier it is for the immigrant to cope with the challenges of entering a new society. Education provides a person with the knowledge, language, conceptual skills, and problem-solving tools that enable him or her to deal better with the demands of acculturation.

To a much larger extent, however, the acculturation process is determined by *post-contact considerations*. The immigrant enters a society with an established set of characteristics determined by its own history, economy, ideology, and policies. The relevant characteristics include the degree of pluralism extant in the host society (e.g., tolerance for and encouragement of ethnic diversity); the positive or negative manner in which the immigrant's group is perceived by the dominant groups in the host society; and the magnitude of social and ethnic group networks available to the immigrant soon after entry (e.g., nature and number of ethnic associations, residential concentration, relevant support groups).

Another factor is the immigrant's "first encounter" or personal experience on entry. How the immigrant is treated by immigration and manpower officials can color the immigrant's perceptions of Canadian society for a long time. There is also an informal "indoctrination process" that occurs when "significant others"—family members, friends, community leaders—attempt to pass on their perceptions of life in Canada to the new initiate.

Sociological and Psychological Models

Sociologists and psychologists have devised many models for explaining how acculturation-related factors interact with each other and how these interactions result in different acculturation modes at the individual and the group level. In this discussion, I adopt a simple but comprehensive scheme that was used by J. W. Berry[11] to summarize the various ways in which acculturation can take place. According to Berry, acculturation is determined by answers to two basic questions: Is it considered to be of value to maintain cultural identity and characteristics? Is it considered to be of value to maintain relationships with other groups?

These two questions are related to the importance that an immigrant, an ethnic group, or even the host society attaches to ethnic maintenance and development. This is variously referred to as heritage maintenance, pluralism, or multiculturalism. On the one hand lies the degree to which the host society desires to foster cultural differentiation in which different ethnic groups are allowed and even encouraged to maintain their cultural heritage. On the other hand is the degree of balance the ethnic group wishes to maintain between preserving its cultural identity and participating in the host society.[12]

Modes of Acculturation

For conceptual purposes only, Berry's scheme assumes that there is a "yes" or "no" answer to each of the earlier two questions. On this basis, four theoretical acculturation modes may be generated (Table 18-4). Although this discussion focuses on how these modes affect ethnic groups, the analysis applies equally to individuals.

TABLE 18-4. Acculuration Modes

Q1: Is it of value to maintain cultural identity and characteristics?		Q2: Is it of value to maintain relationships with other groups?
Yes	No	
Integration	Assimilation	Yes
Isolation	Marginalization	No

A "yes" or "no" answer to the two questions produces four theoretical acculturation modes.

If the answer to both questions is yes, the ethnic group chooses an acculturation mode in which the goals of maintenance of cultural identity and participation in the host society are pursued simultaneously. This acculturation mode, which in sociological jargon is referred to as *integration,* best approximates the policy of multicultural pluralism. The integration option allows for ethnic groups to maintain and strengthen their culture and heritage while concurrently creating an open and inclusive society in which different ethnic groups have equal access to social benefits, privileges, and rights.

If the answer to both questions is no, the result is *marginalization,* an acculturation mode in which the ethnic group loses contact with its own culture and tradition but also remains outside the mainstream of the host society. This is the worst possible mode of acculturation, one that signifies an "identity crisis" for the ethnic group. This results from being alienated from its own cultural history and being marginalized in the host society. Leo Driedger describes this mode as one in which "the marginal person [group] is between two cultures, and not fully a part of either."[13] It is most common among groups that are markedly different in cultural or physical characteristics from the dominant groups in the host society (e.g., visible minorities).

If the answer is yes to the first question but no to the second, the acculturation mode is known as *isolation.* In this mode, the group seeks to maintain its ethnic identity and cultural traditions but voluntarily or involuntarily does not participate in the life of the host society. When isolation occurs by choice, the result is separation; when it is imposed by the host society, the acculturating group experiences segregation.

Assimilation occurs when the second question is answered positively but the first is answered negatively. In other words, the group considers cultural or ethnic maintenance to be less important than acceptance by the host society. The group is prepared to abandon its cultural identity as a price to be paid for belonging to the host society. Except for perfunctory and symbolic gestures, the group abandons its own ethnic identity and adopts the values, beliefs and lifestyle prevalent in the host society. Assimilation takes on a variety of forms, each of which represents a higher level of individual and institutional transformation, and each is determined by factors that are internal to the group or to the host society.[14]

The process of assimilation can be elaborated even further. In *cultural or behavioral* assimilation, the group adopts the overt patterns of the host society. Its primary preoccupation is to "fit in" and not to be different. This transformation includes changes in external behaviors such as dress, mannerisms, and speech. To a certain extent, most groups go through this type of assimilation, certainly in the public domain, where there is direct and unavoidable contact with others from the host society.

In its more extreme form, cultural or behavioral assimilation involves a change in matters more intrinsic to the identity and the cultural history of the group. This includes changes in religious beliefs and practices, moral ideology, and aesthetic and recreational tastes. The group may come to accept, at least verbally, beliefs and values that are prevalent in the host society, although they are contradictory to those of the group's culture. Males and females, for example, may undertake roles that are quite different from those prescribed in the ethnic culture. Tastes in music and dance may change; the individual may shun cultural music and dance in favor of those that are more common in the host society.

When a significantly large number of ethnic groups start gaining access to social institutions, *structural assimilation* occurs. This, according to Milton Gordon, is the most significant type of assimilation, because unless and until it happens, full participation in the host society is not possible. When people with different ethnic backgrounds socialize together, visit each other, and belong to the same social clubs, there are greater opportunities for their children to mix socially, which is more likely to lead to intermarriage. With structural and *marital assimilation* come a sense of "we-ness" and "belongingness." Members of the ethnic group then go through the stage of *identificational assimilation* in which they begin to see themselves as members of the new society.

Gordon goes on to identify three more types or stages of assimilation, which for the study's purposes can be grouped together under the heading of *accepted assimilation*. This occurs when prejudice and discrimination cease, and all the social, economic, and political barriers against members of an ethnic group are removed. Individual members are allowed to participate fully in the civic, political, and economic life of the host society.

Before using this theoretical model to describe how members of the Arab community in Canada have acculturated, some observations need to be made. First, answers to the two questions that define acculturation modes pose a "yes-no" dichotomy. It is, however, possible to describe a group or an individual on a continuum (as being more or less of an isolationist or an integrationist). Second, different individuals within the same group may choose the same acculturation mode in varying degrees or may choose altogether different acculturation modes. Third, individuals may choose an acculturation mode that is quite different from that of the ethnic group to which they belong. As Berry puts it, "if all of one's group pursues assimilation, one is left without a membership group, rendering the other options meaningless."[15] Fourth, groups and individuals may adopt different acculturation modes at different times. An individual or a group may adopt assimilation soon on entry into the new society, but once established, he or she may seek a more integrationist mode. Fifth, questions can be raised about the applicability of Gordon's stages of assimilation to Canada. The model was initially based on the United States' experience and seems to reflect that country's "melting pot" orientation. It is possible that structural assimilation is not as significant in a pluralistic context in which individuals and groups may enjoy freedom from discrimination and prejudice independently of the degree or type of assimilation that may have occurred.

Hyphenated Canadians

One of the central theoretical questions surrounding multiculturalism is related to the degree to which the various groups making up the Canadian mosaic should be encouraged to maintain their own cultural heritage. Some believe that this should be kept to a minimum, arguing that too much ethnic diversity is inimical to the development of national unity and a national ethos. Others have contended that Canadian uniqueness and national unity are predicated on the very concepts of diversity, pluralism, and multiculturalism. In this they echo former Prime Minister Pierre Trudeau's statement to the House of Commons in 1971, when he said, "National unity if it is to mean anything in the deeply personal sense must be founded on confidence in one's own individual identity; out of this can grow respect for that of others." In part, this is a debate about symbols—symbols that give substance to the sense of nationhood of a people.

Historically speaking, the symbols that have dominated Canadian life have been predominantly British and later French in nature. Until recently, this was reflected in the fact that Canada did not have its own national anthem, its own flag, or even possession of its own founding documents. The last three decades, however, have seen a gradual transformation of this society from one that was essentially British or French to one that is becoming uniquely Canadian, and it is the very definition of this uniqueness that has been the cause of so much controversy. Is Canada to seek its uniqueness by fostering national unity through cultural diversity or through cultural homogeneity?

These are no longer purely theoretical questions. "Facts on the ground" are already dictating what kind of country Canada is and will become. A number of noncharter (i.e., non-British and non-French) ethnic groups have a population size and influence that give them political and social power politicians find difficult to ignore. When combined with Canada's well-entrenched official commitment to multiculturalism, it becomes impossible to discount the diverse symbols that Canadians of different ethnic stripes choose for themselves.

One way in which tolerance for multiculturalism may be assessed is by examining the degree to which the culturally "hyphenated citizen" is tolerated. In a society that is open to integration without requiring assimilation, one is allowed, even encouraged, to define one's ethnic identity in a dualistic or a hyphenated manner (e.g., Arab Canadian, Italian Canadian). Hyphenation may also be an indication of the degree to which individuals and groups desire to maintain links with the culture and heritage of their original group. It can therefore serve as a measure of the type of acculturation chosen. In Canada, one would expect hyphenation to be the norm, and a number of studies have shown this to be the case.[16]

One such study was conducted in five major cities (Montreal, Toronto, Winnipeg, Edmonton, and Vancouver) in which respondents from ten non-British, non-French ethnic groups were asked to classify themselves ethnoculturally. They were given four options from which to choose: ethnic, ethnic-Canadian, Canadian-ethnic, and Canadian. Only 36 percent chose the "Canadian" category, the hyphenated categories were chosen by 45 percent of the respondents, and the rest (18 percent) chose a purely ethnic identification.[17] In another study in Winnipeg and Edmonton, respondents were asked to classify themselves and immediate family members (e.g., spouse, mother, father). Fifty percent and 37 percent, respectively, of the Winnipeg and Edmonton respondents identified themselves with their own ethnic group; 10 percent and 8 percent, respectively, as hyphenated Canadian; and the rest as Canadian or "other."[18] This strong identification with the ethnic group was considerably higher when respondents classified their own family members. In the Winnipeg and Edmonton samples, spouses and parents were seen by the respondents as having a much higher identification with the ethnic culture.

Seemingly different results were derived in a national sample conducted in 1974. Only 23 percent identified themselves in terms of their own ethnic group while 59 percent identified themselves as Canadian. It was found, however, that these results were skewed by the fact that respondents of British origin were over-represented in the sample. They overwhelmingly (81 percent) chose the classification "Canadian." Because respondents of British origin equate Canadian with British, they may feel that they lose very little by abandoning their national classification, "British," and adopting the label "Canadian." The same was not true for other ethnic groups in the sample. Even respondents of French origin (66 percent) preferred a hyphenated label (French-Canadian).[19]

A Survey of Arabs in Canada

In a 1993 survey of Arabs in Ontario, when asked to state how they perceived their ethnocultural status, respondents gave answers similar to those of the non-British respondents in the national studies referred to previously. Respondents were given five options: (1) Canadian; (2) Arab; (3) a national of your old country (e.g., Lebanese, Egyptian); (4) Arab Canadian; and (5) a national of your old country and Canadian. The third and fifth options were included to assess the respondents' identification with country rather than national origin.

Almost one-half of the respondents identified themselves as Arabs (31.4 percent) or as nationals of their own country of origin (18.1 percent). The classification "Canadian" was chosen by 8.5 percent, and the remaining 41.9 percent chose a "hyphenated" classification, Arab-Canadian (25.6 percent) and Old Country-Canadian (16.3 percent). On further analysis of the results (Table 18-5), however, significant variations in how the Ontario study respondents identified themselves were found (see Table 18-3). These may be summarized as follows:

1. Respondents born in Canada overwhelmingly identified themselves as "Canadian" (32.8 percent) or hyphenated Canadian-Arab Canadian (37.9 percent), and Old Country-Canadian (17.2 percent). Only 8.6 percent chose the "Arab" label.
2. Respondents who are already Canadian citizens expressed almost twice as much of a preference for a Canadian or a hyphenated label (52.2 percent) than did those whose status is still that of an immigrant (26.8 percent). This is not unexpected because it is hard for a landed immigrant, someone whose passport still belongs to another country, to see himself as Canadian.
3. Respondents who have lived in Canada ten years or more also showed greater identification with the "Canadian" label, with only 31.5 percent choosing the

TABLE 18-5. Label Preference Identification by Percent

Identification Factor	Canadian	Arab[a]	Home Country	Arab Canadian[b]	Home Country and Canadian
Total	8.5	31.4	18.1	25.6	16.3
Country of birth					
Canada	32.8	8.6	3.4	37.9	17.2
Egypt	5.4	28.6	17.9	26.8	21.4
Jordan	8.0	40.0	4.0	36.0	12.0
Lebanon	2.9	25.9	28.8	25.4	17.1
Syria	5.0	52.5	2.5	27.5	12.5
Palestine	9.1	37.4	12.1	26.3	15.2
Other	8.8	45.6	22.1	8.8	14.7
Age					
<30	7.0	33.1	23.8	19.2	16.9
≥30	9.0	31.3	15.8	28.8	15.5
Religion					
Muslim	5.7	45.1	15.9	22.8	10.4
Christian	11.1	20.3	20.3	25.8	22.5
Stay in Canada					
<10 yr	3.1	40.6	24.9	16.4	15.0
≥10 yr	15.0	21.3	10.0	35.8	17.7
Status in Canada					
Canadian	12.4	21.6	13.8	34.0	18.2
Landed	1.8	45.2	26.2	13.1	13.7

[a]Such as Lebanese, Egyptian, and Palestinian.
[b]Such as Lebanese Canadian and Egyptian Canadian.

classification Arab or "national of" and the rest choosing a Canadian (15 percent) or a hyphenated Canadian label (54 percent). When compared with respondents who have lived in Canada ten years or less, there is a fivefold increase in the number who identify themselves as "Canadian" (3.1 to 15 percent) and a significant increase in those who label themselves as hyphenated Canadians (31.4 to 53.5 percent). There is some double counting in these figures, because Canadian-born respondents are included in this group. They accounted for 23 percent of those respondents in Canada ten years or more.

4. Length of stay in Canada coupled with a lower rate of naturalization may explain why Lebanese respondents showed the lowest identification with the label "Canadian" (2.9 percent) and the highest identification with the "Arab" or "country of origin" label (54.7 percent). Almost two-thirds of these respondents have been in Canada less than ten years. They have the highest rate of noncitizen status among all the country groups. Egyptian and Palestinian respondents, two-thirds of whom have been in Canada more than ten years, showed a much higher identification with the "Canadian" label (5.4 and 9.1 percent, respectively) and the hyphenated label (48.2 and 41.55 percent, respectively). Egyptians also have the highest naturalization rate among all the birth countries in the sample.

TABLE 18-6. Percentage Responding Affirmatively to Ethnic Identity Factors

Group	Ability to Speak Arabic	Ability to Read Arabic	Extent of Endo-gamy	Ethnic Organi-zation and Partici-pation	Impor-tance of Culture and Language Retention	Impor-tance of Ethnic Events	Reads Arabic Print Media	Listens to Arabic Music or Watches Arabic Films
Total Sample	93.4	93.7	85.5	24.7	95.0	69.0	52.0	71.6
Length of Stay								
<10 yr	98.3	96.0	90.0	17.8	96.0	68.5	62.0	76.9
≥10 yr	87.5	70.0	81.4	32.8	94.4	69.4	41.6	65.8
Muslims	95.6	90.3	82.3	26.1	97.2	64.3	55.0	67.5
Christians	91.7	77.9	88.3	23.7	92.6	75.0	49.3	75.1
Canadian-born	55.0	17.0	66.0	31.0	95.0	54.0	11.9	40.0

5. Ethnic and national identification varied according to religious classification. More of the Christian respondents identified themselves as Canadians or hyphenated Canadians than did Muslim respondents (59 and 39 percent, respectively). This held true even though length of stay in Canada was not much different for the two samples. What is different, however, is the rate of Canadian naturalization among members of the two groups. Of the total number of Christians who have been in the country ten years or more, 70 percent have taken up Canadian citizenship, but only 53.4 percent of their Muslim counterparts have done so. There is nothing in the data that helps to explain this difference. It may be that Muslims on the whole are more attached to their Arab roots than are Christians. Alternatively, it may be that Christians and Muslims are equally attached to their cultural heritage but that Christians find it easier to acculturate to a "Christian" society.

Another way in which acculturation may be evaluated is by examining people's actual behavioral patterns. Do they marry within their own group? Do they still maintain knowledge of their in-group language? Are their friends mostly of the same ethnic background? To what degree do they participate in their own ethnic organizations? Do they read their ethnic publications, watch ethnic films, or listen to their ethnic music? The findings are summarized in Table 18-6.

Language Use and Retention

As extensive research has shown, the continued use of the mother tongue, especially the ability to read, declines with second and subsequent generations of ethnic Canadians and the amount of time spent in Canada. Given that most of the sample was born in the Arab world, it would be expected that all foreign-born respondents are able to speak Arabic but not necessarily read it. As for Canadian-born respondents, just over one-half can speak Arabic, and no more than one in six can read it.

The Ontario study also asked respondents how frequently they read Arabic newspapers, magazines, or books and how often they listened to Arabic music or watched Arabic films. Fifty-two percent of the respondents indicated that they read Arabic print material with some frequency. This was higher for those in Canada less than ten years (62 percent) and lower for those in Canada ten years or more (41.6 percent). Canadian-born respondents gave a much lower positive response, with less than 12 percent indicating that they read any type of Arabic-print material. The amount of time spent in Canada seems to be the crucial factor in determining the degree of language use and retention.

The number of respondents who listen to Arabic music or watch Arabic-language films was higher for all groupings: 71.6 percent for the total sample, 76.9 percent for those in Canada ten years or less, 65.8 percent for those in Canada more than ten years, and for second-generation Arab Canadians, it was 40 percent. This is partly because watching films and listening to music require less of a facility with the language than does reading.

The use of Arabic among the Ontario study respondents is incongruent with their expressed concern for language and cultural retention. When asked, "How important is it for you to retain the Arabic language and Arab culture?" more than ninety-five percent of the respondents considered this to be very important or somewhat important. Although 85.8 percent of those in Canada for ten years or less considered language retention to be very important, for those in Canada ten years or more, the corresponding figure is 73.8 percent.

Endogamy

Another measure of ethnic salience and persistence is the degree to which there is in-group marriage (i.e., endogamy). If both parents belong to the same ethnic group, it is easier to pass on the cultural heritage (including the native language) of the parents. When respondents were questioned about their marital situation and their views about marriage partners, it was clear that endogamy was the preferred practice. Most (85.5 percent) of married respondents indicated that their spouse is of Arab origin. Nevertheless, the number of endogamous marriages decreased with length of stay in Canada. In-group marriages accounted for 90 percent of respondents who had lived in Canada less than ten years. For those in Canada ten years or more, the rate dropped to 81.4 percent, and for Canadian-born respondents, the rate was considerably lower at 66 percent.

There was a noteworthy variation in the endogamy rates of Christians and Muslims. Christians were more likely to marry one of their own than Muslim respondents (88 and 82 percent, respectively). One would have expected the opposite result. Muslims tend to have a higher attachment to their cultural and ethnic heritage and tend to favor in-group marriage, ethnically and religiously, more than Christians. This variation probably exists because the Christian community in Canada is more institutionally developed than the Muslim community. Its members have been coming to Canada for a longer period and, until recently, in significantly larger numbers. They have developed a complex social infrastructure that is centered mainly on the many churches they have established. Consequently, Christian youths are provided with more opportunities for social interaction with other members of their own ethnic and religious group. Because of the recent arrival of many of its members, the Muslim community is still in the process of developing its social and religious institutions. There are now mosques in all major urban centers, although they tend to be less ethnically homogeneous than are the Arab Christian churches. The mosque is a meeting place for all Muslims—usually of the same denomination—regardless of their ethnic background.

Respondents were asked to indicate if they approved of their children marrying non-Arabs. Almost 61 percent of the respondents expressed disapproval, with males disapproving more than females (62.8 to 56.4 percent); Muslims more than Christians (72.8 to 60.8 percent); and those in Canada less than ten years disapproving more than those in Canada for ten years or more (70.3 to 50.5 percent). Less disapproval was expressed by Canadian- and Egyptian-born respondents (46.5 and 49 percent, respectively) and by those earning $50,000 or more (56.8 percent).

Respondents expressed even stronger opinions when they were questioned about their children marrying outside their religion. Fully 70 percent of the total sample disapproved of their children marrying someone not of the same religion. Males disapproved more than females (73.1 to 62.9 percent); Muslims more than Christians (80 to 70.7 percent); and those in Canada less than ten years more than those in Canada ten year or more (76.3 to 63.5 percent). Of all the groups classified by country of birth, Canadian-born respondents expressed the least disapproval, with less than 40 percent indicating that they do not approve of their children marrying someone outside their religion. With the exception of the Lebanese respondents, more than 75 percent of each of the remaining national groups disapproved of their children marrying someone from outside their religion. A higher level of education, income, and occupational status were positively correlated with a more liberal attitude toward out-of-group and religion marriages.

The respondents' preference for endogamous marriages is not necessarily an indicator of an isolationist acculturation mode. By strongly favoring endogamy, respondents are simply affirming a deeply rooted and widely accepted social practice that does seem to weaken with higher education, income, occupational status, and with what we have dubbed the "Canadian experience"—being born in Canada or living in Canada for a long period.

Social Interaction

A related measure of ethnic identification is in-group social interaction. The more assimilated a person is, the more likely he or she is to socialize and interact with members of other ethnic groups. As Gordon has shown, structural assimilation involves, among other things, a large-scale interaction between members of an ethnic group and those of the host society. Only then do social barriers break down, intermarriage becomes more possible, and social acceptance of the ethnic group by the host society is thereby enhanced. However, this process requires time. It is natural for recently arrived

TABLE 18-7. Precentage Approving of Social Interaction Attitudes

Situation	Minorities Report	Arab Sample	Canadian-born Arab Respondents
Socializing with friends not belonging to ethnic group	92	85	98
Dating someone not belonging to ethnic group	83	54	67
Marrying someone not belonging to the group	77	39	54
Marrying someone not of the same religion	66	30	61

immigrants to want to socialize with people of their own kind. This gives them a sense of security and comfort as they acclimate to their new society. Without a high level of education, occupational status, and income, it takes at least a generation before persons begin to feel less different and more accepted by the host society. Given that most Arab Canadians have been in Canada for a relatively short period, my colleagues and I were not surprised to find that the social ties established by most respondents were with members of their own ethnic group. When they were asked how many of their best friends are Arabs, one in five indicated that all their friends are Arab, and more than 75 percent stated that some or most are Arab.

In comparing these findings with those of *The Toronto Star/Goldfarb Minorities Report* survey of visible minorities in Toronto (Table 18-7),[20] the Ontario study respondents were found to display social interaction attitudes that were quite different from those found in the *Minorities Report*. Even when the responses of Canadian-born Arabs are compared with those of the *Minorities Report*, there are still significant differences. Canadian-born Arab respondents expressed a higher rate of approval for having their children socialize with friends who are not members of their own ethnic group, but they were less approving of having their children date or marry outside ethnic or religious group. Participation in ethnic organizations and the importance attached to ethnic events is another indication of ethnic identification. Of the total sample, 24.7 percent of the respondents indicated that they belonged to some kind of an ethnic or cultural organization and 26.2 percent to a religious organization. "Attending an ethnic event" was ranked first in terms of importance from among a list of five activities. The highest rate of institutional participation was registered by Canadian-born respondents (31 percent) and those who have lived in Canada more than ten years (33 percent).

Experiences of Prejudice and Discrimination

Immigrants from the Arab world face problems that are different from those confronted by many other ethnic groups. British and French immigrants—who choose to live in Quebec—are immediately at home with the culture and lifestyle of the host society. Other North European immigrants may face linguistic problems and a small measure of cultural adaptation, but fundamentally, they are still accepted by the host society as "being like us." Immigrants from all other geographic zones present different degrees of dissimilarity to the host society. Included in this group are Italians, Greeks, Span-ish, Portuguese, East Europeans, and "visible minorities." The latter category includes "nonwhite, non-Caucasian, and non-Aboriginal, comprising people who trace their ori-gins to Asia, Africa, the Caribbean, and Latin America [persons from the Indian sub-continent are considered Caucasian, but not white]."[21] The extent of dissimilarity between these groups and those of the dominant groups, perceived or real, determines the degree of negative stereotyping, prejudice, and discrimination that may exist in the host society.

Viewed as a visible minority in Canada, Arab immigrants face problems similar to those of other minority groups. Moreover, Arabs in North America and Europe suffer from an attack on their culture, identity, and history, an attack that is rooted in the his-tory of the West's association with the Arab world and in the more recent Western attacks against the Arabs (particularly Islam).

Respondents were asked to express their opinion on how Canadians regard Arabs and people from their respective home countries. The study also sought to determine if the respondents thought that Canadians perceived them differently, depending on whether they presented themselves ethnoculturally as Arabs or as members of their own country (e.g., Lebanese, Egyptians).

More than 80 percent of respondents indicated that Canadians regard Arabs rather poorly. Nevertheless, there was a noteworthy variation in responses to the question. A greater number of the Muslim respondents (84.5 percent) indicated a below average or poor regard for Arabs by Canadians; the corresponding figure for Christian respon-dents was 76.7 percent. It may be that Christian Arab Canadians are perceived to be less different by the host society and may therefore have a slightly different accultura-tion experience.

When respondents were asked how Canadians regarded people from their own coun-try of origin, the results were slightly different. In general, respondents felt that Cana-dians had a higher regard for people from their country of origin than they did for Arabs. Even then, 73.9 percent of all respondents indicated that people from their coun-tries of origin are regarded below average or poorly by Canadians. This, however, var-ied significantly by country of birth. It ranged from a high of 80.6 percent for the Pales-tinians to a low of 64 percent for the Jordanians.

Despite the perception of most respondents that Arabs are not held in high regard by Canadians, they do not necessarily believe that there is rampant prejudice and dis-crimination against members of their community. For example, only 30 percent expressed the view that prejudice toward Arabs in Canada is increasing; 16.1 percent thought it was decreasing, and the rest did not know or thought it had not changed (Table 18-8). A majority (55.8 percent) of respondents in Canada for more than ten years and who, because of their length of residency, are in a better position to evaluate this question, thought that prejudice toward Arabs had remained the same or has decreased. Remaining the same is not necessarily good, because it may be that preju-dice toward Arabs was already too high.

Prejudice is sometimes confused with discrimination. Although related, the two are conceptually different. Prejudice has more to do with what people think, discrimina-tion with how people act. One reason why this distinction is important is because

TABLE 18-8. Perception of Prejudice Toward Arabs

Group	Increasing (%)	Decreasing (%)	About the same (%)	Do not know (%)
Total	30.0	16.1	30.4	23.5
Male	31.4	16.0	30.2	22.4
Female	27.0	16.0	31.3	25.8
Muslim	35.9	13.5	31.4	19.2
Christian	23.8	19.0	29.7	27.5
In Canada less than 10 yr	32.5	12.3	26.4	28.8
In Canada 10 yr or more	26.6	20.3	35.5	17.6
Income less than $20,000	41.2	10.8	21.6	26.5
Income $20,000–$34,999	28.9	16.2	31.1	23.7
Income $35,000–$50,000	30.0	14.5	31.8	23.6
Income over $50,000	23.4	21.4	37.7	17.5
Elementary/secondary education	30.5	17.1	26.2	26.2
College/university education	29.6	15.3	31.7	23.4
Occupation—managerial/white collar	29.1	19.7	30.1	21.1
Occupation—skilled/blue collar	35.8	8.4	29.5	26.3
Birthplace				
Canada	25.0	13.3	51.7	10.0
Egypt	23.2	17.9	26.8	32.1
Jordan	24.0	24.0	36.0	16.0
Lebanon	38.2	10.3	26.0	25.5
Syria	17.5	17.5	35.0	30.0
Palestine	29.0	24.0	27.0	20.0
Others	26.5	19.1	27.9	26.5

prejudice and discrimination call for different types of remedies. Prejudice is better treated through education, whereas discrimination is better ameliorated through formal and legislative actions.

The Ontario study respondents did feel that there was discrimination directed against their group but not as much as one would have expected given their perceptions of how poorly Canadians regarded Arabs, their culture, and their way of life. To probe the issue of discrimination further, respondents were asked whether they had experienced discrimination in specific settings. The question was phrased similarly to one found in The Toronto Star/Goldfarb *Minorities Report.* Table 18-9 shows that, when compared with the *Minorities Report,* respondents to the Ontario survey reported a lower degree of discriminatory experiences in all the areas listed. For the total sample, the greatest degree of discrimination seems to have occurred in the workplace. Although less than what was reported for other "visible" ethnic groups, 16.8 percent of the Ontario study respondents reported experiencing discrimination by fellow workers and 14.1 percent by their employers.

There is also a significant degree of discrimination in the schools, with 14.8 percent of the total sample reporting having had such experiences. This figure is considerably higher for respondents who were 30 years old or younger, with more than one in five

TABLE 18-9. Percentage Responding Affirmatively to Perception of Discrimination
Against Respondent

Source of Discrimination	Canada	Egypt	Jordan	Leb-anon	Syria	Palestine	Other	Total	Minorities Report
By fellow workers	25.0	19.3	20.0	12.6	15.0	23.0	11.3	16.8	26.0
By an employer	20.0	22.8	4.0	12.5	7.5	16.0	11.3	14.1	16.0
By the police	6.7	3.5	12.0	8.3	0.0	14.0	5.6	7.9	10.0
At school	41.7	7.0	0.0	15.5	15.0	8.0	11.3	14.8	22.0
By Canada customs	15.0	3.5	8.0	13.1	2.5	11.0	9.9	10.6	12.0
On the street	18.3	3.5	0.0	12.6	12.5	17.0	15.5	12.9	22.0
In government offices	8.3	7.0	12.0	12.1	5.0	12.0	4.2	9.7	8.0
Other	1.7	0.0	0.0	1.9	2.5	3.0	2.8	2.0	N/A

Source of Discrimination	Male	Female	Muslim	Chris-tian	In Canada ≤10 yr	In Canada >10 yr	Under Age 30
By fellow workers	17.3	15.8	21.7	14.2	15.2	19.1	11.5
By an employer	15.3	11.5	14.5	13.8	12.5	16.3	9.8
By the police	8.9	5.5	10.0	6.5	7.4	8.6	4.6
At school	13.5	18.2	15.3	15.3	11.1	19.5	21.8
By Canada customs	9.9	12.1	14.1	8.0	9.1	12.1	9.8
On the street	13.3	12.1	14.1	13.5	12.8	13.2	15.5
In government offices	8.9	11.5	10.0	10.5	10.1	9.3	9.2
Other	1.8	2.4	1.6	2.2	2.0	1.9	1.8

(21.8 percent) indicating discriminatory behavior being directed against them in the school.

A more detailed analysis of the data revealed other noteworthy variations. Canadian-born respondents tended to report a much higher level of discriminatory experience, especially by fellow workers, by employers, at school, and on the street. A disturbingly high number of Canadian-born respondents (41.7 percent) indicated that they had encountered some form of discrimination in the school. This is higher than for any other group classified by birthplace and twice the rate of responses to a comparable question in the *Minorities Report*. We are not sure why Canadian-born respondents would experience more such discrimination. This may be because they are more likely to recognize and object to discriminatory behavior. Respondents who have been in Canada less than ten years reported less discrimination in almost all the areas explored.

Egyptian-born respondents reported the highest degree of discrimination directed against them by employers, with one of five reporting such an experience. These respondents, because of their high academic qualifications, perhaps feel that their employers do not compensate them adequately financially or through promotions. In almost all other areas investigated, Egyptian-born respondents reported less discriminatory experiences than the other national groups. Muslim respondents reported experiencing more discrimination than their Christian counterparts, especially at the hands of their fellow workers.

Conclusions

If the results of the Ontario survey are fairly representative of the views of Arab Canadians, and I believe that they are, it is possible to make the following conclusions. Arab Canadians have sought an integrationist mode of acculturation. Regardless of their sociodemographic differences, most Arab Canadians are aware and proud of their cultural and religious heritage. They are also happy to be in Canada. Their wish to preserve and strengthen links with their ethnic roots is combined with a desire to participate fully in the host society. However, the balance between ethnic maintenance on the one hand and participation in the host society on the other is struck differently by various individuals and subgroups.

The mere choice of an integrationist mode of acculturation is not sufficient to ensure its successful implementation. Integration is a dynamic process in which one normally begins with a preoccupation with cultural preservation and then gradually moves in the direction of social participation. The speed with which integration occurs is a function of such factors as education, occupational status, income level, length of stay in Canada, and to a lesser extent, religion, gender, and age. Moreover, how Arab Canadians are received and treated in the host society will likely enhance or retard the process of integration. Regardless of their socioeconomic and demographic differences, Arab Canadians do have the feeling that the culture and heritage of which they are rightly proud are misunderstood by their fellow Canadians. Attempts at integration can easily be frustrated by feelings of marginalization.

The Arab Canadian community has come of age. Arab Canadians are aware that through their silence they have allowed their culture to be maligned and marginalized. No longer content with this, they have come to the conclusion that it is by fighting for their rights that they and their children can make a better contribution to the society that has adopted them and that has become their new home.

Notes

1. Baha Abu-Laban, *An Olive Branch on the Family Tree: The Arabs in Canada* (Toronto: McClelland & Stewart, 1980).

2. See Jack Shaheen, *The T.V. Arab* (Bowling Green: Bowling Green University Popular Press, 1984); Lorne M. Kenny, "The Middle East in Canadian Social Science Textbooks," In Baha Abu-Laban and Faith T. Zeadey, eds., *Arabs in America: Myths and Realities* (Wilmette: The Medina University Press International, 1975); and *Teaching About the Arabs in Ontario* (Toronto: NECEF, 1989).

3. See Zuhair Kashmeri, *The Gulf Within: Canadian Arabs, Racism and the Gulf War* (Toronto: James Lorimer, 1991).

4. As mentioned by Abu-Laban, *An Olive Branch on the Family Tree*, p. 1.

5. When workers were needed to build the Canadian Pacific Railroad in the 1890s, thousands of Chinese immigrants were allowed into the country. However, during the next fifty years, when "orientalphobia" was widespread among anglophiles, fewer than a 100 Chinese immigrants were admitted.

6. As quoted in Nancy W. Jabbra and Joseph G. Jabbra, *Voyageurs to a Rocky Shore: The Lebanese and Syrians of Nova Scotia* (Halifax: Dalhouise University Press, 1984), p. 7.

7. Jabbra and Jabbra, *Voyageurs to a Rocky Shore,* p. 7. For more on concerns about the ability of immigrants from non-European countries to become assimilated socially and culturally into the white, Anglo-Saxon, Protestant cultural milieu, see Abu-Laban, *An Olive Branch on the Family Tree,* p. 55.

8. The number of Palestinians in Canada is significantly higher than those reported by the census or the immigration statistics. Because they do not have their own state, Palestinians hold the citizenship of various Arab and non-Arab countries, so that when they come to Canada, they are likely to be counted as nationals of the countries from which they have just arrived or of countries whose citizenship they hold.

9. A substantial number of immigrants from Morocco are Arab Jews. Their declining numbers in Morocco may explain why there are now fewer immigrants from that country.

10. Milton Gordon, *Assimilation in American Life* (New York: Oxford University Press, 1964), p. 132.

11. John W. Berry, "The Role of Psychology in Ethnic Studies," *Canadian Ethnic Studies* 22 (January 1990).

12. Scandinavians in Canada, for example, tend to score very low on ethnic identity tests, showing a preference for assimilation; the Hutterities, in their quest to maintain their culture, opt for no more than a marginal participation in the host society.

13. Described in Leo Driedger, *The Ethnic Factor: Identity in Diversity* (Toronto: McGraw-Hill Ryerson, 1989), pp. 329–31.

14. Gordon, *Assimilation in American Life,* pp. 68–83.

15. Berry, *The Role of Psychology in Ethnic Studies,* p. 32.

16. Driedger, *The Ethnic Factor,* pp. 156–63.

17. Driedger, *The Ethnic Factor,* p. 159.

18. Driedger, *The Ethnic Factor,* p. 161.

19. Driedger, *The Ethnic Factor,* p. 157.

20. *The Toronto Star/Goldfarb Minorities Report* was conducted jointly by the *Toronto Star* and Goldfarb Associates. It appeared in the *Toronto Star* as a seven-part series between June and July 1992.

21. T. John Samuel, *Visible Minorities in Canada: A Projection* (Toronto: Canadian Advertising Foundation, 1992).

Therese Saliba

---

19   Resisting Invisibility: Arab Americans in Academia and Activism

> *I went to Lebanon because I believe that Arab peoples and Arab Americans occupy the lowest, the most reviled spot in the racist mind of America. I went because I believe that to be Muslim and to be Arab is to be a people subject to the most uninhibited, lethal bullying possible.*
>
> —June Jordan, *Eyewitness in Lebanon*

African-American feminist critic and poet June Jordan visited Lebanon in the wake of Israel's April 1996 invasion and the massacre of more than 100 civilians in a United Nations camp at Qana. In her "Eyewitness from Lebanon," Jordan calls the video of the Israeli bombings at Qana "the Rodney King video of the Middle East." "But Arab life," she writes, "is less than and lower than African-American life, and so nothing happened."[1] I was elated when I came across Jordan's article in *The Progressive* on my return to the United States. I had been in Lebanon visiting my ancestral homeland when the Israeli military began its 17-day war, which rapidly spread from the South to West Beirut, displacing more than 400,000 refugees. I left Lebanon before the bombing of Qana camp, but I heard the anguish of bloodshed on the television screen, and because I was living in the West Bank that Spring, I also watched Peres and Clinton mouthing their excuses for the bombing on clips from Israeli television. When I came across Jordan's article a few months later, I wanted to embrace her in gratitude for drawing us out of invisibility and for articulating an unqualified indictment of racist attitudes against Arabs and Arab Americans in stronger words than any of us could speak.

Jordan's indictment recalls claims made by Edward Said that "practically the only ethnic group about whom in the West racial slurs are tolerated, even encouraged, is the Arabs."[2] Are Arabs and Arab Americans the lowest in the racist mind of America? In *Unthinking Eurocentrism: Multiculturalism and the Media,* Ella Shohat and Robert Stam argue that political correctness "often degenerates into . . . a competition for oppressed status among the subaltern—victimhood and 'one-downs-personship' as cultural capital in a fluctuating identity stock market."[3] Although hierarchies of oppression signal such dangers, Jordan's and Said's arguments have critical implications: Arabs and Arab Americans remain victims of racist policies, even as they are rendered invisible by the standards of current racialized discourses. It seemed an incredible act of solidarity and recognition for Jordan to travel to Lebanon, to stand in alliance with refugees bereft of families, to bear witness to their lamentations and the right of Lebanese to resist, and to draw analogies between anti-Arab racism and the resonant history of anti-black racism that Americans more readily comprehend.

The purpose of this chapter is to complicate questions of Arab-American identity as they occur in a number of overlapping discourses—American ethnic studies, political and legal discourse, and feminist scholarship—and to examine tensions between theories of identity and practice, academic and political, for rights, representation, and visibility. In *Food for Our Grandmothers,* the first anthology of Arab-American feminist writing, editor Joanna Kadi calls Arab Americans "the Most Invisible of the Invisibles," and argues that both whites and people of color fail to acknowledge our existence except in those moments of political crisis.[4] Activism for Arabs in America has often been reactive, in response to destructive events in the Middle East or to discrimination at home, but our struggle is also an ideological one that takes place wherever education is happening. As Patricia Hill Collins writes, "Teaching becomes an arena for political activism wherever it occurs," in our classrooms, among family, in our communities.[5] Although institutionalized anti-Arab racism has been a major contributing factor to our invisibility, some of our own methodologies of teaching and community organizing have further added to our invisibility. Furthermore, the ambiguous positioning of Arab Americans within the racialized discourses of ethnic studies, legal rights, and feminist scholarship has done more to hinder than to aid Arab Americans in our struggle for representation.

Cultural and literary theorists argue increasingly against identity politics and formulate mutable, hybrid, or borderland identities that allow ethnic peoples to negotiate diverse social and political terrain.[6] For example, in *Culture and Imperialism,* Said argues that the "hybrid counter-energies" of exiles, immigrants, and the marginalized offer "a genuine potential for an emergent non-coercive culture."[7] In a similar vein, Suad Joseph, born Maronite Catholic Lebanese yet critical of Maronite politics, expresses a distrust of identity politics: "often authoritarian, essentializing, fixing, and mandating what one must be in order to belong, to be a member, to have a home."[8] However, poststructuralist feminist and postcolonial discourses, which have often rejected essentialized identities, and political or legal discourse, which supports "affirmative action" policies, provide often contradictory methods of resistance. This leads to "a paradoxical situation where theory deconstructs totalizing myths while activism nourishes them. Theory and practice, then, seem to pull in apparently opposite directions."[9] Within U.S. legal discourse, determining racial categories and fixing identities becomes an intensely political process that affects funding for social agencies and helps to secure civil rights protection from discrimination. Arab Americans, bereft of a racial category, have often been left in obscurity within the academy and in the political arena.

In a highly racialized society such as the United States, racial categories are necessary to gain access to the political power of minority status. Although such categories often lead to the assumption that racial categories and therefore racial identities are fixed, clearly these categories are socially constructed. In *Unthinking Eurocentrism,* Shohat and Stam define identities as geographically and historically situated: "'Identities' are not fixed essences expressing a 'natural' difference; they emerge from a fluid set of historically diverse experiences, within overlapping, polycentric circles of identities. That identity experiences are mediated, narrated, constructed, caught up in the spiral of representation and intertextuality does not mean that all struggle has come to an end."[10] In other words, once we recognize identity as constructed, we need not abandon the struggle for Arab-American rights. In fact, understanding the ways in which Arab-American identity has been "mediated, narrated, constructed" in the past may better help us in determining successful strategies for political and educational influence. The construction of a strategic identity, such as an Arab-American identity woven from the multilayered fabric of Arab life in the United States, may be termed "strategic essentialism" and is "crucial for any multicultural struggle that hopes to allow for communities of identification, even if those communities are multiple, discontinuous, and partly imaginary."[11]

Arab nationalism, which took hold in the early twentieth century in response to European colonialism and Zionism, is one example of a strategic identity movement that sought to gain political power through "the revival of consciousness of the Arab past," with an emphasis on early Islamic history when Arabs had been dominant.[12] Geographically situated "over there" in the Arab world, this movement took on a revolutionary tenor with the rise of anticolonial struggle in Egypt, Algeria, Tunisia, and later Palestine but was largely defeated in the 1967 war. With the vision of Arab unity shattered by successive defeats, betrayals, and intra-ethnic conflict, many Arabs have treated the concept of a unified identity with suspicion, even as they maintain some belief in the ideal of Arabism. In the Americas, pan-Arab nationalism influenced the second and third wave of immigrants, whereas pre-World War II immigrants and their descendants were more comfortable with the designation of Syrian or Lebanese Americans and tended to identify themselves in terms of religion, sect, and their place of origin.[13] Pan-Arab nationalism, or Arabism, informs much of Arab-American activism today as a strategy of organizing diverse groups of Arabs against U.S. foreign policy in the Middle East and racist media images of Arabs, while restoring pride in Arab ethnic heritage that has been treated with contempt and suspicion within U.S. cultural politics.

In the struggle for equality and representation, Arab Americans have undoubtedly lagged behind other recognized "minority" groups, in part because we defy the categories that constitute minority status, but also because Arab Americans have strategically embraced "whiteness" to gain access to privileges conferred by the dominant society. Other groups, such as African Americans, Asian Americans, Latinos, and Native Americans, who gained recognition in the 1960s and 1970s have more recently been influenced by poststructuralist discourses that emphasize "difference" within a particular identity group; Arab Americans are still struggling for basic recognition and inclusion and have yet to interrogate and mobilize the differences within our communities. Deniz Kandiyoti argues that the emphasis within poststructuralist and feminist discourse on "difference" and multiplicity may "potentially degenerate into unprincipled forms of relativism or, on the contrary, lead to more refined conceptions of political alliance and coalition-building."[14] Avoiding the divisiveness of difference, Arab-American activists have often embraced the tenets of Arab nationalism to overcome differences and identify common goals of struggle. Recognition of differences among Arab Americans and between ourselves and other disadvantaged groups has the potential to lead us to building productive political alliances and coalitions. Historically, Soheir Morsy argues, Nasserite versions of Arab nationalism in the 1950s and 1960s embraced pan-Arab, pan-African, and pan-Muslim alliances that stretched across national and racial borders, yet today, "most Egyptians in the United States are not likely to identify with the struggles of other racially or ethnically differentiated groups."[15]

In the present-day context of globalization and U.S. hegemony, the question of productive alliances for Arabs in the United States remains intricately tied to shifting constructions of Arab-American identity. However, as Shohat and Stam assert, in discussions of identity, it is less important to consider "identity as something one 'has,' than identification as something one 'does.'"[16] Do we identify with whites, with people of color, with other Middle Eastern groups, with so-called Third World peoples, with Jews as Semitic cousins, with African Americans, like June Jordan, who have spoken boldly in our name?

The Ethnic Studies Debate

Arab Americans (approximately 2½ million) are often cited as contributing to the "browning of America", but they remain absent from multicultural histories of America and the discourse of American Ethnic Studies. "Ethnicity" theory replaced biological, race-based theories in the 1930s; however, "ethnicity," like "race," remains a nebulous term, often denoting "group formation based on culture and descent."[17] Ethnic Studies emerged in universities across the United States in the late 1960s and early 1970s as a result of highly politicized struggles, led initially by African Americans and then joined by Asian Americans, Native Americans, and Latinos. These groups suffered not only systematic political and economic oppression within U.S. society but also institutionalized exclusion from the Eurocentric curriculum of American educational systems. Thirty years later, these four recognized "minority" groups remain at the core of ethnic studies programs; however, determinants of ethnic studies have fluctuated over time with the inclusion of Jewish Americans and other groups. Nevertheless, the struggle for inclusion within ethnic studies remains a highly politicized battle over definitions of "discrimination" and the right to self-representation and recognition within the educational system and therefore within the larger society.

In a debate that took place regarding a proposed Ethnic Studies requirement at a major northwestern university in 1991, the Jewish Studies department argued that, because of existing anti-Semitism, Jewish American Studies courses should be included, along with ethnic studies courses from the four major ethnic groups in the newly proposed requirement. Some committee members responded that if Jewish Studies were accepted, then other Middle Eastern peoples, especially Arabs, must also be included. A member of the Jewish Studies program protested, arguing that the requirement was meant to address ethnic minorities in the United States, not Arabs in the Middle East. Other committee members asserted the existence of various Middle Eastern populations in this country, and the committee finally agreed to include Jewish and Arab Americans within the requirement because of existing anti-Semitism and anti-Arab racism. However, this decision allowed other departments an entree into the debate; as a result, the Ethnic Studies requirement, founded with the intention of fostering cultural understanding to combat institutionalized racism and anti-Semitism, deteriorated into a watered-down "American pluralism" requirement, which equated all forms of difference and included departments such as Scandinavian Studies.

This debate about the definition of Ethnic Studies illustrates some of the ambiguities surrounding ethnic identities within counter-hegemonic movements, and it addresses more specifically the ambivalent constructions of Arab-American identity within academic discourse. Carried out within the larger context of the Persian Gulf War, this discussion exemplifies a shift in racial formations—inclusion of Arab Americans as a minority group—in part because of recent political events. The common assumption that Arabs exist exclusively in the Middle East and that Arab Americans are irrelevant to American Ethnic Studies is evidenced not only by the seclusion of Arab Studies within Middle East Studies departments, but also by the exclusion of Arab Americans from most U.S. multicultural texts.

For example, in Ronald Takaki's celebrated history of multicultural America, *A Different Mirror,*[18] Arab locales, but not Arab peoples, are mentioned in his introduction, although only as metaphors for the racial tensions and destruction of the 1992 Los Angeles uprising. Takaki writes, "The rioting and the murderous melee on the streets resembled the fighting in Beirut and the West Bank. The thousands of fires burning out of control and the dark smoke filling the skies brought back images of the burning oil fields of Kuwait during Desert Storm".[19] Takaki uses the Arab world as a universally acknowledged symbol of violence and disorder. (Compare this depiction with Jordan's analogy between the destruction of Qana camp and the beating of Rodney King, which focuses on the violation of human lives.) Nowhere else in his 428-page history does he mention Arabs in the Americas or elsewhere, except in reference to the 1967 War, as a point of growing tension between black and Jewish civil rights workers: "after the 1967 Arab-Israeli Six-Day War, SNCC [Student Non-Violent Coordinating Committee] denounced Israel for conquering 'Arab homes and land through terror, force, and massacres.'"[20] When Arabs are mentioned within the multicultural debate, it is often as a point of political tension between blacks and Jews,[21] or as an afterthought, "as the other of Jewish Americans."[22] Takaki focuses his study on Latinos, African Americans, Asian Americans, Indians, Jews, and Irish, with brief references to other American immigrant groups, such as Italians and Poles. In the process, he effectively erases Arabs from the multicultural tapestry of America, reinforces the notion that Arabs exist exclusively in the Middle East, and ironically gives credence to anti-Arab stereotypes as he dismantles the stereotypes of other ethnic Americans.

The multicultural movement, in its attempts to accommodate "difference" within a democratic, pluralistic society, has also reproduced certain hierarchies of difference that leave Arab Americans on the margins. Small indicators reveal that, if we have not entirely entered the ethnic studies debate, Arabs in America have at least gained a toehold. For example, a 1994 multicultural reader includes an essay on Arab Americans under the heading "From Asia—The Model Minorities?"[23] and a recent sociology text on race and ethnic relations in America includes a chapter on Central and West Asian immigrants, with a section on Arab Americans.[24] Although few and perhaps tokenistic, these chapters may be remnants of an awareness of Arab Americans that emerged during the Persian Gulf War, or they may reflect the increasing racial or ethnic diversity and complexity of U.S. society and the educational system's attempt to address this reality.[25] As ethnic studies programs are transformed by growing diversity and by post-structuralist critiques of identity politics, Arab Americans will likely gain more access to representation. However, these new paradigms of ethnicity are doubly edged: as they make space for Arab Americans and others outside current ethnic categories, they may signify a depoliticized, "pluralistic" approach to American cultures that fails to distinguish between historically disadvantaged groups and those with relative privilege.

The Political Debate

Although Arab Americans are legally classified as "Caucasian" and as "white, non-European" by the Bureau of Census,[26] this identification covers over discriminatory and racist practices that define them as "Other," and serves to further disempower Arab Americans in their political struggles. In their book, *Racial Formation in the United States,* Michael Omi and Howard Winant define race as "an unstable and 'decentered' complex of social meanings constantly being transformed by political struggle."[27] Because of the fluidity of racial classifications in the United States, the authors include in a footnote, "there are those whose racial category is ambiguous at present"[28] and mention Arabs as the sole example. This racial ambiguity points to the inadequacy of the current "Caucasian" classification and implies some future resolution. Arab-American organizations have been lobbying for a separate Middle Eastern category (which would include, among others, peoples of Arab, Iranian, Turkish, and Afghani descent) or for a separate Arab-American classification. These two conflicting categorizations, the first proposed by the Arab American Institute (AAI) and the second by the American-Arab Anti-Discrimination Committee (ADC), attest to the difficulty in determining where racial lines should be drawn.

In particular, the 2000 Census debate highlights the community's indecision about how broadly to define their "strategic" or "coalitional" identity. However, in October 1997, the Clinton administration rejected the new categories of Arab American or Middle Eastern. According to *The New York Times,* "the drive ... foundered because groups from *that volatile part of the world* could not agree on whether such a classification would include both Arab Americans and Jewish immigrants from Israel"[29] [emphasis added]. Although this reported rationale invokes familiar stereotypes of violent ethnic divisions, particularly among Jews and Arabs, the more probable reason for the administration's rejection was that granting a category to Arabs or Middle Easterners would encourage other ethnic groups to demand similar representation. As a result of the census defeat, the ADC shifted its strategy and emphasized lobbying for a long form on the 2000 Census to include "the ancestry question."[30] This strategy would help preserve important information on ethnic groups who remain uncounted within the current classifications and their countries of national origin. However, in its appeal to a pluralistic notion of American society as a "nation of immigrants," this compromise strategy tends to equate Arabs and other Third World or ethnic minorities with European ethnic groups and fails to directly address questions of racial discrimination.

The domestic issues in American Arab communities are inextricably linked to the events of the Middle East; one may argue that racist media images of Arabs are the result of oppressive U.S. policies against people of Arab descent, much as critics have argued that anti-black racism is the result of slavery and discrimination, a justification for it, and not vice versa. In the U.S. media, "race" becomes a means of proving Arabs' inferiority. Purported racial features are conveniently invoked to describe Arabs, such as references to "the Arab mind" that repeatedly surfaced during the Gulf War or *The New York Times*' references to Arafat's "pendulous lips"[31] and Ibrahim Salameh's beak-like nose. Racist media images of Arabs serve to reinforce government policy, which operates on the subtext that Arabs pose an international threat to U.S. interests (specifically oil interests), thereby justifying civil rights abuses of Arabs at home and U.S. military and political interventions in the Middle East. During the 1990 and 1991 episodes of Operations Desert Shield and Desert Storm, the ADC documented 150 anti-Arab hate crimes.[32] These discriminatory practices often single out Arabs from other Middle Eastern groups for particularly hostile treatment.

Omi and Winant classify three kinds of racial theories: the ethnicity theory, which locates pressure between assimilation and cultural pluralism; the class theory, which asserts inequality on the basis of social allocation of advantage and disadvantage; and the nation-based theory, which is rooted in colonial territorial acquisition and its color-code system based on racial difference that established relations of dominance.[33] Although early Arab immigrants were seen as unassimilable to American life and sometimes compared with the Chinese and other "Orientals" in their customs and manners, most groups of Arab Americans have proven to be readily assimilable, so much so that efforts must often be made to preserve Arab culture and language among successive generations and to "out" Arab Americans who have gained public attention (e.g., Ralph Nader, Donna Shalala, Paula Abdul, George Mitchell). Although recent Arab immigrants tend to have less economic advantage than their predecessors and frequently face discrimination in the labor force, Arabs maintain a relative economic advantage to other Americans, especially other disadvantaged groups.[34] Given their relative class advantage and assimilation into U.S. society, perhaps the most applicable racial theory for Arab Americans is the nation-based theory rooted in a history of European colonialism and in United States neocolonialism in the Middle East.

This nation-based theory lies at the foundation of Britain's Black Movement, which includes Arabs along with Asians, Latin Americans, Caribbeans, and Africans.[35] The Black Movement defines itself as determined by and opposed to colonial domination and distinguishes this political unity in terms of color. Although British colonial history can be charted and mapped over the terrain of these Third World peoples, United States neocolonialism in these regions and its direct effect on Arab Americans operate in more covert ways.

The racial transformation of Arab identity within this country has been influenced in large part by a second wave of Arab-American immigration, by the formation of Arab-American political organizations beginning in the 1960s, and by a growing resistance among these groups to U.S. foreign policy in the Middle East. In the wake of the Persian Gulf War, Arab Americans emerged as a semi-legitimate minority group. The proliferation of hate crimes against Arab Americans in 1990 and 1991 led Congress to pass bills protecting them from discrimination. In their 1991 questionnaire on racism,

Ms. magazine included Arab American as an identification, along with the other major racial and ethnic groups. In the same year, Kitchen Table: Women of Color Press signed a contract to publish an anthology of Arab-American feminist writings.[36] However, the emerging identification of Arab Americans with racialized politics, with the interests of Latin-, Asian-, Native-, and African-American communities of "color," and with Third World developments has yet to become a space of mutual acceptance, and constructions of Arab-American identity remain riddled with ambiguity.

Legal Discourse: A History of Ambiguity

Nowhere is the ambiguity more clearly reflected than in U.S. legal discourse. In examining four court cases regarding Arab immigration and discrimination, we see a shift in the racial formation of Arabs in the United States from nonwhite, to white, to somewhere outside the limits of racial categories.

In "Early Arab-Americans: The Search for Identity," Michael Suleiman explains that early Syrian immigrants, who were initially classified as "Turks" or "Other Asians," found U.S. racial categories baffling: "The problem of racial identification and citizenship traumatized the Arabic-speaking community for several years early in the century. Indeed to resolve it the erstwhile 'Syrian' community went searching for its roots and emerged to declare itself Arab and hence Caucasian, and therefore, eligible for U.S. citizenship!"[37] This search for their racial roots came in response to a South Carolina District court decision of February 1914 that denied U.S. citizenship to immigrant George Dow on the grounds that as a "Syrian of Asiatic birth," he was not a free white person according to the terms of the naturalization statute approved in 1790. The appeal argued that Syrians were Arabs, "the purest type of the Semitic race," and therefore, had a "better claim upon the White Race than that of the modern nation of Europe."[38] Ironically, the Syrian researchers used white theories of racial purity to claim that Arabs were more purely white than Europeans! This successful appeal reveals how early Arab immigrants initially embraced whiteness as a strategy to ensure their citizenship as "free white persons" under U.S. law; however, similar reasoning also encouraged early, mostly Christian Arab communities to embrace U.S. racist ideologies that set them apart from darker "others" and from Arab Muslims.[39]

Decades later, in 1942, a Yemeni Arab was denied U.S. citizenship by a Michigan District Court decision that stated, "Arabs are not 'white persons' within meaning of statute enumerating classes of people eligible for U.S. citizenship."[40] One argument given for denying the Yemeni's petition was, "Apart from the dark skin of the Arabs, it is well known that they are a part of the Mohammedan world and that a wide gulf separated their culture from that of the predominantly Christian peoples of Europe. It cannot be expected that as a class they would readily intermarry with our population and assimilate into our civilization."[41] This ruling, rooted in what Omi and Winant call the ethnic theory of racial formation, locates racial difference in the pressures between assimilation and separatism; the Arab is considered unassimilable because of his dark skin and "Mohammedan" [sic] religion. This case also signifies a shift in Arab demographics. Early Christian Syrian immigrants were viewed as more assimilable to American culture than the second wave of immigrants, which included more Muslims and

Arabs who identified with Arab nationalism. Peoples classified as "nonwhite" in 1942, as today, are often denied immigration rights. Even though Arabs are presently classified as "Caucasian," "U.S. immigration policy extends preference to Europeans, but not to any Middle Eastern group," revealing how these classifications can be manipulated to favor dominant groups.[42]

In 1942, two years later, the classification of Arabs as "nonwhite" was overturned when an Arab born in Arabia was determined to be "white" and therefore granted U.S. citizenship. The judge argued, "In the understanding of the common man the Arab peoples belong to that division of the white race speaking the Semitic languages.... Both the learned and the unlearned would *compare the Arabs with the Jews* toward whose naturalization every American Congress since the first has been avowedly sympathetic."[43] [emphasis added]. In this case, Arabs attain "whiteness" (and the purported sympathy of the American Congress) by means of the Jews. Because Jews are "white," the reasoning goes, Arabs must also be white. However, this analogy constructs the European or Ashkenazi Jews as the norm and betrays an ignorance of Jewishness as a transracial ethnic identity that includes European (Ashkenazi), Sephardic, Arab, and African Jews (Mizrachim). The assumption of European Jewish whiteness as a measure for Arab peoples who inhabit West Asia and North Africa is inadequate, even if Arabs and Jews share Semitic roots.[44]

This classification confusion resurfaced in a 1987 discrimination case, *Saint Francis College v. Al-Khazraji,* when an Iraqi professor claimed to have been denied tenure because he was a member "of the Arabian race." Al-Khazraji filed under Title 42, Section 1981, a Civil War era law written to protect blacks from discrimination, which "provides that all persons within the jurisdiction of the United States shall have the same right to make and enforce contracts as is enjoyed by white citizens." The statute, however, assumes the nonwhite status of the plaintiff; therefore, the case was initially thrown out of a Pennsylvania District Court, because Arabs are classified as Caucasian. However, in a 1989 appeal to the U.S. Supreme Court, filed jointly with Jewish Americans regarding anti-Jewish slogans written on a synagogue, the court decreed that Arabs, Jews, and all other ethnic and religious groups are protected against discrimination under federal law. In explaining the Court's decision, Justice White wrote that although most people believe there are three major races, Caucasoid, Mongoloid, and Negroid, "many biologists and anthropologists ... criticize racial classifications as arbitrary and of little use in understanding the variability of human beings."[45]

The *St. Francis v. Al-Khazraji* case supports the claim of an "Arabian race" within the arbitrary construction of racial categories. Significantly, this case opened up the category of racial discrimination, much as the inclusion of Arab Americans in the Ethnic Studies debate opened up the requirement to any number of ethnic groups. Once "Arabs" as a category are included in racial politics, it is not in addition to already familiar groups of people of color covered under Affirmative Action, but rather their inclusion leads to a dismantling of those categories. It is also notable that Al-Khazraji was able to get a hearing when his case was allied with a similar case of Jewish discrimination. Most importantly, the Arab-American battle for compensation for discrimination and for recognition as a minority group is taking place in an era when, on the practical level, Affirmative Action programs are being dismantled (e.g., the 1995 decision of the Board of Regents of the University of California[46] and the passage of California proposition 209[47]) and, on the theoretical level, racial categories are declared arbitrary.

Debates in Feminist Scholarship

Arab-American women have participated in debates on racism within the U.S. feminist movement since 1981, when women of color challenged white feminists at the National Women's Studies Association (NWSA) conference and emerged in a coalition of "U.S. Third World Feminists." At the 1982 NWSA conference, Carol Haddad explains how the Third World Caucus condemned the Israeli invasion of Lebanon in a resolution that was met with "hostility and parliamentary maneuvering;" as a result, "the resolution was watered down and effectively defeated."[48] At that same conference, however, Haddad was granted a speaking spot on a panel with prominent women of color for a speech entitled, "Arab-Americans: The Forgotten Minority in Feminist Circles." Similarly, Azizah al-Hibri spoke at the 1983 NWSA conference, condemning the racism in the middle-class white women's movement and their Orientalizing approach to Arab women. In 1994, al-Hibri writes, "The sad thing is, nothing has changed since then."[49]

The June 1995 NWSA conference took place at the University of Oklahoma, a short drive from the site of the Oklahoma City bombing, and reminders of tragedy, yellow ribbons, and memorials to the dead filled the shop windows of Norman. Several factors enticed me to participate in the conference: stories from NWSA in the early 1980s, when U.S. Third World women confronted white feminists and Arab-American women gained some visibility, and an invitation to participate in the first Arab-American feminist reading from *Food for Our Grandmothers*. At the keynote address, representatives from each recognized color group condemned the bombing in Oklahoma City, many called it a racist act, and all of them mentioned the litany of four racial or ethnic groups, but no one mentioned Arabs or Muslims against whom a discriminatory campaign was waged in the wake of the bombing. Our invisibility swelled in the silence and choked my voice. As scheduling would have it, our reading was placed in the same time slot and in a room adjacent to a popular reading by American Indian women. We caught a small group from the overflow. These are structural ways in which our invisibility is reinforced, and I realized then that we are still not a part of people's consciousness when they speak of oppression or injustice.

The debates among feminist academics and activists regarding categories, methodologies, and practice of diverse and "situated" feminisms mirror some of the ethnic studies debates; however, feminist scholarship has provided more in-depth theoretical analysis of political struggle. In Women's Studies, Arab women are emerging from their isolation within Middle East departments to join ranks with other "Third World women." Academia recognizes Arab women as existing within the constructed locales known as the Third World, the South, or the Middle East and North Africa; however, the presence of Arab women among the ranks of what is sometimes called "U.S. Third World feminism" or movements of "women of color" in the United States has been tenuous.

American ethnic models have proven inadequate for understanding Arab-American feminism. As Lisa Suhair Majaj writes, "Arab American feminist articulation is situated at the meeting point of American feminisms, postcolonial feminisms, and the specificities of Arab feminist discourses. As such, it negotiates a complex interaction between 'first' and 'third' world feminisms, situated within a highly politicized context."[50]

The burgeoning scholarship on Arab women and Arab feminist movements within the Arab world has followed certain dominant trends: the publication of Edward Said's *Orientalism* and feminist poststructuralism gave rise to post-Orientalist scholarship, critiquing exoticized, reductive representations of the Oriental or Muslim woman oppressed by her culture. The relationship between feminism and nationalism was also of critical concern; as Palestinian feminist Rita Giacaman says, "In classical western feminist theory, nowhere will you find a serious analysis of the national question."[51] However, outmoded paradigms still prevail in the study of Arab women, including Orientalist stereotypes of Arab society arguing for Western models of Arab women's liberation. Oppositional, post-Orientalist scholarship factors in the multiple forces of oppression, including colonialism, capitalism, imperialism, and social factors on Arab women's lives. However, as Deniz Kandiyoti argues, the history of colonialism and "the historical connection between feminism and nationalism in the Middle East has left an enduring legacy of concerns around the effects of cultural imperialism which has discouraged systematic exploration of local institutions and cultural processes."[52] Similarly, nationalist, Islamist, and other discourses have covered over the heterogeneity of Arab societies. Arab-American feminist scholars, many of them immigrants themselves writing on the country of their birth or second- or third-generation scholars, have often emphasized the complexity and heterogeneity of Arab women's experience. Although it seems impossible to formulate an encompassing theory that can account for the different forms women's struggles have taken in the Middle East, various theories set forth by Arab feminists in the past decade begin to address how these feminisms connect to their specific geographical and historical contexts, as they contribute to the "development of productive feminist agendas."[53]

In contrast, for women of Arab descent in North America or in the diaspora, little scholarship is available documenting the complexities of their lives, including issues of gender, family, assimilation, and discrimination.[54] *Food for Our Grandmothers,* a ground-breaking work in this respect, dismantles racial categories as it problematizes and affirms Arab-American women's claims as part of U.S. women of color movement. Kadi situates the book within the tradition of writings by radical women of color, such as *This Bridge Called My Back,* edited by Gloria Anzaldua and Cherrie Moraga.[55] Although *Food for Our Grandmothers* never received the kind of critical attention suggested by such analogies, it raised important questions about Arab feminist identity in North America, such as the question of color and identification and alliance with other women of color. Arab-American women's push for inclusion in the color movement is tied with a progressive political ideology that stands in opposition to multiple forms of domination; it also exposes the constraints of racialized politics in the struggle for representation.

In "Decolonizing Feminism," Marnia Lazreg, an Algerian feminist scholar teaching in the United States, sets forth an oppositional critique to the racialized politics that have dominated much of feminist studies for the past two decades.[56] Lazreg argues against the term "women of color" and, by implication, the inclusion of Arab women within this category. She proposes "decentering as well as *deracializing* one's self as a precondition" for "developing a form of consciousness among feminists in North America that transcends their sense of specialness and embraces what is human at the heart of womanhood across culture and races"[57] [emphasis added]. Emphasizing a humanistic tradition in Arab studies and women's studies, Lazreg suggests that race is a privilege, a specialness that must be set aside to understand women's lives across religion, nation, and ethnicity. She further critiques the use of color as a shield and argues against the use of the term "women of color" as a reversal of "colored women," one that maintains racist connotations and gives currency to the dominance of Anglo-American feminist discourse and the racialized social relations it was meant to combat.[58] Divisions along skin color, she argues, are grounded in biology, and just as feminists are attempting to dismantle biological assumptions of gender, they should not reinforce biological determinants of race.

Lazreg's critique exposes three important problems: the inversion of the master's language as a form of resistance, the tendency of racial categories to subsume all other forms of difference, and the biological essentialism of much racial discourse. However, by rendering the language of race to the "history of social segregation,"[59] she fails to consider contemporary forms of racial discrimination and the implications of deracializing for Arab women for whom racialization has been imposed from the outside or entirely denied. Nor does she ask if the term "women of color" applies to Arab women in general or more specifically to the Algerian women of her study. Lazreg reinscribes feminist scholarship within categories more resonant in the Arab world—nation, religion, ethnicity—than in North America where racial politics dominate. Categories of color, although confusing in a North American context, have not played a significant role in Arab societies, where ethnic or racial hierarchies are still largely unexamined but where social preference for whiteness remains a colonial legacy.[60] Lazreg does not see invisibility and silence as connected to racial factors, but rather to the erasure of "a rich difficult, and painful history as well as women's struggles through it" by declaring Arab women oppressed, and connected to colonial brands of feminist scholarship that give Islam "privileged explanatory power."[61] According to Lazreg, to decolonize feminism, which still renders Arab women invisible in multiple ways, we must discard racial paradigms as remnants of colonial domination and look for universalizing connections across differences, East and West.

These debates, when focused exclusively on color, miss the point that racial politics exist in response to continuing racist discrimination. If we understand color, regardless of our varied pigmentation, as a metaphor for the postcolonial condition, for neocolonial oppression and domination, it becomes a question of identification with like others with overlapping histories and concerns. Although women of color have more often than not excluded Arab women from such alliances, Arab Americans have also often retreated to the insularity of community and family and failed to examine differences of gender, class, religion, and sexuality within our communities or to confront our own racism in ways that would allow us to build productive alliances with other ethnic groups.

In women's studies, in which the "U.S. Third World feminism" of the 1980s has transformed into "transnational feminism" of the 1990s, space is opening up for Arab women in the diaspora who often negotiate identities across two continents and national identities. In situating feminist theory within the structures of "transnational economic links and cultural asymetries," transnational feminism complicates racialized discourses by emphasizing political, economic, and cultural inequalities alongside gender and by calling for transnational alliances that link domestic issues with United States' hegemony and foreign policies.[62] This methodology has proven more relevant to Arab-American women's scholarship and activism than the current racialized discourses of U.S. ethnic politics.

Conclusions

Given the persistence of anti-Arab racism in the United States, discriminatory government policies, and rising numbers of Arab Americans, racial transformations may lead to more inclusion of Arab Americans within ethnic politics. Paradoxically, however, the gap is widening between theory and policy in decidedly negative ways. On a theoretical level, we see a shift toward more visibility for Arabs in the United States as the racial or ethnic complexity of the country gains critical attention. On the level of policy, however, Affirmative Action statutes are being dismantled at the same time the government is implementing neoliberal policies in the name of "counterterrorism," "personal responsibility," and "legal immigration" that discriminate against immigrant communities in general and Arab Americans in particular.[63] Effective coalition-building among groups adversely affected by these policies seems to be the only way to fight this dangerous political trend that uses racist and xenophobic tactics to pass unconstitutional laws.

As our educational curricula are shaped more and more by worldly events, our teaching becomes activism and our activism a form of education. The push for inclusion of Arab Americans within ethnic politics, ethnic studies, and feminist scholarship is a critical strategy for resisting invisibility. Arabs are labeled Caucasian, Asian, Afro-Asian, non-European, Semitic, Arab, black, or "of color" as racial formations shift with political struggles. It is unclear how long we will inhabit this space of ambiguity that often excludes us from both mainstream and marginalized groups, and it is unclear when and if we will enter an age of "post-ethnicity"[64] in which racialized relations will no longer be a considerable political factor in determining representation.

Notes

1. June Jordan, "Eyewitness in Lebanon," *The Progressive* (August 1996): 13.

2. Edward W. Said, *The Question of Palestine* (New York: Times Books, 1979), p. 26. Said also discusses this point at length in *Orientalism* (New York: Random House, 1978), pp. 284–328.

3. Ella Shohat and Robert Stam, *Unthinking Eurocentrism: Multiculturalism and the Media* (New York: Routledge, 1994), p. 341.

4. Joanna Kadi, *Food for Our Grandmothers: Writings by Arab-American and Arab-Canadian Feminists* (Boston: South End Press, 1994), p. xix.

5. Patricia Hill Collins, *Black Feminist Thought: Knowledge, Consciousness, and the Politics of Empowerment* (New York: Routledge, 1991), p. 151.

6. See, for example, Gloria Anzaldua, *Borderlands/La Frontera: The New Mestiza* (San Francisco: Aunt Lute Press, 1987); and Homi Bhabha, "The Other Question—The Stereotype in Colonial Discourse," *Screen* 24, no. 6 (1983): 18–36.

7. Edward W. Said, *Culture and Imperialism* (New York: Alfred A. Knopf, 1993), pp. 334–35.

8. Suad Joseph, "Searching for Baba: Personal Notes on Rights and Postcolonialities," *Stanford Humanities Review* 5, no. 1 (1995): 141–51.

9. Shohat and Stam, *Unthinking Eurocentrism,* p. 342.

10. Shohat and Stam, *Unthinking Eurocentrism,* p. 346.

11. Shohat and Stam, *Unthinking Eurocentrism,* p. 346.

12. Albert Hourani, *A History of the Arab Peoples* (Cambridge, MA: Belknap Press of Harvard University Press, 1991), p. 309.

13. As Michael Suleiman asserts, "The concept of Arabism or Arab nationalism was [in the early twentieth century] still rather nebulous and weak. Even attachment to a specific political entity (i.e., country) was to come later, after the dismemberment of the former Ottoman provinces." "Early Arab-Americans: The Search for Identity." In Eric Hooglund, ed., *Crossing the Waters: Arabic-Speaking Immigrants to the United States* (Washington, DC: Smithsonian Institution Press, 1987), p. 41. Similarly, Alixa Naff explains that the incipient Arab nationalist movement abroad, with its strong anti-colonialist ideology, seemed to have little impact on Arabs in the new world, particularly among the first wave of mainly Christian Arab immigrants, who "shaped their identities according to religion, sect, and place of origin." Alixa Naff, *Becoming American: The Early Arab Immigrant Experience* (Carbondale: Southern Illinois University Press, 1985), pp. 14–15.

14. Deniz Kandiyoti, "Contemporary Feminist Scholarship and Middle East Studies," the first chapter of her *Gendering the Middle East* (Syracuse: Syracuse University Press, 1996), pp. 1–27.

15. Soheir A. Morsey, "Beyond the Honorary White Classification for Egyptians: Societal Identity in an Historical Context." In Stephen Gregory and Roger Sanjek, eds., *Race* (New Brunswick, NJ: Rutgers University Press, 1994), p. 189.

16. Shohat and Stam, *Unthinking Eurocentrism,* p. 346.

17. Michael Omi and Howard Winant, *Racial Formation in the United States* (New York: Routledge, 1994), pp. 14, 15.

18. Ronald Takaki, *A Different Mirror: A History of Multicultural America* (Boston: Little Brown & Co., 1993).

19. Takaki, *A Different Mirror,* p. 4.

20. Takaki, *A Different Mirror,* p. 408.

21. See, for example, Cornell West's discussion of black-Jewish relations in *Race Matters* (Boston: Beacon, 1993).

22. Joseph Massad argues that Palestinians are defined in "discursive relation to European Jews." Given U.S. constructions of the Arab-Israeli conflict, the same may also be said of Arabs in general. See Joseph Massad, "Palestinians and the Limits of Racialized Discourse," *Social Text* 11, no. 1 (1993): 94. For a fascinating deconstruction of the Arab-Jewish dichotomy, see Ammiel Alcalay, *After Jews and Arabs: Remaking Levantine Culture* (Minneapolis: University of Minnesota Press, 1993). The assumed alliance between African Americans and Arabs, specifically around the Palestinian cause, has not necessarily translated into an effective political alliance. For example, on 25 July 1994, John Lewis, a ranking member of the Black Caucus, along with Newt Gingrich, endorsed a House letter calling on the Clinton administration to revoke any references to Jerusalem as "occupied territory" and to render any Palestinian claims to Jerusalem illegitimate, in violation of international law. See Naseer H. Aruri, *The Obstruction of Peace: The United States, Israel and the Palestinians* (Monroe, ME: Common Courage Press, 1995).

23. See Alixa Naff's article, "Arabs in America." In Joseph Zaitchik, et al., eds., *Face to Face: Readings on Confrontation and Accommodation in America* (Boston: Houghton Mifflin, 1994), pp. 279–88.

24. Vincent Parrillo, *Strangers to These Shores: Race and Ethnic Relations in the United States* (Needham Heights, MA: Allyn & Bacon, 1994).

25. Omi and Winant, in *Racial Formation,* argue that "U.S. society is racially both more diverse and more complex today than at any previous time in history. Racial theory must address this reality . . . [R]acial policy and politics must address it as well" (p. 152).

26. *Washington Report on Middle East Affairs,* (September/October 1993): 62–63.

27. Omi and Winant, *Racial Formation,* p. x.

28. Omi and Winant, *Racial Formation,* Introduction, n. 3.

29. *New York Times* (30 October 1997): 1.

30. See "ADC Action Alert: Ancestry Data Must Be Included in 2000 Census," *ADC Times* 18, no. 8 (December 1996–January 1997): 17.

31. See Michael Kelly, "In Gaza, Peace Meets Pathology," *New York Times Magazine* (27 November 1994): 56.

32. The Justice Department describes "hate crimes" as crimes that "manifest evidence of prejudice based on race, religion, sexual orientation, or ethnicity" and include "aggravated assault, simple assault, intimidation, arson, and destruction, damage or vandalism of property," as cited in American-Arab Anti-Discrimination Committee, *1991 Report on Anti-Arab Hate Crimes: ADC Special Report* (February 1992)(Washington, D.C.: ADC Research Institute), p. 5.

33. Omi and Winant, *Racial Formation,* p. 52.

34. In "The Arab-American Market," *American Demographics* (January 1994): 22–31, Samia El-Badry argues that Arab Americans rank among our nation's leaders in many fields. "They are much like other Americans, except younger, more educated, more affluent, and more likely to own a business" (p. 22).

35. In *Charting the Journey: Writings by Black and Third World Women,* Shabnam Grewal and others argue that "the idea of 'Blackness' in contemporary Britain is 'unmatured' and 'inadequately defined' and that it is "contradictory in its material movements because the unity of action, conscious or otherwise, of Asians, Latin Americans and Arabs, Caribbeans and Africans, gives political expression to a common 'color' even as the State-created fissures of ethnicity threaten to engulf and overwhelm in islands of cultural exclusivity" (London: Sheba Feminist Press, 1988), p. 1.

36. Because of internal problems with the press, the editor, Joanna Kadi, canceled the contract and signed with South End Press (personal correspondence, 1993).

37. Suleiman, "Early Arab-Americans."

38. Quoted in Suleiman, "Early Arab-Americans," p. 44.

39. Michael Suleiman argues that these findings did not lead Syrians to adopt "Arab" as an identity, because it also had a strong association with Islam, from which Christian Arabs chose to distance themselves. Suleiman, "Early Arab-Americans," p. 45. Many contributors in *Food for Our Grandmothers* describe internalized racism within the Arab community and racism directed against other groups. For example, Anne J. M. Mammary writes, "In the face of this anti-Arab sentiment, my family made a home in this country. This home was built with many things, including internalized hatred of Arab peoples along with the racist 'relief' that we are not, in my grandfather's words, 'as dark as black people.' That is, his/our self-definition often came by denying and running from variously deep shades of olive skin and at the same time clinging to the power in the United States that comes from having a sense of self delineation as being 'not someone else'—here not someone darker." See Mammary, "Mint, Tomatoes, and the Grapevine." In *Food for Our Grandmothers,* pp. 250–57.

40. *In Re Ahmed Hassan,* 48 F. Supp. 162148 (E.D. Mich. S.D. 1942).

41. Quoted in Massad, "Palestinians and the Limits of Racialized Discourse," p. 108.

42. See *The Washington Report on Middle East Affairs* (September/October 1993): 63.

43. Quoted in Massad, "Palestinians and the Limits of Racialized Discourse," p. 109.

44. Racial classifications within Israeli society clearly reveal these distinctions lost in the U.S. context. For further explanation, see Ella Shohat, *Israeli Cinema: East/West and the Politics of Representation* (Austin: University of Texas Press, 1989); and Smadar Lavie, "Blow-Up in the Borderzones: Third World Israeli Authors Groping for Home." In Smadar Lavie and Ted Swedenburg, eds., *Displacement, Diaspora, and Geographies of Identity* (Durham: Duke University Press, 1996), pp. 55–96.

45. See Sidney Bernstein, "Supreme Court Review," *Trial* (August 1987): 89. For a full record of the cases, see *Saint Francis College v. Al-Khazraji,* 481 U.S. 604 (1987); and *Shaare Tefila Congregation v. John William Cobb,* 481 U.S. 615 (1987).

46. See, for example, Michael Tomasky, "Reaffirming our Actions," *Nation* (13 May 1996): 21–24. Tomasky argues that the left "must find ways to redefine affirmative action on terms acceptable both to us and to a majority of Americans." Specifically, he points to coalition programs for minorities and economically disadvantaged whites, based on "reasonable moral judgment" rather than on quotas.

47. This proposition, deceptively titled the "Civil Rights Initiative," passed on 5 November 1996.

48. Carol Haddad, "In Search of Home." In *Food for Our Grandmothers,* p. 220.

49. Aziza al-Hibri, "Take Off Your Western Veil." In *Food for Our Grandmothers,* p. 162.

50. Lisa Suhair Majaj, "Arab American Literature and the Politics of Identity" (Dissertation prospectus, University of Michigan, 1994), p. 26.

51. Rita Giacaman, "Palestinian Women, the *Intifada,* and the State of Independence: An Interview with Rita Giacaman," by Graham Usher. *Race & Class* 34, no. 3 (1993): 37.

52. Kandiyoti, "Contemporary Feminist Scholarship," p. 19.

53. Kandiyoti, "Contemporary Feminist Scholarship," p. 17.

54. For emerging new scholarship on Arab-American women, see Evelyn Shakir, *Bint Arab: Arab and Arab American Women in the United States* (Westport, CT: Praeger, 1997).

55. Gloria Anzaldua and Cherrie Moraga, eds., *This Bridge Called My Back* (Watertown, MA: Persephone Press, 1981).

56. See Marnia Lazreg, *The Eloquence of Silence: Algerian Women in Question* (New York: Routledge, 1993), pp. 6–19.

57. Lazreg, *The Eloquence of Silence,* p. 8.

58. Lazreg, *The Eloquence of Silence,* p. 9.

59. Lazreg, *The Eloquence of Silence,* p. 9.

60. For example, when I asked my Palestinian students at Bethlehem University what they thought of color categories and their place within them, some thought of themselves as white, and others said they were brown.

61. Lazreg, *The Eloquence of Silence,* pp. 1, 13.

62. Inderpal Grewal and Caren Kaplan, eds., *Scattered Hegemonies: Postmodernity and Transnational Feminist Practices* (Minneapolis: University of Minnesota Press, 1994), pp. 3, 20.

63. *The Washington Post,* "Flawed Terrorism Bill" (18 April 1996), and the American-Arab Anti-Discrimination Committee have argued that the new counter-terrorism is unconstitutional.

64. R. Radhakrishnan uses the term "post-ethnicity" in "Ethnic Identity and Post-Structuralist Difference," *Cultural Critique* (Spring 1987): 199–220. As he explains, "post-ethnicity" stands for "radical ethnicity" and for a "programmatic, short-term ethnicity" that engages in reconstructing "the very logic of identity," pp. 199–200.

Lisa Suhair Majaj

20   Arab-American Ethnicity: Locations, Coalitions, and Cultural Negotiations

This essay examines the complex location of Arab Americans within the American multiculture. Ethnicity is most often discussed with reference to cultural pluralism, a theoretical model that, in its affirmation of ethnicity, tends to emphasize relatively stable boundaries among groups, but as contemporary Arab-American writing increasingly suggests, ethnicity is articulated within and across boundaries of group identity. This chapter examines the significance for Arab Americans of moving away from cultural insularity and toward a stance emphasizing connections with others. After a discussion of the relevance of theoretical frameworks of ethnicity to Arab-American experience, this chapter explores the work of two contemporary Arab-American writers— Palestinian-American Naomi Shihab Nye and Lebanese-American David Williams— who seek to affirm and assert Arab-American identity while establishing connections across and beyond the boundaries of ethnicity. Their efforts are representative of growing attempts among Arab Americans to situate themselves in relation not only to group identity and concerns, but also to the global multiculture.

Theoretical Negotiations

Discussions of ethnicity are typically situated within paradigms of assimilation or cultural pluralism—interpretive frameworks that reflect, respectively, the conformist pressures exerted on immigrants to the United States during earlier periods, and the current emphasis on celebrating cultural diversity. Central to cultural pluralism is ethnic assertion, or what Charles Taylor calls "the politics of recognition"—the quest for public affirmation of group identity for the purpose of cultural survival.[1] Such assertion is of particular importance to Arab Americans, who have historically been rendered invisible in the American context by their relatively small numbers, by their ambiguous location within American racial and ethnic categories, and by their tenuous status within American political and cultural contexts. Excluded from American citizenship at various times on the basis of being "Asian" or "nonwhite," Arab Americans currently are officially classified as white. This classification, although seeming to grant inclusion in mainstream American society, is ambiguous. Arab-American "whiteness" is at best a merely "honorary" status, one readily stripped away at moments of crisis.[2] (As an example, consider the targeting of Arab Americans during the aftermath of the bombing of the Oklahoma City Federal Building in 1995.[3]) At the same time, classification as "white" means that Arab-American experiences of racism and discrimination often go unaddressed on the basis that "white" people cannot suffer racism. Such contradictions have significant implications for Arab Americans as they attempt to articulate a viable ethnic identity within the American context.

Earlier Arab immigrants, situated within a pre–World War II context that strongly emphasized assimilation, were by most accounts fairly successful in their efforts at assimilating into the American context. Historian Alixa Naff has stated that were it not for renewed Arab immigration in the postwar period, Arab Americans might have "assimilated themselves out of existence."[4] However, Arab Americans now face rising forces of hostility, violence, and discrimination. In contrast to the earlier Arab immigrant population, composed largely of Christians from Mount Lebanon, the current Arab-American community is far from homogeneous. It includes people of many different national origins and religions; recent immigrants and assimilated descendants of earlier immigrants; dark-skinned and light-skinned individuals; people who speak no Arabic, those who speak no English, and those whose dialects are unintelligible to each other; and children of mixed marriages whose hybrid identities locate them at the margins of "Arab" and "American" identity. This increasingly diverse population often finds itself negotiating a political and cultural context that demonizes Arab and Muslim culture while implicitly excluding Arab Americans from perceptions of "American" identity.

A study carried out in 1981 documents the negative attitudes of Americans toward Arabs.[5] A large proportion of respondents in the study held Arabs to be "'barbaric, cruel' (44 percent), 'treacherous, cunning' (49 percent), 'mistreat women' (51 percent), 'warlike, bloodthirsty' (50 percent)"; similarly, respondents viewed "'most' or 'all' Arabs [to be] 'anti-Christian' (40 percent) [and/or] 'anti-Semitic' (40 percent)".[6] Moreover, the study showed that the term "Arab" elicited more hostility than did individual Arab identities such as Lebanese, Egyptian, Saudi, or Palestinian. Such negative perceptions have not dissipated in the late 1990s. As Nabeel Abraham argues, not only does "anti-Arab racism, like other types of racism, [permeate] mainstream cultural and political institutions," but "unlike other forms of racism, anti-Arab racism is often tolerated by mainstream society."[7] The hostility toward Arabs, Muslims, and Middle Easterners in the United States that peaked during the 1980s and that continues to spiral during periods of political tension has not abated. It appears that Arab Americans are one of the few ethnic groups it is still "safe to hate."[8]

Contemporary efforts at asserting and celebrating Arab-American ethnicity are grounded in this intertwined history of earlier assimilationist forces, contemporary hostility, and unclear racial status. In response to these pressures, Arab Americans have increasingly sought to assert their ethnicity on a political and a cultural level. National Arab-American organizations such as the American-Arab Anti-Discrimination

Committee (ADC) and the Association of Arab-American University Graduates (AAUG) work to oppose anti-Arab discrimination, to protect Arab-American interests, and to disseminate accurate information about Arabs and Arab Americans. Meanwhile, Arab-American culture is celebrated and affirmed through national artistic events such as the traveling exhibit *Community Between Two Worlds,*[9] through journals such as *Al Jadid: A Record of Arab Culture and Arts,* and through conferences and books exploring and documenting the experience of Arab Americans throughout this century.[10]

Such ethnic celebration and assertion reflects an important shift away from earlier generations' attempts to deny or hide their Arab identity. However, emphasis on ethnic affirmation is not unproblematic. Celebrations of Arab-American identity are often predicated on an implicit marginalization of individuals who do not fit into community norms (e.g., gays and lesbians). A focus on ethnic celebration may distract attention from problems within the Arab-American community (e.g., urban poverty, deteriorating family and social structures, domestic violence, youth involvement with gangs). Although Arab Americans are highly cognizant of the politicized context situating their attempts at ethnic assertion, a focus on cultural pride may gloss over concerns such as ethnically and religiously motivated anti-Arab violence, employment discrimination, targeting by law-enforcement agents and airlines, and exclusion from resources aimed at improving minority educational, economic, social, and political conditions.

At the same time, the tenuous location of Arab Americans within American political, cultural, and racial frameworks complicates efforts at organizing around a clearly identified minority status. This is evident in the internal debate within Arab-American communities about whether to lobby for official minority status as Arab American. The debate turns on the choice between claiming ethnic (and sometimes racial) distinctiveness as Arab Americans and using this identity as a basis for activism or emphasizing the formal classification of Arabs as "white" and seeking to make inclusion in mainstream American culture a matter of fact, not just nomenclature. The debate points toward a split in the Arab-American community between those who wish to safeguard whatever privileges Arab Americans possess as nominal "white" people and those who feel that Arab Americans have more to gain and more to contribute by identifying with people of color. The tension between inclusion and exclusion that results hinders efforts to organize Arab Americans on a national level and complicates efforts at coalition building between Arab Americans and other ethnic and racial groups.

The narration of Arab-American history in popular and scholarly contexts is informed by this tension between inclusion and exclusion. Consider the 1994 collection of essays, *The Development of Arab-American Identity.* This collection begins by situating Arab Americans in relationship to white immigrant groups of the late nineteenth and early twentieth century and implicitly traces a trajectory in Arab-American history from assimilation through acculturation, awareness, and ethnic assertion. However, the collection also demonstrates the ways in which this transition from assimilation to cultural pride is complicated by forces of politicization, racism, and violence. The concluding essay by Nabeel Abraham documents anti-Arab racism and violence in the contemporary American context. The content of the essay and its placement implicitly disrupt the smooth flow from assimilation to ethnic rejuvenation, forcing readers to shift from a framework of assimilation to one of confrontation and to grapple with the sometimes violent implications of exclusion and difference. Documenting incidents of assault, murder, arson, bombings, vandalism, threats, harassment, and discrimination against Arab Americans, Abraham demonstrates the extent to which "anti-Arab racism continues to lie just beneath the surface of society."[11] He makes clear that, in contrast to white ethnic Americans, who enjoy what Mary Waters has called "ethnic options"[12]— the choice to affiliate with or distance oneself from one's ethnic identity at will—Arab Americans experience their identity not as a choice but as a fact from which they cannot escape.[13]

Central to the workings of ethnicity is the concept of boundary mechanisms. As Frederik Barth observed in the 1969 introduction to his pivotal *Ethnic Groups and Boundaries,* it is "the ethnic *boundary* that defines the group, not the cultural stuff that it encloses."[14] In their celebration of diversity, proponents of cultural pluralism tend to privilege relatively stable boundaries between groups, emphasizing internal group affirmation, cultural specificity, and the distinctiveness of ethnic groups. If it is at the site of the boundary that ethnic delineation occurs, however, it is also here that ethnic transformation and ethnic interaction take place, as groups both police their distinctiveness and come into contact with each other, forging cross-ethnic connections and coalitions.

Although the experience of exclusion and discrimination experienced by groups of color and by more ambiguously located groups such as Arab Americans frequently elicits a reactive focus on ethnic assertion and boundary maintenance, such experiences may also provide the basis for coalitions between similarly marginalized groups. Consider the phenomenon of racism. In a discussion of the stereotyping of Arabs, Ronald Stockton argues that racism has less to do with the actual group being targeted than with the process of maintaining boundaries between "us" and "them." Contemporary stereotypes of Arabs, he asserts, are not specific to Arabs; they are instead based on ethnic archetypes repeated in different contexts with different groups. For instance, "an exceptional proportion of all hostile or derogatory images targeted at Arabs are derived from or are parallel to classical images of Blacks and Jews, modified to fit contemporary circumstances."[15] For Stockton, "Images of Arabs cannot be seen in isolation, but are primarily derivative, rooted in a core of hostile archetypes that our culture applies to those with whom it clashes. When conflict or tension emerges they can be conjured up and adapted to new situations."[16]

As Stockton's discussion suggests, ethnic affirmation requires not just an assertion of group identity, but also a consideration of the broader implications of cultural identities within a multicultural, transnational context: an awareness of how issues affect and unite people across the divides of ethnicity. Groups such as Arab Americans, with little visibility of their own and therefore little power, stand to benefit from forming coalitions with others around issues of common cause—as when Japanese-American, Jewish-American, and Arab-American groups took joint action during the 1991 Gulf War in response to infringements on the civil rights of Arab Americans. Such coalitions make clear that it is possible to bridge the insularity of identity politics without diminishing the specificity of ethnic concerns.

The need to interrogate multiculturalism's emphasis on ethnic insularity has been voiced by critics on the right and the left. Although some commentators view multiculturalism and ethnicity as implicitly threatening to a presumed American "unity,"[17] other critics of multiculturalism speak from a position receptive to ethnic and racial realities, even as they seek a median space between ethnic particularity and a more uni- fied common ground. David Hollinger articulates one such view. Calling for a move- ment beyond multiculturalism as it is currently deployed, Hollinger makes a case for a "postethnic" perspective that would build on, but not be limited by, ethnic identifica- tion and that would infuse the current emphasis on roots with a "critical renewal of cosmopolitanism."[18]

In Hollinger's desired "postethnic" America, the affiliative nature of identities would be emphasized over the prescribed, "ethno-racial groups" would be recognized as con- structed rather than biological categories, and ethnic identity would be treated "as a question rather than a given."[19] The current conflation between race and ethnicity, argues Hollinger, is a result of the extent to which our current classifications depend on classic race thinking even as they seek to escape that legacy. This conflation brings to a point of contradiction "two valuable impulses in contemporary America: the impulse to protect historically disadvantaged populations from the effects of past and continuing discrimination, and the impulse to affirm the variety of cultures that now flourish within the United States."[20] Calling for a more precise distinction between races, which he defines as "culture free" categories that are not "real" but that provide a necessary political tool for affirmative action and cultures, which he defines as spheres of voluntary affiliation, Hollinger proposes that "ethno-racial affiliations" be viewed like religious affiliations, in which individuals possess "the right of exit and also the dynamics of entry" into cultural spheres. By pursuing this parallel, Hollinger argues, educational institutions would no longer need to fulfill the "need for cultural self-val- idation on the part of ethno-racial groups," and affirmative action programs could "continue to occupy the political space that was theirs alone before culture began to take over the ethno-racial pentagon."[21]

Hollinger's understanding of ethnicity as something to be negotiated rather than sim- ply asserted and his emphasis on flexibility and choice within a framework of neces- sary commitments offers a possible point of entry into the problem of negotiating the claims of identity and community. Despite its theoretical promise, however, Hollinger's "postethnic" framework does not adequately account for the complexity of Arab-Amer- ican identity and experience. For instance, Hollinger attempts to "symbolically cut down to size the whites who would otherwise continue to be anomalously unhistori- cized" by defining "white" as "European."[22] However, this definition explicitly excludes Arabs and Arab Americans, despite their official governmental categorization as whites. As non-Europeans racially included in "white" America but culturally excluded from this category,[23] Arab Americans are relegated to an undefined space. Similarly, the dis- tinction between "culture" and "race" fails to account for the extent to which cultural identities such as those of Arab Americans may elicit the same kind of discrimination as racial identities. As a result, Arab Americans are pushed to the margins of available definitions.

Part of the problem lies in the reliance on liberal individualism for an understanding of identity. "A postethnic perspective challenges the right of one's grandfather or grand- mother to determine primary identity," Hollinger asserts. "Individuals should be allowed to affiliate or disaffiliate with their own communities of descent to an extent that they choose, while affiliating with whatever nondescent communities are available and appealing to them."[24] However, although ethnic identity may be a matter of individual choice for some European ethnic groups, whose place in American society is at this point in time unquestioned, for Arab Americans—still subject to identity-based discrimination and to repercussions from political events in the Middle East—ethnicity cannot be understood in isolation from factors affecting the group at large.

More applicable to the Arab-American experience are theories of ethnicity and cultural pluralism that seek to grapple with power relations as well as cultural dynamics and that negotiate ethnic boundaries on both individual and group levels. Two examples include Ella Shohat and Robert Stam's discussion of multiculturalism and Chandra Talpade Mohanty's discussion of ethnic coalitions. In *Unthinking Eurocentrism*, Shohat and Stam critique the cultural focus of liberal pluralism, seeking to move multiculturalism away from essentialist assumptions about identity toward "a radical critique of power relations" and to turn it "into a rallying cry for a more substantive and reciprocal intercommunalism." Their discussion emphasizes "ethnic relationality and community answerability" over issues of "blood" heritage, assuming that the basis for identity and relationships is affiliation rather than kinship. At the heart of this concept of polycentric multiculturalism are identifications that are "multiple, unstable, historically situated, the products of ongoing differentiation and polymorphous identifications." Within this framework, identity serves as a marker both of who one is and of what one does with that information. Similarly, group identities "open the way for informed affiliation on the basis of shared social desires and identification" and for "cultural exchange ... between permeable, changing individuals and communities."[25]

Chandra Talpade Mohanty's discussion similarly emphasizes the process of building coalitions across ethnic boundaries in the context of shared struggle. She calls for

> an 'imagined community' of third world oppositional struggles. 'Imagined' not because it is not 'real' but because it suggests potential alliances and collaborations across divisive boundaries, and 'community' because in spite of internal hierarchies within third world contexts, it nevertheless suggests a significant, deep commitment to what Benedict Anderson, in referring to the idea of the nation, calls 'horizontal comradeship.'[26]

This concept of "horizontal comradeship" turns to "political rather than biological or cultural bases for alliance": rather than being based on ethnicity, race, sex, or class, group identity and action are grounded on the *implications* of such delineations—"the political links we choose to make among and between struggles."[27] It is through such linkages, Mohanty asserts, that issues of racism, marginality, and exclusion can be challenged.

The question of how to establish connections and coalitions across ethnic boundaries is of increasing importance within Arab-American discourse. Given the marginalization of Arab Americans within American culture and the on-going reality of anti-Arab discrimination and violence, the need to focus on protecting and strengthening Arab Americans as a group remains strong. However, it is also increasingly clear that ethnic identity cannot be constructed in isolation. On an ideological level, the insularity that arises from a singular focus on Arab-American issues may result in an obfuscation of the principles of justice and equity that underlie Arab-American struggles, leading to a lack of solidarity with other groups.[28] On a pragmatic level, the anomalous position of Arab Americans within American racial categories means that Arab Americans may be unable to elicit responses to their concerns without affiliating with other minority groups.[29]

Literary Negotiations

Contemporary Arab-American literature increasingly reflects the awareness of the need to forge connections beyond the insular boundaries of group identity. In contrast to earlier Arab-American writers, contemporary writers increasingly seek to articulate identity not only within but also across ethnic lines, from a stance of "reciprocal intercommunalism."[30] Particularly important is the work of Naomi Shihab Nye and David Williams, two writers whose work makes clear that Arab-American identity is not an end goal to be celebrated but a starting point from which to redefine and resituate concepts of identity, relationship, and community.[31] Instead of focusing on "Arab-American" themes to the exclusion of other concerns, Nye and Williams write about a variety of issues, peoples, and locales: Native Americans, Hispanic Americans, South Asians, Lebanese, and Palestinians; immigrants, laborers, and family members; North and South America, Asia, and the Middle East; urban, village, and wilderness contexts; war and poverty; resilience and joy. Their poetry and prose demonstrate the extent to which ethnicity may provide a foundation for new kinds of relationships across cultural divides.

Naomi Shihab Nye

Naomi Shihab Nye is a poet of Palestinian and American background whose work has received much attention within the United States and the Arab world. Daughter of a Palestinian Muslim father and of a European-American, Christian mother, Nye is one of the most widely known Arab-American writers. The author of six books of poetry, a book of essays, a novel for young adults, several children's picture books, and a number of edited collections of poetry, she has been featured on American national television programs such as Bill Moyers' "Language of Life"[32] and is the recipient of many awards and honors, including the prestigious Guggenheim Award. Nye is also increasingly well known in Arab literary contexts; her work has been translated into Arabic and has been included in anthologies of Arab writing.[33] However, Nye's literary activities are not bounded by these two facets of her identity, Arab and American. Her edited collections and her own writing draw on and reflect a wide variety of cultural contexts and sources.

This diversity of subject matter sometimes appears to complicate Nye's categorization as an "Arab-American" poet. For instance, in a 1991 essay discussing the Arab aspects of Nye's work, Gregory Orfalea observes that although Nye

> is the outstanding American poet of Palestinian origin, and one of the premier voices of her
> generation ... of 155 poems in her three published collections, only 14 have a recognizably

Arab or Palestinian content—less than 9 percent. More deal with the Hispanic Southwest where she lives, and Latin America, where she has traveled extensively, than the ancestral homeland of her father.[34]

Orfalea's essay was written before the publication of Nye's recent work, which includes much material on Arab and Palestinian themes. However, it remains true that Nye's poetry cannot be completely accounted for in terms of her ethnic identity, nor can her work be adequately described by a simple division into "Arab" and "non-Arab," "ethnic" and "nonethnic." Nye's writing is undergirded by a consistency of approach best described as a stance of engagement with the world. As reviewer Philip Booth writes, in a discussion of *Yellow Glove*,

> All her [Nye's] questions (and her own response to them) suggest to me an unstated question which seems to inform her best work: How do we come to terms with this world (literally *this world*) we cannot bear *not* to be part of? . . . Nye may not know any more than the rest of us *what to do,* but she knows more than most of us how many people(s) live; and she does justice to them, and to the need for change, by bringing home to readers both how variously and how similarly all people live.[35]

From this stance of listening and narration, Nye forges connections across boundaries of ethnicity, nationality, gender, and class. Although these connections are most often personal rather than communal, they provide the basis for linkages that take on metaphorical resonance. As Nye writes in the poem "Strings," "Tonight it is possible to pull the long string and feel someone moving far away / to touch the fingers of one hand to the fingers of the other hand / [. . .] to be linked to every mother / every father's father."[36]

In preface to the selection of her poetry in *Grapeleaves: A Century of Arab-American Poetry,* Nye writes of the "gravities of ancestry," the sense of "rapturous homecoming" that she experienced on meeting Arab-American writers.[37] Although "all writers are engaged in the building of bridges," she observes, "maybe bicultural writers who are actively conscious of or interested in heritage build another kind of bridge as well, this one between worlds. But it's not like a bridge, really—it's closer, like a pulse."[38] In such passages Nye draws on ethnicity as a foundation for the self. However, the imagery of a pulse not only suggests the notion of ethnicity as a blood inheritance, but also evokes processes of flow and interchange: much as a pulse signals the flow of blood through the body, ethnicity, for Nye, signals communication and interchange. Heritage, Nye suggests, matters not just for what it tells us about who we are, but also for how it informs what we *do,* the ways in which we draw on our cultural identity for our interactions in the world. Although ethnicity does not provide a priori answers, it nonetheless makes it possible to ask necessary, if not always answerable, questions.

An essay about Nye's grandmother's home in Palestine, "One Village," clarifies this sense of ethnicity as the basis for a movement not only backward and inward, but also forward and outward. Describing her return to her Palestinian grandmother's village after fifteen years of absence, Nye at first seeks to relocate herself. "The village smells familiar," she writes. "Whole scenes unfold like recent landscapes." However, the village not only affirms who she is, but also shows her how to listen to differences. "I was a teenager when last here, blind in the way of many teenagers," Nye writes. "I wanted the world to be like me. Now there is nothing I would like less. I enter the world hoping for a journey out of self as much as in."[39]

In this "journey out of self," Nye draws on her ethnic background to make connections beyond the boundaries of ethnicity. Consider the title poem of her first book of poetry, *Different Ways to Pray*. Although Nye clearly evokes her Palestinian Muslim background here, this is not simply an "ethnic" poem. Rather it uses the imagery of an Arab landscape to make a larger point about diversity and commonality. "Prayer," here, is not just the conventional act of religious worship but a generally reverential approach toward life. In addition to the expected modes of kneeling and making pilgrimage (both described with implicit reference to the Palestinian Muslim context), it also includes—in what is for Nye a characteristic homage to dailiness—such activities as "lugging water from the spring / or balancing the baskets of grapes."[40] The pious, Nye suggests, include not only those who "bend to kiss the earth ... their lean faces housing mystery" but also others such as "the old man Fowzi ... Fowzi the fool / who ... / insisted he spoke with God as he spoke with goats, / and was famous for his laugh."[41] Nye's receptiveness here to a variety of perspectives points toward an ability to move beyond conventional boundaries while honoring the identities they delineate.

As the daughter of a European-American Christian mother and a Muslim Palestinian father, Nye has a particular interest in challenging rigid boundaries of identification. In a poem titled "Half and Half" that evokes her mixed background, Nye describes an interlocutor for whom multiple allegiances are an impossible fragmentation: "If you love Jesus you can't love / anyone else. Says he."[42] In contrast, Nye celebrates difference, invoking the possibility of transformation and a wholeness woven of multiplicity: "A woman opens a window—here and here and here— / ... She is making a soup out of what she had left / in the bowl, the shriveled garlic and bent bean. She is leaving nothing out."[43]

"Leaving nothing out" may be viewed as a metaphor for Nye's poetic practice and her approach to identity. Her poems are often about everyday objects and seemingly insignificant incidents, "the things which often go unnoticed."[44] Similarly, Nye draws on all parts of her identity, background, and experience for a wholeness that eschews artificial unity. In an essay about her part-Palestinian son, Nye asks, "Why, if we're part anything, does it matter?"[45] It matters, she suggests, because identity is constructed in relationship to difference. "I had to live in a mostly Mexican-American city to feel what it meant to be part Arab," she writes. "It meant Take This Ribbon and Unwind It Slowly."[46]

"Leaving nothing out" for Nye, as for other Palestinian Americans, also means the need to come to terms with Palestinian history and with a legacy of occupation, injustice, and exile. Given this history, Palestinian-American writers carry the burden of using their talents for Palestinian causes. Nye evokes this burden in "The Man Who Makes Brooms." The poem begins,

> So you come with these maps in your head
> and I come with voices chiding me to
> "speak for my people"
> and we march around like guardians of memory
> till we find the man on the short stool
> who makes brooms.[47]

Given the dearth of spokespeople for the Palestinians in the American context and Nye's stature as a prominent Arab-American writer, it is not surprising that Nye feels the pressure to "speak for [her] people." However, being a "guardian of memory" suggests the task of defending borders, a stance Nye would not be expected to take to readily. She instead chooses to depict the resilience demonstrated by Palestinians in their daily life. Although on the surface a simple evocation of a craftsman in Jerusalem, her poem is a political poem affirming Palestinian experience; as Nye explains in an interview, for the broom-maker to carry out his work with such precision and care under conditions of occupation is "a political act. . . . Politics also involves the dignity of daily life."[48]

In addition to depending on ordinary activities and objects that resonate across cultural lines for her depiction of "ethnic" themes, Nye also draws connections between Palestinians and others. In the poem "Shrines," a response to the massacre of Palestinians in Lebanon at Sabra and Chatila in 1982, Nye writes, "We cannot build enough shrines. . . . If we light candles, we must light a million. / Lebanon, Salvador, Palestine, here."[49] The tragedies of the contemporary world cannot be viewed in isolation. Even Nye's approach to the Palestinian-Israeli conflict is informed by this desire to find points of connection. As she writes in "Jerusalem," "I'm not interested in / who suffered the most. / I'm interested in / people getting over it . . . It's late but everything comes next."[50]

Nye's poems about other peoples and other locales grow out of this sense of connection across even the most intransigent of boundaries. Her work conveys a sense that to tell a fragment of a story—her own or that of someone else—is to forge a link in the chain against erasure. In the poem "Remembered," Nye writes of the "need for remembrance," a "ringing rising up out of the soil's centuries, the ones / who plowed this land, whose names we do not know."[51] The gesture of remembrance carries particular weight for Palestinians, whose history is so often obscured or denied. However, those "whose names we do not know" do not only reside within one's own ethnic group, as is clear in a poem "The Endless Indian Nights." "I lay thinking of Afghanistan," Nye writes, "men who live in caves / eating potatoes till their faces grow longer, their eyes blacken and will not close. / Someone said the world has never forgotten anyone better. / And I vowed to remember them / though what good it would do, who knows."[52] Such poems situate Nye within a global community.

Establishing such linkages is not easy. In the poem "Kindness," Nye writes, "Before you learn the tender gravity of kindness, / you must travel where the Indian in a white poncho / lies dead by the side of the road. / You must see how this could be you, / how he too was someone / who journeyed through the night with plans / and the simple breath that kept him alive."[53] A sense of connection requires not pity, with its implicit stance of superiority, but rather the ability to recognize human commonalities without glossing over the specificity of others' experiences. To arrive at this sense of connection one must move beyond personal experience, viewing oneself within a wider context. You must "lose everything" and "wake up with sorrow," Nye writes; you must "speak to it [sorrow] till your voice / catches the thread of all sorrows / and you see the size of the cloth."[54]

Nye's understanding of her location within this wider context underlies the more joyful linkages that emerge throughout her writing. This is evident in the poem "For Lost and Found Brothers," in which a sense of familial and ethnic connections reverberates outward in widening ripples, suggesting connections that transit the globe:

> For you, brothers.
> For the blood rivers invisibly harbored.
> For the grandfather who murmured the same songs.
> And for the ways we know each other years before meeting,
> how strangely and suddenly, on the lonely porches,
> in the sleepless mouth of the night,
> the sadness drops away, we move forward,
> confident we were born into a large family,
> our brothers cover the earth.[55]

David Williams

The poetry and prose of Lebanese-American David Williams also makes clear the need to make connections with others across the boundaries of ethnicity.[56] Like Nye, Williams is a writer whose work defies simple categorization, making linkages between individual lives in diverse contexts. Throughout his work, Williams traces the ways in which a legacy of Arab heritage may lead not simply to the preservation of insular boundaries of group identity but also to cross-ethnic connections, grounding, as it does in Nye, a movement not only inward but outward as well.

Drawing on his own experiences as a Lebanese American, an activist, and a teacher, Williams writes of war, refugees, poverty, oppression, and injustice. However, his poetry also searches for and identifies sources of hope, affirmation, endurance, resilience, and joy. Situating Arab-American identity within a global and a continental American context, Williams celebrates individual lives while forging connections between Arab Americans and others subjected to the vicissitudes of history, making clear the need for self-criticism and for coalitions across ethnic lines. As one reviewer observed of *Traveling Mercies,* Williams "attempts to find connections in a divided world. . . . In a time that exalts the individual and the virtue of separate heritage, Williams recognizes that true heritage is never diluted by knowledge and understanding of other cultures."[57]

In his poetry collection, *Traveling Mercies,* and in his unpublished texts, *Quick Prism* (poetry) and *Coyote Wells* (a novel), Williams refracts multiple histories through a voice passionate about the "need to join with everyone trying to say something true,"[58] a voice that carries many stories and lives within it. His work points toward the possibility of uniting communities across cultural, ethnic, and national boundaries, even as it honors and affirms individual resilience. The structure of *Traveling Mercies* echoes this insistence on interconnection, moving from a grounding in personal identity and history to a recognition of the wider context of ethnicity and identity. Although the two parts of the book correspond in a general way to a division between personal experience and public testimony, the book interweaves public and private themes, establishing connections between family, ethnicity, and community while situating these within a historical and geographical context that extends from North and South America to the Middle East.

Although grounded in Arab-American realities, Williams' poetry holds the potential of speaking across cultural boundaries to people from many different backgrounds. "Breath," the opening poem of *Traveling Mercies,* brings together themes of ethnic identity, connection, and communal activism in a manner that is at once specific and general. The poem implicitly draws on the links in Arabic between the word for "spirit" and the word for "breath," suggesting that Williams' Arab heritage underlies his poetic perception. However, it refrains from specifically naming Williams' Lebanese ancestry, speaking instead more generally. "The people I come from were thrown away," writes Williams, "as if they were nothing, whatever they might have / said become stone, beyond human patience, / except for the songs."[59] Despite the specifically Arabic resonances of "breath," the poem turns on a sense of common humanity, linking Williams not only to "the people I come from" but also to other peoples "thrown away / as if they were nothing," with whom he can join in common cause. "Breath" invokes the individual, ordinary lives that profoundly matter amid the sweeping devastations of history.

Williams' ability to transform grief into something life-sustaining turns on this recognition of the communal nature of suffering and of the communal efforts required to confront and transform it. Instead of claiming a solitary voice of testimony, Williams seeks to "join that song" of resistance and transformation—a song larger than he is, but one to which his voice is indispensable. He writes, "I'm thirsty for words to join that song—/ cupped hands at the spring, a cup of / rain passed hand to hand."[60] His poetry embodies a faith that what sustains people—poetry, water, bread—can be passed on, "a cup of rain passed hand to hand . . . a clear / lens trembling with our breath."[61]

The need to move beyond ethnic insularity and to recognize commonalities of both suffering and hope emerges with particular clarity in the poem "Available Light." Juxtaposing personal grief over the death of an unnamed girl in Beirut to the historical resonances of a Vishniac photo of the Warsaw ghetto, this poem suggests that, in the same way that historical images make claims on us beyond the specificity of group boundaries, individual suffering may perhaps be best understood by recognizing how our own experiences are reflected in those of others. "When I think of how / you bled to death / during the siege of Beirut," Williams writes, "your face dissolves into grains of silver / bromide, rocks on the moon / we see as a human face." This stark dissolution of grief leads to a more public image, that of the girl in the Warsaw ghetto "who spent the winter in bed / because she was hungry and had no shoes." The two images intertwine, as the connections between the Arab in Beirut and the Jew in Warsaw emerge like shadows in a developing photograph:

> I pick you out among all the lost
> a Jew, an Arab, who both could have passed
> for my daughters, your trace dark crystals
> on a negative, breath on a mirror,
> a steady, invisible light.[62]

Belying the politics of cultural particularity and assumptions about relationships between Jews and Arabs, Williams challenges the most intractable of boundaries. In this and other poems, the possibility of forging connections emerges slowly but steadily, like human features becoming discernible in the moon's far face.

Throughout his work, Williams makes clear that ethnic identity in and of itself cannot always provide a sufficient basis for agency and resistance even though it provides a source of sustenance and strength. Affiliation instead is based on many factors—gender, class, health, the experience of war—none of which can be viewed in isolation. The prose poem "Lasts" makes clear such intersections. "I think of my mother heading back to the shoe factory the morning after her father told her, scholarship or no scholarship, girls didn't go to college," writes Williams. "... I can't help it, I think of the millions killed with no testament but their shoes tossed in a heap, and the others who, being barefoot, are even easier to forget."[63] This linkage between his mother's experience and the suffering of millions suggests that individual experience can never be viewed in a historical vacuum. Although the connections linking people are too often commonalities of suffering, these links also provide a source of sustenance and resilience. "I need to join with everyone trying to say something true," Williams writes, and this communal context lends strength and clarity to his voice. The final lines of *Traveling Mercies* offer a compelling evocation of hope that parallels that put forward by Nye: "Everyone I have ever touched has put more life in my hands, and entered my blood, and lit my brain, and even now moves my tongue to speak."[64]

Nye and Williams draw on their Arab-American ethnicity in their writing not simply to celebrate their heritage, but because this identity has serious implications in the contemporary context. As Williams suggests in the poem "Almost One," in the current American context, Arab-Americans are not quite "white" enough, not quite "American" enough, not quite whole.[65] By recognizing the fragmentation and complexity of their identities and their commonalities with others, however, Arab Americans may begin to join forces with others marginalized by categories of identity or by structures of violence and power. Evoking a radical, polycentric multiculturalism in which essentialist categories of kinship have been replaced by affiliative categories of relationship, Williams and Nye make clear the need to focus on Arab-American ethnicity in relation to other issues and groups and to situate ethnic expression within a context of committed activism. Although their poetry and prose may be read as an affirmation of Arab-American identity, it also should be read as an exploration of how to situate that identity within a contemporary multicultural context in which Arab Americans have a great deal to lose by isolation.

Until now, few have aligned themselves with Arab-American causes, and it could be argued that it is premature for Arab Americans to become involved with the issues of others and that they should instead focus on asserting their own identity within strong cultural parameters. However, at this time of global interconnection, individual causes can no longer be viewed in separation from the global structures of power that situate them, nor can the effects of these structures of power be isolated to a single group. To discuss Arab-American identity requires something more than nostalgia or simple celebration; what is needed is activism and agency on issues of justice, issues that traverse cultural and national boundaries. Whether undertaken from a sense of humanism or from a pragmatic understanding of the need for allies, such communal activism is crucial if Arab Americans are to achieve success in their goals of fighting racism, violence, and injustice and of ensuring a more just and fulfilling future for themselves and others. The result of such communal awareness and agency can only be empowerment.

Notes

Acknowledgment: I am grateful to Souad Dajani and Therese Saliba for reading and commenting on earlier drafts of this essay.

1. Charles Taylor, "The Politics of Recognition." In Charles Taylor et al., eds., *Multiculturalism: Examining the Politics of Recognition* (Princeton, NJ: Princeton University Press, 1994), pp. 75–106.

2. For discussions of the phenomenon of "honorary" whiteness experienced by Arab Americans, see Joseph Massad, "Palestinians and the Limits of Racialized Discourse," *Social Text* 11, no. 1 (1993): 94–114; and Soheir Morsy, "Beyond the Honorary 'White' Classification of Egyptians: Societal Identity in Historical Context." In Steven Gregory and Roger Sanjek, eds., *Race* (New Brunswick, NJ: Rutgers University Press, 1994), pp. 175–198.

3. In the wake of the bombing, amid runaway media speculation on the presumed "Middle Eastern" connection, journalists expressed surprise at government statements that the suspected perpetrators were two "white males," a response that indicated the extent to which "white" and "Arab"—and by implication, "Arab" and "American"—are presumed to be mutually exclusive categories.

4. Alixa Naff, *Becoming American: The Early Arab Immigrant Experience* (Carbondale, IL: Southern Illinois University Press, 1985), p. 330.

5. Shelly Slade, "The Image of the Arab in America: Analysis of a Poll on American Attitudes," *Middle East Journal* 35, no. 2 (Spring 1981): 143–62.

6. Slade, "The Image of the Arab in America," p. 147.

7. Abraham cites the case of a school newspaper that ran an advertisement for a roommate specifying "No Arabs." "One need only imagine the public outcry had a similar notice read 'No Blacks,' or 'No Jews,'" comments Abraham, "to appreciate the level of complicity on the part of the school paper in this bit of racism." See Nabeel Abraham, "Anti-Arab Racism and Violence in the United States." In Ernest McCarus, ed., *The Development of Arab-American Identity* (Ann Arbor, MI: University of Michigan Press, 1994), pp. 159, 190.

8. Unattributed, quoted in Gregory Orfalea and Sherif Elmusa, *Grapeleaves: A Century of Arab-American Poetry* (Salt Lake City: University of Utah Press, 1988), p. xiv.

9. This exhibit, developed and curated by the Arab Community Center for Economic and Social Services (ACCESS) and the Michigan State University Museum, in collaboration with the Detroit Historical Museum, and funded by the National Endowment for the Humanities, opened at the Detroit Historical Museum in March 1998, with the intention to subsequently travel to different cities across the United States. The exhibit features historical and contemporary photographs taken from family albums and from the archives of professional photographers, as well as cultural objects made by Detroit-area Arab-American artists. The exhibit is based on an earlier photographic exhibition presented by ACCESS and the National Museum of American History at the Smithsonian Institution.

10. Examples include Eric Hooglund, ed., *Crossing the Waters: Arabic-Speaking Immigrants to the United States before 1940* (Washington, DC: Smithsonian Institution Press, 1987); Ernest McCarus, ed., *Development of Arab-American Identity*; and Joanna Kadi, ed., *Food for our Grandmothers: Writings by Arab-American and Arab-Canadian Feminists* (Boston: South End Press, 1994).

11. This hostility surfaces, Abraham says, in "ideologically motivated violence" against Arab Americans by Jewish extremist groups (p. 180), in anti-Arab xenophobia manifested through "locally inspired hostility and violence toward ["ethnically visible"] Arab Americans, Muslims and Middle Easterners and their institutions" (p. 188), and in "jingoistic racism," which Abra-

ham describes as a "curious blend of knee-jerk patriotism and homegrown white racism toward non-European, non-Christian dark skinned peoples" (p. 193). See Abraham, "Anti-Arab Racism."

12. Mary C. Waters, *Ethnic Options: Choosing Identities in America* (Berkeley: University of California Press, 1990).

13. See ADC Research Institute, *1995 Report on Anti-Arab Racism, Hate Crimes, Discrimination and Defamation of Arab Americans* (Washington, DC: ADC Research Institute, 1996); and *1996–1997 Report on Hate Crimes and Discrimination Against Arab Americans* (Washington, DC: ADC Research Institute, 1997).

14. Fredrik Barth, ed., *Ethnic Groups and Boundaries: The Social Organization of Culture Difference* (Boston: Little, Brown and Co., 1969), p. 15.

15. Ronald Stockton, "Ethnic Archetypes and the Arab Image." In McCarus, ed., *Development of Arab-American Identity*, p. 121.

16. Stockton, "Ethnic Archetypes and the Arab Image," p. 120.

17. See, for instance, Arthur M. Schlesinger, Jr., *The Disuniting of America: Reflections on a Multicultural Society* (Knoxville, TN: Whittle Direct Books, 1991).

18. David A. Hollinger, *Postethnic America: Beyond Multiculturalism* (New York: Basic Books, 1995), p. 5.

19. Hollinger, *Postethnic America*, p. 106.

20. Hollinger, *Postethnic America*, p. 49. This confusion between race and ethnicity is particularly apparent, Hollinger argues, in the classification of Hispanic or Latino Americans—previously classified as Caucasian and identified according to their country of origin, but now increasingly considered a "race" (pp. 31–32). The lobby for a mixed-race census classification brings these contradictions to the forefront and "threatens to destroy the whole structure" of the ethnic-racial pentagon by challenging the "one-drop rule" (pp. 44–45).

21. Hollinger, *Postethnic America*, pp. 121–129.

22. Hollinger, *Postethnic America*, p. 31.

23. The exclusion of Arabs from American citizenship has on occasion been justified on the basis that Arabs are inherently non-European. In the same way that Jews were once considered a separate "race," Arabs occupy a different space in the American imagination than that indicated by their official classification.

24. Hollinger, *Postethnic America*, p. 116.

25. Ella Shohat and Robert Stam, *Unthinking Eurocentrism: Multiculturalism and the Media* (London: Routledge, 1994), pp. 47–49.

26. See Chandra Tolpade Mohanty's "Introduction." In Chandra Tolpade Mohanty, Ann Russo, and Lourdes Torres, eds., *Third World Women and the Politics of Feminism* (Bloomington, IN: Indiana University Press, 1991), p. 4.

27. Mohanty, Russo, and Torres, eds., *Third World Women*, p. 4.

28. An anecdote will clarify this point. In a discussion about the stereotyping of Arabs in the movie *Aladdin* on the Internet mailing list *Arab-American* in the fall of 1996, one participant commented that, because the Aladdin story is actually Persian, not Arab, Arabs should not feel offended by the stereotyping. The flawed logic in such reasoning becomes clear when one considers the example of Pakistanis and Iranians physically assaulted during the Gulf War because they were thought to be Arab; those injured were doubtless not comforted by the knowledge that it was not their own identity that was being targeted. Such dismissal of discrimination and injustice when it does not directly affect one's own ethnic group ultimately limits the ability to address these problems when they are directed at one's own group. Such attitudes rarefy cultural identification to the point that it loses its meaning.

29. For instance, despite the problems of including Arab Americans under the rubric of "Asian American" (in the case of Lebanese, Syrians, Palestinians, and other west Asians) or "African

American" (in the case of Egyptians, Moroccans, and other North Africans), such classification may be necessary to facilitate Arab-American inclusion within the American context.

30. Shohat and Stam, *Unthinking Eurocentrism,* p. 47.

31. This stance is by no means limited to these two authors. Other Arab-American writing that similarly challenges ethnic boundaries includes Elmaz Abinader's *Children of the Roojme: A Family's Journey* (New York: W. W. Norton, 1991); Diana Abu-Jaber's *Arabian Jazz* (New York: Harcourt Brace, 1993); Etel Adnan's *The Arab Apocalypse* (Sausalito, CA: Post-Apollo Press, 1989); Lawrence Joseph's *Before Our Eyes* (New York: Farrar, Straus & Giroux, 1993), *Curriculum Vitae* (Pittsburgh, PA: University of Pittsburgh Press, 1988); *Shouting at No One* (Pittsburgh, PA: University of Pittsburgh Press, 1983); Joanna Kadi's edited volume, *Food for Our Grandmothers* and her collection of essays *Thinking Class* (Boston: South End Press, 1996); Khaled Mattawa's *Ismalia Eclipse: Poems* (Riverdale-on-Hudson, NY: Sheep Meadow Press, 1995); and Adele NeJame's *Field Work* (Honolulu: Petronium Press, 1996).

32. "The Language of Life" series aired on PBS in the summer of 1995. Nye was also included in the corresponding volume, *The Language of Life.* Nye's poetry books include *Different Ways to Pray* (Portland, OR: Breitenbush Books, 1980), *Hugging the Jukebox* (Portland, OR: Breitenbush Books, 1982), *Yellow Glove* (Portland, OR: Breitenbush Books, 1986), *Words under the Words* (Portland, OR: Eighth Mountain Press, 1995), *Red Suitcase* (Brockport, NY: BOA Editions, 1998), and *Fuel* (New York: BOA Editions, 1998). Her edited anthologies include *This Same Sky: A Collection of Poems from Around the World* (New York: Four Winds Press/Macmillan, 1992), *I Feel a Little Jumpy Around You* (New York: Simon & Schuster Books for Young Readers, 1996), co-edited with Paul B. Janeczko; *The Tree Is Older than You Are* (New York: Simon & Schuster, 1995), *The Space Between Our Footsteps* (New York: Simon & Schuster Books for Young Readers, 1998), and *What Have You Lost?* (New York: Greenwillow Books, 1999). Her prose works include a novel for young adults, *Habibi* (New York: Simon & Schuster Books for Young Readers, 1997), and a collection of essays, *Never in a Hurry* (Columbia, SC: University of South Carolina Press, 1996). Her children's picture books include *Sitti's Secrets* (New York: Four Winds Press, 1994), *Benito's Dream Bottle* (New York: Simon & Schuster Books for Young Readers, 1995), and *Lullaby Raft* (New York: Simon & Schuster Books for Young Readers, 1997).

33. See, for instance, Salma Khadra Jayyusi, ed., *Anthology of Modern Palestinian Literature* (New York: Columbia University Press, 1992).

34. Gregory Orfalea, "Doomed by Our Blood to Care: The Poetry of Naomi Shihab Nye," *Paintbrush* 18, no. 3 (Spring 1991): 56.

35. Philip Booth, "Loners Whose Voices Move: An Essay Review of *Yellow Glove, Further Adventures with You, Descendant,* and *Out in the Open,*" *Georgia Review* 43 (Spring 1989): 162–63.

36. Nye, *Fuel,* p. 86.

37. Orfalea and Elmusa, eds., *Grapeleaves,* p. 266.

38. Orfalea and Elmusa, eds., *Grapeleaves,* p. 266.

39. Nye, *Never in a Hurry,* pp. 49–50.

40. Nye, *Different Ways to Pray,* p. 22.

41. Nye, *Different Ways to Pray,* p. 23.

42. Nye, *Fuel,* p. 60.

43. Nye, *Fuel,* p. 60.

44. Nye, in James Haba, ed., *The Language of Life: A Festival of Poets* (New York: Doubleday, 1995), p. 324.

45. Nye, *Never in a Hurry,* p. 148.

46. Nye, *Never in a Hurry,* p. 148.

47. Nye, *Words under the Words,* p. 127.

48. Nye, in Haba, ed., *The Language of Life*, pp. 325–326.

49. Nye, in Jayyusi, ed., *Anthology of Modern Palestinian Literature*, p. 357.

50. Nye, *Red Suitcase*, pp. 21–22.

51. Nye, *Different Ways to Pray*, p. 11.

52. Nye, *Yellow Glove*, p. 46.

53. Nye, *Different Ways to Pray*, p. 54.

54. Nye, *Different Ways to Pray*, p. 54.

55. Nye, *Words under the Words*, p. 51.

56. This discussion draws in part on my essay "Arab American Literature and the Politics of Memory" in Amritjit Singh, Joseph T. Skerrett, Jr., and Robert E. Hogan, eds., *Memory and Cultural Politics: New Approaches to American Ethnic Languages* (Boston: Northeastern University Press, 1996), pp. 266–290.

57. Ted Genoways, Review of *Traveling Mercies, Prairie Schooner* 69, no. 1 (Spring 1995): 181.

58. Williams, *Traveling Mercies*, p. 69.

59. Williams, *Traveling Mercies*, p. 5.

60. Williams, *Traveling Mercies*, p. 5.

61. Williams, *Traveling Mercies*, p. 5.

62. Williams, *Traveling Mercies*, p. 40.

63. Williams, *Traveling Mercies*, p. 69.

64. Williams, *Traveling Mercies*, p. 65.

65. Williams, *Traveling Mercies*, pp. 66–67.

About the Contributors

BAHA ABU-LABAN is Professor Emeritus of Sociology and Director, Centre of Excellence for Research on Immigration and Integration, at the University of Alberta. He has published widely in the areas of ethnic and minority groups, leadership, sociology of development, and sociology of the Middle East, including *An Olive Branch on the Family Tree: The Arabs in Canada; Arabs in America: Myths and Realities;* and *The Muslim Community in North America.* Dr. Abu-Laban has served as President of the Canadian Ethnic Studies Association and the Association of Arab-American University Graduates.

SHARON McIRVIN ABU-LABAN is Professor of Sociology at the University of Alberta. She is past Chair of the University of Alberta Centre for Gerontology and has served as Associate Chair of the Department of Sociology. Her publications include *Muslim Families in North America, The Arab World: Dynamics of Development,* and journal articles and chapters on the sociology of aging, the family, comparative development, gender, religion, education, and theory.

KRISTINE AJROUCH, Ph.D. is a Research Fellow at the University of Michigan. She has researched how adolescent children of Muslim Lebanese immigrants in the United States form ethnic identities and is working on a book that addresses the acculturation and assimilation processes that second-generation Lebanese and Yemeni adolescents in America live in ethnic communities.

FATIMA AGHA AL-HAYANI was born in Beirut, Lebanon. She holds a B.Ed. in English and French, M.A. in French Language and literature, M.A. in Middle Eastern Studies, and Ph.D. from the University of Michigan at Ann Arbor. Her doctoral concentration was Muslim Jurisprudence and Family Law. She teaches Islam, Muslim Philosophy, and Middle East society and politics in the departments of Philosophy, Sociology, and Political Science at the University of Toledo. She also teaches French and English at the high school level.

RICHARD T. ANTOUN is Professor of Anthropology at the State University of New York at Binghamton. He has written three books on the basis of his research trips to Jordan over the past 30 years: *Arab Village: A Social Structural Study of a Transjordanian Peasant Community* (1972); *Low-Key Politics: Local-Level Leadership and Change in the Middle East* (1979); and *Muslim Preacher in the Modern World: A Jordanian Case Study in Comparative Perspective* (1989). He has also co-edited four interdisciplinary volumes. He has completed the manuscript "Transnational Migration in the Post-modern World" and has begun another entitled "Fundamentalism in Comparative Perspective: Christianity, Islam, Judaism and Change at the Turn of the Century."

BARBARA C. ASWAD is Professor of Anthropology at Wayne State University in Detroit. She has written *Property Control and Social Strategies: Settlers on a Middle Eastern Plain* (1971), edited *Arabic Speaking Communities in American Cities* (1974), and co-edited *Family and Gender Among American Muslims: Issues Facing Middle Eastern Immigrants and Their Descendants* (1996). She served as President of the Middle East Studies Association of North America and has served on the Board of Directors of the Arab Center for Economic and Social Services (ACCESS) in Dearborn, Michigan, for more than twenty-five years.

LOUISE CAINKAR is a sociologist and Research Assistant Professor at the University of Illinois–Great Cities Institute. She specializes in issues of inequality and human rights concerning racial and ethnic groups, immigrants, and migrants. She has published numerous articles on human rights in the Middle East and on Arab Americans. She is completing a book on Palestinian immigrants in the United States that will be published by Temple University Press. As a scholar and activist, Dr. Cainkar also does a significant amount of work with community-based organizations in Chicago.

LAWRENCE DAVIDSON is an Associate Professor in the Department of History at West Chester University. His research focuses on the evolution of American perceptions of Palestine from 1917 to 1948. His work has been published in the *Journal of Palestine Studies, Middle East Policy, Arab Studies Quarterly,* and *Biblical Archaeology.*

ROSINA HASSOUN holds a Bachelor of Science in Zoology and a Master of Science in Biology from Texas A&M University. She received her Ph.D. in anthropology from the University of Florida, Gainesville, in 1995. Hassoun's area of study is the Middle East and Arab Americans. She has published articles in the *Florida Journal of Anthropology, The Link,* and a chapter in *Water, Culture, and Power* (Island Press, 1998), edited by John Donahue and Barbara Johnston. Dr. Hassoun is an adjunct professor at Michigan State University.

IBRAHIM HAYANI is a Professor in the School of Business Management of Seneca College, Toronto, Canada. He has worked as a research economist and policy advisor for the Federal Government of Canada and for the Provincial Government of Ontario. He also worked as a research consultant for the International Centre for Agricultural

Research in Dry Areas (ICARDA) in Aleppo, Syria. Hayani has published numerous articles and research reports, including a comprehensive United Nations–financed study on higher education in Syria to the year 2000 and a study on the Arabs in Ontario for Heritage Canada.

SUAD JOSEPH is Professor of Anthropology and Women's Studies at the University of California at Davis. She has carried out urban and rural fieldwork in her native Lebanon for 30 years. She edited *Intimate Selving in Arab Families: Gender, Self and Identity* (forthcoming). She is also editing a book on *Gender and Citizenship in the Middle East* and co-editing books on *Citizenship in Lebanon* (with Walid Moubarak and Antoine Messarra), *Gender and Citizenship in Lebanon* (with Najla Hamadeh and Jean Said Makdisi), and *Gender, Culture, and Politics in the Middle East* (with Susan Slyomovics).

LISA SUHAIR MAJAJ writes on Arab-American literature and culture and on Arab women's literature. Her recent publications include "Arab-Americans and the Meanings of Race" (in *U.S. Ethnicities and Postcolonial Theory*), "New Directions: Arab-American Writing at Century's End" (in *Jusoor*, forthcoming), and the introduction to Fay Afaf Kanafani's memoir *Nadia: Captive of Hope*. Her creative writing has been anthologized in *Food for Our Grandmothers: Writings by Arab-American and Arab-Canadian Feminists* and *Homemaking: Women Writers and the Politics and Poetics of Home*. She is co-editor of the collections *The Politics of Reception: Globalizing Third World Women's Texts* (forthcoming), *Intersections: Gender, Nation and Community in Arab Women's Novels*, and *Etel Adnan: Scribe of a Scattered Self*.

MOHAMED MATTAR received his Bachelor of Law (LL.B.) and Diploma of Higher Studies in Private Law (D.P.L.) from Alexandria University Faculty of Law. He also has the degrees of Master of Comparative Law (M.C.L.) from the University of Miami School of Law and Master of Law (L.L.M.) and Doctor of Juridical Science (S.J.D.) from Tulane University School of Law. Dr. Mattar has taught at Alexandria University's Faculty of Law, the Arab University of Beirut, and the Arab Maritime Transport Academy in Egypt. He is Legal Advisor to the Embassy of the United Arab Emirates in the United States and Adjunct Professor of Law at Georgetown Law Center.

KATHLEEN M. MOORE is Assistant Professor in the Department of Political Science at the University of Connecticut. Her research interests include religion, law, migration, and the construction of identities. She is the author of *Al-Mughtaribun: American Law and the Transformation of Muslim Life in the United States* (1995). She is writing a book on the emergence of a unique "minoritarian" legal culture among Muslims living in "diaspora."

LORI ANNE SALEM, Director of the Writing Center at Temple University, earned her doctorate in dance history from Temple University in 1995. Her dissertation research focused on images of Arabs in American entertainment and their relation to ideologies of race and sexuality. She has published her work in *Dance Research Journal, Journal of the American Medical Association,* and *Bulletin of the Middle East Studies Associ-*

ation, and has presented papers at the conferences of the American Studies Association, the Society of Dance History Scholars, the Popular Culture Studies Association, and other organizations.

THERESE SALIBA is a faculty member of Third World Feminist Studies at the Evergreen State College, where she teaches courses in women's studies, Middle East Studies, and ethnic literatures. She is an associate editor of *Signs: Journal of Women in Culture and Society,* and her essays on postcolonial literature, media representations, and feminist issues have appeared in several journals and collections. From 1995 through 1996, she was Senior Fulbright Scholar at Bethlehem University, West Bank, and is the producer of the video documentary, "Checkpoint: The Palestinians After Oslo" (1997).

HELEN HATAB SAMHAN is Executive Vice President of the Arab American Institute in Washington, D.C. Samhan has served at the American-Arab Anti-Discrimination Committee as Assistant Director and was affiliated with the American-Arab Association for Commerce and Industry in New York City, where she served as its director of research. In 1996, she organized a "Working Group on Ancestry in the U.S. Census," a national coalition to support ethnic data measurement. Samhan has a Master's degree in Middle East Studies from the American University of Beirut. Her publications have appeared in *Arab Studies Quarterly* and *Journal of Palestine Studies.*

MAY SEIKALY is Associate Professor, Department of Near Eastern and Asian Studies at Wayne State University. Among her publications are *HAIFA: Transformation of a Palestinian Arab Society: 1918–1939* and articles and chapters in *Dirasat; International Journal of Middle East Studies; Der nahe Osten in der Zwischenkriegszeit 1918–1939; Keepers of the Flame: Power, Myth, and Cultural Consciousness in Ethnic Female Identity* (edited by Sondra O'Neale and Cynthia Tompkins, 1998); and *European Maturity and Cultural Difference* (edited by Leila Fawaz, forthcoming).

MICHAEL W. SULEIMAN is University Distinguished Professor of Political Science at Kansas State University. Among his publications are *Political Parties in Lebanon* (1967), *The Arabs in the Mind of America* (1988), *Arab Americans: Continuity and Change* (co-editor, 1989), and *U.S. Policy on Palestine from Wilson to Clinton* (editor, 1995). In 1994 and 1995, Suleiman received an Institute for Advanced Study fellowship at Princeton to write about Arabs in the United States. He has served as president of the Association of Arab-American University Graduates and as a member of the board of directors of the Middle East Studies Association of North America.

JANICE J. TERRY is Professor of History at Eastern Michigan University. She is author of *The Wafd, 1919–1952: Cornerstone of Egyptian Political Power* and *Mistaken Identity: Arab Stereotypes in Popular Writing,* in addition to numerous articles and essays on the media and the Middle East. She has co-authored three college textbooks: *World History; The Twentieth Century: A Brief Global History;* and *A Twentieth Century Reader.* She is an Associate Editor of *Arab Studies Quarterly.*

LINDA S. WALBRIDGE earned her Ph.D. in Anthropology from Wayne State University in 1991. From 1991 to 1993, she was an adjunct faculty member and Assistant Director at the Middle East Institute at Columbia University. She has been teaching at Indiana University's Bloomington and Indianapolis campuses since January 1994. She has published *Without Forgetting the Imam: Lebanese Shi'ism in an American Community* (1997), and her edited volume *The Most Learned of the Shi'a: The Institution of the Marja'-l Taqlid* is being published by Oxford University Press. She is currently writing a book on Shi'a leadership tentatively entitled *The Most Learned of the Shi'a*.

Index